MASTERING THE WEST

Ancient Warfare and Civilization

SERIES EDITORS:

RICHARD ALSTON   ROBIN WATERFIELD

In this series, leading historians offer compelling new narratives of the armed conflicts that shaped and reshaped the classical world, from the wars of Archaic Greece to the fall of the Roman Empire and the Arab conquests.

Dividing the Spoils
The War for Alexander the Great's Empire
Robin Waterfield

By the Spear
Philip II, Alexander the Great, and the Rise and Fall of the Macedonian Empire
Ian Worthington

Taken at the Flood
The Roman Conquest of Greece
Robin Waterfield

In God's Path
The Arab Conquests and the Creation of an Islamic Empire
Robert G. Hoyland

Mastering the West
Rome and Carthage at War
Dexter Hoyos

MASTERING THE WEST

Rome and Carthage at War

Dexter Hoyos

OXFORD
UNIVERSITY PRESS

OXFORD

UNIVERSITY PRESS

Oxford University Press is a department of the University of
Oxford. It furthers the University's objective of excellence in research,
scholarship, and education by publishing worldwide.

Oxford   New York
Auckland   Cape Town   Dar es Salaam   Hong Kong   Karachi
Kuala Lumpur   Madrid   Melbourne   Mexico City   Nairobi
New Delhi   Shanghai   Taipei   Toronto

With offices in
Argentina   Austria   Brazil   Chile   Czech Republic   France   Greece
Guatemala   Hungary   Italy   Japan   Poland   Portugal   Singapore
South Korea   Switzerland   Thailand   Turkey   Ukraine   Vietnam

Oxford is a registered trademark of Oxford University Press
in the UK and certain other countries.

Published in the United States of America by
Oxford University Press
198 Madison Avenue, New York, NY 10016

Library of Congress Cataloging-in-Publication Data
Hoyos, B. D. (B. Dexter), 1944–
Mastering the West : Rome and Carthage at war / Dexter Hoyos.
ISBN 978-0-19-986010-4 (hardcover : alk. paper); 978-0-19-066345-2 (paperback : alk. paper)
1. Punic wars.   2. Command of troops—History—To 1500.   3. Mediterranean Region—
History, Military. 4. Mediterranean Region—History—To 476.   5. Rome—History, Military.
6. Carthage (Extinct city)—History, Military.   I. Title.
DG242.H69 2015
937′.04—dc23
2014015832

CONTENTS

Contents

PART FOUR THE LAST CONFLICT

LIST OF FIGURES AND MAPS

FIGURES

MAPS

All maps prepared by the Author

ACKNOWLEDGMENTS

IT IS A SPECIAL pleasure to acknowledge the encouragement and advice that I have had over a long period of writing. Richard Alston and Robin Waterfield originated the suggestion of a study of the Punic Wars in the context of ancient warfare and civilization. Their vigilant and invariably helpful scrutiny has been matched by that of Stefan Vranka, Oxford University Press's senior editor in Classics, ancient history, and archaeology. I deeply appreciate too their unvarying patience with an author who found his progress slower than he had too-confidently forecast. It gives me immense pleasure to thank the copy editor and book editor for their keen-eyed vigilance with this title. I also thank Sarah Pirovitz at Oxford University Press (New York) for her invaluable help with the artworks in this title. I could not have written this book without the study facilities of Sydney University and Macquarie University, both of which have generously accorded me honorary research affiliateships. The work would not have been feasible, in turn, without the understanding and care of my wife, Jann; our daughter, Camilla; her husband, Anthony; and a tiny granddaughter named Scarlett.

ITALY: THIRD CENTURY B.C.

Mediolanum
CISALPINE GAUL
Ticinus
Clastidium × Cremona
× Placentia
Padus/Po
Parma
LIGURIA
Trebia
Mutina
Bononia
Aquileia
Ariminum
Pisaurum
Fanum
× Sena Gallicia
Arretium
Cortona
Tiber
Metaurus
ILLYRIA

Ligurian Sea

CORSICA
Aleria

L. Trasimene
ETRURIA
Nar
Tiber
Narnia
Pyrgi ROME
Anio
Praeneste
Ostia
LATIUM

Adriatic Sea

Larinum
Gereonium APULIA
Arpi Salapia
Herdonea
Cannae
Canusium
APULIA
Venusia
Numistro
Brundisium

Olbia
SARDINIA
Tharros

Tyrrhenian Sea

Fregellae Teanum
Casilinum Capua
Acerrae Nola
Cumae CAMPANIA
Puteoli Nuceria
Naples Paestum
Beneventum
LUCANIA
Grumentum
Tarentum
Metapontum
Heraclea
Uzentum

Thurii/Copia

Carales
Sulcis

Petelia
Consentia
Croton × C. Lacinium
Vibo Valentia
BRUTTIUM

Ionian Sea

Lipara Is.

M. Heircte Panormus
Solous
Drepana M. Eryx Thermae
Aegates Is.
Segesta
Lilybaeum
Heraclea Minoa
Entella
Cephaloedium
M. Aetna
Enna
Murgantia
Mylae
Tyndaris
Messana
Rhegium
Caulonia
Locri

Hippou Acra
Utica
Carthage C. Bon
Bagradas

Acragas/Agrigentum
Phintias
Camarina
M. Ecnomus
Leontini
Gela
Catana
Syracuse

Mediterranean Sea

Malta

0   100 Mi.
0   100 Km

N
W ◉ E
S

MAP 1
Italy: third century BC.

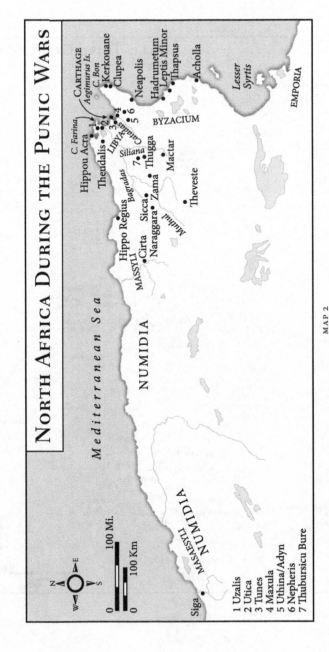

NORTH AFRICA DURING THE PUNIC WARS

Mediterranean Sea

CARTHAGE
Aegimurus Is.
C. Bon
Kerkouane
Clupea
Neapolis
Hadrumetum
Leptis Minor
Thapsus
Acholla

C. Farina
Hippou Acra
Theudalis
LIBYA
Catabathmos
BYZACIUM

Lesser
Syrtis

EMPORIA

Siliana
Bagradas
Thugga
Mactar
Theveste
Zama
Sicca
Naragara
Cirta
MASSYLI
Hippo Regius

Madbul

NUMIDIA

MASAESYLI
NUMIDIA

Siga

N
W E
S

0 100 Mi.

0 100 Km

1 Uzalis
2 Utica
3 Tunes
4 Maxula
5 Uthina/Adyn
6 Nepheris
7 Thubursicu Bure

MAP 2

North Africa during the Punic Wars.

xiv

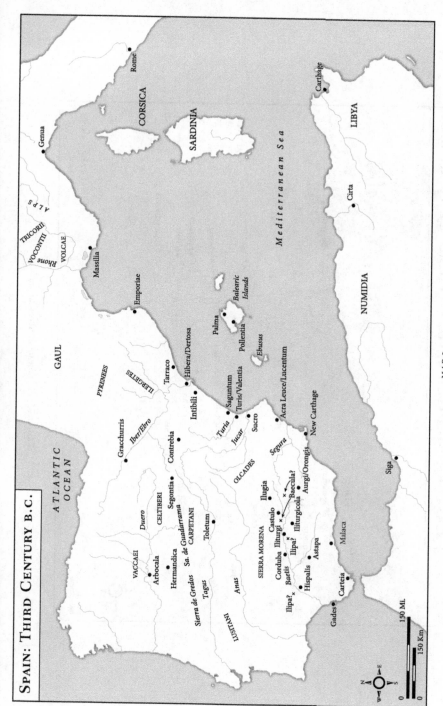

SPAIN: THIRD CENTURY B.C.

ATLANTIC OCEAN

GAUL

ALPS

TRICORII

VOCONTII

VOLCAE

Rhone

Massilia

Emporiae

PYRENEES

ILERGETES

Tarraco

Hibera/Dertosa

Gracchurris

Iber/Ebro

Intibili

Saguntum

Turis/Valentia

Turia

Jucar

Sucro

Contrebia

Segontia

CELTIBERI

Sa. de Guadarrama

CARPETANI

Toletum

Duero

VACCAEI

Arbocala

Hermandica

Sierra de Gredos

Tagus

Anas

LUSTANI

SIERRA MORENA

OLCADES

Segura

Ilugia

Castulo

Illiturgi

Baecula?

Ilipa?

Aurgi/Orongis

Illiturgicola

Corduba

Baetis

Hispalis

Astapa

Ilipa?

Gades

Carteia

Malaca

Acra Leuce/Lucentum

New Carthage

Siga

NUMIDIA

Palma

Balearic
Islands

Pollentia

Ebusus

Mediterranean Sea

CORSICA

SARDINIA

Genua

Rome

Carthage

LIBYA

Cirta

MAP 3
Spain: third century B.C.

N
W E
S

0   150 ML

0   150 Km

XV

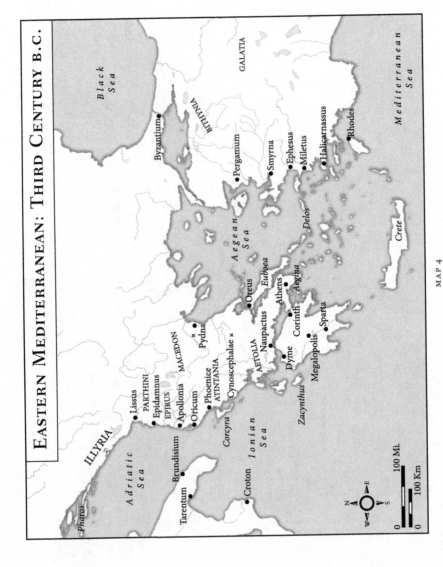

EASTERN MEDITERRANEAN: THIRD CENTURY B.C.

ILLYRIA

Pharos

Adriatic Sea

Tarentum

Brundisium

Lissus
PARTHINI
Epidamnus
EPIRUS
Apollonia
Oricum

Corcyra

Ionian Sea

Croton

Zacynthus

MACEDON
× Pydna
Phoenice
ATINTANIA
Cynoscephalae ×

AETOLIA
Naupactus
Dyme
Megalopolis

Oreus
Euboea
Athens
Corinth *Aegina*
Sparta

Black Sea

Byzantium

BITHYNIA

GALATIA

Pergamum
Smyrna
Ephesus
Miletus
Halicarnassus
Rhodes

Aegean Sea

Delos

Crete

Mediterranean Sea

N
W E
S

0   100 Mi.

0   100 Km

MAP 4

Eastern Mediterranean: third century B.C.

xvi

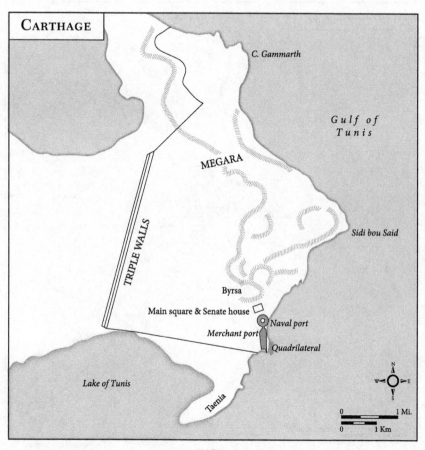

MAP 5
Carthage.

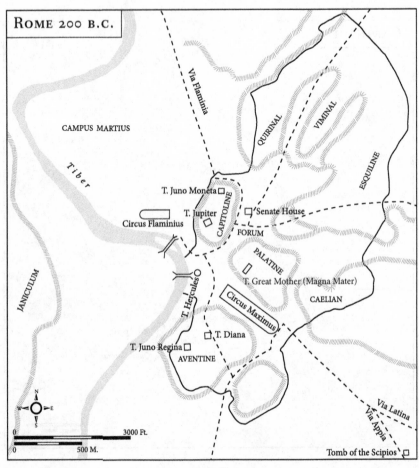

ROME 200 B.C.

Via Flaminia

CAMPUS MARTIUS

Tiber

QUIRINAL

VIMINAL

ESQUILINE

T. Juno Moneta □

T. Jupiter

Circus Flaminius

CAPITOLINE

□ Senate House

FORUM

PALATINE

T. Hercules ○

T. Great Mother (Magna Mater)

CAELIAN

IANICULUM

Circus Maximus

□ T. Diana

T. Juno Regina □

AVENTINE

N
W — ○ — E
S

0   3000 Ft.

0   500 M.

Via Latina

Via Appia

Tomb of the Scipios □

MAP 6
Rome: 200 BC.

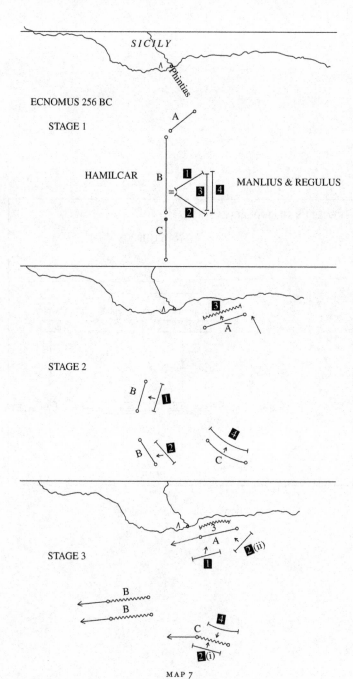

SICILY

Phintias

ECNOMUS 256 BC

STAGE 1

HAMILCAR   B   MANLIUS & REGULUS

A

1

3   4

2

C

STAGE 2

3

A

B   1

B   2

4

C

STAGE 3

3

A

2(ii)

1

B

B

4

C

2(i)

MAP 7
The naval battle of Ecnomus, 256 BC.

xix

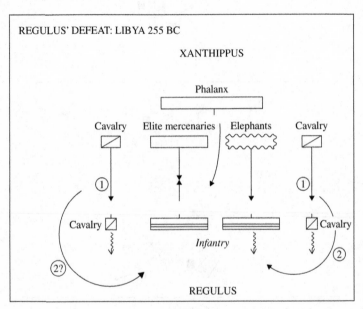

REGULUS' DEFEAT: LIBYA 255 BC

XANTHIPPUS

Phalanx

Cavalry   Elite mercenaries   Elephants   Cavalry

① ①

Cavalry   Infantry   Cavalry

2? ②

REGULUS

MAP 8
Regulus's defeat: Libya 255 BC.

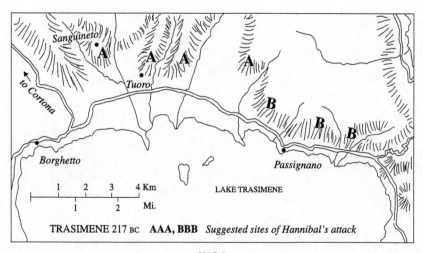

MAP 9

Battle of Lake Trasimene, 217 BC.

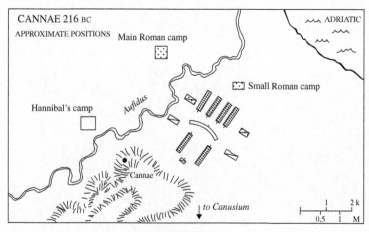

MAP 10

Battle of Cannae, 216 BC.

INTRODUCTION

I N THE THIRD AND second centuries BC the two leading states of the western Mediterranean, Rome and Carthage—both republics, closely linked by trade, and with political and military interests previously focused on differing regions—fought three wars, which decided the fate of their own lands and of those others in the West that were drawn into them. The First Punic War, from 264 to 241 BC, and the Second and most famous, from 218 to 201, were on a scale far beyond most other ancient conflicts—a point made as early as their first surviving historian, the Greek Polybius, himself present during Rome's operations against Carthage in the Third.[1]

The First war ranged over a relatively narrow area of the central Mediterranean: Sicily and its waters and briefly Sardinia and North Africa. Yet the combatants put sometimes huge forces into action—even if Polybius may exaggerate them—and sometimes huge losses befell these. The Second, in its turn, was the most titanic Mediterranean struggle before the Roman civil wars of Julius Caesar's day 200 years later. It was fought across Italy, Spain, the western Mediterranean islands, and North Africa; it also led to Rome's first Macedonian war because Macedon chose to side with Carthage. The Third was more concentrated, this time in North Africa; but it drained far more resources in men, munitions, and money than either side foresaw.

The Punic Wars opened almost by accident, affected the lives and fortunes of millions (not all of them Carthaginians or Romans), destroyed one empire, and launched another. When they began in 264 BC Rome

1

was a rising but middle-level power that had only just imposed her control over peninsular Italy; Carthage was a major state directly or indirectly ruling much of North Africa, Sicily, and Sardinia. When the Third war was launched just over a century later, the situations were almost exactly reversed. How it all happened is a story blended of calculation and (just as often) miscalculation, heroism, cruelty, stubborn resolve, and the unexpected.

The wars' lasting fame rests above all on the renown of two men: Carthage's general Hannibal and his Roman adversary Scipio Africanus, both in the Second. Hannibal's blend of charismatic leadership, risk-taking dash, and tactical genius has always won admiration—even from Romans, once he had passed away—and, from time to time, imitators. If in the end he failed, it was a failure whose brilliance eclipsed most of the ancient world's successful generals. Scipio Africanus was an even greater commander. No less charismatic and risk-taking, he never lost a battle or a campaign, in a career that put Rome on the path to mastery over the Mediterranean West. Ironically, both men died around the same time in self-imposed exile, estranged from their ungrateful homelands.

The conflicts produced a gallery of other notable figures whose memory too has endured. The First war's Marcus Regulus, in a pleasing legend, sacrificed himself rather than urge Rome to beg for peace; Hannibal's father, Hamilcar Barca, saved Carthage in her worst crisis and created her second empire after Rome struck down the first. Against Hannibal, Fabius the Delayer "by delaying restored our fortunes" in the contemporary poet Ennius's proverbial paradox; Claudius Marcellus conquered Syracuse and lamented the slaughter of the scientist Archimedes (himself another figure of note). A young Carthaginian woman, Sophoniba, became queen of Numidia to meet a tragic fate that engrossed later romantic fancy. The Third war owed much to the old and unforgiving Cato the Censor's strident pressure for it, remembered by later ages (inaccurately) as a cry that "Carthage must be destroyed." Scipio Aemilianus, Africanus's adoptive grandson, proved himself another unforgiving enemy of Carthage—as he would be of other accused transgressors, his own cousin among them.[2]

Why the wars erupted and how they were waged are questions still argued, because they still challenge analysis. For a dispute in 264 between Syracuse and Messana, two combative Sicilian cities, to lead to war between Rome and Carthage was and is not an obvious progression. That Hannibal marched to Italy in 218 with a steadily shrinking army, hoping to seduce enough of Rome's allies there to force her to capitulate, appeals to many as a strategic plan of radical brilliance; to others it smacks of foredoomed folly. Why the Carthaginians—reputedly the unmatched masters of Mediterranean naval prowess—should dismally fail against the Romans at sea, in both the First and the Second wars, is another puzzle. The Romans' decision in 149 to force war on an unthreatening Carthage, when continuing trade and peaceful intercourse would have brought them long-term profit, bemused and troubled many observers at the time and still does.

Several related questions are worth asking. Were the Carthaginians, founded from Phoenicia, ethnically and culturally alien to the lands where they lived and ruled and to the Greeks and Romans with whom they traded and warred? Many—or most—modern observers believe it; the ancients were less dogmatic. Again, how did Carthage and Rome, states with many fewer millions of citizens and subjects than any modern great power, sustain conflicts so lengthy and so costly in lives and resources? When Hannibal defeated the Romans in the three great battles of 218–216, his army killed or captured (on a credible calculation) about 120,000 enemies: 13 to 16 percent of the entire adult male population of Italy at that time. What would the wars' outcomes have been if the losing side had won—or would it have made little difference? Why were the ultimate winners not enfeebled after conflicts of such size and stress? Arguably they should have been.[3]

Instead the opposite proved true. On the graves of tens of thousands of dead soldiers and civilians, and the ashes of scores (if not hundreds) of sacked cities and towns, arose one of history's greatest empires. The victors were able to blend their own culture with those of their new subjects to create a civilization that in evolved form exists still. That empire started by mastering the Mediterranean West.

PART ONE

ROME AND CARTHAGE

264 BC

1

TWO REPUBLICS

I N THE EARLY THIRD century BC Rome and Carthage, the leading powers of the western Mediterranean, were both city-state republics like most other western states. The east by contrast was dominated by powerful monarchies—Macedon, the Seleucid Empire, Egypt, and for a time Epirus. The Romans had rid themselves of monarchy more than 200 years before; the Carthaginians, even earlier. Both states were governed along similar lines: executive magistrates elected annually, a consultative house of elders, and official assemblies of citizens for electing the magistrates and enacting laws. In practice both were ruled by small elites that evolved over time.

They shared other resemblances. By tradition Rome was founded in or near 753 by Romulus, a royal descendant of the Trojan exile Aeneas; Carthage, just a few decades earlier, reportedly in 813, by an exiled princess of Phoenician Tyre named Elissa (Dido to Greeks and Romans). In their early centuries, both had had to cope with sometimes dangerous neighbors but over time had come to control broad territories beyond their borders through a network of subordinate allies. By 264 many features of Greek culture had permeated not only Roman society and religion but also Carthage's—and Carthage, not Rome, had the sole non-Greek constitution discussed by Aristotle in his *Politics*. Rome and Carthage had been partners in trade and diplomacy for nearly two and a half centuries, while members of their elites enjoyed reciprocal ties of friendship and hospitality. That they would go to war, and fight not once but three times until one utterly destroyed the other, was far from predictable in 264.[1]

ROME

Rome began as a relatively large city-state on the northern edge of the Latium region, beside a convenient crossing of the river Tiber and close to important coastal salt flats. Disposing of Rome's original monarchy in 509, her leading men set up a republic dominated by elite aristocrats called the patricians and characterized by executive magistrates elected yearly. At first a main member of the religious and military league of Latium's cities, Rome over the next century and a half made herself its dominant power, finally bringing all her fellow Latins under total hegemony by 338. Many Latin states were given Roman citizenship while keeping local autonomy, while the rest had to accept subordinating their foreign and military relations to Rome's.

Even before 338 the Roman republic had expanded beyond its early boundaries. Etruscan Veii nearby, once powerful itself, had been annexed in 396. In 343 the rich Campanian city of Capua, with its subordinate towns, had joined the Roman state to avert a more unappealing intimacy with the warlike Samnites inland. The Campanians acquired the unique condition of "citizenship without the vote": self-governing but able to migrate freely to Rome while accepting Roman direction in foreign affairs and wars, in this much like Rome's autonomous Latin kinsmen. Territorial expansion inevitably and perhaps intentionally brought on a monumental three-war clash with the Samnites down to 283. Despite setbacks, as when her encircled army had to capitulate in Samnium's Caudine Forks pass in 321, and despite other peoples—Etruscans, Umbrians, and northern Italian Gauls—gathering in the 290s to check her, Rome emerged mistress of all peninsular Italy by 270. Her final combat was against the powerful Greek city of Tarentum in the south from 280 to 272. The Tarentines called over the warrior king-errant Pyrrhus of Epirus (who had his own western ambitions), only for him to win a series of pyrrhic victories followed by defeat and departure. In 270 the Romans recovered an allied Greek city, Rhegium on the Sicilian straits, from the mutinous Campanian troops who had appropriated it, and the domination of the peninsula was complete.

FIGURE 1.1
Roman silver didrachm, third century BC.
Image proposed by Sarah.

The ruling elite of Rome also evolved. Early patrician efforts to monopolize or, failing that, control the republic's offices and priesthoods had gradually retreated under pressure from the plebeian majority of citizens. Ambitious plebeian leaders pushed for social justice and economic reform: Magistrates' arbitrary powers were curtailed, the often crushing penalties for indebtedness—a constant purgatory to farmers and traders—were gradually eased, and the plebeians' own voting assembly and magistrates came to exert influence over the whole state. Nonetheless patricians remained respected and resilient out of all proportion to their contracting numbers. Fewer than thirty family groups (*gentes*, singular *gens*) still regularly reached high office in the third century, in contrast to the fifty or so during the fifth, yet among them the great dynasties of the Aemilii, Claudii, Cornelii, Fabii, Manlii, Valerii, and four or five others were sure to attain senior magistracies in virtually every generation. Other patricians, such as the ancient Julii, could manage it from time to time. High office was achieved, too, by a broadening range of eminent plebeian families, some of whom were likewise able to establish virtual dynasties. By 270 the Atilii, Fulvii, Sempronii, and Claudii Marcelli (distinct from the patrician Claudii) had become part of the elite establishment. Patrician and plebeian families very often intermarried.

This flexible oligarchy of office stood at the head of a much larger body of elite citizens. They included the less eminent members of the Senate but chiefly were the well-off to wealthy citizens who took no part in political life. These amounted to about one in every twelve Romans: they were classed as cavalrymen (*equites*) at each five-yearly census, members of the "order of cavalry" (*equester ordo*) who could afford the sizable cost of maintaining a horse and weaponry for war. In 224 BC, of 273,000 citizens registered, 23,000 (8.4 percent) were *equites*.[2]

Rome's political life blended competitiveness and cooperation vigorously. It was becoming the convention that holding junior magistracies should precede holding senior ones, though exceptions could always occur: The hero Marcus Valerius Corvus was consul at twenty-three in 348, and a later hero—Scipio Africanus—would enjoy an even more stellar career from his twenties on. Every ambitious Roman competed with his rivals for votes but, no less important, needed eminent men to support him. Political programs, progressive or conservative, sometimes played a part in these alliances, but it does not look as though family-centered factions or feuds endured over generations, or as though factions existed to push for carefully thought-out political and economic programs or stood for or against Roman expansion. During Hannibal's war Fabius the Delayer disliked and criticized Scipio Africanus, but nothing suggests that their entire *gentes*, friends, and supporters were political adversaries down the decades. Things were different at Carthage, as we will soon see.

Each ordinary magistracy, except the single praetor before 241, existed in colleges of two or more: two consuls, four and later six aediles, several quaestors, and ten plebeian tribunes (in practice, even if not legally, magistrates too). None were paid. Yearly election depended on how the constituent units voted in the very unequally structured, and surprisingly numerous, citizen assemblies. Attaining office—the higher, the better—conferred social eminence and political influence, eagerly sought blessings respectively known to Romans as *dignitas* and *auctoritas*. Ex-consuls commanded the greatest status. Their influence usually carried the day in the Senate; only if sharp divisions among them occurred would a magistrate venture to decide by himself how to act; and as time passed they and their descendants came to monopolize the flattering term *nobiles* (notables), which in 264 still applied to ex-praetors and some ex-aediles as well.

The Senate was a permanent council about 300 strong, appointed by the censors from ex-magistrates and other, invariably well-born, worthies. Its legal powers were limited—for instance, when (rarely) both consuls perished in battle, it appointed one patrician *interrex* after another until fresh elections were held—but its *auctoritas* was vast. Its imprimatur was required before any proposal could be put to the sovereign People. Its resolutions, *senatus consulta*, were almost invariably respected—a sound enough convention when senators were the most experienced and generally the best-informed citizens in the state. Any unusual magistrate who chose to ignore a resolution might find himself promptly obstructed by a colleague or by a plebeian tribune (who had the power to obstruct anything).

The consuls were Rome's heads of state and her principal generals. The praetor dealt with serious legal cases (though he too could command troops as necessary); the aediles, with maintaining the City's temples, streets, and amenities; and the quite youthful quaestors, with finance, under the Senate's watchful eye. Every five years two censors counted the male citizenry and their economic means, assigned or reassigned them across Rome's plethora of economic and voting groups, purged immoral or unwary senators and *equites*, and organized major public projects such as temples, roads, and fortifications. The plebeians' ten tribunes, originally their spokesmen and protectors, now acted as watchdogs over state affairs. At times, too, a tribune promoted one or other popular measure such as freedmen's rights or land grants to poor citizens, to unprogressive senators' annoyance.

During the great Italian wars, military need and common sense had allowed able commanders to attain several consulships (Valerius Corvus had six between 348 and 299) and, if appropriate, have their authority, *imperium*, extended by the Senate for another year as "proconsuls." By 264 this had become unpopular with the elite: Relatively few consuls in the First Punic War—even successful ones—would hold office twice, for one-year commands gave more aristocrats openings for military success and its political benefits. Of course this produced a constant turnover of commanders, with dubious impact on operations, whereas Carthaginian generals could hold their commands for lengthy periods. In a serious emergency, military or domestic, a consul could nominate another leading Roman as dictator, an office with virtually unlimited *imperium* but limited time span. Occasionally, as with Fabius Maximus in 217 (and, two centuries later, Julius Caesar), the People elected him instead. He chose a master of horse (*magister equitum*) and was expected to save the situation as promptly as possible and then abdicate.

Male Romans were enrolled in several formal assemblies. The citizen body was registered in 193 "centuries" to form the Comitia Centuriata, a body that had begun as the people in arms. This elected consuls, censors, and praetors; enacted laws; and could try serious cases. Romans were also allocated in 264 among thirty-three territorial districts (*tribus*), four in the City and twenty-nine covering the rest of Rome's territory (in 241 two more were added when the territory expanded). These—as generally thought, though not all scholars agree—constituted the Comitia Tributa, which elected lesser magistrates and could also legislate. The plebeians' assembly, the Concilium Plebis, was itself organized by tribes. It not only elected the tribunes and two "plebeian" aediles but, remarkably and thanks to the efforts of fourth-century reformers, could enact laws too (these were termed plebiscites). To Romans it was quite natural that these gatherings should vote by their units: the voters' majority in each century or each tribe decided that unit's vote. And it was not thought strange that the largest number of centuries were for relatively wealthy men: eighteen for senators and *equites*, seventy or eighty for other citizens in the highest property class (men worth 100,000 *asses* or above, a third-century fortune), and one century for all propertyless Romans—a century that rarely voted, for voting stopped as soon as a majority was counted, and the counting of course began from the top. Social segregation did not afflict the tribes, but since they convened at Rome, citizens living more than a few hours' travel away could take little part. That these arrangements reinforced the political as well as social supremacy of Rome's aristocracy troubled no one either.[3]

Physically Rome was very large for a third-century city. Eleven kilometers of walls embraced some 427 hectares and an urban population of some 90,000 souls. The census in 265 registered 292,234 male Romans aged seventeen and above (at seventeen a citizen became eligible for army service) living on about 27,000 square kilometers from southern Etruria to Campania. Buttressing the *res publica* were the rest of the peninsula's city-states and cantons, bound to Rome happily or discontentedly by treaties that effectively subordinated each to her military and foreign policies. The old Latin cities not incorporated by Rome enjoyed special privileges, like the thirty Latin colonies—strategically sited cities outside her territory that she had founded with Roman and Latin settlers. The Latins, collectively called the *nomen Latinum*, and the other Italian allies (*socii*) together totaled around 550,000 military-age men, giving the peninsula something like three million people altogether, along with its unknown number of slaves. This Roman military league was not yet a player on the international field, but its resources were already on a par with those of the great Hellenistic kingdoms and of Carthage.

Later Romans cherished a pious view of their heroic ancestors as devout, tough, and honorably unsophisticated, in pleasing contrast to the frivolous Greeks, barbarous Gauls, and devious Carthaginians who surrounded them. That the ancestors were devout is certainly true. Romans knew well that they were under divine scrutiny and that the all-too-easily offended gods, Jupiter at their head, required much cultivation. Foreign deities too sometimes had to be accorded their place, such as Greece's healing god, Asclepius, brought over in 293 as Aesculapius. Signs and portents were monitored by the pontiffs, augurs, and other priests because heaven thus communicated warnings and guidance. In one unique rite, a brood of chickens that accompanied every army and fleet was fed before a battle to see whether they ate well or not—if not, the battle was put off to a better day.

In other features, third-century Romans were far from simple. They practiced trade and diplomacy over much of the Mediterranean, including Carthage. Roman and Carthaginian aristocrats (if not others too) had ties of friendship, sometimes over generations, such as the families of Fabius the Delayer and Carthalo, one of Hannibal's leading officers. Such ties eased arrangements for regular prisoner exchanges and ransoms (thus a captured consul of 260, Cornelius Scipio, could reappear as consul again six years later). Like many Carthaginians, educated Romans read and spoke Greek. In the 240s a Tarentine immigrant, Livius Andronicus, started to stage Latin versions of Greek tragedies and offer his adapted translation of the *Odyssey* to an obviously knowing public. There was already a Latin literature too, notably promoted by the controversial patrician Appius Claudius Caecus (censorial builder in 312 of the Appian Way to Capua and of burgeoning Rome's first aqueduct), with an essay on Roman law and a set of verse aphorisms, including the still popular "Every man is the craftsman of his own fortune." This maxim had a special relevance for Rome, where freed slaves not only were numerous (a fact stressed by no lesser a man than the Macedonian king in 214) but became citizens with only a few civil limitations. As early as 312 Appius had thought freedmen's votes worth cultivating. Rome manufactured goods and also artworks such as the famous Ficoroni *cista*, an elaborately decorated bronze casket under Greek influence, fashioned there around 300 BC for a lady of nearby Praeneste. Roman military skills, as Pyrrhus discomfitedly found, were virtually on a level with those of the Hellenistic east. The state that confronted Syracuse and Carthage fifteen years later was not a farming backwater.[4]

CARTHAGE

Rome's fated adversary was already five and a half centuries old when the two first clashed. One of a number of colonies founded along the North African and southern Spanish coasts by the Phoenicians of Tyre and Sidon—hence the Latin term "Punic"—she had become the richest and most powerful of them on a site geographically ideal for cross-Mediterranean trade. At some date her monarchy had been replaced by republican magistrates, although Greek writers, Aristotle among them, fog the question by regularly terming the fourth and third centuries' chief magistrates "kings" (*basileis*). Adding to the complexity, at least from the mid-sixth century on Carthage was often politically dominated by one or another leading family—the Barcids, Hannibal's family, were only the last of these.

The city stood on what was then an arrow-shaped peninsula nine kilometers from north to south, its built-up area covering some 300 hectares around the southern end. Great encircling walls embraced the entire peninsula, with triple-walled fortifications across the isthmus to its west. Her many enemies discovered down the centuries that Carthage

FIGURE 1.2
Carthaginian silver shekel, First Punic War period.

was impregnable. Within the walls a line of low hills edged the original city. The southernmost hill, Byrsa, was Elissa's first settlement; in historical times it was the city's citadel and the podium for the grand temple of Eshmun (to Romans, Aesculapius) atop a sixty-step stairway. To the north the headland today called Cape Gammarth was backed by Megara, a district of fields, orchards, gardens, and aristocratic villas—all within the city's fortifications.

The Augustan-era geographer Strabo writes that around 150 BC Carthage's population was 700,000. If this figure is valid (there have been doubts), it must cover her rural territories as well. In 264 the city housed maybe some 200,000 citizens and foreigners; its territories, along the coast to the Cape Bon peninsula, perhaps thrice as many. Libya—Punic-dominated North Africa—had perhaps two million more from the coasts to the fertile inland areas around the Bagradas, Siliana, and Muthul rivers. Carthage's kinfolk and allies, other old Phoenician colonies such as Hippou Acra, Utica, and Hadrumetum, were privileged rather like the Latins in Italy: these "Libyphoenicians" had rights of intermarriage and trade with their big sister while contributing to her military enterprises. Utica, the nearest of them, earns special mention in Hannibal's treaty with Macedon in 215. By contrast, the communities of Libya's fertile valleys and plains were more heavily controlled. Though self-governing, they had to pay taxes and supply soldiers, and it was taxation, often harshly exacted, that fed Libyan resentment to produce repeated uprisings—all of them firmly crushed. Along the coasts west of

Libya, small trading ports served as entrepôts and as stopovers for longer trips westward, for example, to southern Spain's own Phoenician colonies such as Abdera, Malaca, and Gades. Over the centuries the Carthaginians tried to keep as much of this lucrative trade as possible in their own hands, as shown in treaties of 509 and 348 with Rome, which the historian Polybius quotes in Greek translation. These banned Roman ships, first from approaching most of Carthage's possessions in Libya, Sicily, and Sardinia, and later from southern Spain too. The archaeological remains of Rome's plentiful third-century "Campanian ware" pottery—jars that carried Roman produce overseas—do not spread far into southern Spain.

In western Sicily and in Sardinia Carthage was effectively hegemon over a range of communities. Towns Phoenician by origin, such as Panormus, Drepana, and Motya in Sicily and Tharros, Carales, and Olbia in Sardinia, were linked to her probably much like the Libyphoenicians, while Sardinia's uplands, largely free of her authority, resisted any efforts to impose it. Carthage's greatest field of stress, though, was Sicily. Its eastern, northern, and southern coastlands were largely Greek, with some of the richest and strongest cities in the Greek world—especially Syracuse and Acragas. The center and inland west were still home to old Sicilian communities, such as Enna and Segesta. Greek Sicily's city-states fought one another with recurrent enthusiasm and had inflicted recurrent headaches on Carthage's allies in the far west. In the early 270s, busy with yet more warfare, they called Pyrrhus over from his stalemated Italian adventure to lead them against the "Phoenicians." Like so many past rounds, this ultimately led nowhere, save back to the status quo.

We know less about Carthage's political system and elite than Rome's, but she was certainly open to newcomers. Phoenician to start with, Carthaginians early on found spouses among their neighbors in Libya, Sicily, and even Egypt. The poet Silius Italicus credited Hannibal's family with descent from Elissa-Dido's brother (without offering any evidence), whereas Hamilcar the Magonid, Carthage's leader in 480, had a mother from Syracuse; and one of the generals during the fatal last war with Rome was a grandson, again on his mother's side, of the Carthaginians' old foe Masinissa, king of the Numidians. Aristotle stresses that wealth no less than birth counted for political success at Carthage; this implies opportunities for well-connected recruits. Noteworthily, no leader in any era is associated with commerce in surviving accounts, despite the city's repute as a hub of commerce. By contrast, some were landed proprietors. One grandee accused of treason in the 350s retreated to his country estate with, supposedly, 20,000 loyal slaves (no doubt an exaggeration), and in 195 Hannibal had a sizable coastal property near Thapsus, 200 kilometers southeast of Carthage. In fact Punic agriculture was so famously productive that the agronomist Mago's encyclopedia of farming was translated into Latin after 146 by decree of the Roman Senate.

The city's institutions only partly resembled Rome's. Two sufetes elected each year (*shophetim* or *softim*) were at its head but, by 264, had only civil functions. Warfare was entrusted to a general (*rab mahanet*, "army head") or generals, who were elected for the war's duration. Inscriptions in Punic, mostly dedications or epitaphs, mention boards of ten or even thirty entrusted with upkeeping temples or paying out funds. A body of accountants apparently supervised all state finances, including customs dues. Aristotle contrastingly and confusingly mentions powerful bodies called pentarchies (boards of five), which, he says, had "supreme control over many important matters": hearing lawsuits; appointing senators to the Court of 104, which judged failed generals; and choosing new members for themselves. How his pentarchies tied in with the larger boards is only one question. Who could belong to a board, who could be a senator and who appointed senators, and what Aristotle means by claiming that pentarchy members could exercise their powers before and after their actual terms of office are even more stressful puzzles.

The Court of 104, obviously not a pentarchy, also had no Roman counterpart. It could handle defeated generals gruesomely—crucifying them was common—though quite a number escaped prosecution, Hannibal included. No doubt much hinged on whom you knew and what you knew about others. One other important office, called the "quaestor" by the Roman historian Livy, saw to the state finances and may be the *rab* ("chief") in many inscriptions of eminent Carthaginians. He had a fixed term and, perhaps, was one of the republic's rather few elected officials.

He also belonged to its senate, called the *adirim* or Mighty Ones, who numbered maybe 300 like their Roman equivalent. Thirty *adirim*, perhaps ex-sufetes, constituted an inner council of much eminence but obscure duties. Like Rome's, the senate at Carthage advised the magistrates, but in Aristotle's account senate and sufetes enjoyed the non-Roman advantage of being able to enact a decision if they both agreed on it. During the wars with Rome, the *adirim* are recorded as rejecting harsh peace proposals, deciding troop movements, and even accepting a Roman war declaration: at least some of these decisions were probably reached as Aristotle describes. Only if senate and sufetes could not agree did the citizens' assembly have a role. This, simply termed "the people" (*ham*), on the other hand, could debate any matter referred to it and, implicitly, could amend this if it chose (Roman assemblies could do neither). How it was structured and functioned is unknown, but, by all the evidence, it accepted political dominance by rich and eminent citizens as willingly as did the Roman assemblies.

By 264 Carthage had a vigorous culture developed from a blend of Phoenician, Greek, Egyptian, and Numidian cultural influences, as surviving tomb decorations, architecture, and artworks show. Her elite knew Greek, not to mention Numidian, and some maybe could speak Latin. Like the Romans, Carthaginians were thoroughly devout, although how far they went in observing omens and portents is not clear. Baal Hammon was the principal god, in close association with Tanit or Tinit, the goddess whom inscribed dedications often call "the face of Baal" (*pene Baal*). The city's protector was Melqart, chief god of Tyre, whom Greeks equated with their Heracles (Roman Hercules); while a very varied assemblage of other deities played their own roles in Carthage's service—among them divinities adopted from other cultures, notably Isis and Bes from Egypt and Demeter and her daughter Persephone from Greek Sicily. Revered too, if Greek and Roman writers are correct, was the deified Elissa (and even Hamilcar the Magonid despite his fatal defeat in Sicily). But easily the most notorious Greek and Roman claim about Carthaginian religion is that they sacrificed children to their gods to avert calamity. The details proffered in written sources about these supposed rites all contradict one another and contradict the cremated remains of stillborn infants and fetuses found in the children's cemetery. Nevertheless, unfairly enough, the lurid stories have always won out.

A TALE OF TWO (OR MORE) TREATIES

As Aristotle attests, Carthage had diplomatic agreements with plenty of foreign states. Other evidence reveals agreements with Athens around 406 and Etruscan cities even earlier and two with Rome. Polybius quotes these two in Greek translation: He dates the first to 509, and most scholars put the second in 348, since Diodorus reports a Roman–Punic agreement in that year. In each, the Carthaginians firmly talk down to the Romans. The treaties restricted Romans from accessing lands of prime trading interest to Carthage without imposing matching restrictions on Carthage's trade with Italy. The 348 treaty even accepted that Carthaginians might capture and loot cities in Latium not subject to Rome—coastal ones, no doubt—so long as they afterward handed these over to Rome. The Romans were not accorded similar leeway in Libya, Sicily, or Sardinia. In reality, these and other provisos reflected principle rather than practice. Carthage had not been seizing places in Italy previously, nor did she do so after 348. These provisos were effectively dead letters from the start. Thus the treaty could be renewed painlessly in 306—even though by now there remained no Latins not subject to Rome and even if the renewal perhaps substituted "in Italy" for "in Latium" (a wording change easy to escape Polybius's eye).

Pyrrhus's victories over the Romans in 279, plus reports already circulating about his ambitions for Sicily, impelled the two states to add a quite separate codicil to this treaty. They agreed that, if either one allied with him, it still was entitled to aid the other if the other was attacked (obviously by Pyrrhus). Their clear mutual fear was that he would try to use one against the other—and the fear was chiefly Carthage's because the badly defeated Romans were indeed thinking of negotiating (until rousingly dissuaded by the aged Appius Claudius Caecus). In the end neither sought the other's help, though in 278 there was a minor joint operation in southern Italy against one of the king's Greek allies.[5]

All the same their pact may have had a notable aftereffect. It very likely prompted the pro-Carthaginian historian Philinus of Acragas to write (as Polybius reports) that Rome and Carthage had once struck a treaty to keep away from, respectively, Sicily and Italy. Philinus therefore damned the Romans as oath-breakers for entering Sicily fifteen years later—a claim with many followers still. His history does not survive, but Roman historians seem to have read it because they tried down the centuries to turn the oath-breaking charge against Carthage. Their flimsy best was to claim that just before Tarentum capitulated to Rome in 272, a Punic fleet appeared offshore; therefore Carthage had not "kept away from Italy." All ignored Polybius's counterclaim that Philinus had made his treaty up. Yet Polybius had found no trace of it, whereas he knew of, and got translated, the texts of the first two treaties in an archive on Rome's Capitoline Hill. Worse, he found no Romans or Carthaginians who knew even those texts. Roman official records did register the two treaties, as do Diodorus and Livy, but not their contents; obviously no details existed at Carthage either. Philinus himself ignored or was ignorant of both.

If real, his treaty necessarily revoked the 348 treaty's permission to Carthage to sack cities in Latin (or Italy). The only dates that would fit it are 306, when a treaty was "renewed" (so Livy writes), or 279. Neither is plausible. In 306 both states were busy elsewhere (Rome with Samnites and Etruscans, Carthage with the resurgent Syracusans); in 279 the situation hardly fitted a pact envisaging cooperation. A less convoluted explanation is that Philinus at Acragas knew of a 279 pact concerning Pyrrhus but not its content and chose to indict Rome under it for invading Sicily. The clumsy later Roman efforts to blame Carthage for the war imply not that they knew of any such treaty but that they had read and were troubled by Philinus.

The two powers themselves fell to blows in 264 on quite other grounds.

2

FIGHTING THE ENEMY

CARTHAGINIAN ARMIES

All advanced Mediterranean states felt the impact of Alexander the Great's military techniques, especially the maneuvering of disciplined cavalry to strike the decisive blow while an agile yet equally disciplined infantry phalanx—a massed formation with formidable impact—charged its enemies with its long *sarisa* spears leveled. Skilled tactics, and warfare across broad regions, called for long-service professionals rather than intermittent citizen levies; the Hellenistic age was an era of mercenaries. Elephants from India or Africa became another (at times unpredictable) weapon; inventive war engines—armored towers and battering rams, catapults firing stones or arrows—figured in sieges. Warfare naturally remained seasonal. Armies were normally immobilized, and sometimes demobilized, during winter, while fleets rarely sailed between October and March because of winter storms.[1]

The Carthaginians took their time about adopting every modern armament. Their infantry formed traditional close-ranked phalanxes of spearmen, but not with the long Macedonian *sarisa*. As late as 341 war chariots were a (not very effective) element of the army shattered in Sicily, a defeat that ended the most energetic of Carthage's efforts to crush the Sicilian Greeks. It was not until 217, when Hannibal refitted his infantry with captured Roman arms, that Carthaginian battle array may have changed: Roman swords and shields virtually required Roman fighting array. Meanwhile, thanks it seems to Pyrrhus's expedition into Punic

Sicily in 278–276, the Carthaginians took up African elephants, smaller cousins of the Hellenistic world's Indian beasts.

Carthage's many but intermittent wars were with the Sicilian Greeks and her Numidian neighbors. They tended to involve much marching, ravaging enemy lands, attacking enemy cities, and maneuvering to fight (or avoid) infrequent major battles. Carthaginian siege engines are not much mentioned—sources admittedly are scrappy—and probably were not very sophisticated. Carthaginian citizens served only as officers or, when military situations pressed, in elite battalions such as the "Sacred Band," which met a disastrous Sicilian fate in 341. By contrast Carthage had led the way much earlier in employing chiefly mercenaries and Libyan conscripts. Mercenaries varied greatly in origins. Cavalry came chiefly from the adept horse-riding peoples of Numidia, along with Gauls later on; regular infantry, from the Iberian Peninsula, Gaul, the Gauls and Ligurians of north Italy, other Italian regions such as Campania, and—the best—Greece (a mid-fourth-century innovation). The Balearic Isles supplied expert light-armed slingers.

CARTHAGINIAN FLEETS

Carthaginians crewed the city's fleets, which for crucial operations could number 100 or even 200 warships. Such large armaments afloat, though, probably called for more crews than Carthage alone could furnish. Probably her Libyphoenician kinsmen, all of them coastal, had to provide quotas of men and ships. Third-century battleships were quinqueremes, each crewed by some 300 oarsmen and able to carry a hundred or more soldiers on deck. Much larger and heavier than the classical trireme, a quinquereme it seems arranged its oarsmen on three lines of benches, one above the other, along either hull. Two men sitting on the top bench pulled an oar, as did two on the middle bench, while on the lowest bench a fifth man handled another oar (hence the name quinquereme). Like triremes and other fighting ships, its bow included an underwater ram sheathed in bronze for smashing an opposing hull. Its size allowed it to carry catapults and other artillery for use against enemy personnel on a hostile ship or hostile shore. Triremes remained in use for escort duty and scouting, while ships called quadriremes (apparently with four oarsmen on each vertical row) often took part too. Flagships even bigger sometimes turned up—Pyrrhus, for instance, boasted a seven-banker that afterward became a Carthaginian possession. How its oarage worked can only be guessed.[2]

Fleets of quinqueremes, even if not accompanied by lesser craft, necessarily covered a broad expanse of sea. Whether the tactic was to ram and wreck enemy ships or to fight side-on to capture them, it required room for maneuver—and if the worst happened, for retreat. All this made a naval battle even harder for a commander to control than one on land. Trumpet calls or drumbeats would be useless over any distance in the confusion of fighting, and flag signaling was yet to be invented. Much depended, therefore, on the experience and pugnacity of ship captains and crews.

The Carthaginians enjoyed and still enjoy a high reputation for naval skills and success. In reality they lost about as many sea battles as they won, even before their disastrous Roman clashes. Given the limitations of ancient naval equipment, it was hard for even a navally strong state to protect its own coasts. Agathocles's invasion of Libya in 310 proved this troublesome truth to the Carthaginians. Their wars had in any case been more military than naval. Those before 264 were essentially land wars in Sicily, Libya, and sometimes Sardinia; fleets played mostly support roles—transporting men and munitions or backing up sieges of Syracuse or other places. Moreover, as late as Agathocles's war Carthage's navy still relied on triremes. It was only later, probably in observing his growing naval strength, that she went over to the modern battleship. It would be tested for the first time when she came to blows with Rome.

ROME

A Roman army until the later fourth, or early third, century had also fielded spear-wielding infantry, formed up in one or more legions. A legion was deployed in three lines, one behind the other, with light-armed soldiers and cavalry in support. By Pyrrhus's day the spear had been replaced in the first two lines by a two-edged short sword for cutting and thrusting, although each legionary also carried two javelins to hurl just before the hand-to-hand clash, and the third line retained its thrusting spears until much later. Roman conservatism over names and symbols ensured that the first-line troops continued to be called *hastati* (spearmen) and the second line *principes* (chiefs, perhaps recalling an era when they stood in front). The rear line more logically kept its old name, *triarii* (third-liners), and consisted of the oldest and most experienced men. *Hastati* and *principes* formed up in ten companies per line called *manipuli* or "handfuls," each consisting of two *centuriae* with (officially) sixty men per century plus its centurion. The *triarii* too were ten maniples and twenty centuries strong, but totaled only 600—a disparity compensated, so the Romans felt, by their experience and reliability. The front centurion of their first maniple was the legion's chief centurion, a formidable veteran always consulted by any intelligent commander along with his senior officers. These were four military tribunes in each legion, not appointed by their commander but elected by the Comitia Centuriata. The consul in command could appoint a trusted fellow senator as his deputy (*legatus*), if he had to be away for any reason.[3]

Roman armies did not use mercenaries, save for rare occasions. Legionaries and Roman cavalrymen were citizens, were entitled to a daily pay of about three bronze *asses* (the earliest Roman coin) for a legionary and ten for a cavalryman, were recruited from men above a minimum property qualification—determining this was a task of the five-yearly censors—and had to buy their own equipment. As a result the poorest Romans, who had no assessed property, were not liable to conscription save in emergencies. This saved them from becoming casualties but equally cost them the much-prized prospect of sharing in booty. Before 264 an army was not normally kept in being beyond a single year's campaign or, exceptionally, beyond two. The Latin states and Rome's other Italian allies had to raise contingents of infantry and cavalry too when ordered to (they were not allowed to fight their own wars), each commanded by a prefect—contingents equal to or greater in numbers than Rome's and equipped in the same style. Some experienced allied troops were selected to form an elite unit of *extraordinarii*, and some of these received the honor (and peril) of being the Roman general's bodyguard.

A regular infantryman's equipment consisted essentially of chain-mail body armor (if he could afford that) or a bronze plate over the chest, a protective helmet, sometimes greaves, and a large oblong shield, together with sword and javelins. His heavy wooden shield, edged with iron strips, could protect a soldier up to his neck; a metal boss nailed to its outer side could push back or even topple an opponent. The light-armed men, called *rorarii* and later on *velites*, carried a lighter, round shield, a chest protector, sword, and javelins; as for light troops everywhere, their tasks were to harass and soften up enemy formations before battle and press the pursuit afterward.

A legion theoretically numbered some 3,000 in its three infantry lines, a sizable body of *velites* (about 1,200 by the early second century but perhaps fewer three generations earlier), and a 300-strong cavalry force, the *equites*. A consul led two legions to war; a praetor, one if needed. With the allied contingents a consular army could total 18,000 or more; a praetor's, half that. Fielding two consular armies—the norm in a big war like Pyrrhus's—put stressful demands on Rome and the allies alike, for it meant taking up to 40,000 able-bodied men from their farms or other occupations for much of the working year. Roman and allied men aged seventeen and above numbered perhaps 850,000 in 264, but of course those above forty-six were therefore liable for further service only in emergencies. The legions and allied forces had to be levied from the rest.

The countryside not only supplied nearly all the fighting men but also suffered much of the damage from the fighting. The costs and problems of transporting supplies often forced an army to live mostly off the land and off towns and communities near where it was operating, while trying to prevent the enemy from doing the same. Military doctrine was simple. A general sought out enemy forces for battle or could choose to attack enemy strongholds or ravage enemy fields. Both choices could bring in movable booty—goods, animals, and captives for enslavement, prime attractions for hard-fighting soldiers and officers. Either choice could also bring on a battle, which both armies usually preferred to fight on fairly level ground.[4]

Battle, normally or at any rate notionally, took the form of confronting the enemy infantry with the legions in their three-line array. The *hastati* delivered or received the first assault, with the *principes* coming up to reinforce them. The *triarii* were held back until it was time to launch a final blow against the foe—or cover a measured retreat. At all times the formations had to keep their cohesion, for any breakup of the ranks could set off a rout. Cavalry would fight the other side's cavalry or, if opportunity offered, would join in attacking its infantry. Subtle maneuver was necessarily rare, for Roman armies did not comprise long-serving professionals. The nearest that Italian warfare came to subtle maneuver was an ambush: most famously the Samnites entrapment in 321 of both consuls in the Caudine Forks, a narrow valley east of Capua, forcing their bloodless surrender. Sieges in Italy saw few (or none) of the sophisticated assault engines used by Hellenistic powers, as in Alexander's siege of Tyre in 332. Rather, they were resolved by starving out the defenders, seizing the place through an insider's betrayal, or giving up and going away.

At sea Rome had instituted no naval force bigger than an occasional squadron of twenty triremes, and that not until 311. This minor navy performed unimpressively when it did put to sea, but it could be useful in causing annoyance: in 282 ten ships were sent to sail past Cape Lacinium in southern Italy, breaking a treaty and so provoking Tarentum into war. Who built and crewed such triremes is not clear: most likely some of Rome's coastal allies, as they would do on a greater scale in the First Punic War. The escalating demands of that war, nevertheless, would put Roman citizens onto the rowing benches too.

PART TWO

THE FIRST PUNIC WAR

AND AFTERMATH

264-218

3

SICILY AND ITS SEAS: 264–257

SICILY AND ITALY AFTER PYRRHUS

Romans and their Greek friends later asserted that down to 264 Carthage was an aggressively expansionist power, with deep designs on Italy as well as Sicily. This claim was used to justify Rome's decisions, first to send military aid to the Mamertines of Messana on the straits facing Italy and later to drive the Carthaginians even from their own dominion in Sicily's west. That the claim was untrue did not matter, nor did later generations realize that it was untrue.

Carthage's war with the Sicilian Greeks had petered out around 274, leaving her—as usual—where she had started, ruling the western territories up to the river Halycus. Syracuse was now headed by a young aristocratic general named Hiero, whose military concern was much nearer home. The Greek city of Messana had been seized a decade and a half earlier by an unemployed force of mercenaries from Campania; ironically, their old employer had been Agathocles, until he died in 289. Lawless, bellicose, and greedy, the new owners of Messana called themselves Mamertines after the Campanian war god Mamers (Mars to the Romans) and lived up to the name by attacking and plundering their neighbors, then by aligning themselves with Carthage against Pyrrhus, and afterward by impartially raiding the Carthaginian west as well. Hiero's first effort against them, probably around 269, was beaten off, but he was too strong to be counterattacked. A second offensive, most likely in early 264 (though conventionally dated to 265 or even earlier), finally shattered the

Mamertines at the Longanus river near their city. Penned within their walls and expecting assault, the survivors were saved at the last moment by a (not entirely unexpected) *deus ex machina*, Carthage. It was plainly not in her interest for Syracuse to aggrandize itself with Messana, when just a couple of decades earlier Agathocles had dominated practically all of Greek Sicily, so her general in Sicily slipped a small protecting garrison into Messana. Hiero could not afford a clash. He withdrew to Syracuse and consoled himself, like Agathocles, with the title of king.

Rome had spent the years following the defeat of Pyrrhus and surrender of Tarentum in confirming her control of Italy. Tarentum, like the other Greek cities, became a dependent ally. Rhegium, diagonally opposite Messana and also a Greek colony, was liberated in 270 from a rogue Campanian garrison that, ten years before, had imitated its Mamertine kinsmen to seize the city. Just as the Tarentine war had in Roman propaganda been fought to save Rome's south Italian ally Thurii (another of the Greek cities) from Tarentum's encroachment, the restoration of Rhegium to its exiles was treated as a proof of Roman loyalty, *fides*, toward an ally. Italian warfare, though, was far from over—the heel of Italy, the Sallentine peninsula, was next brought into the Roman orbit; rebellious communities in the northeast were subdued; and when in 265 Etruscan Volsinii's serfs drove out their overlords, a consular army laid siege to the city to restore it to its aristocrats.

None of these activities yielded particularly profitable booty. Tarentum had sensibly made terms rather than be sacked; the proceeds from other areas must have been middling at best, while Volsinii was dangerous— the consul Fabius besieging it was fatally wounded, and the siege dragged on. Polybius indicates that in 264 ordinary Romans were dissatisfied and as a result keen to find better returns elsewhere.

THE CRISIS OVER MESSANA

Continuing Roman wars and Carthage's opportunistic takeover of Messana might well look like trajectories toward an inevitable conflict. King Pyrrhus supposedly remarked, as he sailed defeated from Sicily in

276, "What a fine wrestling ground we are leaving to the Romans and Carthaginians!"—an alleged foresight that some biographer probably invented for him in hindsight. That war between the two was foreordained was the standard view of ancient historians and is held by most modern scholars too.[1]

The situation was in reality more complicated—one important reason being that the surviving historical accounts leave some critical details unclear. If Hiero's crushing victory was in 269 rather than five years later, why did the Mamertines wait until 264 to ask Rome for help, and (more crucially) for help against whom? Presumably not against the Syracusans but, rather, the Carthaginians, who by then would have been holding Messana's citadel for half a decade. This gap is not in any surviving account: they have events from the Longanus to the first Roman campaign in Sicily all in fairly swift sequence. The Romans crossed to Sicily led by the consul Appius Claudius Caudex, whose twelve-month term began in about May 264, and in the first year of Olympiad 129, which began in July. It is likely that, as Polybius firmly implies, the Mamertines' defeat, rescue by the Carthaginians, and appeal to Rome all happened in the preceding months.

Polybius states clearly that the decimated freebooters not only turned to the Carthaginians—which makes eminent sense, as the Punic general was closely following events and could act fast—but also appealed to Rome. This logic was both sound and devious. It scarcely suited them to be under a Punic thumb permanently, whereas their Roman kinsmen (the Mamertines, ex-Campanians, used this loaded term in their appeal) could protect them just as efficiently against Syracuse, yet leave them free to carry on as before in Sicily; or so they might gamble. The appeal, though, did not meet a ready acceptance at Rome. The Senate's debate was lengthy. As Polybius tells it, senators could not reach a decision: on the one hand, they judged that Italy was threatened by an expansionist Carthage, yet, on the other, could see that helping brigands like the Mamertines was wholly unjust. They recognized, too, that aid to Messana sat uneasily alongside Rome's exactly opposite treatment of the Campanians at Rhegium six years before. As a result even the backing of the consuls, Appius Claudius Caudex and Marcus Fulvius Flaccus, failed to sway a majority to favor the appeal. With the Senate deadlocked, the consuls took a dramatic step: they put the proposal for aiding Messana directly before the Comitia Centuriata. The People, says Polybius, needed little persuasion. Worn down by all the recent wars, they grasped at this opportunity for "great and obvious benefits," plainly meaning war booty. The Mamertines were accepted as allies in need of help—just as Thurii had been, and others before that—and Claudius was bidden to levy troops for the task. Fulvius returned to besieging the stubborn serfs in Volsinii, who surrendered later in the year.

The central puzzle of 264 is Rome's intended enemy. Who moved the Mamertines to appeal? Every surviving ancient writer—except one—insists or assumes that it was Carthage. By claiming that she was aggressively expanding her power across the Mediterranean, they justified Rome's decisions first to aid the Mamertines and later to drive the Carthaginians from their own historic holdings in the island's west. The claim was not true—Carthage's areas of control had not expanded in a century and a half—but that did not matter. One later historian, Cassius Dio, tried his hand at Thucydidean-style analysis: Each side, Romans and Carthaginians, coveted the other's possessions; each feared the other's greed; therefore war was inevitable. Neat as this may look, it ignores other relevant issues.

No source denies that once Claudius crossed the straits and freed Messana from a siege by its protectors-turned-enemies and a revitalized Hiero, he and then his successors in 263 concentrated entirely on fighting Hiero, while the Carthaginians retired to western Sicily. Nor is there dispute that, well before the Roman army reached the toe of Italy, Carthage's garrison in Messana had gone. It was bloodlessly dismissed by its protégés, a step the Mamertines were entitled to take, whether or not they were instigated by a military tribune sent over by the consul (as Dio—alone—writes) and even if they achieved it by mixing persuasion with pressure. Sending away unwanted protectors was not an act of war. Carthage's ensuing decision to send fresh troops over and lay siege to her ex-friends definitely was. This was not a move due somehow to Roman manipulation, nor one that the Romans could have predicted. In fact, if Rome was looking for a Punic war, she should have deterred her new allies from ejecting the garrison so that she could claim to be rescuing them from oppressive occupation. At the very least she could have bidden the Mamertines to massacre the departing garrison on some pretext, which would certainly have provoked Carthage into desired hostility.

Not only did Rome focus on Syracuse after Claudius raised the siege of Messana, but once the consuls of 263 made peace terms with Hiero, one left with his army for Italy. This again does not fit the idea that the war had been planned against Carthage, with Hiero simply getting in the way. Syracuse had proved too strong an enemy for a single consul, even the vigorous Appius Claudius; cutting the forces in Sicily in half to tackle Carthage made no sense. It was only when she launched a major buildup of her forces, in 262 at Acragas, that two new consular armies returned to the island, to launch the first direct confrontation with Carthaginian forces since Claudius rescued Messana. Even then, the war remained confined to Sicily, another feature that ill fits ancient and modern views of Rome in 264 already intending to fight her old treaty partner.

There is a final, obvious point. If from the start the Romans wanted war with the premier maritime power in the western Mediterranean, it would be sensible of them to have a modern navy ready—or failing that, to launch one as soon as they could. But no Roman navy appeared until four years into the war, when they finally accepted that they could never defeat Carthage if they stuck to fighting in Sicily against her perpetually replenished armies. On all the probabilities, the enemy that the voters envisaged in 264, because they feared its potential danger to Italy and expected to garner "great and obvious benefits" if they struck first, was Syracuse.

The Carthaginians' attack on Messana, in turn, made clear that their concern all along was not Mamertine well-being (no one ever imagined it was) but to possess an eastern Sicilian satellite invaluable for checking any threat that might develop against their own territories on the island. Previously the Mamertines had done that job independently, and the Carthaginians had seen no need to get involved, but the brigands' debacle had changed the situation. As she had done against Agathocles in 314, so now Carthage intervened again, first to check Syracuse and then a second time when she saw her brief hold on Messana passing to a state even more powerful than Hiero's. It was Rome, not Carthage, that had been extending her territorial mastery over the last half century, and in 270 this reached the opposite shore of the straits. The *adirim* could not assume that it would stop there.

The news of Rome taking on the Mamertines as allies flustered the Greeks of Sicily no less. Hanno, the new Punic general, easily won over Acragas—the strongest and richest Greek city after Syracuse and, like Syracuse, an ancient and recent foe of Carthage—and then received alliance overtures from Hiero in turn, which he naturally welcomed. When he marched across the island to besiege Messana, Hiero joined in. And when the consul Claudius arrived at the straits to find the two improbable allies beleaguering the Mamertines, both Hiero and Hanno refused point-blank his offer of talks. For a power supposedly looking for war, this Roman offer was paradoxical. Even if war with Carthage was the true aim, Hiero—who had set off the whole crisis and still had unfinished business with the Mamertines—could not have been ignored. Appius Claudius's real surprise must have been to find a Carthaginian, not just the Syracusan, army outside Messana. Tellingly, his offer to negotiate was made, as Diodorus shows, to the king.

Hiero's reply berated the Romans for boasting about their virtuous loyalty to allies and then taking up thugs like the Mamertines: he declared that Rome's true motive was greed for his island. It cannot be doubted that exactly the same suspicion was in the minds of the Carthaginians. Hanno, though, was acting carefully. When the consul tried to send ships over to Messana, they were intercepted by the Carthaginian fleet and driven back, but Hanno then sent back the ships and crews he had captured. He added a colorful warning: The Romans should stay friends with Carthage, or they "would not dare even to wash their hands in the sea." The message was plain. Carthage wanted to stay at peace with Rome, provided that the Romans stayed out of Sicily.

This was not a message that Appius Claudius could accept. If he had to call off the war, he must do so from what would at least look like a position of strength, and that meant he had to take his legions over to Sicily and there face down the besiegers. The crossing to Messana with a full fleet of transports did succeed under cover of night—Hanno was tougher in words than in performance and even lost a quinquereme when it ran aground near the Roman landing. Even so, Claudius renewed his offer to the besiegers, with a warning that war was the alternative, only to meet renewed rejection. He marched at once—against Hiero; struck him hard enough to impel the Syracusans to retreat all the way home; and then did the same, in a hard-fought battle, to Hanno. Hanno, tellingly, had not flexed a muscle to help his ally and now lost all interest in continuing operations: he too retreated, all the way to the west, leaving Claudius free to advance on Syracuse.

EXPECTATIONS IN 264

In sum, the Romans' actions in 264, as opposed to later writers' claims about their thinking, strongly imply that Rome had factored in Hiero as the enemy, not Carthage. Other items reinforce this conclusion. The popular belief that aid to the Mamertines would bring in "great and obvious benefits" would make much more sense. North Africa's wealth was unreachable, and even looting western Sicily would entail a war inevitably long, dangerous, and costly. Syracuse and its allies, by contrast, were rich, and their territories were accessible just across the straits, with Messana an ideal bridgehead. The Senate's anxiety about an expansionist threat to Italy would fit Hiero's vigorous revival of Syracusan might. In older senators' lifetime, Syracuse had been a match even for Carthage and after 300 had brought much of Greek Italy under its dominance; now Roman hegemony over Greek Italy was less than ten years old.

One author, the epic poet Silius Italicus, three and a half centuries later, outlined the Romans' aim in 264: they judged it "noble to aid Messana against the arms of the Sicilian tyrant." It would be interesting to know his source. This aim, not war with Carthage, fits the situation and the events. But in 263 Hiero changed from enemy to ultimately revered friend of Rome, and within his own time memory of the greater war easily overshadowed the original one.

Carthage's responses to the complications escalating out of Hiero's Longanus victory no doubt seemed necessary and inevitable to the *adirim*: all the same they proved a disaster. Rescuing Messana was a standard tactic in her centuries-long brawling with Syracuse. It did not bring over any other Sicilian state with it. Nothing (except Roman and Greek hindsight-thinking) suggests that Messana was to be a Punic steppingstone to Italy. But losing Messana was a blow that had to be rectified, both for Carthaginian prestige and because letting Roman power into Sicily—even if the only target planned was Syracuse—presented a prospect plainly intolerable. Roman energies, the Carthaginians surely reckoned, would not limit themselves to the island's east, especially when so many Greek states had traditionally bitter relations with Carthage. On the other hand, Carthage was unenthusiastic about fighting the state that had beaten Pyrrhus. Claudius's victory over Hanno, hard-fought as it was, was enough to make her pull back and leave resistance to Hiero. A city that had fought Carthage herself to a standstill for more than 200 years could surely wear the Romans down in their turn.

THE FIRST ENEMY: SYRACUSE

The First Punic War was unusual. It had not been intended as such by any of its participants. It began as an east Sicilian contest between Rome and Syracuse but shifted to a Punic war, properly speaking, after little over a year. Then it continued for a quarter of a century, "the longest, most persistent, and greatest that we know of," in Polybius's judgment. In contrast to most wars, where the combatants aim from the start at each other's homeland, it was fought mostly outside both. The Carthaginians never tried to invade Italy, and the Romans' one attempt on Libya was a disaster. It pitted a previously land-bound military power against one of high naval repute—and the naval newcomers won. Its outcome was the birth of the Roman empire.

Appius Claudius's defeat of Hiero outside Messana was hard-won, but Hiero—left to fight without help from Hanno—drew his own conclusion about Roman–Punic relations and retreated, yet again, to Syracuse. Hanno's failure to intervene in the battle was probably not due to collusion but, rather, excessive caution, and he was punished the next day when the energetic consul won another hard battle to force the Carthaginians, too, to retreat. They abandoned the scene entirely to return to the west, leaving the coast (literally) clear for Claudius to advance on Syracuse. The siege, though, proved a fiasco: like the Athenians' disastrous attempt during the Peloponnesian War a century and a half before, and the Carthaginians over and over more recently, the Romans could make no impression on the impregnable fortifications. Facing the usual effects of a failing siege of Syracuse—supply shortages and dysentery—and Hiero's renewed refusal to talk terms, Claudius in his turn beat a retreat to Messana as the campaigning season closed and then took his legions back to Italy, except for a garrison to protect Rome's new friends.

Neither the king nor the Carthaginians chose to exploit this discomfiture (which cost Claudius a triumph). This was a further miscalculation, especially by the Carthaginians, who could at least have tried to bar the straits against the new consuls in 263. Manius Valerius Maximus and Manius Otacilius Crassus were thus free to take up the military initiative—once more against Syracuse. Two consular armies were more than Hiero could afford to resist, least of all when he saw that during their advance south more and more Sicilian cities sent them offers of friendship, from as far away as Halaesa on the north coast, 120 kilometers west of Messana. Some usefully sent military forces too. When Catana resisted, it was captured without great effort and suffered the usual plunder: a Catanian sundial became a notable installation in the Forum at Rome (though it was another hundred years before the Romans realized that its calibration was inaccurate there). Discontent with the stubborn king began to surface in Syracuse. Hiero asked for terms.

The war had plainly not brought the "great and obvious benefits" that Roman voters had been promised. Against the obvious expectation in 264, Syracuse had proved too hard a nut for one consul and army to crack. More troubling still, Carthage was now an enemy, and word had probably reached Valerius and Otacilius of an expedition being readied, at last, to aid Hiero. They offered the king lenient terms: to restore war captives free of ransom (there cannot have been many, unless Mamertines taken at the Longanus were included) and pay an indemnity of 100 talents (600,000 drachmas)—equivalent to about a year's salary for 5,000 legionary soldiers, though Hiero had to pay only a quarter of it on the spot and had fifteen years for the rest. The real damage was to the greatness of Syracuse. It was now left as a small kingdom in southeastern Sicily, which Hiero would carefully and neutrally rule for another forty-eight years.[2]

Soon after the terms were agreed, a Carthaginian fleet put in at Xiphonia, a harbor thirty kilometers north of Syracuse (at today's Augusta)—"but on learning what had been done," Diodorus writes, it departed. Earlier arrival might have kept Hiero in the war, but without him the expedition would meet disaster against 40,000 Roman and allied troops. It was rational, therefore, to withdraw—but at the same time it seems that this encouraged the consuls to infer that the Carthaginians were unwilling to face Roman forces in Sicily.

THE WAR BECOMES PUNIC

Sundials and other spoils notwithstanding, the booty from Rome's Syracusan war cannot have been anywhere near the expectations of 264. So many cities had prudently declared their support that the areas and amounts of looting had been limited. But Carthage was still at war with Rome, no matter how cautiously; and the consuls' defeat of Syracuse had given some restive subject allies of Carthage in the far west thoughts of defecting too. All this explains why, after Otacilius returned to Italy, Valerius marched his two legions into western Sicily in hopes of fresh successes and plunder.

The fullest account, by Diodorus, reports him winning over the important cities of Segesta—which claimed a kindred descent from Trojans, useful in dealing with Rome—and Halicyae, and capturing three very obscure places but failing against two called Macella and Adranon, all (it seems) in Sicily's west. Tyndaris, on the north coast only fifty-odd kilometers from Messana, failed to join the pro-Roman movement only because a Carthaginian fleet at the nearby island of Lipara swooped to seize the leading Tyndaritans as hostages. Valerius tackled none of the Carthaginians' coastal strongpoints, such as Panormus, Drepana, or Lilybaeum (the successor city to destroyed Motya); plainly he was not interested in serious confrontation. Equally he was untroubled by serious enemy resistance. The Carthaginians almost certainly lacked forces large enough to take on the legions, even if they could deter them from major centers. When Valerius returned to Italy and Rome, he celebrated a triumph (which Otacilius did not share) in March 262 "over the Carthaginians and King Hiero" and gave himself the extra name Messalla as a boast about rescuing Messana.[3]

This western raid ended any lingering chance that warfare in Sicily might come to a negotiated or just tacit close (as it had ten years earlier between Carthage and Syracuse). Since Valerius's raid showed that defensive inaction was not going to discourage the Romans, Carthage overhauled her military policy between late 263 and the new campaign season in 262. Fresh mercenary forces were enlisted from as far away as Iberia, Gaul, and Liguria, and these along with contingents from North Africa took station at Acragas—Agrigentum to the Romans—which was still her ally. But even now these troops' purpose was probably defensive: to deter any new raid or, if one did occur, to attack it. There was no counterraid into the east against Rome's newly minted allies, nor, more mystifyingly, did the navy, despite its grip on Tyndaris and Lipara, try to stop the next pair of consuls from ferrying over another four-legion army in spring 262. Left to Carthage, there would have been no Roman war even now.

This was not a conclusion obvious at Rome. The growing armament at Acragas/Agrigentum seemingly foreshadowed a powerful, if belated, Punic riposte to undo the taming of Syracuse and rescue of Messana. The new consuls, Lucius Postumius Megellus and Quintus Mamilius Vitulus, scotched this supposed scheme by marching on Agrigentum and laying it under siege. This was no easy proposition. The city was large and well defended, and the besiegers had nearly as much difficulty obtaining supplies as the besieged, even though their new friend Hiero did his best with deliveries. After five painful months of blockade, the Romans were menaced by a new Punic army arriving late in the year from Africa.

Its commander was Hanno, probably the same who had performed less than gloriously outside Messana in 264—and who, in spite of having supposedly 50,000 foot, 6,000 horse, and sixty elephants, was just as uninspired now. Apart from a few skirmishes, he was content to remain encamped close to the Roman siegeworks, no doubt waiting for hunger pangs over the winter to defeat the enemy rather than try it himself. Only after two more months, when starvation in Agrigentum outweighed that in the Roman forces, did he accept battle early in 261. The rout of his army (the Romans even captured most of his elephants) sealed the city's fate. Its defenders got away by night, but the Romans sacked it comprehensively and sold 25,000 Agrigentines as slaves, including no doubt to other Sicilians. Though Hanno miraculously suffered only a fine when he went home, the Carthaginians were now confined to their western Sicilian territory, plus a few isolated points elsewhere such as Lipara.

THE ROMANS AFLOAT

Puzzlingly, given this impressive victory, neither Postumius nor Mamilius gained a triumph, the military parade into the City that was a consul's acme of glory: perhaps because the campaign had incurred heavy losses (although Diodorus's claim of 30,000 foot, versus 540 horse, looks contrived). Its impact was momentous, all the same. The Senate, in Polybius's words, now "expected to be able to drive the Carthaginians off Sicily altogether, and thereby to advance Roman interests enormously." This had not been part of expectations in 264 or even 263. It was an extraordinary aim. The Carthaginians had been a masterful presence in Sicily for nearly 300 years, immovable by even the strongest combinations of Greek cities. They could put forces into the field to equal or outnumber two consular armies, and they had powerful fleets—as they showed in 261 by launching raids on Italy's coasts. The Romans nevertheless set themselves to rid Sicily of these tenacious foes with the usual two annual armies and (at first) to do it without a modern navy.

In this project they were notably helped by the enemy's failure, yet again, to prevent their forces from crossing to Sicily—a failure, whatever its cause, that was disastrous to Carthage's prospects. Had Punic warships harried the straits of Messina as vigorously as they did Italy's and Sicily's coasts, Rome might have found it impossible to keep control of eastern Sicily, far less operate deep into the west. Instead, every year one or both consuls took up operations where their predecessors had left off, and the Carthaginians found themselves more or less permanently enmeshed across central and western Sicily. The stalemate to which land operations were reduced in 261 was offset only by the raids that they launched from Sardinia against the Italian coasts. These inflicted little overall damage on the Romans even if they garnered some plunder and prisoners. Unintendedly they inflicted more serious damage on Carthage. Italy's exposure to seaborne attack was one incitement to Rome to build her own navy. The project (we happen to know) was strongly backed by Valerius Messalla, but—in one of the odder Roman inconsistencies in this war—he was not one of the new fleet's commanders. That task was given to two completely untried new consuls.

Polybius's story of how the ships were built reads almost like overexcited fiction. The Punic quinquereme captured by the Romans outside Messana in 264 served as a model for 100 ships, built in two months perhaps in the harbor of Ostia at the mouth of the river Tiber. Meanwhile their oarsmen learned rowing technique (or at least its basics) on benches set up on dry ground to match a quinquereme's layout. The building method is not in fact fiction, for the skeletal remains of a smaller Carthaginian warship, sunk in the shallows of Lilybaeum (Marsala) harbor around 241 BC, show that it had been constructed using specially marked timbers—in other words, following the ancient equivalent of a blueprint—and the same could have been done by craftsmen after taking apart the captured quinquereme. Training oarsmen on land was done at other times too, for example, in 37 BC when the triumvir Octavian (later the Emperor Augustus) was preparing to face his naval rival Sextus Pompey. The fleet also counted twenty triremes, probably not built at the same time (as Polybius assumes) but belonging to the squadron originally formed in 311.

A new navy was one thing; skilled rowers, another. Even crews recruited mainly from coastal allies would not have taken part in naval operations before, except maybe some Tarentines. Facing one of the leading maritime powers of their time, the Romans finally hit on a remarkable device to even the odds. Polybius, the only detailed source, describes it as an adjustable plank bridge with railings, slotted at one end to fit round a pole on a quinquereme's forward deck, and with a metal spike under its other end. This bridge—called a "raven"—could be raised up by a rope and pulley, swung in different directions, and then dropped onto the deck of a hostile ship to embed the spike. A Roman boarding party would then rush over. For this contraption to work, the quinquereme had to place itself more or less alongside its target even when this was maneuvering to ram it at an angle. For some moderns this is too improbable to be true, causing Polybius to be suspected of wildly misunderstanding some simpler tool (like grappling irons). Whatever the device, in the mayhem of battle all the advantage might be expected to lie with the navally adept Carthaginians—yet in the first major collision between the two fleets, in 260, they suffered a shattering defeat.[4]

The consuls that year divided responsibilities at first, with Gnaeus Cornelius Scipio taking the new fleet and Gaius Duilius taking the army in Sicily, only for Scipio to get himself and a squadron of seventeen ships captured in an incautious descent on the island of Lipara. The Carthaginian admiral Hannibal (no relation to Rome's famous later foe) then had a narrow escape himself when his squadron ran unexpectedly into the main Roman fleet; but with his remaining forces he engaged Duilius, now his opposite number, off the town of Mylae west of Messana. This was not only the first great sea battle between Carthaginians and Romans but, it seems, the first for the Carthaginians in their modern fleet of quinqueremes. No doubt much planning, training, and practicing had been done, but all of it could not fully equip crews and captains for the realities of quinquereme combat, and this showed. In their efforts to ram the enemy, Carthaginian quinqueremes fell prey to the "ravens"— even those battleships that rowed around behind the Romans for a rear attack. Up to fifty Punic ships, about half Hannibal's fleet, were captured or sunk; his own flagship, the "seven" originally belonging to Pyrrhus, was taken, though he himself nimbly escaped again; and the human losses were 7,000 dead—probably most of them drowned—and 3,000 captured, if later sources are accurate (Polybius gives none).

SICILIAN STALEMATE

Yet the outcome was an anticlimax. Duilius returned to land and won some more successes: he relieved Segesta from a Punic siege and captured Macella. A lengthy siege of an inland fortress called Mytistratus, on the other hand, got nowhere, and then, in the conventional way, Duilius went home to celebrate a triumph in 259 and put up two columns in the Forum adorned with the rams from captured enemy ships. Successful as he was, he never held another consulship, even though he would be censor in 231. As noted earlier, a curiosity of the First Punic War is how few consuls held the office more than once, even though multiple repetitions had been common in previous wars. Not just Duilius but also Claudius Caudex, Valerius Messalla, and Valerius Flaccus were never reelected. By contrast, Duilius's colleague Gnaeus Scipio, exchanged or ransomed from Carthage and now adorned with the teasing sobriquet Asina (She-ass), was consul again in 254, presumably thanks to his patrician eminence.

Hamilcar, Hanno's successor in Sicily—unrelated to Carthage's later leader Hamilcar Barca, it must be added—skillfully retrieved some of the situation after Duilius's departure and during 259, defeating a force of Sicilian allies of Rome near Thermae east of Panormus, taking Camarina on the southeast coast and Enna in the center through betrayal, and altogether baffling the hapless new consul Aquillius Florus. The other consul, Lucius Scipio (Asina's brother), took the fleet to harry Corsica and Sardinia. In Corsica, he tells us himself in his epitaph, he captured the Carthaginian port of Aleria. Later writers credit him with capturing Olbia on Sardinia's northeast coast, and he did hold a triumph claiming victories in both islands. These hits at the Carthaginians, even if in a secondary war theater, scotched further enemy raids on the Italian coast, and the disarray they inflicted seems to have persisted into 258, when the next naval consul, Sulpicius Paterculus, descended on Sardinia. His only serious opposition came not on the island but from naval forces under the admiral Hannibal (the loser at Mylae). Sulpicius defeated him so soundly off Sulcis that the surviving Carthaginian crews, driven ashore, saved the Court of 104 the trouble and crucified Hannibal themselves. Yet Sardinia and still more Corsica were strategic sideshows. Punic naval raids on Italy from there did small damage, neither disrupting Rome's war effort nor paving the way for a proper invasion—a move the Carthaginians never chose to make. If the Roman expeditions were practice runs for Africa, as sometimes suggested, they were dubious and dangerous: they carried no large land forces, faced no major fortified city on the scale of Carthage, and (for obvious reasons) learned nothing of the defenses of Africa or its coastal landscapes. What probably was learned was that neither island was important enough, in strategy or plunder, to concern Rome; she ignored them for the rest of the war.

On land in Sicily the Romans blunted recent enemy successes by retaking both Camarina and Enna, thanks to Sulpicius's colleague Atilius Caiatinus, and storming Mytistratus at last, as well as some lesser places near Agrigentum. These operations over, both sides seem to have been baffled about what to do next on land: a few maneuvers and skirmishes were all that marked the following year. At sea another, less momentous, victory was won over a Carthaginian fleet off Tyndaris, enough to earn the victorious consul Gaius Atilius Regulus a triumph. A brief excerpt from the poet Naevius's almost contemporary epic on the war attests a brief raid on Malta as well. If not another plunder hunt, this may have been a preliminary to the invasion of Libya in 256; but if so, it was ill conceived—Malta was not on any direct route to Carthage's heartland, and the raid alerted the Carthaginians to their enemies' growing confidence at sea. A program of frenetic shipbuilding ensued in both Italy and Africa, as the war took a momentous new turn.

4

AFRICA AND AFTER: 256–249

PRELUDE TO INVASION: THE SEA BATTLE OF ECNOMUS

To be at war with an overseas enemy for eight years—four of them with
a matching navy—and only then assail the enemy heartland was a rare
abstinence in ancient history. The Romans, even after 261, had plainly
persisted in believing that they could win a purely Sicilian war and
Carthage would in the end accept this. By 257 it was clear that this would
not happen; and it seemed just as clear that taking the chief Carthaginian
strongholds of Panormus, Drepana, and Lilybaeum was more or less
beyond their ability. The following year therefore saw a powerful fleet put
to sea, carrying both consuls and their armies, with Libya as their target.
According to Polybius, the quinqueremes numbered 330, bearing the
expedition's soldiers along with the crews, 120 soldiers to a ship. This, if
accurate, means that nearly 140,000 men sailed from the mustering point
at Phintias on Sicily's south coast—an armada larger, proportionate to
population, than the forces crossing on D-Day. There is no way of checking the figures, because later ancient writers echo or even exaggerate
Polybius's. Skeptical modern revisions go no lower than 250 quinqueremes, whose crews and passengers together would still come to more
than 100,000 men. Two or even three times the size of the first grand fleet
of four years earlier, this one needed far more crews than the coastal
allies could supply. For the first time, Roman citizens too must have been
recruited for naval service, most from the propertyless class who

otherwise were not called up. Rome's invasion of Africa, then, was one of the most massive operations in ancient history.[1]

In this war's typically less-than-imaginative way, neither consul had previous experience of command, even if they must have seen fighting, for instance as military tribunes. Lucius Manlius Vulso was a patrician of ancient family, but the last Vulso to hold consular office had done so in 400, and the last Manlius—not a close kinsman—in 299; the Manlii's claims to a consulship may have become too insistent to ignore. His original colleague, Quintus Caedicius, son of a past consul, was distinguished only by dying soon after entering office, thus clearing the way to be replaced by a Regulus—yet not Gaius Regulus the victor at Tyndaris but his kinsman Marcus, consul eleven years before, whose military leadership had been limited to the heel of Italy and whose diplomatic skills were to prove disastrous. What prompted the voters at Rome to elect first Caedicius and then Marcus Regulus will never be known, but again domestic politics must have been stronger than military considerations.

The grand fleet sailed to Sicily, passed Syracuse, and embarked the legions assembled on the south coast at Phintias beside a steep headland called Ecnomus. Rather than wait in home waters and hope to intercept the invaders there—the Carthaginians could not forecast where they might arrive—Carthage's fleet sailed to Lilybaeum and then eastward along Sicily's south coast looking to fight. Polybius reports that the admiral Hamilcar (the loser at Tyndaris) led 350 ships and 150,000 men, colossal figures again. If accurate, each Punic quinquereme too carried 120 soldiers; obviously Hamilcar had to meet the threat of the boarding-bridge "ravens," and an obvious countermeasure was to have plenty of troops aboard ship. Equally obvious is the question why, after four years, the Carthaginians had no better answer—no ravens of their own for counterattacking or improved rowing skills for eluding the ravens and ramming enemy quinqueremes farther aft. But Hamilcar had a plan.

He deployed most of his fleet in extended line abreast, while nearest the coast his left wing sailed line ahead. The plan was to tempt the approaching Romans, with their narrower array, to assault his thin-looking center and then outflank them on both sides. This was a fairly basic tactic, although applying it would not be easy. By contrast, the fleet formation that the consuls adopted was unique. Supposedly for security against enemy ships' superior speed, the two leading lines formed a V shape: behind the two flagships rowing side by side, the lines moved in echelon (not prow to poop). Their third line, towing the expedition's horse transports line abreast, completed the triangle, and the fourth acted as rearguard, again line abreast. This fairly complex pattern must have needed prior practice, perhaps on the way south from Italy and in the waters off Phintias (and if so, Hamilcar probably came to know about it). Yet it was surely not easy to cohere over long distances or under pressure. In practice it quickly fell apart.

Manlius and Regulus did just as Hamilcar wished, pressing into and pushing back his center so that their lines became readily vulnerable to side attacks. His right wing under Hanno (the loser at Agrigentum in 261) swung out and around the consuls' lines to strike at their rearguard. His left wing swung into line abreast to take on the consuls' third line, which had to cut the horse transports loose but soon got into trouble close to shore. This near-catastrophe was retrieved by the Romans' fierce fighting spirit and able use of the ravens. In the center, Hamilcar was driven off with serious losses, allowing Regulus to turn and rescue the fourth line from Hanno and Manlius to save the third. Significantly, the Carthaginian left had pressed that division close inshore but, fearful of its ravens, then hung back—plainly lacking room for agile maneuvers. The outcome of one of the greatest battles in naval history was that the Carthaginians fled to Lilybaeum after losing ninety-four ships, sixty-four of them captured, versus twenty-four Roman vessels sunk and none taken.

REGULUS IN LIBYA

The battered invasion fleet had to return to Messana to refit, but when it sailed anew for Africa it met no opposition. This was a strange nonevent, for the Carthaginians had had exactly the same amount of time to do their own refitting. Instead their naval forces disappear from the record for a year. Reaching the Cape Bon peninsula, the consuls took over the port of Aspis (Clupea to the Romans) and, predictably, spent time plundering the wealthy neighboring countryside, along with freeing numerous Roman and Italian war prisoners enslaved there, while they awaited instructions from the Senate. Why they needed instructing is far from plain. Consuls had *imperium*, their obvious goal was to crush Carthage, and this pause in hostilities enabled the Carthaginians to organize resistance. Then the Senate's decree, when it came, was extraordinary. Manlius was to sail home with the freed war prisoners, the loot, and 20,000 Libyans captured in the countryside. Regulus was to stay with forty ships, 15,000 infantry (meaning his consular army), and just 500 cavalry.

It looked like gross overconfidence—yet, extraordinarily again, Regulus prospered. He was materially helped by Punic ineptitude. As they had done against Agathocles in 310, the Carthaginians judged multiple generals a necessity and appointed two more, Bostar and Hannibal, as well as bringing Hamilcar from Sicily with 5,000 foot and 500 horse. This worked no better than in 310. When Regulus besieged a town called Adys or Adyn, probably Uthina fifty kilometers by road south of Carthage, all three stationed themselves on a steep hilltop nearby even though they had plenty of cavalry plus elephants—forces better suited to level ground. Perhaps they disagreed on how best to act; certainly they did not view the enemy below as a threat. No doubt they were shocked when Regulus launched a bold dawn attack. The routed army fled to Carthage, leaving him unopposed. He marched north to seize Tunes, then a small town on the shore of its lake only eighteen kilometers west of Carthage.

The Romans now blocked land access to the city. Many Libyan towns began offering support, while Numidian raiders into western Libya spread terror across the countryside. Many refugees fled to Carthage, probably encouraged by Regulus: their numbers would worsen pressure on the *adirim* and sufetes. By now autumn must have been turning into winter, making supplies to Carthage by sea difficult, even dangerous. The Carthaginians accepted Regulus's call to negotiate.

Rome had victory virtually in hand. Carthage was isolated, much of Libya was in revolt, and operations in Sicily had ground to a halt. Little besides the western strongholds there remained under her control. Even though fresh forces were being gathered at Carthage, the authorities had to reckon that Rome, in turn, would reinforce Regulus. They probably expected his peace terms to require them to surrender remaining prisoners, limit themselves to Sicily's far west, and pay an indemnity like Hiero (though a larger one). What they did not expect were Regulus's actual terms. Only the much later historian Dio states details, and not all of them are believable; but besides the standard restoration of Roman prisoners of war and ransoming of Carthaginians captured by Rome, Regulus did probably demand that both Sicily and Sardinia be forfeited, and heavy reparations to cover Rome's war expenses. True, Sardinia was not mentioned when peace finally came fifteen years later; but by then Rome too was eager for an end.[2]

Unless his paradoxical intention was to force a final battle that he was confident of winning, Regulus misjudged not only Carthage's strategic state but his own. He assumed that the Carthaginians were utterly desperate, and he was anxious to achieve a glorious conclusion to preempt being replaced by a new consul. Yet after weeks of campaigning his army cannot have kept up its original numbers; nor had any reinforcements arrived. Nor, it seems, had he recruited any Libyans or Numidians, so the 30,000 troops in late Roman accounts are fanciful. With an army under 15,000 strong Regulus expected to impose a crushing peace on Carthage, a feat that had eluded Agathocles, even though he could not capture the city and the arriving spring allowed it to be reprovisioned. An army was being rebuilt in the ample spaces within the walls, assembling fresh levies and mercenaries from Spain, Gaul, and Greece. The Carthaginians rejected his terms.

TWO ROMAN DISASTERS

The new mercenaries included a Spartan, Xanthippus, a veteran of that city's classic military culture. As Polybius tells it, he lectured his incompetent superiors so forcefully about their troops' woeful training and morale that they put him in charge of reinvigorating them. This looks like Greek special pleading. Hamilcar at least was an experienced general, and it cannot have been news that improvements were needed, even if the generals did judge Xanthippus best qualified to make them. When campaigning began again in spring 255 they had the sense, too, to continue following his advice—it was hardly revolutionary—to operate on level terrain, bring the enemy to battle, and exploit their cavalry superiority and elephants. The Carthaginian army numbered only 12,000 infantry, which must have been roughly the same as Regulus's, but its 4,000 cavalry vastly outnumbered his, and he had nothing to counter its ninety-odd elephants.

Regulus chose not to fight in the hilly country around Tunes or to undergo a siege there. He marched away to find open ground. Somewhere between Adyn and the Cape Bon peninsula, sometime in late May or in June 255, the clash took place. Here Xanthippus's tactics were strikingly inventive. The elephants and elite mercenaries side by side formed the first line, the rest of the infantry stood behind in phalanx formation, and the cavalry as usual were on the wings, this time with the other mercenaries. Regulus deployed his legions in two closely packed divisions side by side—supposedly he thought this was how to cope with elephants—with the light-armed *rorarii* in front and his exiguous cavalry forming the usual wings. The infantry that clashed with the mercenaries made good headway, but the elephants' charge against the other division bowled its leading ranks bloodily over. After the Carthaginian cavalry routed their opponents, they swung round to attack this division in its rear; at the same time the main Carthaginian phalanx moved into action against the wearied other Roman division.

Regulus's army, trapped on every side on the open fields, was virtually annihilated. Two thousand did escape to make a perilous journey back to the bridgehead at Aspis; a mere 500 were captured—the consul among them. The rest had been slaughtered. Xanthippus's tactics, to keep the Roman center occupied while its wings were swept away and then use his own wings to break it up, were essentially what Hamilcar had tried to do navally at Ecnomus. His tactics even more closely resemble Hannibal's at Cannae forty years later and Scipio's at Zama. A more immediate outcome was that the skillful Spartan was thanked by his employers and then dismissed: Carthage's appreciation at being saved by a foreigner was not unalloyed. Romans later liked to visualize him being secretly murdered by Punic perfidy, but in reality he seems to have gone to work for the king of Egypt.[3]

Roman defeats as calamitous as this were rare; the last had been in 390, at the hands of the Gauls, outside Rome itself. The capture of a consul was unprecedented. The disaster killed the invasion of Libya—even though Aspis was still in Roman hands, an unenthusiastic Carthaginian siege failed, and a Roman expedition still larger than before was being readied. The invasion had been a paradigm of mistakes and missed opportunities on both sides: Regulus left with a strangely small army to prosecute it, making no effort to cultivate the restive Libyans and Numidians, setting impossible peace terms, and finally fighting on terrain more or less gifting victory to Xanthippus. The Carthaginians did themselves no good by laying up their fleet after Ecnomus, practicing a hesitant strategy and shoddy battle tactics until Xanthippus intervened, and afterward getting rid of him in favor of citizen generals no more inspired than before.

The end of the African affair soon came. From Sicily a Roman fleet no less than 350 strong set sail for Aspis. The new consuls, Fulvius Nobilior and Aemilius Paullus, had aimed to bring reinforcements, but now all they could do was rescue Regulus's survivors. The Carthaginians could launch only 200 ships to intercept them off Cape Bon (Cape Hermaea to Polybius). Not surprisingly they were soundly defeated, with no fewer than 114 warships and their crews captured. The Aspis rescue succeeded; a raid on the nearby island of Cossura followed, and then Fulvius and Aemilius sailed for Sicily with some captured quinqueremes added to the fleet. Cheerfully ignoring their pilots' advice that its southwestern seas were dangerously storm-prone "between the risings of Orion and Sirius" (that is, the period July 4–28), they were hit by a gigantic tempest off Camarina. It shattered their armada as thoroughly as they had shattered the Carthaginians: eighty ships out of 364 got through.[4]

Whether the fleet still carried ravens and they destabilized ships in the storm is not known, though it has been suggested. Ravens are not heard of again after Ecnomus, nor when or why they disappeared. The Sicilian storm caused one of the greatest naval disasters in history. The ships' crews, accompanying troops, and captured enemy personnel must have totaled far more than 100,000—and some three-quarters of them drowned, although perhaps some from the foundered ships made it to shore to be succored, like the surviving ships' crews, by Hiero's Syracusans. Whatever the precise losses, the human cost to Rome and her allies was massive. Fulvius and Aemilius astonishingly still gained triumphs for their naval victory. Political influence trumped abominable seamanship.

THE SICILIAN SEESAW

There would be no repeat invasion of North Africa. With Sardinia and Corsica out of play too, both sides focused their hostilities on the ravaged western parts of Sicily for another fourteen years. The Roman war was not Carthage's only concern. The Numidians who had raided Libya during the invasion also needed attention, and this was applied by Hamilcar, one of the three recently victorious generals. It was the start, it seems, of a new phase of expansion, which over the next seven or eight years would take Carthaginian dominance farther west and southwest into the nearer parts of Numidia—first under Hamilcar and then under a younger general named Hanno, perhaps a political ally. Carthage's aim was probably not just wider security against western raids but new sources of revenue. The long, grinding, and expensive struggle against Rome was ratcheting up demands on Libyans for tribute in money and produce; gaining power over fresh grain-growing territories, such as those in the west and southwest around Sicca and Theveste, was a distinct attraction.

This helps explain why the Carthaginians kept essentially to the defensive even after destroying the Roman invaders. To Sicily, still in 255, they dispatched some reinforcements and 140 elephants, but—despite Polybius insisting that they meant to challenge the Romans head-on—their forces made little effort to exploit enemy disarray while they had the chance. A new general, Carthalo, did retake Agrigentum—only to burn it, demolish its walls, and abandon it. A new 200-ship building project did not lead to much. By contrast the Romans rebounded from their disasters to take the initiative in the new year. They built a fresh fleet, and two more consular armies took the field, led by Atilius Caiatinus, who as consul in 258 had already commanded in the island, and, as his colleague, none other than a reelected Scipio Asina. As suggested earlier, his new consulship was probably thanks to family eminence, as suffering rapid capture by the Carthaginians in 260 was no recommendation. But the two executed a dazzling and rare feat of arms: a combined land and sea assault to capture Panormus, the chief city of Punic Sicily. After taking Cephaloedium on the north coast and making a thrust—it may have been a feint—at Drepana, they pounced on Panormus beside its broad bay with 300 ships, disembarked troops and siege engines, and in short order forced it to capitulate. Carthalo, who had beaten off the thrust on Drepana, was nowhere to be seen. For once the episode comes with some believable figures (from Diodorus). Fourteen thousand residents went free for a ransom of two *minae*—200 drachmas—per person, whereas a poorer 13,000 were sold into slavery.[5]

This was enough for a wave of other places to defect, including the Phoenician colony of Soluntum just east of Panormus. Now very little of Sicily remained in the Carthaginians' hands: the strongholds of Lilybaeum and Drepana, Thermae Himeraeae near Panormus, the island of Lipara, Heraclaea Minoa (possibly deserted), and Selinus inland, which, a few years later, was evacuated and its inhabitants moved to Lilybaeum. For the harried peoples of middle and western Sicily the war was unmitigated horror—place after place sacked; countryside plundered or ravaged; cities once rich and flourishing, such as Agrigentum and Panormus, gutted. Disasters like these had happened before in the struggles between Carthage and her Sicilian Greek opponents, but none of those wars had lasted so long or ranged so widely. Only the island's east was spared. There Hiero's small but comfortable realm was enjoying prosperous times and taking care to stay in Rome's good books, as did his ex-foes at Messana.

After 254 Carthage had no serious prospect of winning the war. She was penned into Sicily's western coastal districts, her generals now reactive rather than aggressive—Polybius's claim that they felt supremely confident because the Romans feared their elephants is hardly supported by his own or any other account of the campaigns from 253 to 250. Carthage showed no interest in a counterinvasion of Italy, not even into its south, where at least some of the recently subdued peoples—Tarentum and the Bruttians, for instance—might have been sympathetic. Her navy did very little of note even after a third Roman disaster at sea in 253 shut down Roman naval operations. All this listlessness strongly suggests that Carthage would have been ready to settle for a compromise peace. She may even have made an overture in the late 250s, giving rise to one of Rome's best-known legends. Supposedly the captive Regulus was sent home on parole to urge making terms; but instead he commanded his countrymen to fight on and then honorably sailed back to suffer a hideous death. In more banal fact, it seems, he died of privations in captivity, and his embittered widow at Rome, entrusted with lodging two distinguished Carthaginian prisoners, let them starve until one died; the other was saved only because the tribunes learned of his plight just in time. The patriotic legend that overlaid this may be based on a real Punic overture.[6]

The Romans were not minded to compromise, although their fortunes continued to vary. In 253 another 300-strong fleet ruined a profitable raid against Libya's east coast, first by almost foundering amid the treacherous shoals of the Lesser Syrtis gulf (the Gulf of Gabès) and then by running into a massive storm as it sailed for Italy from Panormus across open sea. No fewer than 150 ships were lost, with an unknowable number of lives, not that that prevented the consul Sempronius Blaesus from celebrating an African triumph. On the other hand, the navally disenchanted Romans gave up shipbuilding for a decade (according to Dio they even passed a law vetoing it), though in 252 they did capture Lipara island. Thermae Himeraeae, abandoned by its residents in favor of Lilybaeum, fell too, further squeezing Carthage's Sicilian foothold. But with these modest successes Roman efforts ran out of steam. The casualties at sea and the war's expenses—less and less matched by booty—encouraged her not only to leave her fleet small but in 251 even to halve her forces in Sicily. The consul Lucius Caecilius Metellus kept himself and his forces at Panormus, an inglorious posture that lasted all the same for months, if the widespread view is right that he and the Carthaginians clashed there at harvest time in 250.

The opposing general Hasdrubal came under pressure to do something. He took the military initiative—Carthage's first in four years—to move out from Lilybaeum with strong forces and more than a hundred elephants to attack Panormus, sometime in June. This suited Metellus well. The elephants with some Punic troops were sent up uselessly against Panormus's fortifications, to be harassed and finally maddened by volleys of missiles from the battlements and from light-armed fighters just outside the walls. Hasdrubal began to lose control of his army as confusion spread through its ranks. Then Metellus's infantry charged out from a gate diagonally opposite Hasdrubal's left. Most of the Carthaginian troops were killed or captured, and all the elephants were captured too (they were later slaughtered at Rome). If, as Dio reported, a Carthaginian fleet now turned up, it was too late. Hasdrubal suffered the predictable and painful fate of a beaten Carthaginian general, and this was Carthage's last land offensive in the war.

THE DISASTERS OF 249

The Romans of course were hugely encouraged. The new consuls for 250, Gaius Atilius Regulus, who had held the office in 257 (the defeated Regulus's brother), and Manlius Vulso, who had been Regulus's colleague, were already organizing fresh naval and legionary forces for a drive against the last Punic strongpoints, the fortress ports Lilybaeum and Drepana. Carthage had been in the same position in 277–276 against Pyrrhus, but that king had been undone by his own allies' defections— not a prospect to worry the Romans, whose military grip on the rest of the island was unchallengeable. In any case they were using no Sicilian allied forces by now, not even from Hiero. With 200 ships and four legions, they laid siege to Lilybaeum.

Inept on the offensive, the Carthaginians were contrastingly resourceful in defense. For once they had appointed vigorous and aggressive generals: Himilco in command at Lilybaeum; Hannibal and his colleague Adherbal, who brought in reinforcements; and Carthalo, last heard of six years before. Even a private citizen, another Hannibal, played a brief but notable role. The Romans had innovated by building siege engines—catapults and battering rams with protecting sheds—but, despite damage to the walls, Himilco and his men beat back every assault. An effort to block the harbor, sinking several vessels laden with stones near its entry shoals, failed because winds and currents scattered the hulks and allowed the reinforcements from Carthage to sail in. The reinforcements brought Lilybaeum's original 7,000-strong garrison up to 20,000, including Greek and Gallic mercenaries, while Adherbal sailed with the city's 700 cavalry to Drepana and from there vigorously harassed the besiegers.

Later on, various fast single Punic ships also managed to evade Roman warships to maintain communications with Africa, once a repeated example was set by the bold Hannibal, nicknamed "the Rhodian," in his specially designed quinquereme. Unluckily for him, eventually one of the other blockade runners, a quadrireme, got stuck on some of the underwater Roman rubble and was captured. With it a Roman crew managed to overhaul and board him. Both vessels then served to stop other blockade runners, leaving Lilybaeum even more isolated than before. Nonetheless the fortress city continued to be impregnable. A Greek captain named Alexon foiled a tentative mutiny by some of the garrison's Gallic troops, and sometime later enterprising Greek commandos succeeded in burning all the siege engines to ashes with the help of a friendly breeze. The Romans resigned themselves to a close blockade by land as well as sea.[7]

These episodes probably extended over 250 and into 249. The blockade-running escapades must have occurred mostly before or after the winter, for sailing was especially perilous between November and February. The besiegers ran low on supplies and, predictably, suffered torments from dysentery—badly enough, it seems, for half the soldiers and some of the fleet to be withdrawn yet again. Then the fierce fightback by the garrison and Adherbal's harassments from Drepana took a heavy toll on those remaining. Once more, probably during autumn and winter, Hiero of Syracuse had to shore them up with gifts of grain. Adherbal now also took to raiding Italy's coasts with his fleet, a renewal of unpleasant Punic attentions after an eight-year break.

All these frustrations spurred yet another Roman effort in 249. One of the consuls, Publius Claudius Pulcher—probably a son of Claudius Caudex, the Mamertines' friend—took over the siege. Sent 10,000 fresh recruits for his depleted crews, he formed the plan of seizing Drepana from the sea, while his colleague Lucius Junius Pullus organized a supply convoy for the besieging army. Claudius was a character—as painted by Diodorus, anyway—in the exemplary tradition of his patrician *gens*: haughty, harsh, and headstrong. He embarked at night for Drepana with 123 ships, aiming to take Adherbal by surprise by sailing directly into the town's narrow harbor. Cicero and others tell a famous story: when the chickens aboard the flagship revealed heaven's disfavor by refusing to eat, the consul declared, "Since they won't eat, let them drink," and had them flung over the side. The quip and the dunking look too smart to be true, but possibly enough Claudius, sure of victory, did disregard the chickens' omen.

Heaven duly proved hostile: Adherbal was not taken by surprise. He put to sea at the head of 130 or so ships crammed with troops, skirting Drepana's offshore islets on their open northern side to assail Claudius's ships as they rowed in line between the islets and the shore toward the harbor entrance. A fine Roman confusion followed. Some ships that had entered the harbor, and others coming up to it, had to pull round to get out. The rest had to turn to meet the Carthaginians now coming in from the west. Close to the shore, with little room to maneuver—and plainly no longer raven-equipped—most were overwhelmed. Claudius, bringing up the rear, made it back with about thirty other ships to the anchorage outside Lilybaeum. Ninety-three more were captured with their crews or were run aground and abandoned. The captures and captives were sent to Carthage. Diodorus claims that 20,000 of Claudius's men were lost, in Carthage's only major victory at sea.[8]

The other consul, Junius, was already on the way with 120 warships escorting 800 supply transports. Miscalculated overconfidence was not limited to Claudius. Junius put in at Syracuse to gather further supplies, sending ahead via the south coast 400 laden transports with a small escort under two quaestors. This was a mistake that a more experienced commander and a bigger escort might (perhaps) have avoided. The dynamic Carthaginian officer Carthalo had already arrived at Drepana with seventy more quinqueremes. Adherbal added thirty of his own and sent Carthalo out by night to attack the battered Roman fleet anchored near Lilybaeum. His dawn onslaught was seconded by Himilco's men making a sortie from the city, throwing all the Roman forces into uproar and confusion. Carthalo carried off or damaged a few enemy vessels and, probably more important, revictualed the besieged city. Even so, this was just the first of his feats. Next he sailed south to intercept the quaestors' convoy, so alarming them that they put in to shore at Phintias, where they could protect their ships with catapults from its fortifications. Carthalo still managed to tow away a few cargo ships, but bigger prey was coming from the east: an unsuspecting consul with 400 more transports and the bulk of his fleet. Junius had rather more than 100 quinqueremes, yet on sighting Carthalo's advancing force he chose not to engage but to anchor beside the harborless rocky coast near Camarina, seventy kilometers east of Phintias, still watched by the enemy—until stormy weather approached. Thereupon Carthalo sailed past to round Cape Pachynus into calmer waters south of Syracuse, leaving the two separated Roman fleets to be smashed to pieces by the gale. The crews escaped to land, but nothing seaworthy was left except two quinqueremes, which bore the hapless Junius to Lilybaeum to take over command from Claudius.

Neither consul, Rome's most inglorious pair in the entire war, had a happy outcome. Junius did succeed in seizing the height of Eryx, overlooking Drepana and crowned with a temple of Phoenician Astarte (identified with Greek Aphrodite and Roman Venus, but a cult and site notorious for sacred prostitution). His nemesis Carthalo soon arrived, however, and in a skirmish captured him—the third consul to fall into Punic hands. Tradition had it that Junius had disobeyed omens against fighting and later committed suicide in Rome (he no doubt came home in a prisoner exchange in 247). Publius Claudius, annoyed at being told by the Senate to appoint a dictator (who would outrank him) to mend the situation, annoyed the Senate in return by nominating a family dependent named Claudius Glicia. The inevitable furor forced Glicia to step down and be replaced by a much more seemly person, Atilius Caiatinus—consul back in 258 and 254, a kinsman of the Regulus cousins—who appointed Metellus, the hero of Panormus, as his master of horse. Publius Claudius on leaving office was prosecuted by two tribunes (the charge is obscure) and fined a substantial 120,000 *asses*. This verdict, and his death not long after, may have soothed his fellow citizens' anger. All the same they had to face the reality that the high hopes of the past two years had ended in grief and disaster.

5

STALEMATE AND CHECKMATE: 249-241

AN INTERIM BALANCE SHEET

Carthage's successes in 249 were her greatest in the war, and for them she could thank a remarkable trio of commanders: Adherbal, Himilco, and Carthalo. Rome by contrast had sunk to a dispiriting nadir of failure, which continued to blight her efforts afterward. Lilybaeum and Drepana continued under siege by each year's consuls, with little to show for it. Carthalo raided Italy again in 248, and so did his successor in following years. Instead of fleet-building, the Romans simply built defensive coastal colonies, Alsium and Fregenae north of Rome and Brundisium on the Adriatic. The census in 246 registered just over 241,000 citizens, a 17 percent fall from 265. Interpretation is debated because the census figure for 251 is uncertain (297,000 or 267,000), but the steep drop cannot be unconnected with Rome's recent war losses. The Italian allies must have suffered heavy losses, too.

Not only had Carthage comprehensively beaten down her opponent, but she was triumphant in North Africa. Her furious repression of the Numidians who had attacked Libya in 256–255 brought mastery over the fertile territories farther inland. Around 247 a new general, Hanno—supposedly nicknamed "the Great"—captured Theveste 300 kilometers southwest of Carthage. Sicca too, 100 kilometers to Theveste's north and 180 west of Carthage, was probably another gain.[1]

It is all the stranger, then, that the victorious leaders of 249 disappear from the scene within a year. Carthalo, the last of them, disposed of mutinous mercenaries in 248 after raiding Italy (he dumped them on deserted islets) and then found himself superseded. The new general, Hamilcar, nicknamed Barca, remained in command until the war's end. At Lilybaeum the garrison was now led by one Gisco. In Libya, Hanno the Great looks like another newcomer, for he was in public life at least till 203. For a corps of successful commanders to be dropped wholesale suggests politics: one hitherto dominant faction abruptly losing ground to a rival. Failure to exploit the victories of 249—for example, to try to expel the Romans from western Sicily—and the costs of the interminable war could have influenced the switch. State finances were struggling. Carthage tried to borrow 2,000 talents from Ptolemy II of Egypt (a very large sum, equivalent to twelve million drachmas); he declined to lend. Roman and Italian privateers were preying on North African merchant shipping and raiding Libya's coasts. They became numerous enough even to sack Hippou Acra, eighty kilometers to Carthage's north.[2]

Hanno held the Libyan command and primacy in Carthaginian politics for the rest of the 240s. The conventional view of Punic politics makes him the leader of the supposedly conservative landowning aristocracy, hostile to commercial interests backing Hamilcar Barca. Certainly the two did fall out around 240, and from then on Hanno was consigned to political impotence. Yet in 247 Hamilcar cannot have been his enemy: Hanno and his supporters had no reason to let an enemy be given command in Sicily, still less keep it for six years. Hamilcar in 247, on the other hand, looks not like a political equal but like an ally. It was Hanno who earned enthusiasm for his western conquests and ruthless exploitation of the subject Libyans; in Sicily Hamilcar had to operate on military and financial shoestrings. He too was relatively young, says his biographer Nepos, but he nonetheless had three daughters close to marriageable age. Then, just before or after he took up his military command, the first of three sons arrived. Hamilcar named him Hannibal after his own father.

In Sicily both sides' options had shrunk. The besiegers of Lilybaeum and Drepana, lacking effective warships, could not stop supplies from getting in. On the other hand, they were not going to leave off. The theory that affairs were now in the hands of a peace-inclined group, headed by the Fabii, rests merely on three successive Fabii—two brothers and their cousin—being consuls from 247 to 245 and achieving little. Yet their colleagues were Caecilius Metellus in 247 (the victor at Panormus); in 246 Manius Otacilius, who had campaigned in Sicily back in 263; and then Gaius Atilius Bulbus in 245. Peace-mindedness at Rome's highest levels is not at all plausible. Fabius Buteo in 247 actually managed to seize one of Drepana's offshore islets, despite Hamilcar Barca's efforts. The problem was that no further success followed. The Romans could not take either port, and Hamilcar could not make them give up. After another raid on Italy, he turned to an entirely new strategy, one with more than a hint of improvisation.

He occupied a coastal height called Heircte or Hercte near Panormus, accessed by few and steep paths, with a harbor at its foot where he could moor his warships. Heircte was probably Monte Castellaccio, part of the block of mountains some ten kilometers west of Panormus, topped by a broad plateau 600–800 meters high and with the little port and harbor of Isola delle Femmine below. Despite being watched by Roman forces at its foot, Heircte proved impregnable for three years. At the same time it enabled Hamilcar to continue his occasional Italian raids and also to launch attacks on enemy strongpoints in Sicily. An incomplete excerpt from Diodorus mentions one such, against a fort called Italium near a town, Longon, in the territory of Catana, perhaps an attempt on an east-coast fort. From time to time he may have sailed over to Drepana and Lilybaeum to hearten the garrisons—and to Carthage, for his second and third sons, Hasdrubal and Mago, arrived between 246 and about 241, born surely there and not on his mountaintop. Yet his military activities were essentially futile. The raids were little more than local irritants, while the Romans kept him equally busy at Heircte itself fending off their attacks. By 244 Hamilcar judged that it had failed as a stronghold. He took the Romans by surprise when he pounced on the Eryx massif behind and above Drepana. The small town on the ridge halfway up the mountain was emptied of its hapless residents, who had to move to Drepana.

Hamilcar's transfer was only partly successful. His forces on the ridge were sandwiched between the legions encamped below outside Drepana and troops garrisoning the summit with its sacred temple. Later, apparently while he was away, a contingent of unruly Gauls among his troops tried to hand Eryx town over to the Romans, were foiled, and promptly deserted. The position gave access to the sea along a single road, and so he could bring up supplies, but over the next three years his every attempt at breaking Drepana's siege failed. Intermittent fighting, with varying outcomes, left the situation unchanged, although Diodorus happily illustrates Hamilcar's chivalry with an incident in 243. After an unexpected defeat outside Drepana in which disaster facing an officer named "Vodostor" (Bostar in Punic) was barely averted by the gallantry of 200 cavalrymen, Hamilcar requested a truce to bury the dead—a standard courtesy—but was refused by the consul Fundanius. Then fortune swiftly turned against Fundanius; soon he suffered serious losses and had to seek a burial truce himself. This the Carthaginian granted, remarking that he was at war with the living but at peace with the dead.[3]

The anecdote reveals more than Punic chivalry (a quality not often acknowledged by Greek or Roman authors). The combatants' numbers were small; the clashes made no change to the military balance; and not only did the siege wear on, but—tellingly—Hamilcar seems to have had little to do with Lilybaeum except for an occasional visit. There the garrison commander was the hard-working Gisco, who held his men's respect but could only endure. Naval raids on Italy ceased. So did reinforcements from Carthage, even if individual ships could still make the crossing. Crucially, funds to pay the troops at Eryx and in the ports ceased arriving too. The authorities perhaps were stingy, but on the other hand, putting large quantities of money—actual coinage—aboard ship when enemy privateers were on the prowl would be asking for trouble. Besides, with the garrisons shut up in the ports and Hamilcar's men encamped on their ridge, there was little to spend their pay on. Hamilcar made do by promising the men plentiful rewards once the war was over.

The Carthaginians in fact had no idea how to end the war short of asking for terms. Arguably, they might send over huge (and hugely expensive) new forces to Hamilcar with orders to destroy the Roman armies and dictate terms. But Hamilcar had shown no ability for winning pitched battles, and the Romans no inclination to negotiate after defeats. Neither reinforced nor rejected, he was left to hang on in

Sicily. Very likely no other potential general wanted his job, Hanno the Great least of all. At the same time the Romans did not, apparently, overexert themselves at the ports and Eryx: no fresh assaults, no attempts to bribe any of the garrison mercenaries or even mount better blockades of the harbors. When the Gauls at Eryx deserted to them, their knowledge of or contacts with fellow mercenaries were not utilized. They were sent up to guard the sacred temple on the mountaintop (they happily looted it). It looks as though each side was waiting for something to turn up or for the other side to collapse in simple exhaustion.

THE FINAL DICE THROW

New political personalities appeared at Rome in late 243: Gaius Lutatius Catulus and his brother Quintus Lutatius Cerco. They backed—probably they led—a successful drive to build a new grand fleet and put an end to Lilybaeum and Drepana. Invading Africa was the obvious further aim. Roman funds were so low that a public loan had to be organized, or, rather, a sponsorship plan. One or more men of means undertook to fund a warship and defer reimbursement until victory. Just as Rome's first fleet had been modeled on the Punic quinquereme captured outside Messana, now this one was based on Hannibal the Rhodian's exceptional craft. "Ravens" were not judged necessary; maybe the trim of the ships was not suitable. Two hundred were built, Catulus was elected consul for 242, and as praetor the voters chose Publius Valerius Falto—clearly an ally of the brothers, for he worked ably with Lutatius in the operations that followed. Lutatius's brother Cerco, in turn, in the midst of the new drive would be elected consul for 241. It was Catulus, with praetor Falto an unusual second-in-command, who took the new fleet to Sicily in summer 242. His colleague Postumius Albinus, who was also the *flamen* (special priest) of Mars, was conveniently declared ineligible for command by Rome's new Pontifex Maximus (chief pontiff)—none other than Caecilius Metellus of Panormus fame and likely enough another proponent of dash.

The timing of events that followed is a puzzle. Lutatius and his fleet reached western Sicily at the start of summer, Polybius says. There he infused the sieges with fresh vigor, cutting off Drepana's harbor from the open sea (we are not told how) and likewise blocking off Lilybaeum, despite suffering a serious thigh wound in one combat. Hamilcar Barca was powerless to interfere. More strangely his home authorities took very long to organize a response. The relief fleet with troops and supplies under yet another Hanno sailed only in spring 241, for it was intercepted and totally defeated on March 10 (so writes the later historian Eutropius, the only source with a date).

The Carthaginians supposedly had had trouble finding trained seamen. Polybius contrasts Lutatius's skillful oarsmen, who had all summer to practice, with Hanno's new and unhandy crews. Yet Carthalo's and Adherbal's sailors cannot all have died or emigrated—though perhaps some old hands were unenthusiastic about joining up yet again. By contrast, some warships could have been broken up since 249 or were unseaworthy for other reasons, and repairs, still more so replacements, took time. The small warship discovered in Marsala's harbor, an auxiliary it seems to the fleet of 241, was newly built; and worth notice is how in 218, when the next war opened, a sizable minority of the already lean Punic navy was again unseaworthy. The news of Lutatius's fleet must have mentioned that his quinqueremes were highly up to date, even perhaps that they matched Hannibal the Rhodian's. Hannibal's exploits imply that his ship had been unique at Carthage; with him and it now out of reach, the best that the Carthaginians could do in 242 would be to try to upgrade older warships and build new ones as best they could. It would all take time and maybe some false starts. Their crews might practice on land, like the Roman beginners in 260, but again as in 260 actual training at sea was essential; this had to wait until the fleet was ready to float. Then autumn and winter arrived to close down all but emergency sailing until the new year.

Winter made the state of rations at Lilybaeum, Drepana, and Eryx much worse thanks to Lutatius's tightened blockade. News could still slip through to and from Africa, and so a disastrous decision was made: to launch the fleet, 250 strong, loaded with both relief supplies and fresh mercenary troops. The plan—such as it was—involved delivering the supplies while the Romans were not looking (or were somehow navally distracted), taking on Hamilcar and his best troops from Eryx, and then going into battle with the enemy fleet. Early March, though, was far from the best season for a risky venture like this. And the Romans did not fail to learn of the fleet's approach. Lutatius and Falto readied theirs, took aboard the best land troops, and intercepted Hanno near Hiera, outermost of the Aegates islands—the last thing Hanno wanted, weighed down as his ships were with grain and rather green troops. The only features favoring him were a fresh westerly that made rowing harder for the Romans and the bravery of his crews, but though they inflicted losses, the battle was soon over. Fifty ships sunk, seventy taken, and a varyingly reported (4,400 to nearly 10,000) haul of prisoners ended Carthage's last effort to save Punic Sicily.[4]

Hanno with the survivors sailed home, where the Court of 104 dealt with him in the usual way. Lutatius and Falto had lost thirty of their own quinqueremes, and another fifty were badly damaged, but now they commanded the sea. On land the defenders of the ports and Hamilcar's men on Eryx ridge were starving. The authorities at Carthage dared not risk a new invasion of Libya. They no doubt knew that the subject Libyans were in a bitter mood. Maybe too they feared Libyphoenician resentment at a quarter-century of fruitless war, coastal Roman raids, and now privateers' harassment. Hamilcar received a dispatch authorizing him to negotiate.

Lutatius's terms were predictably hard: especially a total Carthaginian evacuation of Sicily, a war indemnity of 2,200 talents payable over twenty years, Punic prisoners to be ransomed whereas Carthage must of course repatriate her captives ransom-free, and a fee—effectively a ransom too—of eighteen drachmas each to allow Hamilcar's soldiers at Eryx to leave. Hamilcar stared him down over two other intentionally humiliating demands—that his men surrender their arms and hand over their Roman and allied deserters—with a dignified firmness that prompted the beginnings of an enduring Roman respect. At Rome, nonetheless, enough people took umbrage at the consul's supposed lenience for ten special envoys to be selected, senators no doubt, and sent to amend his terms. The chief change was financial. The indemnity went up to 3,200 talents (19.2 million drachmas or about 192 million *asses*), and its calendar went down: a thousand to be paid at once and the rest over only ten years, probably to ensure that Carthage would be too starved of funds to consider any new war. Perhaps for the same reason "the islands between Sicily and Italy" (which must mean chiefly the Lipara chain) were added to the evacuation clause. But the terms were reasonably statesmanlike. Each side's allies must be respected, and not recruited, by the other (the earlier version had covered Syracuse alone), and neither should recruit troops from the other's lands (this guarded Rome's claims on Italian manpower) or set up fortified places there.[5]

The Carthaginians were in no position to argue—even if Hamilcar believed that they should have fought on. The treaty was agreed in May or June, and he sailed for Carthage, leaving Gisco to organize the troop removals. To settle affairs in Sicily, Catulus as proconsul was joined by his brother Cerco, now consul. Some states, such as the Mamertines who had started it all, became formal allies of Rome like Syracuse; others (it seems) remained in an informal relationship under Roman hegemony. Catulus and Falto returned to Rome for triumphs on October 4 and 6, leaving the harried Sicilians to make a start on recovery. Their old freedoms to fight one another and play major roles in the affairs of the western Greek world were lost forever. The word "province" was not yet applied, but something momentous had happened: the birth of the Roman empire. The Romans of the time did not see it this way—for years they did little with their new possession, four-fifths of the island—but Sicily was their first extra-Italian territory, in a series that would climax one day with Rome ruling from the Atlantic to the Euphrates.

CONCLUSIONS

The First Punic War, according to Polybius, cost the belligerents over a thousand battleships: he reckons 700 of Rome's and 500 Carthaginian. The lives claimed by battles and storm disasters outdid the losses from virtually any earlier war. How many more were killed or died—in sieges, sackings, and land-ravagings across western Sicily in particular but also in campaigns and raids elsewhere—could never be calculated. Overall, the Romans suffered worse material losses from the willfulness of the sea, and their misreading of it, than from their enemies. The outcome was a triumph all the same. For the first time, Roman mastery stretched permanently beyond Italy. Simultaneously, the Mediterranean's older great powers learned that another had asserted its potential.

Rome enjoyed many lucky strikes between 264 and 241. Above all, no other threats arose to distract her—no hostilities with north Italy's Gauls (why they kept quiet is unknown), no revolts by Italian allies, no disputes with peoples across the Adriatic. This respite could not have been foreseen. Gallic conflicts and Italian wars had been rife down to the 270s; nor was it long before others erupted again, together with the first trans-Adriatic war. By 264 domestic social stresses—popular agitation over debt levels and over plebeians' access to legal and political rights—had eased too, and the touchy issue of land grants to poorer citizens arose only in the later 230s. By contrast, the two decades of Punic war were (on the evidence) far less troubled. Rome enjoyed the benefit, too, of staying free from enemy invasion throughout, apart from intermittent coast raids (most of them in its first years and then between 249 and 244).

On the other hand, most Roman war-waging was mediocre. During the Italian wars it had been standard for Roman forces to attack hostile heartlands directly and go on attacking till their opponents sought terms. Against Carthage, all but two years of land war, in 256–255, were limited to Sicily plus raids into Sardinia. In Sicily, where the principal Punic centers lay on the coasts, only one amphibious operation was launched (the one that took Panormus); even where a fleet and army stood alongside the same city, like Drepana in the 240s, they operated apart. Crucial decisions—or lack of decisions—could be bizarre. Even after the Punic war proper superseded the Syracusan in late 263, a grand fleet remained at best a gleam in the eye of a few leading men (Valerius Messala's according to Diodorus) for two more years. Though the new navy under Duilius then showed what it could do with legionaries' help, Africa stayed uninvaded for four years more. The victory of Ecnomus gave a Roman army of more than 30,000 the entry to Africa, but it was quickly slimmed to 15,000 with derisory cavalry strength. Regulus's intransigent sabotage of his own peace prospects hardly needs underlining. The heavens played a part in Rome's naval misfortunes (in 255, 253, and 249), but so did the unseaworthy overconfidence of consuls.

Political appointments were a problem. Rather than reelect battle-winning consuls or extend their military commands as proconsuls—a regularity in Italian wars after 327—the Romans chose new yearly pairs. Dio underlines the inefficiency of replacing commanders every year outside Lilybaeum and Drepana. In fact the inefficiency was longer and deeper. It reflected Rome's competitive political life, a competitiveness made easier partly because Italy was never seriously menaced, partly because most Carthaginian generals were not vastly abler. Roman aristocrats and voters could feel that a wide range of notables were entitled to seek glory through high office, in contrast to the old days when military leadership was confided repeatedly to veteran generals. As a result voters' choices seem seldom based on military needs or even experience. Messala and Duilius, like Lucius Scipio and Sulpicius Paterculus (the victors in Sardinia in 259–258), never won second consulships. Those who did succeeded only after lengthy breaks—Manius Otacilius with a seventeen-year gap after 263, Gaius Regulus (victor at Tyndaris in 257) not again until 250, Manlius Vulso (co-victor at Ecnomus in 256) likewise only in 250, Caecilius Metellus in 251 and 247. Moreover, in contrast to the successes of their first terms, none achieved much of note in the second. The only pair to do better the second time around were Atilius Caiatinus, who, after run-of-the-mill campaigning in 258, collaborated in capturing Panormus four years later, and his then collaborator Scipio Asina, Carthage's prize but ransomed captive. Aurelius Cotta and Servilius Geminus, twice colleagues in 252 and 248, did nothing remarkable either time; and the only notable achievement of Sempronius Blaesus (253 and 244) was helping to lose half a fleet in the storm of 253.

Carthage managed her war no better. Unenthused about it from the beginning, she then responded as she had done to her Sicilian Greek foes—using large armies and large fleets essentially to protect Punic territories in the island's west, though sometimes doing so via strategic offensives. Her fleets rarely cooperated effectively with the land forces or had much independent impact. Yet from 264 she faced a new kind of foe and novel strategic problems: no enemy center readily accessible to attack, in contrast to Syracuse or Acragas in former times (raiding Italian coasts was no substitute); no ready means, therefore, of putting meaningful pressure on Rome to seek terms; and a much more demanding role for the navy, which had to fight giant battles with more costly warships—and far heavier casualties—than ever before. Carthage's generals, nearly all of them admirals only secondarily, faced tests greater than their ancestors had. At sea only the unusual duo in 249, Adherbal and Carthalo, shone when tested. Her only other generals of some skill were the two Hamilcars, first the general in Sicily from 260 to 255 and then Barca. Polybius's gushing praise of Barca, all the same, as "the commander who must, for his intelligence and daring, be given pride of place above all the rest" on either side, is overblown. Hamilcar's long tenure was basically a holding pattern, without major battles and with minimal impact on enemy operations.[6]

Serious miscalculations damaged Carthage's war-making too. Despite her hard line toward Appius Claudius at the straits of Messina, she did nothing to support Hiero until too late. Annihilating Regulus in 255, together with the Mediterranean helpfully shattering the rescue fleet, opened the opportunity to take initiatives by both sea and land; instead Panormus was lost the year after. Adherbal's and Carthalo's still more impressive victories might have been exploited at least to free Drepana and Lilybaeum, if not reopen a broader offensive against the baffled—by now even demoralized—Romans. Their actual upshot was that Adherbal and Carthalo disappeared. Worse, over the next several years Carthage ran down her fleet and maintained Hamilcar in Sicily on a limited budget of men and funds—again until too late. Reluctant to fight in 264, and after 254 plainly unable to win the war, by 247 she was less keen than ever, continuing it only because the Romans would not let up and perhaps hoping that the vigorous Hamilcar could find a way to frustrate them into negotiations. He turned out to have no solution, and it was Rome that cast the final and crushing throw of dice.

6

BETWEEN THE WARS: 241–218

ROME AFTER 241

Having thrown the Carthaginians out of Sicily after their 300-year stay, the Romans did little with the island. Some communities were formal allies, notably the Mamertines and Syracuse. The others, including those taken from Carthage, were also left largely to themselves but forbidden to take up arms (unless Rome demanded it) and probably were expected to supply grain and other goods to Roman authorities if called on. Apart from making Carthage repatriate Sicilian hostages, Rome took no known steps to help communities recover from the ravages of war, though Hiero may have been kinder—after all, it was in Syracuse's interest to have prosperous neighbors. Inscriptions show that around 242, even before peace, Camarina and Phintias on the south coast set up ceremonious interstate relations with the prestigious Aegean island of Cos, for all the world like independent polities; they seem to have been on the mend from their earlier misfortunes.

Hiero trod carefully in this new scenario. Rome must receive due respect—he visited the City in 237, bearing gifts of grain and taking home plaudits—and never be crossed, yet at the same time he tried to present Syracuse as something like the independent power it once had been. So during Carthage's postwar agony of mercenary and Libyan revolt, he exerted himself to send over plentiful food and munitions to her: he judged it essential for one great power not to dominate all. Polybius lauds his statesmanship—but promptly indicates that there was no risk in it, because the Romans sent aid too.[1]

In Italy the city-state of Falerii thirty miles north of Rome, once a formidable neighbor but now mighty only in its citizens' minds, chose 241 and the expiry of a fifty-year truce to renew its own war. This was an unusually fatuous own goal. Falerii was overwhelmed in six days, its walls razed, and its survivors transplanted from their hilltop to flat land nearby. Yet Falerii may not have been the only Italian ally to feel resentment, even if no one else dared show it. Italians had got little out of the war apart from campaign booty and privateering, even though they had made equal (or greater) contributions and suffered losses at least as heavy as Rome's. King Hiero's grain was for Rome; any Italians keen on a share would have had to go there—and then ask. If Rome shared any of the war indemnity with her allies, it is kept quiet in our sources.

Peace between Rome and Carthage had not long returned before fresh friction arose, sometime in 240. Italian merchants fell foul of Carthage by trading with the rebels in Libya holding her by the throat. Arrested and locked up at Carthage—no fewer than 500 of them—they prompted a protest embassy from Rome. Of course the Carthaginians could not afford a quarrel and released them at once. Rome in turn, gratified at the compliance and also worried at the prospective anarchy in Libya, exerted herself to help her ex-enemy. Traders from Italy were banned from dealing with the rebels, and Carthaginian requests for supplies were readily met; the treaty clause against recruiting troops in Roman-ruled territories was suspended, and—on a reasonable surmise—so were installments of the indemnity while the revolt lasted. Probably in 239 an appeal to Rome from Carthage's sister city Utica, desperate for help against rebel besiegers, was refused. She also rejected (then or in 238) a call from Sardinia's rebel mercenaries, who had massacred the Carthaginians there and, Mamertine-style, sought Rome's patronage. Roman support, like Hiero's, contributed to Carthage's crushing of the rebellion in late 238 and early 237. It made the next stage of relations with her all the more extraordinary.

THE TRUCELESS WAR

Required by the treaty to remove Punic forces from Sicily, the Carthaginians faced the uneasy problem in summer 241 of demobilizing more than 20,000 unemployed veteran mercenaries—chiefly Spaniards, Gauls, Ligurians, and southern Italians—and Libyan conscripts, all of them owed several years' pay. Hamilcar, who had kept them loyal by making lavish promises, now resigned his command to go into private life, probably the price for avoiding prosecution by embittered opponents. Negotiating with the soldiery was Hanno the Great's task, and he made a sorry hash of it, trying to beat down the men's claims on the plea that the war they had fought had impoverished their employer. Late in 241 his replacement, Gisco, Hamilcar's old and respected deputy, did commit Carthage to pay the arrears in full to the troops, now encamped with their families at nearby Tunes. It was too late. A malcontent faction in the army, led by the Libyan soldier Mathos, a Campanian deserter from Rome's forces (and therefore a Roman citizen) named Spendius, and Autaritus, the leader of the Gallic contingent, exploited the troops' continuing resentment and suspicions to engineer a coup. They overthrew, murdered, and replaced the army's commanders and excited a general rebellion across Libya. Carthage's heavy-handed exploitation of her subjects during the war, gouge-taxing townsmen and farmers and relentlessly punishing defaulters, had built up hatreds that needed only this opportunity to spill over. Reinforced by reportedly 70,000 Libyan volunteers, the rebels blockaded Carthage from Tunes and besieged her nearby allies Utica and Hippou Acra. The mercenaries in Sardinia followed fashion: they slaughtered every Carthaginian they could catch and seized the island.

Hanno was outside Carthage with the small army he had led since 247. He could make little impression on this tidal wave of insurrection except help Utica and Hippou Acra to hold out. Nor did an expedition to regain Sardinia prosper—its mercenaries lynched their commander (still another Hanno) and joined the rebels. Carthage relied on her massive fortifications, accessibility by sea, and the hastily reappointed Hamilcar. With another small army recruited from citizens and fresh mercenaries—and some rebel deserters—he sortied from the city probably early in 240, aiming to undermine the insurgency by winning over or subduing the Libyans inland. The strategy was high-risk. Although he won a quick victory over Spendius on the banks of the river Bagradas north of Carthage, he later got himself boxed in on a narrow plain by Spendius and Autaritus holding the hills above and joined by just-arrived Numidian allies. As Polybius tells it, one young Numidian commander, Naravas, so admired the famous general that he took his men and changed sides, helped him defeat the rebel forces, and was promised one of his daughters in marriage.

As Hamilcar's and Naravas's operations in the hinterland proceeded, probably during 240 and into 239, the rebel high command on the coast resorted to atrocities to cement their own followers' loyalty and terrorize opponents: gruesomely slaughtering Gisco and his companions, mutilating war captives, and murdering critics in their own ranks. Hamilcar's brutal retaliation included having prisoners trampled by his elephants (a savagery borrowed from the Greek east) and harrying rebel communities with fire and sword. Polybius stresses that it was these mutual excesses that gave the "Truceless War" a special horror.

Predictably, instead of cowing resistance Hamilcar stiffened it. He had to call on Hanno—most likely still holding ground near Utica and Hippou Acra—to reinforce him. This nearly led to fresh disaster, for the two generals quarreled so bitterly that operations came to a stop. The *adirim* at Carthage, called on to decide between them, took an unusual if not unique step, giving the choice to the soldiers—most likely the Carthaginian personnel—in the combined army. Sensibly these voted for Hamilcar, who, despite intermittent misjudgments, was plainly better at war. Hanno was not deposed from his generalship but went back to Carthage, where probably he headed its defenders. The soldiers' vote, though, badly hit his political power. It would be men close to Hamilcar—notably another son-in-law, Hasdrubal, already a popular favorite—who would profit by Barca's ongoing successes, no doubt joined over time by many more in the elite who saw that Hanno's day was done.

Meanwhile the rebellion surged on. Utica and Hippou Acra caved in, freeing their besiegers to join the main rebel army at Tunes. The

rebels put out coins, many of them Carthaginian silver shekels overstruck with symbols such as a lion, bull, horse, or Melqart in profile,
with the legend "Of the Libyans" (in Greek letters: *Libyon*). The coinage was apparently to pay foreign traders; many surviving examples
come from Sicily. What national or ethnic consciousness there was
among the Libyan peoples is opaque. The only other evidence for
cooperation was the mercenary and largely Libyan army under
Mathos, Spendius, and Autaritus, joined for a time by another Libyan
commander named Zarzas. The rebel communities' role was to send
them recruits and funds—a task repeatedly disrupted by Hamilcar's
cross-country raids.

Probably between autumn 239 and spring 238 Mathos hardened the
blockade of Carthage into a full siege—presumably attacking the walls
with troops and any available siege engines—while Hamilcar, Hanno's
more amenable successor Hannibal, and Naravas focused on disrupting
Mathos's links to the interior. As a result Carthage's besiegers themselves
came under virtual siege. Over time they began to starve. When Spendius
launched a new campaign against Hamilcar, during summer 238, he
ended entrapped at a place called the Saw—apparently beside a steep
mountain ridge—where the rebel army was starved into begging for
terms and then was massacred on a pretext. Spendius, Autaritus, and
Zarzas were taken back to the hills around Tunes and crucified there.
Mathos, still full of fight, struck back: Hamilcar's unlucky colleague
Hannibal was routed, captured, and crucified on Spendius's cross, with
thirty high-ranking Carthaginian captives slaughtered at his feet.
Hamilcar marched away to the Bagradas.

The *adirim* recovered their nerve. A senior delegation to Hamilcar, accompanied by Hanno himself—so acknowledging his rival's superiority—recon-
ciled them enough to cooperate in destroying Mathos. The final act of the
war was played out in Byzacium, near Hadrumetum and Leptis Minor.
What was left of Mathos's army was crushed; Mathos himself fell into
Hamilcar's hands to be dragged through Carthage's streets and killed. Soon
enough the whole of Libya and finally Utica and Hippou Acra capitulated, at
the end of 238 or early in 237. Carthage abstained from savage reprisals,
instead imposing terms bearable enough to keep the Libyans loyal

throughout the next Roman war. This sensible policy must be credited to Hamilcar, the new leader of the republic.

The Truceless War's cost in lives, property, and money must have been heavy. Polybius numbers the rebels slaughtered at the Saw alone as 40,000; the number may be exaggerated but no doubt was large, and this was only the biggest of many battles. Restoring Carthage to prosperity was urgently needed. Hamilcar and his group were clearly forming plans even before hostilities in Africa closed. An expedition was readied to retake Sardinia (the native Sardinians had expelled the mutineers), as was a much larger one under Hamilcar himself to acquire new dominions in Spain. But now Carthage's historical trajectory collided in totally unforeseen fashion with Rome.

THE SARDINIA CRISIS

Rome had materially aided Carthage since 240. And she had not accepted the invitation from the mercenaries in Sardinia to annex it. Yet, when these, expelled by the locals to Italy, appealed anew, she abruptly began readying forces to do just that—then denounced Carthage's planned expedition as really aimed against Italy. In the face of appalled Carthaginian protests, Rome added (or substituted) the allegation that they had maltreated, even murdered, many of the Italian traders arrested in 240—an exercise in surreal logic, given that the traders' case had been settled very amicably. To ram the bully-point home, consuls and Senate arranged for the Comitia Centuriata to declare war. Neither Polybius nor Roman tradition offers any coherent explanation. Polybius in fact calls it "an act of sheer injustice" and one cause of the war to come. Later writers, Greek and Roman, oscillated between claiming farcically that Sardinia had been ceded in 241 (as one of "the islands between Sicily and Italy") and painting lurid pictures of hapless merchants being covertly drowned by Punic villains—a lie first dished up by the Romans themselves in 237 as another ground for war.

Arguments that only now were Romans realizing Sardinia's attractions, or were remedying a strategic oversight in not demanding it in 241, do not convince. Roman forces did not land there until 235, and Sardinia's main use for decades afterward was as a hunting ground for booty-hungry consuls or praetors. The real motive very likely was that the military and political triumph of Rome's old and unconquered opponent Hamilcar, plus word of Carthage's intended overseas expeditions, triggered alarm. True, Romans had no sympathy for rebellious allies and subjects and had willingly lent help against them; but a vigorously reviving Carthage, led by her ablest general and already aiming to project her power overseas, was a different prospect. It was only four years since she had lost Sicily. Romans, judging others by their own ingrained instincts, might forecast that if Hamilcar's Carthage retook Sardinia, trying to retake Sicily might prove an irresistible temptation.

The Carthaginians yielded. They had to accept a treaty revision, not just to cede Sardinia but to pay Rome another 1,200 talents and pay this at once. This exaction, bigger than the down payment in 241, is often lost sight of; but not by Polybius. It was probably to cripple further any chance of Carthage fighting a major war for which she would have to build a modern fleet and hire plentiful new mercenaries. Just paying off the original war indemnity, at 220 talents a year, would not be enough of a check. Still, the fact that she did pay the new indemnity with no known delay, and Hamilcar then began to conquer Spain with his seasoned army, suggests that maybe Carthage complied too readily with Rome's *diktat*. Had she refused, begun building a new navy, and met any Roman invasion with Hamilcar as general, she might have changed her own and Rome's history, in her favor. Instead the lasting impact of the Sardinia crisis was to kill off the fragile chance of the two states rebuilding friendly relations and to recharge the latent mistrust that each held for the other. Its immediate sequel for Carthage was the Barcid empire in Spain.

ROME VERSUS GAULS AND ILLYRIANS

The Gallic peoples of northern Italy, then called Cisalpine Gaul or Cisalpina, had not troubled the peninsula for more than forty years, but during the 230s relations soured anew. Gauls in southeastern Cisalpina had lost land to Rome after 283 and resented the Latin colony of Ariminum founded there in 268. Rome in turn made friends with the non-Gallic Cenomani and Veneti dwelling between these Gauls and the Alpine foothills—another irritation. Clashes over Ariminum with the Boii, the leading people of southern Cisalpina, in the early 230s were followed by a law in 232, brainchild of a vigorous plebeian tribune, Gaius Flaminius, to open up the annexed Gallic land to poor citizens. Yet the Gauls took years to react, giving the Romans and their allies invaluable time for preparation. When invasion from the north loomed in 225, very large forces were levied: two consular armies, another legion under a praetor, a four-legion reserve army at Rome, a legion in Sicily and one at Tarentum, and supporting allied contingents, to a total of some 210,000 troops according to Polybius. The legions sent to Tarentum and Sicily—of all places the least in peril from Gauls—are worth noting. So is the fact that one of the consuls first went to Sardinia.

The invading Gauls came from all the Cisalpine peoples, chief among them the Insubres of the northwest and the Boii, and from across the Alps a body of professional warriors called Gaesatae, making an army of 50,000 foot and an unusually numerous 20,000 horse. After some opening successes and plentiful plundering, they were met in Etruria not only by one consul, Lucius Aemilius Papus, marching across from Ariminum, but by his colleague Gaius Atilius Regulus (nephew of Africa's invader), sailing over from Sardinia at just the right moment. Near Cape Telamon the Gauls, drawn up back to back against the legions closing in from both sides, were almost wiped out, though it cost Regulus his life. Italy was saved.

The initiative shifted to Rome. Between 225 and 222 consuls campaigned across Cisalpine Gaul, steadily spreading Roman control up to the fringes of the Alps. The feisty Flaminius as consul in 223 won the decisive victory that forced the Boii to submit. The following year his successors, Gnaeus Cornelius Scipio and Marcus Claudius Marcellus, subdued the Insubres in two hard battles. Marcellus's victory at Clastidium would inspire the poet Naevius to compose perhaps the very first Roman history play; Flaminius as censor in 220 had Rome's first great northern road built from the City to Ariminum, in counterpoise to the existing southerly Via Appia, to ensure communications with the new territories. Two years later a pair of Latin colonies, Placentia and Cremona, were founded not far apart on the middle stretch of the Po. With the untypically large number of 6,000 colonists each, their task too was to help control the region—as the beaten but still truculent Gauls well knew.

Rome was assertive in other places also. During the 230s there were clashes in the northeast with the warlike Ligurians of the Apennines. The Sardinians after 235 found their new overlords uncongenial and put up stubborn resistance. So did the Corsicans when Roman forces ventured there—making Rome's possession of either island shakier than in Sicily, even though in 228 or 227 a new annual praetorship to govern them was created along with one for Sicily (which Flaminius was the first to hold). More serious antagonism arose in 230 in yet another region. The Illyrian lands across the Adriatic were a mixture of local states; the chief Illyrian kingdom under its queen Teuta was encroaching, in standard expansionist style, on its neighbors as far south as the Greek colonies of Apollonia and Epidamnus and the island state of Corcyra. Rome intervened, much to the relief of the Greeks—and of some Illyrian communities—when Italian traders were plundered, and some murdered, by Illyrian privateers. A grievance so much like the one in 240 over traders arrested by Carthage looks provocatively convenient; solicitude for harassed merchants only rarely influenced Roman diplomacy. The resulting war saw both consuls of 229 sent with large forces, legionary and naval, to choke off Illyrian expansion. They removed Teuta, put the kingdom under a pro-Roman Greek in her service named Demetrius of Pharos, and brought a sheaf of Adriatic Greek states into Rome's circle of friends: Apollonia, Epidamnus, and Corcyra in particular.

Then, to mark her entry into eastern international affairs, Roman ambassadors the following year visited several mainland Greek states to pay their respects—the Aetolian and Achaean Leagues (both with a strong interest in Adriatic events), Athens, and Corinth (second-rank cities now but hugely prestigious). One state not treated to a visit was the kingdom of Macedon, recovering strength after a period of weakness and also having interest in Adriatic lands. Macedon must have felt at least a little concern about Rome's arrival on that scene but in the 220s was preoccupied with other business.[2]

THE BARCID ASCENDANCY: HAMILCAR

Hamilcar Barca and his army landed at Gades during 237. Besides the small and prosperous Phoenician colonies dotted along the south coast—Malaca, Abdera, and Sexi were others—Spain south of the river Tagus was a mosaic of warlike peoples centered on strongly fortified little towns. It was well developed socially and economically, exploiting both fertile agriculture and very rich mineral resources: silver above all. Hamilcar set about conquering it. From 237 to winter 229–228 he pushed Carthage's dominion eastward through the broad Baetis river valley and surrounding lands. His methods varied from diplomatic charm to the same ruthlessness that he had used in Libya. One captured lord, Indortes, was blinded, castrated, and crucified, but his 10,000 warriors were freed unharmed—a combination of cruelty and clemency to impress their neighbors.

Hamilcar's leadership of the republic depended on victory and its profits from Spain. These he supplied in exemplary fashion. "With horses, arms, men, and money he enriched the whole of Africa," says his biographer Nepos, predictably emphasizing the military benefits. Spanish soldiers, long recruited as mercenaries, could now be levied in even greater numbers—disciplined, well armed, tough, and loyal. In the tradition of Alexander and other conquerors of foreign lands, Hamilcar also created a city. Diodorus calls it Acra Leuce, "White Fort" (probably at or near Roman Lucentum, today's Alicante), as perhaps Hamilcar himself did. Spanish silver was used by him and afterward by his successor Hasdrubal for impressively designed coins displaying standard Punic icons—horse, elephant, palm tree—on one side and, on the other, portraits of Carthage's city god Melqart adorned with club and lion skin, in other words identified with Hercules: another sign of Carthage's responsiveness to Greek cultural themes.

FIGURE 6.1
Hannibal's oath: a Baroque-era depiction.

Hamilcar's military deputy was his equally able son-in-law Hasdrubal. They were accompanied to Spain by his nine-year-old eldest son, Hannibal. Hamilcar, bitter at Rome's ruthless behavior over Sardinia, first made little Hannibal take an oath "never to be friendly to the Romans" (figure 6.1)—a promise that his son was still stressing forty-five years later. It certainly persuaded Polybius of Hamilcar's anger against Rome, though he classes it as only one of the motives for the war. Later, in hostile retellings such as Livy's, Hannibal swore to be Rome's enemy forever—usefully making his father's plan even plainer.

Hannibal showed promise from the start. In Spain he received first-class training in warfare under his father, along with a Greek education under an erudite Spartan, Sosylus, and a Sicilian named Silenus. In time his younger brothers too, Hasdrubal and Mago, joined their father to live the military life. Much later on, Romans and their Greek friends (like Polybius) looked back on this family warlord-cluster as the core of a deep-seated Punic plan initiated by Hamilcar for a war of revanche and revenge against Rome.

This was not how contemporaries saw Hamilcar. The Romans had no quarrel with Carthage during his leadership or Hasdrubal's. According to Dio, an inquisitive embassy sent from Rome to him in 231 could find nothing to criticize (and this late story may be made up). Cato the Elder, later a veteran of the Second Punic War, ranked him with Themistocles, Pericles, and the admired Roman war hero Curius Dentatus, while his contemporary Fabius Pictor blamed the war not on him but on Hasdrubal and Hasdrubal's evil influence over Hannibal. More telling still, Hamilcar, who well knew the importance of navies for fighting Rome, did nothing to improve Carthage's—or to encourage his successors to do so. His military attitude to Rome was very likely defensive. By the time he died, Spain alone could put into the field 50,000 foot, 6,000 horse, and (reportedly) a hundred elephants, a force not seen in Carthaginian territories since the early days of the First Punic War. Carthage and her new Spanish domains had to be strong so as to deter or, if worse came to worst, fight off any Roman attack. They did not need to be strong enough to attack her.[3]

HASDRUBAL'S TIME

Hamilcar perished on campaign in mountainous southeastern Spain during winter 229–228. Hasdrubal was elected general to replace him, first by the army in Spain (at any rate its citizen cadres) and then in proper form by the citizens at Carthage. This novel procedure had a precedent of sorts from the Truceless War, when the troops in the field chose Hamilcar over Hanno. It was a foregone conclusion anyway. The Barcids were making Carthage rich and powerful again, and the only opposition of any note was Hanno's limited (probably shrinking) group of supporters. Hasdrubal continued expansion: when he perished in 221, Carthaginian hegemony reached north to the Tagus and from the east coast to the Atlantic. He maintained 60,000 foot and 8,000 horse, plus 200 elephants if we can believe Diodorus. Carthage's hold on Libya was firm too, especially as Hamilcar around 236 had sent his son-in-law over to crush a "Numidian" revolt—most likely a rising in the regions annexed to Punic Libya between 254 and 247—with similar harshness to Barca's in Spain.

Even more than Hamilcar, Hasdrubal took on the trappings of a modern Hellenistic grandee. Perhaps now a widower, he married the daughter of a Spanish king. Later he encouraged or arranged a Spanish bride for his young brother-in-law Hannibal, a girl from the wealthy inland city of Castulo (Silius Italicus calls her Imilce, a Punic name). He was also "acclaimed general with supreme power by all the Iberians," says Diodorus, whose excerpt does not explain how this was done.

A scenario is not hard to envisage. Hasdrubal's own great foundation was a city he called simply Carthage—Polybius calls it New City, a correct translation—replacing an old town named Mastia on Spain's southeastern coast. It was complete enough by 226 to arouse comment at Rome and no doubt elsewhere. Laid out between a saltwater lagoon and one of the best harbors in the Mediterranean, the new Carthage stood on five hills, four crowned each with a temple to a god revered by Carthaginians and Greeks: Polybius names them as Asclepius (Punic Eshmun), Hephaestus (perhaps the god Kusor), Aletes (unknown but probably Spanish), and Cronus (Baal Hammon). The fifth housed a splendid palace for Hasdrubal himself. Rich silver mines lay around the city, which at once became the capital of Punic Spain. To mark the achievement Hasdrubal would certainly have held a solemn rite of dedication, and very probably that was when the leaders of Gades and other sister colonies, and the kings and chieftains of the Spanish peoples within Carthage's sway, all met to acclaim him their paramount leader. The gesture was symbolic, not practical—it did not deter an affronted Spaniard from assassinating him five years later—but the symbol was important, not just for foreign eyes but equally for his fellow citizens at African Carthage, a place that neither Hasdrubal after 236 nor Hannibal, his brother-in-law and from 224 his cavalry general and deputy, visited in person.

Worth notice is that in Hasdrubal's choice of principal gods for his new city there was no place for Melqart. This does not well fit the general modern view that the Barcid leaders all had a special place for Melqart in their hearts and rites. The finely crafted silver shekels that they struck in Spain portraying Melqart as his Greek alter ego Heracles, complete with lion skin and club, do depict him at various ages from youthful to elderly, but it is a dubious step to infer that this means they really depict Hamilcar, Hasdrubal, and Hannibal—still more dubious that this was a claim to virtual kingship in Hellenistic style. The shekels bear no lettering (a contrast to Hellenistic royal issues), but of course Melqart/Heracles would be recognizable—and it made sense to put him on coins struck in Spain, where he did bask in special reverence, with a temple at Gades that was claimed to be almost a thousand years old. Hannibal took care to offer him ceremonies and vows when readying his expedition to Italy. The Barcids themselves cherished many Phoenician/Punic divinities, as not only the temples at New Carthage make clear but also, and more strikingly still, the long list of gods and goddesses that heads Hannibal's oath in his alliance treaty with the king of Macedon in 215—where Baal Hammon (as Zeus) and Tanit (as Hera) hold first place.[4]

ROME'S "TREATY" WITH HASDRUBAL

The Romans chose to recognize Hasdrubal as the ruler that he was. They had their reasons. By 226 the mounting war preparations in Cisalpina were causing consternation. Hasdrubal's splendid new city, Polybius assures us, caught their attention too, if not in the way the generalissimo might prefer. Their two republics had not had formal contact in years—not since 237 if Dio's embassy story is fiction—and precisely this lack left Rome unsure of how the vigorous Barcids might view her Gallic crisis. Two actions resulted: preventive military moves as mentioned earlier and a new embassy to Spain, probably as soon as sailing allowed in spring 225. There was scant military reason to spread out sizable forces, to Tarentum, Sicily, and even Sardinia, if Romans feared only the Gallic onslaught (even if some Sardinians had rebelled, they could have waited). It makes sense if the aim was to deter, or at worst fight off, attack from overseas—which could only come from the Carthaginians. The same spread of forces would recur in 217, when the threat from Hannibal's invasion became dire.

The envoys negotiated a succinct accord with Hasdrubal: "The Carthaginians are not to cross the river Iber in war." While scholarly debate still occurs about which river was the Iber, almost certainly it was the Ebro (as everywhere else in Polybius and other sources). By now Hasdrubal's hegemony was near or at the rivers Tagus and eastward-flowing Júcar. Polybius stresses via a domestic metaphor— Hasdrubal as an ill-tempered dog or horse—that the Romans "stroked and soothed" him so that they could deal with the Gauls, but they would have conceded him nothing if either of those streams (still less the Segura even farther south) was the *ne plus ultra*. Polybius stresses, too, that the accord said nothing else about Spain. Livy, Appian, and others write in extra provisos—which very conveniently fitted later Roman propaganda blaming Hannibal and Carthage for the war of 218, especially a proviso guaranteeing security to Saguntum on the Mediterranean coast. Livy does not help the case by locating Saguntum fatuously "midway between the two empires"—between the two banks of the Iber, then—nor does Appian by turning it into a Greek colony north of that river (no doubt misusing Emporiae, which was both).

On the other hand, as is often remarked, however silver-tongued the envoys might have been, it would be peculiar for Hasdrubal to feel soothed by promising Rome not to cross the Ebro. A spoken, not written, concession from Rome is very likely: she would ignore what he did in the other 80 percent of Iberia. In 225 the Ebro was a long way off, and the Iberian interior held much promise. What mattered was to let the envoys have the reassurance that Hasdrubal and Carthage would keep well away from the crisis with the Gauls, and in return he received an implicit guarantee of real value. The Pyrenees would have been a more obvious demarcation line, but they would have put him—had he ever reached them—next to southern Gaul. Since southern Gaul was sending the warrior Gaesatae to join the Gallic offensive, the Romans would not have ruled out getting involved there in turn. The Ebro by contrast signaled that, if the two "empires" did expand, Spain's northeast would still be buffer territory between them.

Meantime a small and well-off place like Saguntum might certainly feel anxious, sited more than 170 kilometers south of that stream. Polybius writes that the Saguntines started friendly contacts with Rome "many years before Hannibal's time" (which opened in late 221)—probably then during the envoys' Spanish trip, which very probably took in Saguntum along the normal coastal route. No source explains why the Saguntines were so afraid of Punic hegemony. Timely submission could have made them allies, valuable enough to be cosseted. Most of southern Spain had become a well-organized mosaic of communities, some closely supervised (though details are obscure) but many others ranking as allies and remaining autonomous. But afraid they were, and they later showed that they would die to resist it.[5]

The accord was not ratified at Carthage, as it was a military undertaking given by her chief general (not a nicety appreciated at Rome). Nonetheless it served its purpose. The Romans could concentrate on the Gauls and then on other northern—and Adriatic—ventures; Hasdrubal, on warfare, consolidation, and politics. The Saguntines did not give up calling for Rome's attention but were benignly ignored every time, until matters took a new turn half a decade later.

HANNIBAL IN CHARGE

Hasdrubal was assassinated late in 221. His brother-in-law, cavalry chief, and effective deputy, Hannibal, was acclaimed the new general in the same way as Hasdrubal had been: first by the army in Spain, which probably again means its Carthaginian personnel, then at home—unanimously, Polybius states—by the citizen assembly, the *ham*. Like his predecessors, he became in practice leader of the Carthaginian state, though leaving affairs at Carthage and in North Africa to his Barcid kinsmen and supporters, who continued a near-monopoly of magistracies and a majority among the *adirim*.

Twenty-six years old, Hannibal had not set foot in Africa since he was nine. He and his Spanish wife had a little son (if Silius the poet is not simply inventing one), and by now both his brothers, Hasdrubal and Mago, were on active service with him. He led, too, a cadre of highly competent officers inherited from his father and brother-in-law and destined to play their parts in one of history's most famous military ventures. One was Hanno son of Bomilcar, whom Appian calls Hannibal's nephew; if he is right, Hamilcar Barca had had a third daughter married to a Carthaginian, besides the wives of Naravas and the just-murdered Hasdrubal—all of them a good deal older than their brothers. Another Mago, nicknamed "the Samnite," was both Hannibal's closest friend, says Polybius, and his rival in military exploits (and fondness for money). Maharbal, Carthalo, and a third Hasdrubal were to help win the battles of Lake Trasimene and Cannae, and Maharbal would make an undyingly remembered gibe at Hannibal.

Hasdrubal had left unfinished business in central Spain, for the new general immediately moved against a restive people, the Olcades, most likely in the La Mancha region. A lightning autumn campaign took their chief town by assault, subdued their region, and—as expected of a Barcid leader—gathered plenty of booty to be shown off at New Carthage and shared out among his appreciative soldiery. In this first campaign, Hannibal confirmed the energy and resourcefulness he had shown as Hasdrubal's deputy, and he did so again the following year with a far more wide-ranging expedition beyond the Tagus and the Sierra de Gredos mountains as far as the Duero river. This was an attack—quite unprovoked—on the Vaccaei, the grain-rich people of the northwestern plains, again for booty and probably, too, to show that Carthage's new generalissimo was as formidable as those before. Their towns Hermandica and Arbocala were taken by assault, but Arbocala was a slower and harder prize than its predecessor: a harbinger of siege difficulties to come. The campaign was only an extended raid, imposed no permanent rule on the Vaccaei, and brought Hannibal more trouble when the powerful Carpetani to their south, between the Guadarrama and Gredos ranges and the Tagus, attacked his returning army. Since the Carpetani had let him pass northward, they must have been previously on friendly terms (or had been promised a share of his plunder), but refugee Vaccaei and also Olcades roused them to war.

This brought on the first, and least known, of Hannibal's great victories, fought near Toletum beside the Tagus. Outpacing a reported (probably overestimated) 100,000 Spanish warriors, he crossed the river to take position a short distance beyond; then when most of the warriors splashed across, they were slaughtered on its banks or in the water by his forty elephants and his cavalry. He then recrossed the river to rout the rest of the enemy. The victory, according to Polybius, completely intimidated everyone as far as the Ebro. In two strenuous campaigns over twelve months the new general had spread Carthaginian military power over nearly as much territory again as Hamilcar and Hasdrubal had.

THE AFFAIR OF SAGUNTUM

Carthage in 220 was prosperous, secure, and mistress of a territorial empire larger than ever before. Hannibal may have been politically inexperienced, but his faction will have included plenty of long-standing and knowledgeable supporters. Rome in 220 was equally secure, mistress of a fledgling dominion in north Italy and Italy's neighboring islands, and pushing her fields of interest and involvement eastward.

Roman public life was as competitively open as Carthage's was straitjacketed. Hannibal's Roman contemporaries included Quintus Fulvius Flaccus, Quintus Fabius Maximus, the brothers Gnaeus and Publius Cornelius Scipio, Lucius Aemilius Paullus, Marcus Marcellus, and the popular (enemies called him the demagogic) Gaius Flaminius—all of them consuls during the 230s and 220s except Paullus and Publius Scipio, who followed in 219 and 218. All of them had military experience to their credit, even if sometimes limited (Fabius Maximus, twice consul, had fought only a war with the Apennines' Ligurians). Politically they could be strongly divided. Fabius disliked both Flaminius's land-grants program and Flaminius himself, while Flaminius managed to be at odds with a large number of his fellow senators most of the time. Campaigning in Cisalpine Gaul in 223, he received a senatorial recall notice, which, Nelson-style, he avoided reading until after victory; in 218 he alone in the Senate spoke for a law to stop senators from engaging in mercantile business that distracted them from their duties. Aemilius Paullus's colleague in 219, Marcus Livius Salinator, fined for misappropriating booty from a new Illyrian war, was so disgusted at the verdict, and at his fellow senator Gaius Claudius Nero, whose hostile testimony caused it, that he washed his hands entirely of public life for years, only to reemerge with decisive impact late in the Second Punic War.

Neither state showed any sign of wanting a war with the other, still less of needing one. Rome's interests were northward and eastward. In 221, the year after finishing with the Cisalpine Gauls, she thought it good to send the consuls to Istria, in the northeastern corner of the Adriatic, to subdue its peoples too. Two years later the troublesomely ambitious activities of the Illyrian regent, Demetrius of Pharos, led to the consuls

Aemilius and Livius crossing the Adriatic with very large forces to drive him out and reaffirm Rome's hegemony, loose as this was. Demetrius fled to the king of Macedon; this would bring consequences later. If Rome was going to fight a new war (people in 219 might suppose), it would be eastward versus Macedon, a kingdom invitingly beset by many troubles.

Meanwhile Carthage and Hannibal still had much of northern and western Spain open for warfare. Had Hannibal chosen that option, he would have discovered the northwest's prolific gold mines, which instead waited to benefit Augustan Rome. If yet more victories and conquests were wanted after that, Numidia and Mauretania were conveniently accessible from both Libya and Spain—and with much of western Numidia ruled by Syphax, an ambitious foe of Naravas's Punic-friendly Massyli, a pretext was ready to hand. None of this happened. Instead, Rome and Carthage went again to war.

This time Saguntum was the small town playing the role that in 264 had been Messana's. After studiously ignoring its messages about Barcid Spain for years, the Romans abruptly paid attention during 220. This no doubt resulted from learning how Hannibal's military drive north was spreading Carthaginian dominance even to the Ebro. Polybius declares that his victories left no one south of that river inclined to resist. No doubt many peoples took care to send him friendly assurances; sending hostages might seem a sound move too. Two Roman envoys, Valerius Flaccus and Baebius Tamphilus, were dispatched to New Carthage, where they awaited his return from the north. This was sometime in September or early October, for the safe sailing season closed during November, and they had Carthage to visit as well. Their message was not particularly ingratiating—the new general was "solemnly admonished" both to keep away from Saguntum, "because it lay in their [the Romans'] trust," and also from crossing the "Iber."

This pair of demands has fueled the argument that the "Iber" must have been not north of Saguntum but south (Appian's notion). Other evidence mentioned earlier nonetheless weakens that view. Rome's concern was that Hannibal's hegemony should not progress toward—and eventually over—the Pyrenees into Gaul. Greek Emporiae, 300 kilometers north of the Ebro and on good terms with Rome, already was striking coins on Carthage's shekel standard: not a military impact, but it suggested the possibilities. Saguntum was showing itself a useful lookout on Barcid Spain. Interdicting it to Hannibal (even though it stood in territory implicitly conceded to Hasdrubal) brought an extra gain: it would depict Rome as having some control over Carthage's empire—if Hannibal obeyed. The gesture backfired when Hannibal turned the argument around, accusing Rome of maliciously intervening in Saguntum's internal affairs. For at some stage the Saguntines had sought Roman arbitration over a bitter factional contest, and Rome's agents—maybe Valerius and Baebius themselves en route to New Carthage—had fixed matters drastically by putting one faction's leaders to death. Hannibal now promised to right the claimed wrong: a virtual guarantee that he would attack the town. The baffled ambassadors went on to Carthage, to receive no better response.

Hannibal had been silent about the Ebro demand. His reason is not hard to guess. Within Spain, beyond the Ebro appeared the only promising region left to conquer. By intervening on the Saguntines' behalf Rome may have delayed such a project, for he clearly inferred that her long inattention to Spain was now replaced by a dangerously intrusive interest. If he buckled, the intrusions would multiply. If he stood firm, it could spark war—at latest, when he did cross the Ebro—but a firm stand, coupled with Rome's developing trans-Adriatic interests, might avert that. Hannibal did not for a moment consider buckling.

Yet probably he was mistaken about the Romans' attitude. His rocket rise as Carthage's leader had troubled them enough to act to bring him back to earth: no move on Saguntum, no transgressing the Ebro. It was all bluster. Essentially they wanted Punic expansion to come to a stop so that they could be sure of quiet in the west while they carried on their business eastward. They had no planned fallback should Hannibal refuse to comply. Despite his snail's-pace siege of Saguntum throughout 219, nothing was done except to keep debating whether to do something—and to launch a new Illyrian war. If Hannibal had followed up his outburst to Valerius and Baebius by equally doing nothing on either Saguntum or the Ebro, it looks likely that there would have been no Hannibalic War. Rome's bluff and his misreading of it ensured the reverse.

THE OUTBREAK OF WAR

In spring 219 Hannibal led forth his army to attack Saguntum. Ignoring his earlier propaganda about righting its wrongs, he claimed that the Saguntines had mistreated neighbors (those of nearby Turis, it seems) whose own wrongs he would right—he was now, after all, the neighbors' hegemon. Like the discarded claim, this too appropriated the Romans' cherished theme of *fides* (loyalty) to allies. His prey proved hard to crush. Strongly fortified, Saguntum held out against assaults for seven and a half months, teaching the same lesson as Arbocala had: where a stronghold was determined to resist, it could inflict frustrating damage. He himself suffered a thigh wound, Livy reports, and had to hand over operations temporarily to Maharbal. All Carthaginians must have wondered how Rome would react. Had two consular armies landed nearby backed by the Roman navy, Hannibal could have been in serious difficulty. It was no doubt a relief to learn that the consuls Aemilius and Livius had gone in the opposite direction, to Illyria. Nevertheless, after Saguntum fell he chose to make preparations for a war he plainly judged more than likely.

Roman historical tradition was unhappy at this train of events. Not only Livy but Cicero and later Dio too date Valerius's and Baebius's embassy to the siege. Livy compounds this by putting the siege into 218, followed by Hannibal's invasion of Italy and opening victories—only to concede soon after that this chronology is impossible. As already mentioned, Hasdrubal's accord was rewritten in pro-Roman histories to exempt Saguntum from attack, and—although this showed that for Romans the "Iber" was indeed the Ebro—some historians thought it a good idea to put them beyond that stream too (Appian, for example). The purpose of these convulsions was simple. Rome could not be revealed as having done absolutely nothing for the besieged Saguntines, yet equally no one could deny that, rather than send them military help, she sent troops to Illyria. So the best that could be done was to make Valerius and Baebius go to Spain during the siege. Of course they then had to be shown putting a different demand to Hannibal: not to abstain from but, rather, to stop besieging Saguntum.

The final nail in this gimcrack structure was to depict the Saguntines as allies of Rome all along, for this made Hannibal violate not only

Hasdrubal's accord but Lutatius's peace, which had guaranteed the integrity of both states' allies. None of these manipulations works. The chronology is false, the Saguntines on all available evidence were never allies (however much they longed to be), the embassy was in 220 and the siege and sack were in 219; and in 219 the Romans did nothing.

Polybius very possibly took his contrastingly unsensational and coherent account from a non-Roman source such as Silenus or Sosylus. They were on Hannibal's side, but neither would have helped his case by falsely putting the embassy into 220 and at New Carthage, had it really arrived during 219 outside Saguntum, or by having the envoys add a demand not to cross the Ebro. Less plausible is how Polybius interprets developments. He shares the near-universal Greek and Roman opinion that Hamilcar had schemed a revenge-war plan, Hasdrubal strengthened Carthage for it, and Hannibal launched it (only Fabius Pictor left Hamilcar out of the indictment). Again, though less conventionally, Polybius holds that by 225 at latest Rome foresaw war and made the Ebro accord simply to win breathing space against the Gauls; for him, Hannibal's pugnacious response to the envoys simply confirmed that they had foreseen rightly. Of course Polybius then has to explain why Rome chose to fight in Illyria precisely while Hannibal was tied down at Saguntum. His explanation is lameness itself: that the Romans expected to have plenty of time for both, only for Hannibal to "preempt" them by taking Saguntum and invading Italy. In reality, the easy Illyrian war was over by midsummer 219, when Hannibal was still mired in his siege. He did not march for Italy until late spring 218. The victorious consuls of 219 could have set off directly for Spain—or even more decisively, for Carthage—to launch the supposedly inevitable war on a much better footing than their successors would.

As just mentioned, during 219 vigorous senatorial debate did occur on what to do. The outline can be detected in Dio's rhetorical version, even though he places it—impossibly—during Hannibal's march to Italy a year later. Not only must many senators have seen the attack on Saguntum as intolerable defiance by ex-enemies who had not learned the lesson of 241, but there were obvious further questions about the Ebro if Hannibal got away with his defiance and about Carthage's current attitude to Rome overall. Others urged caution—partly, no doubt, because Rome was committed in the Adriatic and partly because war with Carthage, over a faraway town about which most Romans knew nothing, promised much pain for uncertain gain. Even on the consuls' triumphant return from Illyria no decision followed, not even for a diplomatic gesture on Saguntum's behalf. The Senate (not for the first time if we recall what happened in 264) was deadlocked.

The news of the sack, on the other hand, at last pushed senators into favoring strong reaction. This was a fateful decision. The only possible reaction now was to threaten Carthage with war if Hannibal was not punished—and Roman aristocrats had enough Carthaginian guest-friends and other contacts to know that he would not be. As the sack took place late in the year, even a swift decision to send an ultimatum (Polybius stresses that it was swift) could not be acted on until sea travel became reasonably safe. This accounts for the ex-consuls from 219 being among the five selected (Livius Salinator's prosecution would come later): their successors Publius Scipio and Tiberius Sempronius Longus replaced them on the Ides of March, just around the time that sailing reopened. The mission was led by Marcus Fabius, almost certainly Marcus Fabius Buteo, the most senior living senator—consul in 245 but still full of vigor.[6]

Reaching Carthage, Fabius put a flat alternative to the *adirim*: hand over Hannibal and his war council to Rome or accept war. He refused to go into any debate. Carthage's spokesman—probably one of the sufetes—replied that the guarantee of allies did not apply to the Saguntines as they had not been Roman allies in 241, and he even read the text out to prove it. Logically this was beside the point, for the Saguntines were not allies even now. Yet Rome's ultimatum was implicitly treating them as current allies; since the Carthaginians could not disprove this, the sufete brought in his red herring about the peace treaty. Fabius promptly declared quite falsely that "because the treaty had been violated" there was no room for discussion, a claim that can only have confirmed his hearers' suspicions.

Neither they nor he brought the Ebro accord into the argument over Saguntum. Possibly enough Fabius did mention the accord to the *adirim*: for instance, that Rome was not only angered at their general defying the warning about Saguntum but concerned that he would equally defiantly go on to transgress the Ebro. The Carthaginians, Polybius writes, judged the accord irrelevant because it had been an agreement with Hasdrubal personally. He does not add the plain point that it was geographically irrelevant too. Since Hannibal soon enough did cross the Ebro—after Rome declared war—some Romans later on and their Greek friends could fog the war guilt debate to add this to his list of bad faiths, by rearranging chronology and Spanish geography to place it south of Saguntum, just as they happily asserted that the town had been Rome's formal ally when attacked.

Since the Carthaginian senate gave the embassy no satisfaction, Fabius Buteo theatrically let fall a fold of his toga to announce that he gave Carthage war. With nemesis-laden enthusiasm the *adirim* welcomed the gesture, and the Second Punic War was launched.

PART THREE
THE SECOND PUNIC WAR
218–201

7

HANNIBAL'S INVASION

STRENGTHS AND STRATEGIES

In the end, as both Hannibal and Scipio Africanus were to say, it was about "honor and power"—in Latin, *dignitas* and *imperium* (figure 7.1). Roman *dignitas* suffered from the loss of face over Saguntum and the blow to her carefully cherished claim of loyalty, *fides*, toward threatened allies (the Saguntines being now enlisted as such). Power was even more in question if Hannibal could not be curbed: the anxiety seen in 225, about Carthage possibly looking to regain Sicily and Sardinia, surely revived by 218. At the same time a successful Punic war would mean military renown and booty from both Spain and Africa for the victorious generals and troops. Whether the Romans were thinking of Spain as a desirable permanent possession is more doubtful. Just as Sicily had not received a regular praetor for over a decade after 241 and would not be regularized in administration or taxation until 210, Spain after this war would remain a military district until 197, while systematically exploiting even its mining wealth started later still. In 218 it ranked simply as a Punic stronghold to be dealt with.

For Carthage and Hannibal the issues were still simpler. The Romans had shown ill-faith in 237 over Sardinia—Polybius insists that their injustice rankled—and suspicions in 225. Next they abruptly decided to champion Saguntum and order Hannibal to keep to Hasdrubal's accord. At both Carthages this had to look like the start of a forward thrust, not merely to prevent wider Punic expansion but to push it back. After all, in

FIGURE 7.1
Hannibal (perhaps a Renaissance-era bust), Naples Museum.

225 Rome had in principle conceded Saguntum, under the same accord that in 220 she had commanded Hannibal to respect. The blow to Carthage's *dignitas*, had she given in, would have been disastrous: a state that had risen from disasters to a stature even greater than before could not afford to lose that much face.[1]

Livy rightly stresses that "no other states or nations that have come into conflict had greater resources than these two peoples, nor had the combatants themselves ever been stronger or more powerful" as in the fateful year 218. Rome's census at the time of the Gallic invasion registered 273,000 citizens, 23,000 of them ranking as cavalrymen (*equites*).

The Latin and other Italian allies numbered almost half a million more. Not all were of fighting age, as the census included men over forty-six, but to meet the Gallic crisis 52,000 Romans and 138,000 allies had been levied, although only about a quarter of them actually saw combat. For the new war Rome levied six legions—four for the consuls Publius Cornelius Scipio and Tiberius Sempronius Longus, who were to invade Spain and Africa, the others for a praetor in Cisalpine Gaul where the Insubres and Boii had rebelled—and with them just over 44,000 allies, for a total of rather more than 70,000 troops.

Even though Carthage is generally thought of as the underdog, the reality was different. By 218 the ravages of previous wars were largely healed, while Punic Spain was another prime recruiting ground. As noted earlier, Hasdrubal had 68,000 horse and foot in Spain, with supposedly 200 elephants though probably fewer in fact (in 218 Hannibal had only fifty-eight). Hannibal increased his forces further. His military arrangements during winter and spring 219–218—he himself recorded them—transferred 20,000 mostly Spanish troops to North Africa and Carthage and stationed 12,600 chiefly Libyan soldiers in Spain with his brother Hasdrubal. All could be supplemented by local levies, though not the twenty-one elephants he also left. He himself marched from New Carthage with thirty-seven elephants and 90,000 men, although detachments and losses in his trans-Ebro campaign would reduce troop numbers. To start the war, then, Carthage fielded 122,600 horse and foot, a mobilization more than 50 percent larger than Rome's.

Naval strengths were another matter. The Romans had 220 warships— requiring some 66,000 men if all were fully crewed quinqueremes. By contrast, the once-grand navy of Carthage was in a bad way after twenty Barcid years. In Spain Hannibal had a mere thirty-two immediately serviceable quinqueremes, seven smaller ships, and twenty-one under-manned craft. At Carthage at least fifty-five ships were seaworthy (they were soon sent into Sicilian and Italian waters on minor missions), but probably not many more. More would be built in coming years, but the Carthaginians' long-languishing naval prowess would not return. Had the consul Sempronius sailed for Africa, his assigned objective, with his army and 160 quinqueremes, it would have been impossible to stop him.[2]

Both powers were thinking of a short war. Each planned a decisive blow: Rome, the double offensive against Libya and Spain; Hannibal, a strike into Italy via the Alps—his only offensive option due to his naval inferiority. The Romans plainly did not realize the size of the opposition they would have met in Spain: Sempronius's colleague Publius Scipio had the usual consular army of two legions and allies, altogether just over 24,000 troops, plus sixty warships. For Hannibal, invading Italy was essential. His sole alternative would have been to wait to confront the Romans in Spain, with no certainty that meantime their invasion of Libya would be defeated. Hannibal gambled that invading Italy would save Libya, was confident that he could crush opposition there till he had Rome at his mercy, and reckoned that this would compel her to accept his terms.

Reality soon intervened to force dramatic changes to each side's plans. Hannibal's army was whittled down to a hard core, a quarter of its original size, by the time it reached Cisalpine Gaul. Meanwhile his approach induced the Senate to recall Sempronius from his just-begun expedition, though (as we shall see) the expedition to Spain would go ahead under Scipio's elder brother Gnaeus while Publius himself returned hastily to Cisalpina. Publius's original departure from Rome had been held up. The rebellion in Cisalpine Gaul caused his original army to be given to a praetor, Manlius, to deal with it (Manlius would fail dismally), and Scipio had to raise another. These modifications to the initial strategies had a profound impact on how the war developed. Arguably they caused it to last seventeen years.

WAR AIMS

It is not likely that Rome had voracious designs in 218, for instance to satisfy trading and financial interests aiming to make Spain an economic milch cow, still less to annex Punic Africa. Her likely war aims were to defeat the Carthaginians so thoroughly that they would never be a major power again: this meant ending their dominion in Spain, forcing the Barcid faction from power, and of course amassing as much plunder—and for her aristocracy as much glory and status—as possible. Some

Romans no doubt hoped to go much further and see Carthage sacked and her leaders crucified. But neither happened even when the bitter struggle ended.

Hannibal's and Carthage's original war aims were no doubt simple too: Rome must be crushed and her network of Italian alliances cut away and attached to Carthage instead. Western Sicily, Sardinia, and Corsica would become Carthage's again. Dominant from the Atlantic to the Adriatic, she would become the greatest power in the west and fully a match for the leading Hellenistic kingdoms of the east—and all this under the leadership of the Barcid house. Just possibly Hannibal intended to annex some Italian territory too. Livy reports him offering a detailed list of rewards to his soldiers before their first battle in Cisalpina: land tax-free in Italy, Africa, or Spain (whichever they chose); payments of silver if they preferred these; and Carthaginian citizenship if they wanted it. Land grants and citizenship were typical rewards for retiring Roman veterans in later centuries, but they were not unique to Rome (Alexander the Great had settled veterans all over his new empire), and measures like these were plain necessities if victory over Rome was to be made permanent.

But the expectations of 218 did not last beyond 216. The enemy's refusal to talk terms led Hannibal to enlist Macedon and Syracuse, states outside Italy, as allies to force the Romans to spread their military efforts. In turn he had to take his new allies' ambitions and needs into account. This ironically spread out his and Carthage's efforts too, on land and by sea. Similarly his political colleagues at home found that they had to pay attention to the affairs of Numidia, where internal struggles finally created a unified kingdom—an outcome ultimately catastrophic for Carthage.

ALPS AND ELEPHANTS

Hannibal appointed his brother Hasdrubal to replace him as commander in Spain with the troops mentioned earlier, while keeping their youngest brother, Mago, as a senior officer. Preparations took time, so that the grand army left New Carthage sometime in late May or early June 218. It would arrive on the northern Italian plains five and a half months later, around the time of the setting of the Pleiades, Polybius reports—thus early November. Hannibal's friend and biographer Silenus recorded a famous dream of the young general en route to the Ebro. The gods gave him a divine being as a guide, who forbade him to look back; then when the disobedient Hannibal did so and saw a monstrous beast ravaging the countryside, his guide told him that he saw the ravaging of Italy and he must press on. Reminiscent of the Orpheus and Eurydice myth—Hannibal had a sound Greek education—but with an upbeat ending, the dream seems genuine, and it undermines his enemies' claims of amoral atheism.[3]

One modern concept (unmentioned by ancients) makes the general appropriate the aura of Heracles—equated with Melqart, as noted earlier—to impress the Greek world. Heracles in myth journeyed from Spain to Italy driving along the giant Geryon's stolen cattle, one of the heroic labors that earned him ultimate divinity; and later embellishments outfitted him not only with cattle but with an army for overcoming the Italians. That this was a theme expected to arouse Italian enthusiasm is not very plausible. No more plausible is the common notion that Hannibal's propaganda was aimed primarily at winning over the Italian Greeks, militarily the feeblest of Rome's allies. He needed, and knew he needed, backing from the powerful peoples of Italy's center and north. Yet there is no trace of him juggling with Italic deities or myths to achieve this—despite which he did win many over, even if it took time.

In any case Hannibal as Herculean propagandist, like Barcids as Melqart enthusiasts above all, rests on flimsy suppositions. From Spain to the Rhône the army marched partly along the route sometimes (but not often) called "the road of Heracles"—later the Via Domitia across southern Gaul—and in a speech in Livy the consul Scipio, in 218, mocks him as claiming to rival Heracles, but neither item helps. Next, in Hannibal's famous dream his youthful god-guide is optimistically assumed on no evidence to be none other than the mythical hero; yet, given the (modest) resemblance to Orpheus's myth, the youth should arguably be the disappointed singer. Much likelier, in any case, for Hannibal he was a Punic deity pure and simple, even if not now identifiable.[4]

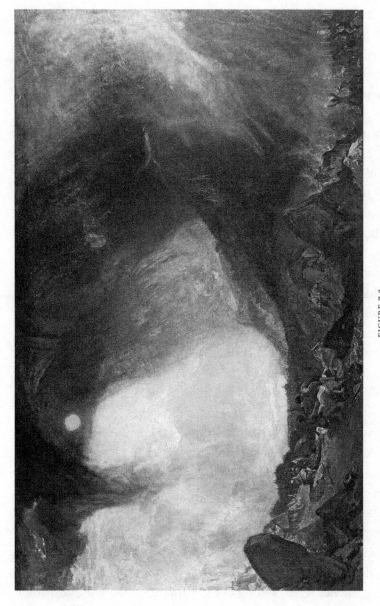

FIGURE 7.2

Hannibal crossing the Alps, envisioned by J. M. Turner, 1812.

Hannibal did not press on as single-mindedly as his godly guide urged. He spent a considerable time subduing hostile Spanish peoples north of the Ebro, with heavy losses. He then had not only to leave a sizable force to hold the northeast but to dismiss another sizable contingent, Spanish troops unwilling to follow him across the Pyrenees: in all, more than 20,000 men. He also left behind the army's heavy baggage, clearly to speed up the march—a sign that the campaign had taken longer than foreseen, bringing a risk that the army might run into winter before reaching Italy. Now leading 50,000 foot and 9,000 horse, he crossed into Gaul with the carefully cultivated goodwill of the local peoples as far as the Rhône. This march suffered strange, and probably unexpected, new losses: at the Rhône his army was down to 38,000 foot and 8,000 horse. No battles had been fought, provisions were plentiful, and Polybius does not explain the loss, a silence that quite possibly goes back to Hannibal's or his friends' tactful accounts. Nor is there any trace of garrisons being left along the route as some scholars surmise. The likeliest explanation is that, as the Alps neared, some soldiers' enthusiasm departed and—officially or illicitly—so did those soldiers themselves, to enjoy instead the attractions of late summer in Languedoc and Provence or to tramp home.

Massing on the far side of the Rhône (it was now around mid-October), the unfriendly Volcae tried to block Hannibal's crossing but were skillfully driven off by a surprise maneuver. His nephew Hanno took a division across upstream and fell on them from the rear, while the rest of the army crossed to strike them in front. This entrapment tactic became a Hannibalic trademark. Just then Publius Scipio, en route at last for Spain with his army, put in at the mouth of the Rhône three days' march to the south (the Rhône in 218 reached the sea several kilometers farther north than today). When a skirmish between cavalry scouts revealed his nearness, Hannibal chose to march northward rather than face the approaching consul. No doubt anxious to cross the Alps before winter, he gained fresh supplies in a region called The Island from friendlier Gauls, probably the Vocontii just east of the Rhône, before setting out northward on the last, most strenuous, and most famous section of the great march. Meanwhile Scipio sent his ex-consul brother Gnaeus on to Spain with the army and doubled back to Cisalpine Gaul to take command of its two legions.

Avoiding Scipio may have been a miscalculation, like the laborious trans-Ebro campaign. Had Hannibal chosen to fight, it is hard to imagine him and 46,000 seasoned troops being beaten by the consul with half as many, and a major victory would have both opened the easier coastal route to Italy and scotched the threat to Spain. Without that threat, Hasdrubal in Spain would have had minimal trouble sending reinforcements through Gaul to his brother as needed. The war might well have climaxed much sooner and much more on Carthage's terms.

The crossing of the Alps became and remains—unfairly—Hannibal's most famous exploit (figure 7.2). Shameless rhetoric and poetic fancy, paraded especially by Livy and Silius Italicus, proffer a vivid drama of desperate endeavor in snow-clad wildernesses of crags, landslides, and savage barbarian attacks. Of course Livy, and surely even Silius, knew that to arrive in Cisalpine Gaul early in November, the invaders had to cross the range during a Provençal autumn, although the army did meet snow and ice (as is usual) on and around the final pass. It did meet some hard fighting too. The warlike Allobroges north and east of the Dauphiné Alps, no more impressed than the Volcae at a foreign army marching through their lands, launched attacks as it mounted a gorge in that area, perhaps in the Vercors range overlooking the river Isère. This example was imitated some days later farther on, probably in the Drac river valley, by the Tricorii after an initial show of goodwill. Like the Volcae, both sets of attackers were beaten off, but the Tricorii at one point posed the greatest threat of the march—splitting the army in two overnight, though they could not exploit this—and over the next week or so mounting hit-and-run strikes that took a toll mainly on the pack animals, as Hannibal's forces headed for the final pass. Even so, over the fifteen days from entering the mountains to reaching Cisalpine Gaul, the troops experienced serious fighting only on four or five. Both Polybius and Livy make it clear that en route they gained plenty of supplies: first from the Vocontii, then when the army captured a well-stocked Allobrogian town (it may have been today's Grenoble on the Isère), and after that from other Gauls on the route—probably the just-mentioned Tricorii—before these turned hostile. A Punic army staggering through snowfalls and snowdrifts, under endless assaults, is purely an imaginative construct.

Argument and romancing about Hannibal's Alpine march started not many generations later. The Alps were opaque to third-century Greeks and Romans, and tribal and place names were unfamiliar enough for Polybius to decide that he would spare his readers their tedium. The romancing is especially vivid and vexing in Livy. His basic factual framework comes from Polybius, with extra details from other unstated sources, plus a good deal more from a jumble of fancy and invention. Some of his extra details are believable, going back in the end perhaps to Hannibal's historiographer friends Silenus and Sosylus: the Vocontii; their Rhône valley neighbors the Tricastini, through whose land (still called *le Tricastin*) Hannibal marched; and the Tricorii on the other side of the Vercors massif. This zigzag route is plausible for an army aiming to elude Roman observers: along the Rhône to the Isère, over to the Drac valley, and from there to the high Alps and the pass. Such a route would best lead to the Montgenèvre pass or one of its neighbors such as the Larche—each a fairly easy climb up from Gaul, followed by a steep descent down to Italy. Other candidates (the best known are the Col du Clapier and the Traversette, both farther north) are much more difficult to fit into what evidence we do have.

Any solution certainly has to be teased out with care and caution from Polybius's largely name-free narrative and Livy's clumsily executed story. Livy makes Hannibal cross the lower Durance river 150 kilometers south of the Vocontii (he describes the river's flat, broad, and variable course accurately) only after leaving Vocontian territory to march, contradictorily, northward. His men are then shocked to come face to face with the high Alps—buried in snow and ice—and with the equally frozen, and very unfriendly, inhabitants. Well might the men be shocked: in reality they were in Provence in early or mid-October. The hostile mountain people supposedly stiff with frost were actually the Allobroges (Polybius exceptionally names them), whose territory covered mainly the rolling uplands east of modern Lyon, although it did extend, too, to the high Grande Chartreuse massif along the upper Isère. The true, still-autumnal Alps were still days away—and to reach them from the land of the Tricorii necessarily required crossing the upper, narrow Durance. This must explain Livy's confused mention of it.[5]

The last stage of all was the steep descent to the Cisalpine plains, all the harder because a landslide had swept away part of the path and it took three days to rebuild. This was the locale for two other famous moments: Hannibal cheering his dispirited troops by pointing out Italy's fertile plains below and then breaking up a huge rock blocking the path by heating it with a bonfire of felled trees and pouring vinegar over it. Vinegar was certainly so used by farmers, but both tales break down in contradictions. The vinegar story (not in Polybius) requires many large trees; yet both Livy and Polybius emphasize that the area was treeless. In any case the landslide had taken away some 300 meters—one and a half *stadia*—of the path; there was no place for Livy's massive rock. Meanwhile Polybius has the plains (including the site of Rome) on view from the pass itself; but no army-suitable pass offers a view of Cisalpina's plains. The north Italian Livy perhaps knew this—but he could not leave out so famous a tale. He rationalizes it by moving the view and Hannibal's cheering speech to a spur farther down the descent. Yet no route descending to Italy seems to have a viewing area large enough for 26,000 troops. At best Hannibal pointed out a view to his officers, told them to pass the news on—and maybe lived long enough to see it become a rhetorically magnified literary piece.

THE TICINUS AND THE TREBIA

The army that stumbled down into early November's Cisalpine Gaul was disheveled and starving, had lost most of its pack animals, and on Hannibal's count consisted of 8,000 Spanish and 12,000 Libyan infantry and 6,000 cavalry as well as the thirty-seven elephants, none of which apparently had perished. Hannibal's losses since crossing the Rhône amounted, therefore, to 3,000 horse and no fewer than 18,000 foot—almost half the forces at the Rhône and a disconcerting drop to just 44 percent of the 59,000 who had crossed the Pyrenees with him two or three months before. It is incredible that in four or five weeks since the

Rhône, with five or so scattered days of fighting Allobroges and Tricorii and another week of hit-and-run attacks, he can have lost more than 20,000 men, more than he would lose in all in the three great battles to come. Certainly many soldiers were killed, while others perhaps were too injured to keep going, but the unpleasantness of the march's final stages very probably prompted fresh desertions—not so much in the mountains as after the army had made it to autumnal Lombardy and before Hannibal took the count.

Those who stayed needed time to recover, which for a while left them open to damaging attack had Roman forces been nearby. Publius Scipio, however, needed time too, to reach the legions in Cisalpina and make preparations. As soon as practicable Hannibal picked a fight with the nearby Taurini, who had resisted his overtures. Sacking their town (one day to be Turin) and slaughtering its defenders usefully terrified other communities nearby into submission, as well as impressing his allies the Insubres and Boii farther east and no doubt providing his indigent troops with welcome plunder. He then quested south, while the consul moved up and over the river Po, both expecting a clash. Around the start of December, near where the Ticinus river joins the Po, their cavalry forces, the generals at their head, clashed in Rome's first battle with Carthage since the Aegates in 241. Hannibal engaged the enemy squadrons in front, while his agile Numidians on each wing worked their way round to charge the Roman rear—successful envelopment again—and the Romans broke. Scipio, badly wounded, was saved either by his seventeen-year-old son and namesake or (in Coelius Antipater's downbeat version a century later) by a Ligurian slave accompanying his master. He retreated to Placentia but, when his allied Gallic contingent deserted to the enemy, recrossed the Po to a strong position by the river Trebia and waited for his recalled colleague.

In a small portent of things to come, Dasius of Brundisium, commanding the garrison of Clastidium, a well-stocked town near the Trebia, betrayed it to a very pleased Hannibal—the first defection to him of a Roman ally in Italy. He promptly freed Clastidium's garrison of Latin and other allied troops, a first gesture of conciliation to the Italians whom he hoped to prize from their hegemon. Meanwhile Gallic warriors in their thousands came in, seeing him as their liberator from Rome's recently imposed control. When Sempronius Longus with his legions arrived to join Scipio, they faced the Carthaginians across the Trebia with a combined army of four legions and their allied units—38,000 foot and 4,000 horse. A pitched battle was certain, even though by now winter had emphatically arrived too.

Roman historians, and Polybius too, chose to paint here the first of a series of black-and-white contrasts between colleagues in command: Sempronius combative, overconfident, and ignorant of the military genius of his foe; the wounded Scipio wisely but ineffectually cautious. In reality, whether or not Scipio did have doubts (and we might wonder what his son was thinking), all other Romans were looking for a grand victorious battle that would smash the invader. On December 22 or 23 (the time of the winter solstice), a teasing foray by Numidian cavalry over the river to the gates of the Roman camp brought out the entire army in battle array. Yet it was woefully ill-prepared: early in the morning, mostly unfed, amid sleeting rain, men and horses had to ford the freezing chest-high stream and then be harassed by the Numidians as they marched across broad open ground to attack Hannibal's comfortably prepared troops. Although his infantry totaled only about 30,000 even with the new Gallic allies, his 10,000 cavalry outnumbered the enemy's more than two to one. His own sharp eye for terrain had picked out another asset the day before: a long and deep watercourse near the battleground, full of brambly undergrowth, where he now placed his brother Mago with a thousand elite Numidian infantrymen and another thousand cavalry. Sempronius and his men had no idea they were there.

The Romans swiftly ran into serious trouble. On each wing Hannibal's cavalry swept away theirs, leaving their infantry vulnerable first to his light-armed footmen and then, much worse, to Numidian cavalry turning back onto the field. Still, even while the Roman infantry's flanks began to lose order, the bulk of the formation pressed into the Gallic infantry of Hannibal's center and then the Libyans stationed behind. Sempronius might yet have forced a draw—if Mago's Numidians had not charged from their hidingplace into the Roman rear. The army began to break up. Its front ranks actually pierced through the opposition, but all the rest either were slaughtered in the pouring rain by Hannibal's cavalry and elephants as they fled back toward the Trebia or were taken prisoner. The 10,000 infantry who had broken through could do little but leave the shattered field as fast as they could for the relative safety of Placentia fifteen kilometers away. Sempronius, with most of his cavalry and some infantry, also made it to Placentia, to be joined by Scipio.

LAKE TRASIMENE

Hannibal's battle losses had been chiefly among his Gallic contingents, but the bitter winter that lasted into early 217 killed many other soldiers and horses, as well as all but one of the elephants he had brought to Italy. Again he released his non-Roman Italian captives ransom-free, and now he gave them a message: he was in Italy to free its peoples from Roman rule and restore to them the cities and lands taken from them. The weather was now so atrocious that he spent several months virtually immobile, perhaps at Clastidium. Livy has him try unsuccessfully to seize more Cisalpine supply depots and even cross the Apennines in the teeth of storm and snow, but these seem later inventions to fill this inactive period. Nevertheless, to crush Rome's will to resist and win over the other Italians Hannibal had to demonstrate his military mastery in the heart of the peninsula. Nor did his Gallic allies expect anything less. Indeed, over the winter they became riskily restive—enough to impel the general himself, so the fairly improbable story goes, to disguise himself with wigs and unusual clothing to escape some resentful Gaul's dagger.

Only in early May, when he could be sure of finding forage for the army and fodder for the horses, did he march with something over 50,000 men. Etruria was his opening objective but not his ultimate goal. Once ships could sail again he apparently communicated with Carthage, perhaps via one or more Greek or foreign merchant ships from a Cisalpine port: for a few months later seventy Punic ships—Carthage was building up her navy at last—arrived via Sardinia at the Italian coast near Pisae expecting to link up with him. Seventy ships could bring welcome funds, though not large reinforcements; but early in 217 Hannibal may have had something bolder in mind, even perhaps a strike at Rome by land and water.[6]

Meanwhile the Romans rebounded fast from their defeat. During the winter the combative Gaius Flaminius was chosen consul, along with Gnaeus Servilius Geminus. Ancient writers paint Flaminius as rash to the point of impiety—their posthumous payback for the catastrophe at Lake Trasimene—but in fact the consuls cooperated in a joint strategy that recalled how Rome had dealt with the Gallic invasion eight years before. With freshly levied reinforcements, Flaminius positioned himself at Arretium in the heart of Etruria, and Servilius stood at Ariminum beside the upper Adriatic. Hannibal would have to try to evade one or the other to march south. They may have reckoned that in evading one he could be shepherded into confronting the other and so be caught between both— or even that indecision might keep him in Cisalpina while they converged against him. Flaminius was confident, too, that in pitched battle he could defeat the invader on his own, although his army totaled only 25,000 horse and foot. The Senate meantime authorized additional legions: per- haps two to garrison Rome and certainly others for Tarentum, Sicily, and Sardinia, obviously to guard against possible naval attack. In 218 a Punic squadron had briefly raided farmlands around Vibo in southern Italy, and likely enough word had come (from deserters, prisoners, neutral traders, or Hiero at Syracuse) of warship-building at Carthage.

With his Gallic contingents, Hannibal in 217 was at the head of more than 50,000 troops. His best prospect was to defeat one if not both consuls, master central Italy's countryside, and then either advance on Rome or move through Italy pressuring her allies to change sides. Since a fleet at Carthage was readying to rendezvous with him in Etruria, the advance on Rome looks like his chosen option, a joint operation to hem her in by land and sea. The campaign did not start entirely well. Crossing the Apennines into northern Etruria after the bitter winter, the army had to flounder through floodlands, probably from melting snows, along the middle course of the Arno river. A nightmare four-day passage through the sodden and stinking marshes took a heavy toll not only on the Gauls forming the army's center, and on the cavalry in the rear (many horses lost hooves), but also on the pack animals—most perished—and on the general himself. Hannibal rode on his last surviving elephant, but an infection already developing in one eye became so severe that its sight was lost.

As the battered army regrouped on dry ground south of the Arno, Flaminius just possibly could have seized the opportunity to close with it before it (and Hannibal) could recover balance. Fiery as he was, however, the consul was no strategist. He chose to wait at Arretium nearby to see what would come next—which, foreseeably, was the enemy slashing and burning through opulent Etruscan fields, farms, and orchards south of Arretium and between the cities of Saena (today's Siena) and Cortona and then turning east toward Lake Trasimene. To Flaminius these movements probably seemed exactly what was wanted, for Hannibal moving eastward meant moving closer to Servilius, with Flaminius in pursuit. Servilius indeed was marching west and planning to send his cavalry ahead to reinforce his colleague.

Hannibal had his own plan. He halted on the hillsides running parallel to Trasimene's northern shore (the precise site is debated), deployed his troops along them, and then waited for the Romans to arrive. On June 21, a morning of unusually dense mist over the lakeshore, they did—the army in long columns of march, men's armor piled in carts or on pack animals, and no scouts roaming ahead because Flaminius imagined the enemy to be miles beyond. When the Carthaginian forces came rolling down the mist-laden hillsides, his men barely had time to snatch their armor and weapons. They could not form regular battle lines or see what was happening at any distance, and many could not even cluster together in their normal maniples. Flaminius had no way to organize a fightback except among the troops nearest to him, the *triarii* (third and veteran line) of his legions. Polybius claims that he fell into panic; Livy, by contrast, depicts him coolheaded and resolute. Livy's report looks more plausible, coming from a usually harsh critic, but perhaps at the outset the consul did have a spell of horror and despair, visible to some who survived.

Strung out over three, four, or more kilometers of lakeshore and wrapped in the morning mist, the legionaries and allies nevertheless organized themselves into groups, managed to put on some armor and seize their weapons, and fought back. Many will have been veterans of past campaigns such as the Gallic invasion. Flaminius's example must have been imitated down the line by the military tribunes and the allied contingents' prefects. As a result the battle was no abrupt rout. It lasted three hours. The Romans' improvised fighting units were gradually broken up, and as one gave way some of its victorious maulers could move to reinforce their comrades against another. When Flaminius was speared to death by an Insubrian nobleman, word spread along the already faltering lines to cause a wholesale collapse, save for 6,000 men in the vanguard who pushed through to higher ground and made for a nearby village—only to be rounded up overnight by Maharbal leading a detached force. Ten thousand Romans and allies were killed on land or in the lake's shallows; 15,000 fell into Hannibal's hands including Maharbal's haul. That agile commander followed this up a few days later by wiping out the cavalry that Servilius had sent ahead. Two thousand died, and the other 2,000 had to surrender. This left the surviving consul with no cavalry arm and effectively stranded in the northeast. The only other Roman military forces in Italy were those at Rome herself and the legion at Tarentum. Flaminius's conqueror stood only four or five days' march from the City.

In two great clashes only six months apart Rome lost some 55,000 citizen and allied troops, dead or captured. For the ancient world these were colossal disasters, comparable to the Persians' defeats by Alexander the Great eleven decades before. Even so, Trebia and Trasimene would pale into the shadows before yet another Hannibalic triumph, just over a year to come. Before then, all the same, the invaders would experience a first and unpleasant taste of Rome's peculiar stubbornness in warfare.

FABIUS'S TACTICS

Hannibal could have marched on Rome with little trouble in June and July 217. Etruria's countryside was well stocked, and there was practically no one in the way. His officers expected it. Maharbal indeed may have urged his leader to send him ahead with the cavalry, on a five-day dash to seize the City by surprise—though this advice is recorded only a year later. An alternative would have been to march down to the Etruscan coast to keep watch for the prearranged fleet from Carthage and then advance on Rome in tandem with it. The Senate did expect Hannibal to come. The walls were manned, and bridges up and down the Tiber were broken down. Even if there were two new legions already in the City as some scholars believe, against 50,000 victorious enemy troops they could have done little except share the starvation or venture out to be destroyed. With Rome invested by land and a Punic fleet in the Tiber, the war might have ended rapidly.

Instead Hannibal decided to march to the Adriatic. Prisoners and deserters, or the spy at Rome who was unmasked the following year, could tell him of Rome's 110 ships patrolling the Tyrrhenian Sea to make any Punic fleet's approach perilous. Although he had lost only about 1,500 men by the lake, the rest of his troops and also the horses were suffering the effects of a hard battle, the noxious Arno marshes, and the fierce Cisalpine winter. He expected that the Adriatic coast down to Apulia promised better conditions and that thrusting so far into Italian territories would hurry on the defections he needed. To the same end he again released all his non-Roman captives with the seductive message of Carthage as liberator. After he fitted out his Libyans with captured Roman weapons, ten days' march through bountiful countryside brought the army to the east coast, then to advance south through the lands of the Praetuttii, Marrucini, Frentani, and others into Apulia, amassing food, wine, and movable plunder en route—more in fact than the troops could manage. By Hannibal's order they also slaughtered all the adult men they came across, even though few can have been Romans in those parts of the peninsula. Either the general did not know this, or he was ruthlessly resolved to spread wide the terror of Punic arms. Like his troops' enthusiastic looting of everything in sight, it did him no good with the very peoples he wanted to entice.

In Apulia the men had leisure to recover from their ailments and exertions, while they cured the horses of mange by bathing them (says Polybius) in old wine—perhaps an antiseptic cleanser. Before long the invaders were literally fighting fit again. The Romans gave them no trouble, with the weakened Servilius in no condition to move against them and time needed for levying fresh forces. Three aristocrats from Capua in Campania, captured at Lake Trasimene, had told Hannibal just what he wanted to hear: that Campania was seething with anti-Roman feeling and ripe for changing sides and the three would foment this once released. But neither Capua nor any other city in Italy shifted loyalties when the invaders arrived outside. Hannibal perhaps began to think of summoning his brother Hasdrubal from Spain with fresh forces, although the order would not be sent until the following year (and Hasdrubal would ignore it).

The Romans were once again regrouping. For the first time since Atilius Caiatinus in 249, they appointed a dictator for warfare. As Servilius could not reach the City, the Comitia Centuriata for the first time in history, probably on a praetor's proposal, chose both the dictator and his master of horse: Quintus Fabius Maximus, consul in 233 and 228, and Marcus Minucius Rufus, consul in 221. These were not obvious choices. On campaign as consul—sixteen years earlier—the now elderly Fabius had had no grimmer enemies to face than the northern Apennine Ligurians. Minucius had fought the northern Adriatic Istrians no more sensationally. By contrast, their peers included Lucius Postumius Albinus, one of the subduers in 229 of the Illyrian queen Teuta; Quintus Fulvius Flaccus and Titus Manlius Torquatus, who in 224 had overcome the Boii; Marcus Claudius Marcellus, the victor of Clastidium in 222; and Lucius Aemilius Paullus, the co-commander against Demetrius of Pharos just two years before. An added oddity of the choices was that Fabius and Minucius disliked each other—although no sound evidence backs up an old theory that the dictator headed a cautiously conservative political faction whereas Minucius belonged to a supposed populist and assertive opposing one. It was not the last choice of unlikely collaborators during this war.[7]

Fabius publicly condemned the dead Flaminius for acting rashly: a hint, unnoted by all, of the contrasting strategy that he was planning. Taking over Servilius's army and two new legions and allied units, he advanced with a good 30,000 troops into northern Apulia—where, instead of seeking a new battle, the Romans simply shadowed the enemy, keeping to higher ground, harassing foragers, and cutting off stragglers.

Broadly this recalled Hamilcar Barca's harassment strategy against the Romans in Sicily thirty years before. Hannibal, failing to provoke or ambush his suddenly coy opponents, marched from Apulia through Samnium's mountains—plundering and ravaging again—down to Campania's *ager Falernus*, the fertile plain along the west bank of the lower Volturnus river. He hoped (fruitlessly, it turned out) that the Capuans would change sides once he was close by and that ransacking the *ager Falernus* would at last provoke his arm's-length pursuers to fight. Instead Fabius's army, seething but obedient, looked on from the heights of Monte Massico just to the west, week after week. Minucius as well as many of the military tribunes were all for battle and furious at their chief, but Fabius was readying his own scheme.

It came into action sometime in September, when Hannibal decided to withdraw to winter in Apulia. Fabius garrisoned Casilinum beside the Volturnus, to block him from crossing to the plains around Capua and to shepherd him back the way he had come, via a pass not far north of Capua (Polybius calls it Eribianus; Livy, Callicula). Fabius occupied the pass with 4,000 men and waited on a height overlooking it. Hannibal found the pass blocked only when his booty-laden army was too near to swing away elsewhere without risk. He faced being shut up over autumn and winter in the ravaged Falernian district, with Romans on three sides and the sea on the fourth—but extricated himself with one of his most famous stratagems. Two thousand unfortunate cattle, selected from the livestock booty by his quartermaster Hasdrubal, had bundled branches tied to their horns and set on fire and then were driven in the dead of night by light-armed troops toward a saddle in the heights beside the pass. Literally and metaphorically in the dark, the Romans holding Callicula left it to counter the supposed breakout, expecting the dictator to bring support. Fabius rightly suspected a Punic ruse, wrongly assumed that he could not thwart it, and so kept his troops in camp. Hannibal marched untroubled through Callicula and then sent troops back the next morning to bring in the doughty light-armed force, while its Roman attackers suffered heavy casualties. Back in northern Apulia, he seized a small town called Gerunium or Gereonium, thirty-five kilometers north-west of the Latin colony of Luceria and fifty or so from Arpi, killing all its inhabitants because they resisted. Even more cautious than before, Fabius followed along every upland height available.[8]

Hannibal's all-too-easy (it seemed) escape from destruction fueled Romans' criticisms of the delaying dictator. Even the funds for him to ransom 247 Roman captives left over from the latest prisoner exchange were held up. The odium was not allayed when Fabius returned to the City for religious duties. Left in command, Minucius harassed enemy forces foraging for supplies and even came close to attacking Hannibal's camp before being beaten back. Hannibal tweaked Fabius's unpopularity by ostentatiously sparing an Apulian estate of his from plunder, a familiar ruse—the Spartans harrying Attica at the start of the Peloponnesian War had used it against Pericles—to hint at an unseemly understanding between them. Fabius promptly sold the property (to an unknown optimist) and used the proceeds for ransoming the captives.

Nonetheless and no doubt to his chagrin he suffered an official humiliation that was also a constitutional anomaly. By vote of the People, his master of horse was made his equal in authority (*imperium*): in effect giving Rome two dictators, even though the point of the dictatorship was its being unique and supreme. That it could be doubled distressed later Romans—so Livy argues that Fabius was really only a "pro-dictator" (an otherwise unknown conceit) through having been elected, not nominated by a consul. Third-century Rome was less prone to technical hair-splitting than later ages; Minucius probably remained master of horse formally, yet in practice was Fabius's colleague (and on the surviving base of a statue dedicated to Hercules calls himself dictator). The consul Servilius was sent to command the fleet at Ostia and raid Africa; his new colleague Atilius Regulus, it seems, had charge of Rome's garrison.[9]

Fabius and Minucius now took two legions each, remaining fairly close to each other to shadow the invaders. As autumn advanced, Hannibal's crucial need—short of a victorious battle—was to scour the countryside for supplies to take his men, horses, and captured livestock through the winter. Fabius's obvious aim was to thwart this as far as possible, whereas (we are told) Minucius was heedlessly keen to force a battle, which he felt he could win. This weakness Hannibal exploited by enticing him to attack what looked like unaccompanied light-armed troops on a hilltop.

The Carthaginians then came up in full force, and too late the Roman discovered that other enemy troops had been hidden in dips and hollows nearby, a stratagem recalling the Trebia battle nine or ten months before. All that saved Minucius's army was the timely arrival of Fabius's legions, which compelled the enemy to retire. Hannibal must have realized that this could happen but probably had hoped to cut Minucius to pieces first. The chastened co-dictator publicly confessed his errors (in Livy's highly moral account), reunited his troops with Fabius's, and from then on loyally did as he was told.

Minucius's stagy confession is too good to be true, while the saga of his headstrong incaution suspiciously recalls the alleged rashnesses of Sempronius Longus and Flaminius. Just conceivably, Fabius and Minucius had agreed to cooperate—aiming to starve down the Carthaginian army over winter or even force battle if they could catch Hannibal in unfavorable circumstances between their forces (like the consuls' maneuver against the Gauls at Telamon eight years earlier). Then, arguably, Minucius acted too hastily, and neither commander reckoned with the risk of a Hannibalic ambush. Given Fabius's soon-to-be-sanctified reputation as the Delayer who saved Rome, even the earliest Roman historians of the episode—including of course his kinsman Pictor—might well recolor it to his glory. Minucius, dead within a year, could not protest, and Hannibal's historians would not be interested.

In any case it was the last affair of the 217 campaign. The co-dictators laid down their magistracy as its six-month maximum neared, leaving Servilius and Regulus to take over their armies.

CANNAE

In Apulia the next six or seven months were largely uneventful. Hannibal and the consuls (who became proconsuls when their year expired in March 216) did little except conduct intermittent skirmishes. Servilius and Regulus were under orders from Rome not to risk a battle, and Hannibal found them impossible to seduce. In practice Fabius's cautious strategy continued, which was the antithesis to Hannibal's needs. He could not obtain further Gallic warriors from distant Cisalpina, not in serious numbers anyway, yet no Italian states would defect to him even if he received the trickle of deserters usual in any war. No new Punic fleet tried to make contact. Over winter and spring Apulia (above all the districts he had scoured) could not supply the lush provisions that his army had enjoyed in eastern Italy and Campania after Trasimene. Livy credibly reports that he feared even that his veteran Spanish troops might desert. In fact the news from Spain, if he and the army did hear it, was worrying. Gnaeus Scipio during 217 inflicted a serious defeat on Hasdrubal by land and sea near the mouth of the Ebro; then Publius Scipio as proconsul brought reinforcements, and the two began to extend operations southward even as far as Saguntum. Libya too was hit. Servilius Geminus's fleet had carried out its coastal raid during the summer—the first of many attacks that the Carthaginian navy found itself incapable of warding off.

Had the new consuls in 216 maintained Fabius's methods throughout the year, Hannibal's invasion would have been in difficulties if not near disaster. But the Romans' caution through the first half of the year was not because they had been converted by Fabius. A resolve to make an end of the invasion through overwhelming force led to consuls being elected who were judged able to apply it: Lucius Aemilius Paullus and a new-comer, popular and forceful, named Gaius Terentius Varro—one of the backers of the law equating Minucius with Fabius and a political figure in Flaminius's mold. Every ancient source disdains Varro, Polybius included: a butcher's son, hostile to the ruling elite, ignorant of warfare, heedless of wise advice. The abuse came about because he commanded the greatest army that the republic had ever seen and supervised its destruction. His patrician colleague, dead on the battlefield, could be contrastingly portrayed as a harassed if ineffectual martyr to patriotism and folly. Varro's case was not helped either by Aemilius's family being closely linked to the Scipios, patrons later on of Polybius. Varro thus became the fourth member of the quartet of allegedly rash generals whose moral and military failings could be satisfyingly blamed for the battle disasters of 218 to 216.

His and Aemilius's joint task, decreed by the Senate, was to confront Hannibal with a massive army and finish him. They were authorized to levy twice the usual number of legions and matchingly large numbers of allies. As normal, they would command the army on alternate days. With two other legions raised for Cisalpine Gaul, the two with the Scipio brothers in Spain, a legion of marines at Ostia under Claudius Marcellus (now a praetor), and possibly again two garrison legions for the city of Rome itself (*legiones urbanae*), the state had 130,000–140,000 soldiers in arms, citizens and allies, as well as the crews for at least 110 warships—more than 170,000 men all told. The consuls commanded eight legions, each with an unprecedented 5,000 infantrymen, and allied forces more or less equal in number, for a total of 80,000 foot, including the light-armed *velites*, and 6,000 horse, plus a contingent of 1,000 Cretan archers and slingers sent by Hiero. The cavalry were still fewer than Hannibal's 10,000, but the Romans expected the juggernaut of legionary and allied infantry to decide the matter.

FIGURE 7.3
View of the battlefield of Cannae from the nearby hill, with modern commemorative column.

To Hannibal this readiness to fight was a relief, perilous though clashing with such numbers would be. Despite being smaller, his army was the most seasoned and versatile that Carthage had ever fielded, and he could count on his enemies' lack of tactical sophistication, a skill he and his officers had in abundance. He surely reckoned that if this giant among Roman armies could be decisively beaten, Rome would have no choice left except to seek terms. Sixty years earlier two heavy defeats by Pyrrhus had induced her to negotiate, even if nothing came of it at last. Half a century before that, Alexander had overthrown the Persian monarchy in a triad of battles against ever larger Persian armies. A third victory in Italy, if overwhelming enough, would be—Hannibal clearly thought—the circuit breaker. It remained only to find ground suitable for a killer blow. He decided to find it elsewhere in Apulia.

When in July he and his hungry army marched from Gerunium to capture a well-stocked Roman military depot at Cannae, an abandoned town close to the river Aufidus about 100 kilometers away, the consuls followed. The region below Cannae's hilltop, down to the Adriatic three and a half kilometers away, looked ideal for a juggernaut battle (figure 7.3): a coastal plain reassuringly free of hollows, deep watercourses, or ridges and more than broad enough for a vast army to maneuver. After some skirmishing, the two armies encamped just west of the river, with a smaller Roman camp being set up beside the eastern bank. Wary of Hannibal's superior cavalry, the consuls avoided battle on the very flat plain along the west bank of the Aufidus, choosing its eastern side where the almost equally level ground stretched southward to meet Cannae's abrupt hill. Afterward Roman tradition pretended that Aemilius was against fighting there but that Varro still opted for it on a day when he held command. In fact the consuls were under orders to fight, and the eastern side looked safer for containing the Punic cavalry while Rome's infantry mass overwhelmed its opposition.

Just after dawn on August 2, the two sides deployed beside the Aufidus, the Roman right wing and the Punic left—both cavalry as usual—edging the river. With about 15,000 men left to hold the two camps, the Romans on the field numbered some 70,000 horse and foot. The infantry center, under Servilius Geminus, was more tightly arrayed than usual. Less space separated the maniples, and each maniple formed up with fewer men than normal in its front and more in the ranks behind. The obvious aim was to build overwhelming impetus into the infantry attack while the cavalry—Roman on the right wing under Aemilius Paullus, allied on the left with Varro—dealt with Hannibal's cavalry. Varro's position has drawn comment on the assumption that commanding generals regularly took station on the right wing. In reality it was not all that standard a practice: Hannibal positioned himself initially with his brother Mago in the center, just as Scipio would do at Zama. In any case it was normal, indeed necessary, for generals to move around the battlefield as much as possible to inspire their men, restore morale where needed, and react to developments.

Hannibal's array was carefully thought out. It involved immense risk, but in his situation risk was justified, for defeat meant destruction. The Spanish and Gallic cavalry, under quartermaster Hasdrubal, formed his left wing beside the river; the Numidian cavalry, his right under his nephew Hanno. This was a conventional arrangement. By contrast his center was radical: there his Spanish and Gallic infantry were deployed in a long and shallow convex line, with open ground directly behind. The Libyan infantry were drawn up in two columns, one behind each end of the convex arc, with the open ground between them; almost certainly they were invisible to the Romans as these tramped forward, shouting and clashing their weapons amid clouds of dust. By now Hannibal can have had only 8,000–10,000 Libyan infantry and perhaps 6,000 or 7,000 Spaniards, even though most losses so far had fallen on the Gauls. Fully aware of their numerical inferiority, even some of Hannibal's senior officers were uneasy watching the close-packed enemy masses. Hannibal teased a particularly queasy friend, Gisco, by commenting that there was one thing about them that his friend had not noticed: "Although they are so many, not one of them is named Gisco!" The joke cheered everyone up.[10]

History's textbook envelopment battle followed. While Hanno's Numidians grappled with the Roman allied cavalry, Hasdrubal beside the river drove the Roman cavalry off the field, prompting the consul Aemilius to move over to the infantry in the center to stiffen efforts there. The densely packed Roman and allied infantry struck Hannibal's Spaniards and Gauls, pushing them into disciplined but unbroken retreat. Most of the infantry were not actually in combat but steadily pushing forward in a tightening mass as the front ranks hacked at the enemy. The next two crucial events happened probably around the same time.

Hasdrubal did not pursue the routed Roman cavalry for long but instead wheeled his squadrons around behind the Roman infantry mass, to strike the allies' cavalry wing in the rear as it fought the Numidians, dissolving it into rout in its turn. Meanwhile the legions and allies had now pushed back the Spaniards and Gauls so far that the Libyans on each side of the open ground could pivot their own array to attack the enemy's crowded flanks. The Roman center began to lose cohesion as the men faced foes on three sides—and then Hasdrubal, leaving the Italian allied cavalry to the pursuing mercies of the Numidians, turned his own cavalrymen against the legions' rear. The trapped formations steadily shrank as virtually Hannibal's entire army, including its largely fresh light-armed spearmen and archers, cut them down.

As darkness fell, all that remained of the most powerful army that Rome had ever fielded were the garrisons holding the camps and some survivors escaping the slaughter on the plain. Estimates vary for the losses. Polybius claims 70,000 foot and 5,600 cavalrymen killed, but more plausible are Livy's more restrained figures: 45,500 infantry and 2,700 cavalry dead, just over 19,000 captured (two-thirds of them when the Roman camps surrendered). Meanwhile 14,550 eventually rallied around Varro at Canusium twelve kilometers to the south, unmolested by the exhausted conquerors. Dead were Varro's fellow consul Aemilius, his predecessor Servilius Geminus, the ex-dictator Minucius, Aemilius's and Varro's quaestors Atilius and Furius, and twenty-nine of the forty-eight military tribunes. Fate, though, decreed that among the surviving nineteen was young Publius Scipio, son of the proconsul in Spain. Hannibal's victory cost blood as well as effort and genius—5,500 infantry (1,500 of them his Libyans and Spaniards) were killed along with 200 cavalry—but the fields below Cannae were strewn with the ruins of the army that was to have been his nemesis.[11]

The Romans never forgot Cannae and never forgave Hannibal. The total of dead, Romans and allies together, had now passed 100,000 since the war began. That is, up to one in every seven Italian men of fighting age alive in August 218 was dead by August 216. Livy remarks accurately enough that "no other nation would not have been crushed by such an overwhelming disaster." Polybius, equally admiring, judges that the excellent qualities of their constitution were what enabled the Romans to pull through. Indeed in Roman memory it was not so much the monstrous casualties—even today the size of a large town—that took prime place but, rather, a cherished image of indomitable resoluteness, resilience, and selfless cooperation among all citizens. Like Great Britain's admired national rallying-round in the wartime 1940s, the image embodied a great deal of truth (intermittent exceptions only proved the rule).

Resoluteness and cooperation against Hannibal were vital in Cannae's aftermath. Just as after Trasimene, no Roman forces stood between him and the City. Once again the Romans, and his own officers, expected a direct march there to terminate the war. Maharbal certainly urged it, even though this time it could not be a fast five-day march but, rather, a purposeful advance after a few days' rest, driving uprooted refugees ahead to fill the beleaguered City with more and more hungry mouths. Although the praetor Marcellus at Ostia sent 1,500 naval personnel up to the City, they would have made little difference. Not only could Rome itself have been blockaded—even from access along the Tiber—but this would have shattered the loyalties of even more allies than Cannae soon did. Organizing fresh forces would have been next to impossible for the Senate and magistrates within the walls or for the surviving consul and his shattered remnants. By contrast the sufetes and *adirim* at Carthage could have sent whatever reinforcements Hannibal wished: they had at least 27,000 troops immediately available and elephants too, plus transport.

Hannibal decided otherwise. His decision has been defended often—the army was exhausted from its orgy of killing (though after a few days' rest it was on the march again); Rome lay three weeks' march away, across Samnium's mountains (yet the army knew these well and soon crossed them anew); he lacked siege engines (but some could have been made, using the forests in Latium, Samnium, and southern Etruria—or supplied by defecting cities); the Romans could have raised more troops (though with most surviving Roman authorities shut up inside the City this would have been problematic, and in any case such new troops would be raw recruits tackling veterans); he could not count on unstinting support from Carthage, where jealous enemies might prefer to see him lose (this argument ignores every known fact). None of these supposed obstacles was insurmountable; one or two, as just noted, did not exist. Hannibal's second self-denial, capping the first after Trasimene, cost Carthage the war.

8

HANNIBAL'S ZENITH

DEFIANCE AND DEFECTIONS

Hannibal in fact expected peace. He did not even move against the few thousand Roman survivors whom Varro was pulling together at Canusium a half-day's march away. Besides freeing his Italian prisoners as usual, this time he told his Roman captives that he was not fighting a war to the death but, rather (as already mentioned), one "about honor and power." Along with letting them choose a delegation to Rome to appeal for ransom, he appointed his chief cavalry commander Carthalo as his spokesman to offer talks, while he advanced with the army into Samnium and then Campania. What Carthalo would have proposed remains one of history's most intriguing unknowns. At word of his approach, the newly appointed dictator Marcus Junius Pera sent an order to him to leave Roman territory (he had perhaps got as far as Latium). The Senate and the dictator would not grant ransom, even though this left thousands of soldiers—who could have formed at least two legions—to be handed over to slave traders.

Rome's defiance was clear. In a renowned gesture, when Varro did return to Rome he was met by crowds of ordinary citizens as well as senators and publicly thanked "because he had not despaired of the state," a reference to his efforts following the disaster. The war would go on even after the third and worst disaster in as many years. While Marcellus's naval recruits came up from Ostia, he sent his legion of marines to hold Teanum on the Via Latina, the main inland road from Campania to the

City, in case the enemy moved that way. He himself was sent to Canusium to take over command of the Cannae survivors and march them to Casilinum in northern Campania. Next, unhindered by any further onslaught from Hannibal, the republic began to organize fresh armies. As dictator, Junius Pera—either nominated by Varro if the consul had now come to Rome or else elected by the People like Fabius in 217—organized fresh forces including men too old and teenagers too young for a normal levy; 8,000 slave volunteers called *volones*, who were promised freedom in return for loyal service; and even 6,000 imprisoned convicts and debtors who volunteered. Another concurrent dictator, the elderly Fabius Buteo, who had delivered the war declaration two years before, had to appoint no fewer than 177 notable Romans to replenish the desperately thinned-out Senate. Embarrassingly to future Roman generations, human sacrifice found a place among the religious acts taken to placate the angry gods: a Gallic and a Greek couple were seized and buried alive in the Forum Boarium, the cattle market near the Tiber.

Roman resolve did not falter even when frightful news arrived from Cisalpine Gaul that the legions and allies there, 25,000 men under Postumius Albinus, consul-elect for 215, had been massacred in a forest ambush. The army was trapped as trees with sawn-through trunks crashed around its marching columns, leaving survivors to be slaughtered by the Boii; Postumius's skull was covered in gold to become a ritual cup for the Boian priests.

Still the bad news did not stop. At last Italian allies started to rethink their loyalties: first of all some in Apulia such as the important cities of Arpi, Salapia, and Herdonea, and then many communities in semirural Bruttium in the southwest, a process encouraged by the arrival of Punic forces detached by Hannibal. Livy, oligarchic to his bones, insists that Italian defections were all forced by the bloody-minded masses on unwilling pro-Roman aristocrats. In reality his own narrative shows that the reverse often happened too—it did at Arpi—and, in other cases, disenchantment with Rome bridged all classes. When Hannibal entered Samnium after Cannae, the town of Compsa went over to him because one powerful aristocrat (his name was Statius Trebius) had enough popular backing to scare his family foes, the Mopsii, into decamping with their supporters. Before long, of Samnium's four peoples the only one still faithful to Rome was the Pentri, the northernmost. The Samnites had been Rome's toughest opponents in the fourth century and had not been fully brought under control until Pyrrhus's time; Samnite recruits would make a valuable contribution to Hannibal's army strength.[1]

In Campania the general won a still richer prize—Capua, the region's chief city, with its special, limited form of Roman citizenship. Capua amply compensated him for failing to capture Naples, twenty-five kilometers south, though he was still anxious for a secure harbor to improve communications with Carthage. Many in Capua's elite had close ties with Roman aristocrats—Pacuvius Calavius, Capuan leader at the time, was son-in-law of a patrician, Claudius, and father-in-law of Livius Salinator, the disgraced consul of 219—but they resented how their wealthy and cultivated city was subordinated to Rome's demands and directions and how their limited Roman status kept them from seeking Roman magistracies. So although the promises of Hannibal's three Campanian captives the year before had come to nothing, Cannae prompted a sea change (even though 300 young Campanian aristocrats were with the Roman forces in Sicily). Calavius and his close friends, notably the influential Vibius Virrius and the city's current chief magistrate, Marius Blossius, were authorized to contact Hannibal to negotiate friendship and alliance. No doubt they, and all the other allies who changed sides in 216 and 215, expected that the war would soon end. The more defections that came Hannibal's way, maybe one more mighty victory too, would end Rome's resistance and liberate them forever. The one outcome that none foresaw, unless in nightmares, was a dozen more years of destructive conflict—most of it across their own territories.

HANNIBAL'S NEW ITALIAN ALLIES

How carefully Hannibal had to tread in dealing with important defectors is clear in the terms he struck with Capua: its continuing independence, freedom from all Carthaginian interference, and a guarantee against forced recruitment of Campanians. Livy's report of him almost immediately breaking the treaty by having Capua's leading pro-Roman, Decius Magius, seized and shipped to Carthage (though contrary winds instead bore Magius to Egypt and asylum), may exaggerate: Calavius and company must have been glad to get rid of an opponent who might have turned the populace against them. Certainly Hannibal could not afford casual high-handedness with new allies. When other Italian cities and peoples changed sides, they too—or at least important ones such as Locri in 215 and Tarentum three years later—had to be guaranteed continuing self-government and no forced levies of men, munitions, or money. Locri's treaty expressly guaranteed that the city would keep control of its port, obviously its crucial economic resource. Defecting states did not change alliances just to replace one insistent hegemon with another. For them, being freed from Rome's control essentially meant being free to choose their own friends and enemies once more, resume feuding with neighbors, and form their own relations with peoples in and outside Italy—the same expectations that Syracuse would have a year or so later when it broke its alliance with Rome. Capua had still grander ideas: to replace Rome as hegemon of Italy.

All these calculations, some clearly incompatible with others, depended on one assumption: that once peace came, Hannibal and his men would go home. Livy reports him assuring the Capuan senate that their city would indeed become the ruler of all Italy. This of course presupposed that Carthage would not. It was a promise he could not keep and surely knew he could not. Once forced into peace, Rome would have to be supervised, and the best means of doing that would be a continuing Punic presence in the peninsula. Besides, if left to themselves, the liberated Italian states assuredly would soon come to blows with one another, leaving the path open for even a shrunken Rome to reassert mastery—or for an ambitious Macedon from across the Adriatic. As mentioned earlier, Hannibal had promised rewards of Italian land to his troops—no doubt aware from the start that annexing Italian territory and settling veterans and other colonists there would be essential to a *pax Punica*. None of this could be admitted to the eager Italians who from late 216 on chose to pin their hopes to his banner.[2]

Almost at once other problems showed themselves. Capua and her satellite cities, conventionally called "the Campanians," lay in northern Campania. Traditional rivalries and more amiable bonds with Rome kept virtually all the rest of the region loyal to her: not only important seaports such as Naples, Puteoli, and Cumae but strong inland cities including Casilinum, Nola, Acerrae, and Nuceria. Although discontented groups could be found in them (at Casilinum the Roman garrison massacred suspected traitors, at Nola accused Punic sympathizers would be executed), they were too few to push their cities over to the Carthaginians. Hannibal persisted nevertheless. His aim was plainly to create a large, coherent bloc of territories, allied or subject, across central and (he hoped) southern Italy to match—better still, outmatch—Rome and her still loyal supporters. Campania was the wealthiest region in Italy. Controlling all of it, including its ports, could be decisive.

Extending the bloc beyond Capua was the problem. He tried more than once to seize Naples, failing each time. He did force Nuceria and Acerrae to surrender and sacked them, taking care to let their residents leave first—massacring or enslaving non-Roman Italians would tarnish a liberator's image—and then early in 215 devoted time to starving out the stubborn garrison of Casilinum on the Volturnus, despite the efforts of Junius Pera's master of horse, Tiberius Sempronius Gracchus, to keep the men provisioned from outside. But repeated moves in late 216 and after against the strongpoint of Nola failed. This was now defended by Marcellus, whose unquenchable energy in the war would make him one of Rome's military icons. At the same time Marcellus's energy was bounded by caution and common sense: he would not hazard a pitched battle. Roman sources' claims of smashing victories by him outside Nola are excited exaggerations at best—at one stage, an impossible corps of Carthaginian elephants materializes in Livy—but neither in 215 nor again in 214 did Hannibal's attacks on the city succeed. He did no better with an attempt on Cumae in 215. Nor could he induce or entice the other enemy forces in Campania into battle. Fabian tactics had returned: Fabius Maximus, consul once again in 215, and his colleague Gracchus guarded strategic centers such as Cales inland and Cumae and Puteoli on the coast, avoiding combat and taking opportunities to ravage Capua's lands.

The victor of Cannae was becoming bogged down in Campania, paradoxically so near to Rome and yet so far.

His fortunes went better farther south. Before entering Campania in late summer 216 he had detached his brother Mago with troops into Lucania and Bruttium to gather more allies and attack recalcitrants—a task taken over by their nephew Hanno when Mago sailed to Carthage to report the glorious news of Cannae. The bulk of the Bruttians and also Locri and Croton, two of the coastal Greek cities in that region, joined the cause (but the Bruttians had to be restrained from assaulting a much-depopulated Croton). By contrast, Rhegium on the straits of Messina refused to turn its coat—and likewise the small Bruttian town of Petelia north of Croton. In fact Petelia held out against its besiegers, rebel Bruttians and Carthaginians under Hanno's lieutenant Himilco, for an agonizing eleven months, bereft of aid from its distant hegemon. Only when its people ran out of tree bark and leather to eat did they surrender on terms. The Carthaginians' persistence is strange. Though strongly sited on a mountaintop, Petelia was no great prize; it played no part in the rest of the war, and its stubbornness uncomfortably underlined Punic limitations in sieges. Perhaps Himilco overestimated its worth. Rhegium, on the other hand, would have been a major prize—yet was not attacked at all until 211 and even then only briefly and unsuccessfully. Southeastern Italy too resisted Hannibal's liberation call, at any rate for some years more.

The pattern of the new alliances formed in 216 and 215 showed up another flaw. Even in regions where most communities changed sides, such as Bruttium, Samnium, and Apulia, hostile centers remained. Latin and Roman colonies in such regions were important strategic points, could not be seduced, and were almost impossible to capture—Venusia on the borders of Samnium and Lucania, for instance, Beneventum in the heart of Samnium, and Cales north of the Volturnus. Even after the Greek cities in the southeast did defect in 213–212, Hannibal's allies formed not a continuous swathe of southern Italy but territorial clumps intermingled with others still on Rome's side, where Roman armies could find supplies and security when needed. It was the perfect recipe for a relentlessly grinding tug of war.

Hannibal was already thinking ahead and thinking, too, beyond Italy. The news from Spain continued to be bad. Around the start of 215 the Scipio brothers' formidable land and sea victory over Hasdrubal at the Ebro's mouth both confirmed his loss of the northeast that Hannibal had subdued three years before and threatened the whole eastern coast (they even reached Saguntum, briefly). When his brother Mago assembled at Carthage the 12,000 foot, 1,500 horse, and twenty elephants planned for Italy, he and they were ordered to Spain instead. Around the same time, a second similarly sized expedition sailed to Sardinia to back up locals rebelling against Rome; one of the deputy commanders was a Barcid kinsman, again a Mago. Only a much smaller, separately levied reinforcement of 4,000 Numidians finally made its way to Hannibal, transported to Locri by his likely brother-in-law Bomilcar, now Carthage's chief admiral, and escorted to Hannibal by Bomilcar's son Hanno. At least these troops had forty elephants with them and a large sum of money—exactly how much is uncertain, but either 500 or even 1,000 talents, a valuable addition to his campaign chest (three or six million drachmas). With the Numidians perhaps came a new and capable Libyphoenician cavalry officer, Mottones of Hippou Acra, very unusually a non-Carthaginian; Mottones does not appear in earlier events but by 212 was one of Hannibal's most trusted lieutenants.

These force dispersals do not signal that Hannibal's enemies at home had won back enough strength to thwart his needs and sabotage the war. Even if, arguably, Polybius is excessive in affirming that Hannibal had total control on all fronts, enemies powerful enough to decide military deployments would have been the opposite of clever in giving command, or subcommand, of every dispersed force to a Barcid kinsman or backer. In reality, by 215—unlike 216—Hannibal did not need to press for large reinforcements, because his Italian allies were providing troops. His nephew Hanno, sent off again to operate independently in the south, soon commanded a regular army 18,000 strong, mainly of Bruttians and Lucanians. Already in 215 Hannibal's Samnite allies were complaining, without success, about the numbers of their soldiers serving with him, because without them Samnium lay helpless against Marcellus's vengeful ravaging from Nola.

The Samnites' complaint, so early after Cannae, illustrated a problem for the invaders that would worsen over time. Hannibal could march anywhere he liked in Italy; but so could the Romans. Cannae brought Fabius's strategy back to stay, and with variations painful for Hannibal's allies and Hannibal himself. Rather than try a new doomed battle against him, the Roman commanders fell upon Rome's ex-allies and made their lives wretched. The unpleasantly scattered mosaic of defector states was both vulnerable to ravagings and hard for Hannibal to defend. Instead of leading a focused offensive against Roman armies or Rome herself to end all resistance, he would be occupied for years marching and countermarching over central and southern Italy, seeking new allies or protecting—or rescuing—ones he already had. The Romans found too that, without Hannibal in charge, forces such as Hanno's could be vulnerable. Despite victories from time to time by either side, the war in Italy was now essentially stalemated.

HANNIBAL'S OVERSEAS ALLIES: MACEDON AND SYRACUSE

A telling sign that the original invasion plan had had to be jettisoned came in 215 again, when for the first time Hannibal and Carthage accepted another great power as an ally. Macedon, under the young and aggressive Philip V, disliked Rome's interventions in Illyria. Philip had given asylum to Demetrius of Pharos when the Romans tumbled him out in 219. With ambitions of his own in coastal Illyria, and the Greek world watching the titanic battles in the west with guarded fascination, the king judged—just as Rome's defecting allies did—that Cannae would end the war, would wreck Rome as a great power, and would make Carthage hegemon of the western world: it was therefore the right moment to become a friend. His envoy, Xenophanes of Athens—despite being intercepted en route in Apulia by the praetor Marcus Valerius Laevinus and having to pretend that his mission was to Rome—reached Campania to negotiate with Hannibal.

Very fortunately the resulting treaty's Greek text survives in an excerpt from Polybius, in the form of the oath sworn by Hannibal and his advisers to the gods of Carthage, Macedon, and Greece—the one direct statement by Hannibal that has come down to us—followed by the terms mutually agreed on. Xenophanes on Philip's behalf no doubt swore a matching version. In Hannibal's oath proper, Carthage's gods and goddesses are all given Greek names, leaving it unclear and debated exactly which deities are meant—though the first two in the list, Zeus and Hera, must be Baal Hammon and Tanit. Heracles (surely Melqart) comes fifth. Together with a piously generalized promise of mutual protection, the two states undertook in standard fashion each to have the same enemies as the other (with the wary exception of "those kings, cities, and peoples with which we have sworn agreements and friendships"). Macedon was to help Hannibal in his current war, and Hannibal was to include in any peace with Rome a ban on her warring against Macedon afterward. His peace terms would also end Roman control over Illyria and the Adriatic Greek states, enforce Demetrius's restoration over his "friends" in the region, and—of especial note—declare that "if the Romans ever make war on you or on us, we shall aid each other as needed."[3]

The treaty's practical benefit to either signatory was nil. Xenophanes was caught again, this time on his way back, by a Roman naval patrol off Cape Lacinium, and the treaty was discovered. Another, more successful copy must have reached the king, but his ensuing Roman war, fought entirely on the eastern side of the Adriatic, was a depressing failure, and the peace that he finally made in 205 paid no attention at all to Hannibal or Carthage. The treaty's practical effect, instead of profiting either leader, was to embitter Rome unnecessarily and irremediably against Philip, with disastrous consequences in the end for his dynasty and realm. As for Hannibal, it is not highly likely that he would have welcomed a Macedonian army to Italy, least of all if headed by an assertive twenty-three-year-old king. Greek kings had a history of coming over in arms, summoned to aid the local Greeks against their non-Greek foes but then becoming unscrupulous would-be empire-builders; Pyrrhus was only the most recent. Indeed the Italian Greeks might prefer even an ambitious Macedonian rescuer to one from Africa. But the treaty shows that Hannibal expected Rome to continue existing, and in some strength—for a totally dismembered or annihilated Roman state would not pose a war threat or require a clause on collaborative defense against her.

The treaty's relatively temperate terms—some diplomatically ceremonious rather than realistic (Macedon was never going to help Carthage against enemies in Spain, for instance, nor would Carthage send troops in a clash between Macedon and the Seleucid empire)—were not to the liking of patriotic Roman historians. They invented more satisfying terms, as Livy's preposterous version shows: not just a massive invasion of Italy by Philip but the cession of all the peninsula, including the city of Rome, to Carthage—followed by a Carthaginian expedition eastward for war "against any peoples the king might choose." It is not the only case where Livy deliberately ignores a sound source (here an actual documentary text) to purvey more sensational fare.

Also in spring or summer 215 another foreign situation turned Carthage's way. Hiero of Syracuse, aged ninety and predeceased by his only son, Gelo, finally died after fifty-four years of rule. His unquestioning support for Rome had lost popularity as one Roman disaster followed another; even Gelo had grown restive. When Gelo's precocious fourteen-year-old son, Hieronymus, became king, the royal council was dominated by Gelo's son-in-law Adranodorus and a faction keen to exploit the international situation to revive Syracuse's power in Sicily. Hannibal swiftly responded to their feelers by sending over one of his chief lieutenants, another Hannibal—perhaps the friend nicknamed the Gladiator—and two resourceful officers, brothers named Hippocrates and Epicydes, whose Syracusan grandfather had settled in Carthage. Frustrating efforts by Appius Claudius Pulcher, the praetor in Roman Sicily (son of the naval loser at Drepana in 249), to keep Syracuse allied to Rome, this pair and Adranodorus guided the boy king into a treaty with Carthage that—unrealistically, and the Carthaginians knew it—promised sovereignty over the entire island to Syracuse (Hieronymus kindly conceded Italy to Carthage). This pact, too, accorded with Hannibal's revised grand strategy, though his namesake and the Syracusan envoys sailed to Carthage to arrange it. Macedon and Syracuse as allies would wring even greater exertions from Rome and therefore (all Carthaginians surely calculated) would undermine both her resistance to Hannibal in

Italy and the expedition harassing Hasdrubal in Spain. Should fortune favor, the combined pressure could even force her finally to talk peace.[4]

Yet widening the war was also a partial defeat for Carthage. Hannibal's original war plan assumed a one-to-one struggle—a rerun of the previous war without sea battles and with the outcome reversed. The revised scenario brought in more actors with major roles. Hannibal, the reviser, had to take their claims and interests into account if a future settlement was to last. He surely realized that, if this meant Syracuse ruling all (or even most) of Sicily and Macedon becoming hegemon of the lower Adriatic, and maybe protectress of the Italian Greeks, while Carthage dominated the rest of Italy including a curbed Rome, it would not be a settlement likely to last. In any case, Carthage's freedom of action in the current war was now that much more limited.

THE ROMAN FIGHTBACK

The year after Cannae saw the Romans radically change how they fought the invasion. Dangers and strains were immense. As more and more Italians switched sides, especially the hardy Samnites (the Pentri excepted) and populous Campanians, the recruitment pool shrank to Roman citizens themselves, Latins, and the peoples of central and northern Italy. Conversely, military needs grew. In 215 fourteen legions—perhaps 75,000 Romans and as many allies—were in the field, more than twice as many as the six levied at the confident outset of war three years before. Six legions operated in Campania—two each under the consuls Fabius and Gracchus, two with Marcellus—and another two in Apulia commanded by Marcus Valerius Laevinus, one of the year's praetors. In Sicily Appius Claudius's two legions consisted chiefly of the survivors of Cannae; their somewhat unfair lot, decreed by the Senate, was to serve out the war there without remission or discharge. Two others were sent to Sardinia to cope with its revolt, and in Spain the Scipio brothers continued to occupy Hasdrubal's attention. The navy had about 120 quinqueremes (out of the original 220) in service. The Adriatic fleet had to be increased because of the new collision with Macedon, but the naval menace from Carthage was small—in fact each year from 217 to 215 Roman squadrons raided Libyan coasts, followed by another five visits over the next decade.

From 215 the Second Punic War changed character. Head-on battles with the invincible invader were rigorously avoided (later tradition had to invent some, or exaggerate skirmishes, to enhance Marcellus's reputation as "the sword of Rome," balancing Fabius as "the shield") in favor of ravaging his allies and where possible reconquering them. The overall aim must have been to starve the invaders slowly but steadily of support and supplies. This was a strategy of draining drudgery and attrition, with no certainty that it would work. Hannibal might circumvent it by winning over an unconquerable number of Italian states, by focusing his efforts on ravaging Rome's own territories, and—if fortune favored him—by trapping and annihilating Roman forces no matter how cagily they maneuvered. Yet, short of levying even more forces for a risky counterinvasion of Libya, Fabian strategy was the best of the available bad options.

A group of tested commanders was emerging. Fabius, consul in 215 and again (his fourth time) in 214, was the doyen; Marcellus, who would be his colleague in 214, was the next most outstanding; still others were Tiberius Gracchus, Quintus Fulvius Flaccus, and Valerius Laevinus. These men did not quite monopolize the consulships and therefore the high commands of the next seven or eight years, but not many others joined them. Those who did, notably Appius Claudius in 212 with Fulvius and Titus Quinctius Crispinus in 208 with Marcellus, collaborated satisfactorily with the doyens. Similar stability of command had prevailed in Spain since 218–217, where the Scipio brothers continued as proconsuls.

Fabius, Marcellus, and the others were not automatically close friends or allies, though Marcellus and Fabius shared some family links, as did Fulvius and Laevinus. Such connections were common in the relatively small social envelope of the Roman elite; that did not avert disagreements, clashes, and even occasional political dodges. Marcellus abdicated the consulship of 215 after being elected with Gracchus (in place of the ill-fated consul-elect Postumius, killed in Gaul), because, just as he took office, the gods via a roll of thunder pronounced themselves unhappy—two plebeians had never before shared the highest magistracy. Since the gods were interpreted by the augurs and, in the ensuing revote, he was replaced by the most senior augur, human instead of heavenly interference is usually suspected—perhaps rightly. But equally the Romans were highly sensitive to anything they judged as a sign or portent, especially at critical moments, and the election won by Marcellus occurred because of Postumius's disaster, which itself had followed the horror of Cannae: events easy to judge as due to displeased divinities. At such a juncture, anything that seemingly crossed heaven (like the unheard-of lack of a patrician consul) might well not be risked.

Instead Marcellus gained the consulship for 214, with Fabius again elected as patrician colleague, again after an unusual contretemps. This time it showed Fabius willing to antagonize his own kinsman Titus Otacilius Crassus (who was also Marcellus's half-brother). When that hard-working ex-praetor, in charge of the fleet at Lilybaeum since 217, was plainly about to be elected one of the consuls, his venerable uncle-in-law as presiding consul insisted to Otacilius's loud disgust that his kinsman lacked the necessary abilities, while the other candidate (a totally unmemorable Aemilius Regillus, *flamen*—the special priest—of the god Quirinus) had religious impediments to holding consular office. Since Fabius himself was elected instead along with Marcellus, Otacilius's accusation that his uncle was acting for personal benefit has been shared by many historians: a verdict more plausible than the suspicion over Marcellus's thunder-thwarted experience the previous year. It would be hard, all the same, to hold that Rome would have done better in 214 with Otacilius and Regillus; so if Fabius did intend personal advantage, it nonetheless was a plus for the state too.

When not holding office, all these leaders could be continued in their commands—the technical term was "prorogued"—if the Senate extended their *imperium*. Used only occasionally during the First Punic War, prorogation now became common both for ex-consuls and for various ex-praetors who also held a military command. Publius Scipio, in Spain from 217, had been a proconsul from the start; possibly his brother Gnaeus, at first his deputy or *legatus*, then received formal appointment too. Marcellus in turn was, it seems, compensated for his abdication in 215 by being formally designated praetor with consular *imperium*; then after his consulship the following year, his *imperium* was continued as proconsul from 213 to 211 inclusive. Gracchus in similar style continued operations in central Italy as proconsul when his own office ended; and the harried Otacilius's praetorship in 217 was followed by many years (before and after his failed quest to be consul) as propraetor, all of them commanding the Lilybaeum fleet. Even Varro, the antihero of Cannae, was kept on to do useful military-administrative tasks out of harm's way in Picenum, until 213; years later he was made a propraetor for security tasks in Etruria.

This flexible use of extended *imperium* responded to the demands of a war with so many separate fronts. By 214 Rome was operating military forces from Spain to Illyria and in Italy alone was maintaining three groups of armies under several commanders—Campania, Apulia, and the two City legions—not to mention a legion with Varro in the northeast. Two years later there would be even more. The system of military commands through annual magistracies with the resulting constant rotation of commanders, which had proved barely satisfactory in the first war, was thus neatly modified to fit new circumstances: so neatly that the modifications would outlive the war.

STRESSES OF WAR

Financially and economically the war was inflicting more disaster. Trade and business must have been harmed, even if no source is interested enough to report on them. Rome's trade with other parts of Italy will certainly have stopped or been badly interfered with, while Punic fleets at least intermittently on the prowl would worry, maybe deter, many a sea trader. Plunder and destruction spread especially over southern Italy. Hannibal's land ravages mainly blighted Roman allies' possessions but spread terror widely. Fabius, when dictator and later when consul, tried to deny plunder to the Carthaginians by issuing (in 217) a scorched-earth order to the areas that Hannibal was traversing and by ordering (in 215) all grain in loyal districts to be delivered to fortified centers before June 1—though how well obeyed his orders were may be wondered (there were no functionaries to supervise them); they were not repeated in later years. The Romans too laid waste to hostile territories such as Capua's; although in 215, and maybe in later years, they cannily waited until crops were ripe and then reaped them for themselves.

Raising funds to pay the state's costs (chiefly military and religious) had become a serious problem too. In the year of Cannae a finance commission of three, called *triumviri mensarii*, was appointed to supervise income and spending and kept busy until at least 210. Not only was the property tax or *tributum* levied from the start, but in 215 double *tributum* was required, and at one level or other the tax was levied throughout the war. But of course the number of citizens paying it was lower than the prewar number, due to the thousands of casualties and because so many (indeed more and more) soldiers were on service. Late that year the Senate and magistrates were driven to asking munitions providers to take up contracts for supplying food and clothing to the forces in Spain on trust; the *res publica* promised to pay when funds were available and meanwhile to insure cargoes. Plenty of providers did comply—although in 213 and 212 it came out that at least a few had preferred to practice fraud with shoddy goods and bloated, even fictitious, insurance claims.

For state finances the next year, 214, was especially critical. Not only did contractors (probably rather few) for public building projects have to accept promises too, in lieu of cash, but orphans' and widows' trust funds were taken over as, in effect, state loans, earning interest (the state presumably returned the funds to their executors after the war). Not to be outdone, the former owners of slave volunteers (the *volones*) put off payment for these now freed warriors until war's end. Yet none of this was enough for ongoing costs, as still another war loomed in Sicily. This called for more ships to be commissioned, which meant finding crews and their pay. How the authorities met the need throws instructive light on Rome's administrative and social norms. The Senate required private citizens to foot the bills according to their means as registered in the census of 220. Those assessed at 50,000–100,000 *asses* must furnish one sailor with six months' pay, and those worth 100,000–300,000 *asses*, three with a year's pay. The affluent citizen worth 300,000 to one million was called on for five sailors on the same pay; the rich (one million plus), no fewer than seven; and senators—whether in the superband or not—eight.

Livy supplies all these items and mentions no further acts of patriotic financial selflessness until 210. In that year Marcus Valerius Laevinus as consul prompted first his fellow senators, and then Romans in the cavalry order (the *equester ordo*) and everyone else who could afford it, to donate much or most of their gold and silver possessions and their funds in coin to the *triumviri mensarii*. The laudable result was that all the year's military expenses were met. Whether contributions like these occurred in other years is not known, but obviously not even senators could hand over the bulk of their possessions year after year—least of all if each was meeting the annual upkeep of several sailors. Revenues like expenses no doubt fluctuated, scattered though details are. Other money-raising steps had to be taken in 209 and 205, yet in 204 and (it seems) 202 some of the sums raised by the communal contributions six years earlier were actually repaid to their donors.[5]

FIGURE 8.1
Carthage's enclosed ports: artist's reconstruction.

Generous self-denial was not universal. As just mentioned, some supply contractors for Spain preferred fraud as the road to riches. Substandard cargoes went missing, and inflated insurance claims were then presented. The ringleaders were well-connected *equites* (even if Livy is anxious to declare them simply Etruscans): Titus Pomponius of Veii, who in 213 was commanding a detached allied force in Lucania and got himself captured, and Marcus Postumius of Pyrgi, who—Livy then discloses—was kinsman of an aristocrat, Gaius Servilius Casca (one of whose descendants would make a name for himself as Julius Caesar's envious assassin). The affair was at first hushed up by the authorities, anxious not to upset the entire community of suppliers, but in 212 Postumius was fined the heavy sum of 200,000 *asses*. A virtual riot in the Forum by friends and fellow contractors followed, forcing the consuls Claudius and Fulvius to intervene—the upshot being that Postumius and many of the rioters disappeared scot-free into exile. We may wonder what the three finance commissioners, the *triumviri mensarii*—in office as late as 210—were doing amid this turmoil and, still more to the point, whether this can have been the sole serious case in the whole war (and not just the sole recorded one) of defrauding public funds.

Carthage's war finances and economics can only be surmised. Coastal raids apart, Libya was spared enemy attack until 204, and down to 209 so was most of southern Spain. No doubt thanks to hard effort, money was sent to the armies at various times: in 215 Mago took to Spain no less than 1,000 talents—in Roman terms sixty million *asses* or six million *denarii* (the new coin introduced just a few years later, equivalent to a drachma). The sum that Bomilcar ferried to Hanno at Locri that same year was 500 or even again 1,000 talents, as already noted. Ten years later Mago, now trying his military luck in Liguria, received substantial funds from home (no figure is recorded) along with troops. Carthage's funds must have come mainly from Libyan taxes, customs dues, and levies or loans from citizens, though southern Spain's revenues probably came in until Scipio Africanus began to play havoc with them from 209 on. Overseas trade probably suffered, although serious danger perhaps befell only ships that passed too near Roman-held ports or ran into Roman squadrons at sea.

At some date, quite likely during this war, the Carthaginians had the money to construct the two famous artificial ports, one behind the other, where the lake of Tunis's shoreline meets the sea. Shipping normally docked or moored alongside the city's seaward walls or in the lake of Tunis; maybe, too, the now-submerged quay called Falbe's Quadrilateral already existed. But in wartime greater security was vital. Both ports were invisible behind their walls. The outer, commercial port, entered from the sea via a narrow channel, was rectangular; a short canal linked this to the circular naval port beyond, with a man-made circular island in its center. Ship sheds on this island and along the port's shore opposite could house all or most of the Punic navy, even when this totaled some 200 quinqueremes. From there it was only a few minutes' walk to Carthage's main square, with Byrsa hill just beyond.

Although only a little archaeological evidence from the site can be dated earlier than about 150 BC—when no Punic navy existed at all—the original dual project was carried out, more likely, during the late third century. The decade after 218 fits best. Before then the navy had declined drastically, as mentioned earlier, whereas soon afterward Carthage was putting large fleets to sea. Mago had sixty quinqueremes escorting his army to Spain in 215, and the concurrent expedition to Sardinia, about as many; and admiral Bomilcar four years later reportedly had no fewer than 185 all told, in two divisions, for a vain effort to save Syracuse. Large, though not as large, Punic fleets operated over ensuing years too—in 208 as far east as Greek waters. Even at the very end of hostilities the navy's total complement, from skiffs to quinqueremes, reportedly stood at 500. Secure ports and large fleets make sense together, and with the Romans raiding the coasts eight times from 217 to 205, the ports afforded security to the navy as well as to merchants plying whatever overseas trade Carthage still had.[6]

THE MILITARY SEESAW IN ITALY

Nobody realized it at the time, but during 215 the war in Italy took on a rough equilibrium. Hannibal was still winning successes: the defections in the southeast, the alliance with Philip V, and friendly young Hieronymus's accession at Syracuse. The Romans, however, suffered no more defeats in battles, proved that they could foil assaults on key centers such as Naples and Nola, and—ominously—started to pick on Carthage's allies. The Samnites underwent unfriendly attentions, first from Fabius capturing a few small places and then more painfully from Marcellus (the ravagings that prompted their unsuccessful plea to Hannibal). While Marcellus's supposed victories over Hannibal outside Nola must be exaggerations at best, he did impress a few enemy soldiers: 272 Spaniards and Numidians deserted to fight for Rome (all were rewarded handsomely when the war was over). It was a minor event but a small sign of how Hannibal had lost the unquestionable momentum of previous years; and when he marched away to winter in Apulia at Arpi, Fabius took to laying Campanian fields waste. The following year Tiberius Gracchus, as proconsul operating in Samnium with his two legions of *volones*, near Beneventum caught Hanno's detached army of 18,200 mostly southern Italian recruits and pulverized it—reportedly Hanno got away with a mere 2,000 men, chiefly his African cavalry. The consuls of 214, Fabius and Marcellus, retook Casilinum on the Volturnus, the prize that had cost Hannibal so much time and effort to win only the year before.

While in 215 Rome had maintained fourteen legions from Italy to Spain, the year 214 demanded even more to cope with new as well as existing military theaters: Sardinia fresh from its revolt, Cisalpina to face the hostile Gauls, Brundisium by the Adriatic because of the new war with Philip. Not only Campania but Apulia each had a four-legion army operating to watch (but not fight) Hannibal, while parking two reserve *legiones urbanae* at Rome was now established practice. With the two ex-Cannae legions continuing their unthanked duty down in Sicily, Varro doing likewise with his one in Picenum, and the brothers Scipio in Spain, twenty legions and their allied complements were under arms—a colossal undertaking, even if older ones were by now somewhat depleted, and all the more striking after so many important defections.

Hannibal's forces were still large too. Not only had he the main army and Hanno the secondary one (at least until Gracchus routed it), but many of the new allies were protected by his garrisons against Roman forces. Arpi, for example, hosted no fewer than 5,000 such troops; Locri, an unknown number; and likewise even Capua according to Livy.

A reasonable estimate would put at least 60,000 soldiers under Carthage's standards in Italy around 212. By now the larger part must actually have been Italian, chiefly Lucanians and Bruttians but also some Samnites and Apulians—plus one known Etruscan, a youngster from Tarquinii named Felsnas Larth who died eighty years later, aged 106. His epitaph survives, proudly commemorating that he had stayed at Capua and fought "alongside Hannibal and his people [*hanipaluscle*]." There may have been others, for by 208 some Etruscan cities' fidelity was suspect enough at Rome to have Varro, still in harness, commissioned to investigate. As late as 204 the Romans prosecuted various Etruscan aristocrats for pro-Punic intrigues—this time with Hannibal's brother Mago, now campaigning in Liguria.[7]

Yet Hannibal could not mobilize all his allies' manpower for his own armies. With Roman forces so widespread, allies wanted and needed to keep as many of their own men at home—hence the Samnites' complaints to him in 215. Frustratingly in turn, neither he nor they could organize a more coherent way of fighting the enemy, for example, with strategically located joint armies for confronting the various Roman armies across Italy. The very nature of their support for Carthage precluded a unified war leadership such as Rome exercised over her allies or as the Barcids exercised in Spain over theirs. Instead of being a firm basis for his grand design, they became a chain that started to hobble him.

In 214 and 213 nevertheless, Rome faced a widening ring of hostile alliances that ratcheted up pressure. Macedon was now one of the growing band of enemies, although Valerius Laevinus as propraetor quickly scotched Philip's incursion into Illyria. Syracuse's turn toward Carthage was scotched too, at first—but not killed. The precocious boy king was assassinated in 214, and republican government was reestablished, but eventually faction-feuding, open violence, and pro-Punic intrigues put the brothers Hippocrates and Epicydes, Hannibal's half-Syracusan officers, into power and pitted Syracuse once more against Rome. In Spain the Scipios' successes of 218–215 were replaced by stalemate. In Italy in 214, the best that could be done against Hannibal was to disappoint his various endeavors against coveted strongholds: first the port of Puteoli near Naples and then Nola, where he was held off yet again by Marcellus, now consul; and when he left Campania on a bid for Tarentum, he found it too strongly garrisoned. Keeping to the strategy of hitting Carthage's allies when Hannibal could not protect them from hurt, Fabius meantime exploited Hanno's rout at Beneventum to reenter Samnium and capture a number of towns—Compsa among them.

Hannibal was further damaged the year after by losing Arpi to one of the new consuls, Fabius's son and namesake (this Fabius's one notable achievement). For Hannibal the blow was worrisome on more than one count and was partly his fault. When a leading citizen of Arpi, Dasius Altinius, defected to the Romans (taking along a large cache of gold), the general thought he would make an example of the man's family to deter any other disloyalists (Livy claims he was furious too about the gold). He burned Altinius's wife and children alive. This achieved the opposite. As soon as Roman soldiers broke into Arpi during a rainstorm, its 3,000 armed townsmen changed sides—and so did the Spaniards in the Punic garrison. Numbering nearly a thousand, these stipulated only that their 4,000 comrades (at a guess, Libyans and Numidians) be let go. Arpi had been one of the first places to join the cause after Cannae, and these Spaniards were the second lot among Hannibal's veteran soldiers to abandon him; these were troubling signs for the invader.

Because of Rome's multiplying military theaters, the year 213 brought more legions into action than even the year before—twenty-two in all, for Sicily's ex-Cannae pair under the propraetor Appius Claudius was joined by another two when Marcellus was assigned to the island as proconsul. Hannibal, watched by eight legions in army groups from Campania to Apulia and Lucania, could move where he willed yet still not bring about a decisive battle. For part of the summer he marched around the Sallentine peninsula, garnering a few small allies (Uzentum is mentioned), and he also brought Consentia in Bruttium back under control after a brief pro-Roman flirtation. These were far from the crushing successes that he needed three years on from Cannae. The one field success of 213 was when Hanno, with a revived southern army in Lucania, defeated an irregular enemy force under Pomponius of Veii, the shady munitions supplier turned military officer and now captive—again no very productive feat. Bad news came from Sicily, where Syracuse was now under siege by Marcellus. Then just in time to relieve the frustration came a major coup, Hannibal's first in nearly three years. At the end of the year or early in 212, Tarentum changed sides.

TARENTUM AND HANNIBAL

Tarentum had once been the most powerful city in the south and only two generations before had fought Rome, unsuccessfully despite Pyrrhus's help, to remain such. Since then it had been only the most important of the Greek city-states under Rome's hegemony, subject to the usual duties of furnishing ships, crews, and munitions for Roman wars, no doubt too suffering its share of naval losses in the First Punic War. Its other noteworthy contribution in this century was Livius Andronicus, Rome's first poet, but by Hannibal's day Tarentines felt aggrieved at how they and their city were treated by the hegemon. The city had received a Roman garrison in 217 (as in 225) to ward off any attack, but the Romans had grown distrustful of Tarentine loyalty. A number of hostages, no doubt from elite families, were in lax custody at Rome along with others from Thurii, another southern Greek city under suspicion. When they all made a failed escape attempt during 213, they were summarily put to death. The bitterness this caused in their home cities prompted a venturesome group of young Tarentine aristocrats, plainly with backing from their seniors, to contact Hannibal (three days' march away) with a scheme to bring their city over.

On the prearranged day, sometime during the winter of 213–212, they and other plotters opened two of the gates on Tarentum's eastern, landward side to let him in with 8,000 troops. The Roman garrison commander, Livius Macatus, barely got away into the impregnable citadel, sited on the narrow peninsula that all but blocks off Tarentum's spacious harbor from the sea. Every Roman captured in the city was slaughtered. Early in 212 Thurii got rid of its small Roman garrison and let in Carthaginian troops, while Tarentum's neighbor Metapontum seized its opportunity when its Roman occupiers were transferred by sea to reinforce Tarentum's citadel. Another Greek city, Heraclea, seems to have joined the pro-Punic rush too, leaving Rome without a single significant port from the heel of Italy down to the toe at Rhegium.

This was a serious loss for Rome, yet not a killer one. Naval contingents from Tarentum and its Greek neighbors had—it seems—played little part in Rome's major fleets recently; such crews are not mentioned at Ostia or elsewhere (whether as hostages, mutineers, or laudable models of continuing loyalty). In fact Tarentum's fleet, twenty strong, was moored in its harbor. It had to be rolled through the city's wide streets on wagons—a bright idea of Hannibal's that much impressed the Tarentines—to reach the open sea and help blockade the citadel. Hannibal's own military efforts, though, had no recorded help from either Tarentine or other Italian Greek warships. Nor did he acquire Greek recruits for his armies. If his new Greek friends contributed funds to his coffers, it left no mark in the sources. The south coast was certainly lost by Rome, but this did not prevent her from keeping Livius and his men going (with difficulty, true) in the citadel.

The greatest peril was that Carthage would use the freedom of Italy's south coast to land reinforcements for Hannibal or that Philip of Macedon would come over with an army. Yet neither happened. Philip had been chased away from the Adriatic in 214 by the intrepid Laevinus, whose fleet from then on deterred him from naval ventures. The only time a sizable Punic fleet, in turn, appeared at Tarentum was Bomilcar's in 212, after it dodged combat with a Roman fleet near Syracuse. Bomilcar had at least 130 quinqueremes, his remit being to help starve out the enemy-held citadel; and no Roman fleet came to trouble him. Yet he failed almost farcically. After enduring months of his fruitless efforts, in 211 the Tarentines begged him to leave because, while the besieged Romans were coping on very short rations, his hosts found it impossible to feed his tens of thousands of crewmen. That was the end of Punic attempts to exploit their theoretical dominance of the Ionian Sea coast.[8]

The southern Greeks' defection was not Hannibal's only success in 212—although some of the others have at times been doubted. First came the death of the energetic Tiberius Gracchus: operating as proconsul in his usual theater, Lucania, he was assassinated by a trusted but turncoat Lucanian officer while leading his *volones* to join the consuls in Campania. Some of Livy's sources reported Hannibal giving the dead proconsul a military funeral with full honors; others held that he could recover only Gracchus's head but had Carthalo bear this honorably to the Roman camp for funeral rites. Next—as Livy tells it—after being baffled in his effort to save Capua from siege, he scored an actual battle victory of sorts, the first since Cannae, over a detached Roman force in Lucania, destroying 16,000 irregulars led by an officer named Centenius Paenula. More importantly, some weeks later he faced the praetor Gnaeus Fulvius Flaccus with 18,000 men near Herdonea in central Apulia, sprang an ambush from woods behind them when they attacked, and annihilated most of them, though not Fulvius. Both victories can cautiously be believed, despite the doubts. Centenius's army was not the sole detached Roman force to operate (most of them ingloriously) in southern Italy during the war, though its size may have been exaggerated; and Fulvius was afterward prosecuted for losing his army and driven into exile. Roman tradition and friendly Greek writers, it can be added, were not prone to invent Roman defeats to enlarge Hannibal's glory.[9]

Yet once again none of these successes brought him great profit. Gracchus was replaced by other vigorous commanders; even more significantly, slaughtering tens of thousands of Romans in one season now had practically no impact on enemy morale or on the strategic balance that was developing—or, rather, imbalance. During the same summer of 212, the Romans laid siege to Capua. On this hinged the future of the war in Italy.

THE SIEGE OF CAPUA

For the campaigns of 212 the Romans, despite the loss of nearly half of Italy to the invaders, fielded an unprecedented number of legions: twenty-five in all—fifteen in various regions of Italy; four in Sicily (where there was not only Syracuse to be dealt with but also a new Carthaginian army); and the others in Cisalpina, Spain (where the Scipios soon launched a renewed offensive), and Sardinia. Those that had been in service for several years were probably under strength, for instance, the Scipios' two in Spain (they had received no reinforcements since 217) and the two Cannae legions in Sicily, which fought hard every year and were repeatedly beefed up with other disgraced soldiers, such as Herdonea's survivors. Gracchus's *volones* dispersed after his murder, leaving twenty-three. Even if many were under the theoretical norm of 4,200 foot and 300 horse each, more than 75,000 Romans must have been under arms, maybe more than 80,000, with roughly the same number of Latin and other Italian allies. At the same time, at least 120 warships were in service in various theaters: something like 36,000 sailors (Romans and allies together). By even the most tentative reckoning, during 212 and again in 211 up to 200,000 men were fighting for Rome and her remaining allies—close to one in every three military-age Romans and a similar proportion of loyal Italians. No other ancient state was remotely capable of such an effort.[10]

The effort was needed, for Rome and her allies were surrounded. Central and northern Italy, some strongholds in the south, Sardinia with Corsica, and Spain above the Ebro were Roman-controlled. Sicily— Roman province and Syracusan state—was engulfed in war. In sharp contrast, Carthage's projection of power had never extended as far as it did now. She and her generalissimo had Libya, Punic Spain, Cisalpine Gaul, and more than half of southern Italy under control or in alliance, as well as Macedon. In Africa the Numidians were divided between a generally pro-Punic east dominated by the Massyli (whose ruling family had included Hamilcar Barca's presumed son-in-law Naravas) and western parts largely controlled by the Masaesyli and their crafty king Syphax (whom the Scipio brothers were busily courting from Spain, without much profit). Objective onlookers between 215 and 212 at least would surely conclude that if Rome survived at all, it would only be by accepting Hannibal's terms and Carthage's hegemony.

They would have been wrong. In 212 the Romans launched two new offensives. The Scipios struck into the heart of Punic Spain, as we will see in the next chapter; the consuls Quintus Fulvius Flaccus and Appius Claudius Pulcher moved against Capua. That city had long been harassed and was low in food, but when Hanno tried to bring over supplies gathered in Samnium, his camp near Beneventum was surprised by Flaccus (brother of the gormless Gnaeus), and he was driven off back to Bruttium. Hannibal preferred not to lock himself and his army up in Capua to share in the looming siege. He put 2,000 men in to reinforce the defenders, while he waited elsewhere. Fulvius and his colleague then arrived. When they were joined by the praetor Gaius Claudius Nero and his army, the would-be capital of postwar Italy was invested by six legions and allied contingents—more than 40,000 infantry and cavalry.

Failing to bring on a battle with the consuls before Nero arrived, Hannibal marched away southward, leaving Capua to fend for itself. This was when he soothed his feelings by smashing first Centenius's irregulars and then Gnaeus Fulvius's army at Herdonea, before making his way to Tarentum, still hoping to prize Livius Macatus and his men out of its citadel (and again failing). As already noted, the victories led nowhere. Instead Hannibal was effectively shackled: he could not force the Romans either to lift their siege of his principal ally or to meet him for a decisive battle. There were no reinforcements to be had from Carthage—so much for controlling virtually the entire south coast of Italy and for Bomilcar's great fleet—and his brother Hasdrubal, ordered so long ago to march over from Spain, was preoccupied as usual. Philip V in turn was useless as an ally. His interest in places west was limited to taking over Illyria and other Adriatic lands, his efforts at this were thwarted by the Romans, and he was repeatedly distracted by challenges elsewhere—notably in the Peloponnese and against his southern neighbor the Aetolian League, which in 211 became allied with Rome. Neither her operations against him nor the war in Sicily where Syracuse was about to fall distracted Rome's implacable attention from Capua.

By the end of 212 the city was surrounded with almost impregnable siegeworks. For 211 Claudius, Fulvius, and Nero were continued in command as proconsuls and propraetor, beating back desperate Capuan attempts to break the ring. Hannibal's long delay in reacting once he had retired to the south is hard to explain, for he did nothing of note during autumn 212. Only in the new year, after the Capuans had failed in their own efforts to break the siege, did he march for Campania with a picked force that included his remaining thirty-three elephants. He and the besieged then concerted moves, they again striving to break out on one side of the city while he fought to smash a way through the enemy fortifications on the other side. The Capuans were driven back again, although Appius Claudius was badly wounded (to die some weeks later of the wound). Hannibal's own assault very nearly succeeded, but in furious combat over the bodies of three heroic elephants Fulvius's fighters stopped him. As he had done the year before, Hannibal broke off the attack and—just five days after arriving—marched away.

He did not return to the south this time but pushed north toward Rome. His intention—or, rather, hope—was to pull enough besiegers after him to enable the Capuans to break the siege. The Romans then and later assumed that his true aim was to surprise and capture the city of Rome, but with the force he had that would have required almost miraculous luck. An extra hope, though, may have been to bring the pursuing Roman forces to battle. Even if these were reinforced by the two new, untried City legions, a climactic victory at Rome's gates would surely compel her to peace at last. At the very least, breaking the siege of Capua might yet push the rest of Campania—Naples, Nola, Puteoli, and the others—into rethinking their loyalties, with the tantalizing possibility that that, too, could bring the Romans to terms. All these were very long shots. Hannibal had with him a relatively small force, including more cavalry than usual as he had left much of the infantry in Bruttium. He had no siege engines or artillery (the military baggage too had been left behind) and no time to build any. He may have encamped eight kilometers north of Rome before being spotted, as Polybius rather unconvincingly claims—but Fulvius had been told by deserters where he was headed and sent word to Rome.

Like the crossing of the Alps and his refusal of Maharbal's advice after Cannae, the march on Rome in 211 was remembered as one of the climaxes of Hannibal's saga. His troops ransacked the prosperous countryside, which had never hitherto been touched by the war—even a revered grove of the Sabine goddess Feronia thirty kilometers north of the City, a sacrilege that alarmed his own men and boosted propaganda about their leader's ungodliness. Stories, engaging even if not true, were told: how, on camping by the Anio river even nearer the City, he learned that a body of troops had just left Rome for Spain and that the ground where his army stood had also just been sold at a normal price; and how he retaliated by declaring the bankers' shops around the Forum for sale too.

Exactly what countermeasures the Romans took is varyingly reported. According to Livy, Fulvius Flaccus left Capua for Rome with 16,000 select troops (equivalent to two legions with allies, a consular army). Polybius states that the consuls, Fulvius Centumalus and Sulpicius Galba, happened to be enrolling two legions there when Hannibal arrived. It may well be that the previous year's *legiones urbanae* were still there, too, not yet assigned to another theater as was usual. No fewer than 1,200 Numidian cavalrymen, deserters from Hannibal, were also within the walls—they caused great though short-lived panic when they rode through the streets to take up assigned positions. At all events the City was well garrisoned, well enough for Centumalus and Galba to lead their troops outside the walls in battle array—and for Hannibal to decline battle (or for the heavens to intervene with massive rain and hail, says Livy instead). This more than any other incident suggests how limited his numbers were. The consuls even pursued him for a time as he retired southward, and he had to fight them off, losing a good deal of his booty in the process. So ended his third missed opportunity since 217 to strike lethally at his enemies' heart. It would be his last.

Hannibal left the environs of Rome reckoning that by now at least part of the forces hemming Capua would have come after him. Within a few days he learned that the siege was unbroken: even if Fulvius Flaccus had set out to reinforce Rome, Appius Claudius still ringed his besieged allies. To the amazed anger of both the Capuans and his own officers there (they wrote him a harsh letter, which the Romans intercepted), the general did not reappear. Instead he marched right through Samnium, Lucania, and Bruttium to Rhegium—a march of at least 700 kilometers and three to four weeks—hoping to seize that city by surprise. He swept up a lot of Rhegines who were working their fields but made no impact on the town. Where he went next is not recorded, but it may have been to Tarentum to view Bomilcar's fleet in its unavailing efforts against the Romans in the citadel. He did not march back to Capua.

Capua was out of options. Its chief anti-Roman leader, Vibius Virrius (Pacuvius Calavius, his predecessor, had disappeared from the scene, perhaps dead), and twenty-seven other hard-liners held a splendid feast and poisoned themselves. Plenty more remained to meet summary execution by Fulvius when the city surrendered. Naturally enough it was treated severely—though nowhere as savagely as (for instance) Thebes had been in 335 by Alexander the Great or Jerusalem would be by Rome in AD 70. Many upper-class Capuans and their families were enslaved, others were lengthily imprisoned, Capua's entire territory was declared Roman state land, and the city itself was stripped of legal existence to be run instead by commissioners, *praefecti*, from Rome. Ordinary Capuans were ordered out, leaving the city to their freed slaves and to its foreign residents, while they themselves were to be settled elsewhere (a penalty not, it seems, thoroughly carried out). Everyone of course lost their Roman citizenship. Similar penalties were imposed on the Capuan satellites Atella and Calatia. The booty from the captured city was immense. More than 2,000 pounds of gold and 31,200 of silver, gathered up from Capuan senators, were only the most noticeable quantities.[11]

The Romans' exhilaration at Capua's capitulation was partly dimmed when news came that the Scipios in Spain had been totally defeated and the brothers themselves killed. The Senate quickly commissioned Claudius Nero to take a relief force over, while leaving to 210 a decision on what to do for the longer term. The most serious worry was that Hasdrubal would seize his opportunity at last and march for Italy. Conversely this must have been Hannibal's lively hope. Losing Capua effectively shut him out of Campania; Samnium was open to Roman revenge, and his allies in Apulia were too. With no prospect of forcing Rome to terms by battle, and with Roman armies ranging widely through all pro-Punic Italy—whereas he could barely encroach on the regions loyal to his foes—he had forfeited virtually all strategic advantage. Were Hasdrubal to march, on the other hand, the situation could still be retrieved. It was Hannibal's and Carthage's misfortune that Hasdrubal would not march for another three years.

9

THE WAR BEYOND ITALY

THE FIRST MACEDONIAN WAR

Philip V had come to his throne as a small boy in 229 and then became effective ruler in 221. Macedon generally looked south and east, but Rome's Illyrian interventions incited plenty of attention and suspicion. It was an Aetolian envoy to a Greece-wide peace conference at Naupactus, in July 217, who warned his fellow Greeks—and Philip in particular—to beware of "the clouds now gathering in the west" because, whether Rome or Carthage won their war, Greece and Macedon were in danger of those clouds coming to settle on them. Philip chose to work with the Carthaginian cloud, a decision that would bedevil the rest of his long reign. He had no need at all to get involved, and benign neutrality (like Egypt's in both wars) could have enabled him to reimpose Macedon's old hegemony in Greece, strengthen his often-imperiled northern frontiers, and be much better prepared to face whoever came off best across the Adriatic.

That Macedon's interest in allying with Hannibal was strictly to do with the eastern Adriatic is clear enough, both from the treaty terms of 215 (noted earlier) and from events. Already in 217 the king had ventured with a fleet of light warships into the southern Adriatic, only to retire ingloriously when word came of approaching Roman quinqueremes. Three years later and now Hannibal's ally, he tried again. Oricum, another Greek colony, was taken, and Apollonia fifty kilometers farther north was menaced. Again it ended ingloriously when Valerius Laevinus landed troops. Surprised in a night assault on his camp outside Apollonia, Philip had to flee "half-naked" (according to Livy) and then burn his ships to prevent Laevinus capturing them, before he and his surviving troops struggled home across the mountains. The Romans now held the coasts, while Philip busied himself in 213 with the Peloponnese and afterward with subduing the restless highlands of Atintania and the Parthini, between coastal Illyria and his kingdom. Only then did he return to the Adriatic to seize the port of Lissus, up the coast from Apollonia.

This had an unfortunate result. Laevinus negotiated an alliance with Philip's inveterate foes the Aetolian League, making a treaty not only summarized by Livy—more accurately than he did Philip's with Hannibal—but partly preserved in a damaged inscription. The Aetolians were promised Roman military support, both states pledged not to make a separate peace with the king, and other anti-Macedonian states were welcome to join in (with Sparta, the Illyrian ruler Scerdilaidas, and Pergamum across the Aegean mentioned). The surviving inscribed provisos detail how captured cities and booty were to be handled—basically, the Aetolians would keep the real estate, while the Romans could take the movables. The war soon widened to mainland Greece and even the Aegean Sea—the first time that those regions were to experience Romans in war and an omen for the future.

Philip's own allies, apart from Carthage, included the Achaean League (homeland of the not-yet-born Polybius) and his neighbors Epirus and Acarnania, but they provided little more than local help. In 209 a fleet from Carthage actually arrived off Corcyra; typically enough it did nothing of note—maybe Bomilcar was in charge—either then or when it briefly reappeared the following year. Philip had generals of his own yet always chose, or needed, to take personal command in a major campaign and so spent the next six years racing from one military threat or opportunity to another: against the Thracians on his northern frontiers, and in central and southern Greece and the Aegean against the Aetolians, Romans, and a growing range of foes (notably Pergamum from 211 and Sparta from 209).

The Romans played a carefully limited role in all this. Their main aim was to keep Philip too occupied in the Greek world to threaten Italy.

Laevinus in 211 captured the island of Zacynthus and now or later (the date is not certain) Dyme, an Achaean city at the entrance to the gulf of Corinth. During 210 he and the Aetolians took Anticyra on the northern shore of the gulf of Corinth, but thereafter Roman involvement was mostly naval, under Laevinus's successor, Sulpicius Galba. Galba occupied the island of Aegina in 209 with the Pergamene king Attalus and then in 208 operated in Euboea to take (and of course loot) the town of Oreus, though before long Philip recaptured it.

Over several years after 211 the redoubtable king gained the upper hand over all his other adversaries, the Aetolians included. Finally in 206 these struck a separate peace with him, much to Roman annoyance. Although a small Roman expeditionary force was sent over to protect Epidamnus and Apollonia the following year, hostilities soon came to an end. Peace was settled at the Epirote city of Phoenice, with Philip keeping most of his conquests in Illyria's hinterland, notably Atintania, but letting go of Rome's other friends such as the Parthini. Nowhere else in Greece or the Aegean was mentioned in the treaty, though Greek states that had supported one side or the other added their names to it—Pergamum and Sparta on Rome's, the Achaeans and Epirus on Macedon's, for example. Carthage was not added, however, even though she was still Philip's ally and had taken part (no matter if ingloriously) in his war, and though his treaty with her had strongly implied that neither signatory would make peace with Rome without the other. Of course by 205 Carthage looked unlikely to prevail against Rome; the king's pragmatic snub was predictable. Yet the peace of Phoenice proved nothing but a five-year truce before a new clash between him and the Romans.

SARDINIA

In the war's first years Sardinia had a small role to play. Its peoples had not taken kindly to Roman rule since 237. Once Roman forces went over in 235, several years of fighting and a good few consular triumphs were needed before peace more or less reigned. Even at the time, some Romans may have entertained suspicion that Carthage was behind the Sardinians' unfriendliness to their new masters. Cato the Elder, born in 234, would later claim that several Punic treaty breaches occurred before 219 (though his details are missing); and, as noted earlier, the Gallic invasion looming in 225 sent Roman forces not only to Tarentum and Sicily but to Sardinia as well—a consular army, in fact.

After Hannibal's opening victories in the war, it again made sense to send a legion to the island as a precaution against the Carthaginians. No doubt it helped too with enforcing the heavy payments of tribute and grain that Rome imposed on the locals. These demands naturally increased Sardinians' discontent. After Cannae, restive chieftains led by one Hampsicora invited Carthage to aid them in a planned rebellion. As some communities stayed loyal to the Romans, based at Carales on the south coast, while the folk of the island's mountainous interior were largely independent, and as the rebels' main stronghold was Cornus on the west coast, the rebellion may have arisen in that region. Old Phoenician colonies there such as Cornus, Tharros, and Othoca probably kept in touch with their former hegemon more easily than others nearer Carales could. Hampsicora's contact at Carthage was an aristocrat named Hanno, influential enough to win the city's backing for the revolt and no doubt a Barcid supporter, though not a kinsman. He and one Mago, who was related to Hannibal, were appointed lieutenants to a Hasdrubal, who with about 12,000 troops sailed for Sardinia in 215.

Everything went wrong. Their fleet was so thoroughly deranged by a storm that it fetched up in the Balearic Isles 500 kilometers away, needing repairs. Hampsicora's rebellion could not wait, but Titus Manlius Torquatus (the first consul to campaign in annexed Sardinia, twenty years before) had already landed at Carales with reinforcements and soon inflicted a defeat on the Sardinians. When Hasdrubal finally arrived and joined them for another effort, Manlius smashed the combined armies. Hampsicora's son Hostus was killed, all three Carthaginian leaders were taken prisoner, and with Hampsicora's own suicide and the fall of Cornus the rebellion collapsed. The island continued to be garrisoned by Roman legions (two until 207, a single one thereafter) but caused no further alarm except in 210, when an enterprising commodore named

Hamilcar raided first Olbia's countryside on the northeast coast and then Carales's, to sail home laden with plunder.

THE SIEGE OF SYRACUSE

The boy king Hieronymus's murder in 214 led to a tumultuously messy restored republic. His uncle and aunts, suspected of a monarchic plot, were savagely murdered in their turn. Hannibal's agents, the half-Syracusan brothers Hippocrates and Epicydes, now gained a foothold toward power by being elected among the new generals. The native-born Syracusan leaders were anxious to preserve peace with Rome; but Hippocrates, at Leontini with Syracusan troops and some mercenaries and Roman deserters, soon provoked strife by raiding the nearby Roman province. Marcellus, now proconsul in Sicily, captured Leontini, but the brothers managed to win over the main Syracusan army and seize power in the city, with a suitable massacre of opponents. Early in 213 they came under siege by Marcellus and his subordinate, the propraetor Appius Claudius Pulcher.

Hannibal and Carthage thus got the Roman–Syracusan war they had wanted, but it did them little good. Although it kept four legions busy, and then in 212 a fifth, this failed to ease pressure on Hannibal and his allies in Italy (or on Roman operations in Spain, for that matter). The conflict also called on Carthage's resources: quantities of troops, fleets, and munitions had to be sent to help her beleaguered ally. For Syracuse the war was a purposeless disaster. Even if it could somehow be won with Punic aid, there would be no Sicilian hegemony as Hieronymus had daydreamed; rather, Syracuse would be yoked forever to Carthage's supremacy.

Syracuse was surrounded by massive walls that took in not only its urban areas—the island of Ortygia (sometimes called Nasos, "the Island") and the adjoining mainland suburbs of Achradina, Tyche, and Neapolis—but also the broad triangular plateau of Epipolae beyond. The great city had never been captured, despite the best efforts of Athens in 415–413 and Carthage repeatedly down to 280. Marcellus at first shared this ill-luck when attacking Achradina's sea walls, while Appius Claudius assaulted the northern land wall at the massive Hexapylon gate. They found the defenders using unique war machines devised by Syracuse's mathematician and scientist Archimedes (a kinsman of the just-extinguished royal family)—sophisticated catapults firing missiles lethally through wall embrasures, wooden beams swinging out over the walls to drop boulders and lead blocks onto attacking ships and men, and other beams fitted with iron claws or hooks on a chain dropped onto ships to upend them. No reliable source mentions polished mirrors or shields for focusing sunlight to set ships on fire, but Archimedes may have devised strongly burning missiles of pitch to hurl at them. Marcellus sourly nicknamed him "this geometrical Briareus," after a hundred-armed giant in myth. He gave up assaults in favor of a blockade, dangerous though this was with Carthaginian aid to Syracuse coming.[1]

The relief army that landed at Heraclea Minoa in western Sicily during 213 was powerful: 25,000 infantry, 3,000 cavalry, and even a dozen elephants. Its general, Himilco, on the other hand, was one of the most second-rate leaders in Carthaginian history and thus a valuable, if unintended, aid to the Romans. He did win over Agrigentum, restive at Roman rule like many other cities, and then marched to Syracuse, picking up Hippocrates and some Syracusan cavalry en route. These were the miserable remnants of Hippocrates's rash decision to take 10,000 defenders out of the city to meet up with Himilco—they had met up with Marcellus instead. Outside Syracuse, Himilco positioned his forces not far from the Roman camp. He then did very little, and Marcellus, outnumbered and probably aware that a further legion was coming, avoided a clash too. Himilco by contrast had less excuse for coyness, and still less after admiral Bomilcar evaded the Roman fleet to sail into Syracuse's Great Harbor with fifty-five quinqueremes. A concerted attack on the Romans, including by Epicydes from the city, could have achieved results. Instead Himilco chose to try cutting off the legion now marching overland to Marcellus. The outcome was farcical. He assumed that it was coming by an inland route and headed that way, whereas it came by the coast road.

Now faced by a much stronger enemy, Bomilcar sailed away, and Himilco tried something different. He abandoned his camp to move inland and try winning over other rebel-minded Sicilians. Murgantia, in the hill country 120 kilometers to the northwest, welcomed his Punic wiles and massacred its Roman garrison. This led to a Roman atrocity at nearby Enna, a strategically critical site. The fearful garrison commander there, one Pinarius, inflicted his own preemptive massacre on its citizens. Marcellus tolerated the atrocity as noxious but necessary—a paradox lost on Sicilians, many of whom not only defected to Himilco but contributed soldiers. That general opted not to use his strengthened forces against Marcellus but to retire to Agrigentum for the winter. Marcellus, with Titus Quinctius Crispinus now his propraetor (Appius Claudius had been elected consul for 212), meanwhile worked out how to succeed where Athens and Carthage had failed.

Although a pro-Roman plot within Syracuse to betray it was bloodily repressed by Epicydes, a cheerful festival of Artemis in spring 212 lowered the defenders' guard in Epipolae. Marcellus's men climbed over the wall near the Hexapylon gate, seized this and then the entire district, and before long pushed the crucial fortress of Euryalus into capitulating. The story goes that the panorama from Epipolae of the historic city below moved the hard-bitten general to tears; he knew what he and his men would do to it once they took it. The mood soon passed. When the Tyche and Neapolis districts also fell into Roman hands, the defiant Epicydes was left holding only Achradina and Syracuse's oldest center, Ortygia island, and hoping for Punic rescue. Both Himilco and Bomilcar at last made vigorous efforts. Himilco, Hippocrates still in tow, again encamped just south of the city alongside the Great Harbor and near the Roman camp defended by Crispinus. Bomilcar reappeared in a sequence of comings and goings—arriving with ninety quinqueremes, lending fifty-five to Epicydes, and then sailing home to return in a few days with no fewer than 100 more. It was Carthage's greatest armada since 241.

Now the allies launched a concerted assault on the Romans. Marcellus, occupying the captured sectors of the city with the bulk of his army, was assailed from Achradina by Epicydes. Crispinus in their camp was challenged by Hippocrates's Greeks and perhaps some of Himilco's troops (the rest were falling sick). Syracuse's last chance had arrived. So too had a critical moment in Carthage's war with Rome. If the Romans could be crushed—and still better, Marcellus be slain or taken—the rest of Sicily would be at Himilco's mercy, while Bomilcar with his well-honed skill at evading enemy fleets could deliver fresh troops to Hannibal.

All the attacks failed. At the same time something even grimmer was befalling the Carthaginians—plague, perhaps typhus, always a danger when the marshlands edging the Great Harbor were contaminated with refuse from an encamped army. Himilco's was not the first Punic army to fall victim there, but it suffered the worst. Most of his men perished; he and Hippocrates did too. Marcellus saved most of his by bringing them all up into Epipolae, while Bomilcar made a hasty exit (untroubled as usual) from Sicilian waters. Perhaps he assumed optimistically that the Romans would be just as plague-ravaged, for not long after he was on his way back—now at the head of 130 quinqueremes escorting 700 supply ships, in a final mission to break the siege.

This time the weather played him false: he could not round Cape Pachynus. Epicydes could sail down alone to join him, but so could Marcellus with his own 100 ships. It would have been a portentous test of his skills to lead a Roman fleet into a major battle with the Carthaginian navy for the first time since the Aegates—had the choppy seas and Bomilcar's nerves allowed. Instead Carthage's worst admiral in history raised sail for flight. The transports were ordered home, and he swung his quinqueremes away (the winds must have changed) to Tarentum, where, as shown earlier, his performance then and in 211 was to be no less cringeworthy. Epicydes fled to Agrigentum to join its garrison commander, Hanno.

Late in 212 Achradina and Ortygia finally capitulated. The mercenaries and deserters tried to prevent it by killing as many Syracusan opponents as they could, but a Spanish mercenary captain named Moericus soon let himself be persuaded by his brother, an auxiliary in Marcellus's army, to open the gate near Arethusa's fountain in Ortygia to a Roman task force, while the proconsul made a loud diversionary attack on Achradina. The diehard resisters fled, and the Roman army flooded in and (as Marcellus had promised) were let loose to plunder. Killing Syracusans was forbidden, but that was not always obeyed, certainly not by the soldier sent to fetch Archimedes. He impatiently slew the "geometric Briareus" when his summons was ignored by the old scholar, intent (we are told) on geometry diagrams drawn in the dust. Marcellus provided more tears, a respectful burial, and apologies to the family. It was, from Rome's point of view, an acceptable if regrettable collateral cost of mastering the first great Greek metropolis to challenge her in war, back in 264, and garnering huge amounts of booty—including valuables looted from temples, which earned the proconsul criticism at home—to enrich troops, commanders, and Rome herself.

SICILY: THE FINAL STAGES

Hanno and Epicydes were still holding out at Agrigentum with troops including a body of Numidian cavalry. Hannibal sent over a new officer to take command of these, the Hippou Acra cavalryman Mottones. Full of enterprise, Mottones infused new energy into operations in early 211, shoring up morale among the remaining allied Sicilian towns and then badly harassing Marcellus's army when the proconsul marched west. The Carthaginian forces waited by the river Himera. Success then sank yet again into farce. Hanno found Mottones's prowess so irritating that, as soon as the Hippacritan departed to deal with some mutinous Numidians at Heraclea Minoa, he chose to offer battle without him. The Numidians with the Punic army promptly opted out, handing Marcellus an easy victory. This did not end resistance, however, for the proconsul now departed for Rome, the consulship in 210, and greater challenges.

Fresh forces came over from Africa: 8,000 foot and, tellingly, 3,000 Numidian horse. Hanno had to rein in his resentment and allow Mottones a free hand to ravage the lands of cities loyal to Rome. A few other cities were won over again, notably Macella north of Heraclea and, once more, Murgantia. Yet all was pointless. Hanno and Mottones had no chance of inflicting anything worse than harassment on their adversaries. Marcellus's successor in Sicily, the praetor Marcus Cornelius, first had to pacify his own resentful troops—most of them the veterans of Cannae, who wanted to go home after all their exploits—but then brought Murgantia and some other rebel places under control later in 211 (Moericus and his comrades were given Murgantia in reward for services rendered). In 210 arrived the experienced Marcus Valerius Laevinus, Marcellus's consular colleague, who with typical decisiveness marched on Agrigentum. There Hanno had given himself the pleasure of sacking his much abler, non-Carthaginian, detested lieutenant. Mottones's command went instead to Hanno's son. This fresh outbreak of ineptitude defeated itself: Mottones and his men promptly opened the gates of Agrigentum. Hanno and Epicydes ignominiously got away by commandeering a small merchant ship to sail for Carthage. The troops and townsfolk they abandoned suffered predictable fates, slaughtered in the fighting or afterward sold. Carthage's efforts in Sicily ended forever. Most of the rebel Sicilian cities surrendered; six that held out—we have no names—were subdued by force; and the island lay ready for Roman retribution.

Laevinus, aided by a new praetor, the historian-to-be Lucius Cincius Alimentus, reorganized its affairs firmly and, given the wartime conditions, reasonably fairly. Syracuse of course lost its independence, so that the island province now embraced all Sicily. Agrigentum suffered far worse: its leaders executed, its surviving inhabitants enslaved (not for the first time in its history), and the city left empty for some years until loyalist Agrigentines were allowed back. Other rebel places no doubt underwent penalties too, but, on the other hand, Laevinus was keen to see agriculture and trade recover and acted to encourage them. His penalties, therefore, were perhaps not always harsh on communities, even if defecting leaders suffered. To the same end he may have regularized the province's tax system—if one did exist before 210—or else he set one up: maybe the tithe on produce used in Hiero's kingdom. It certainly applied to the whole island in later times and won glowing praise for its fairness, from Romans anyway. More immediately, he rid Sicily of a body of armed desperadoes—4,000 homeless exiles, runaway debtors, and even wanted criminals, who had taken a leaf from Mottones's book by terrorizing communities. Laevinus let them loose over southern Italy instead, against Hannibal's allies. Sicily gave no further trouble; it even started to regain some prosperity over the next few years.

INVADING SPAIN

Rome's original war plan was to invade Libya and Spain together. Although its Libyan arm was aborted late in 218, the Spanish expedition had gone ahead under Gnaeus Scipio (nicknamed Calvus, "Baldy"), Marcellus's fellow consul in 222. The small Greek colony of Emporiae near the Pyrenees, an offshoot of Rome's friend Massilia in Gaul, had been left untroubled by Hannibal and now served as Scipio's landing place. With some 20,000 infantry and 4,200 cavalry, along with forty warships, he set about clearing northeastern Spain of Carthaginians. He defeated the area's commandant, Hanno, at Cissis (the older name for the coast city Tarraco) and captured him and his Spanish ally Indibilis, lord of the powerful inland Ilergetes. Livy's often muddled narrative of Spanish events next brings the Barcid Hasdrubal himself north to cross the Ebro twice, do not very much, and then retire, but at best he came and dithered only once. As Livy tells it (Polybius is silent), Gnaeus Scipio asserted military control over the coast and nearby inland districts before establishing his lasting base at Tarraco and settling down there for the winter. Tarragona's surviving sections of massive "cyclopean" walls and gates attest its role from then on as the Roman operations base.

Gnaeus (like all his fellow countrymen) surely expected Rome to demolish Hannibal before long, send reinforcements to Spain, and thus enable him to overturn the enemy in the peninsula soon. Meanwhile he awaited another foray by Hasdrubal from the south, which duly occurred in 217. Gnaeus briskly sailed down to the Ebro's mouth with thirty-five quinqueremes, some from Massilia; engaged the Punic fleet of forty while Hasdrubal and his men watched onshore; and roundly beat it with sterling work especially from the Massiliots. Rather than try to turn the tables with a land offensive, Hasdrubal tamely went south again, leaving the coasts open—Livy reports, though Polybius is silent again—to a lengthy raid by the Roman fleet all the way down (it seems) to Lucentum, the Romans' name for Hamilcar Barca's colony Acra Leuce, even assailing the isle of Ebusus. Gnaeus held back from invading Punic Spain, although once his brother Publius arrived later in the year, with 8,000 more troops and thirty quinqueremes, the two chose to make a foray 160 kilometers beyond the Ebro to Saguntum. Hasdrubal was distracted by hostilities in central Spain with the Celtiberians (Livy claims that the Scipios had suborned them), and his east-coast commander, Bostar, had no keenness to take on three legions and allies. He even let himself be tricked by a local grandee into freeing the sons of regional Spanish lords held as hostages at Saguntum; they were taken to the Scipios, who earned Spanish plaudits by sending the boys home.

During the following year Hasdrubal was sent a not very exciting reinforcement of 4,500 troops from Carthage and then an order to drop everything and march to Italy. Instead he found himself having to fight a revolt in the south, his territorial heartland, by a people called the Tartessii. Whether these were actual descendants of the ancient south-western kingdom of Tartessus, in the mining-rich Río Tinto region, or were some of the Turdetanian peoples of the Baetis valley given an evocative old name by Livy's source, they were stout opponents—raising much of the countryside against Carthage. This left Hasdrubal no time to focus on the Romans until 215. Why the Scipios failed to exploit his troubles is hard to divine. Had they struck southward while his hands were full, they might not only have wrecked his plans for Italy but even destabilized Punic power in Spain.

Hasdrubal launched his own offensive in 215, having quelled the Tartessii (temporarily at least) and of course encouraged now by the news of Cannae, still more by his brother Mago's timely arrival with reinforcements: 12,000 foot, 1,500 horse, twenty elephants, and as mentioned before no less than 1,000 talents. Mago was perhaps responsible for the army's battle array, too, when it confronted the Romans outside the town of Hibera (later called Dertosa Ilercavonia) near the Ebro's delta. With his cavalry forming both wings as usual, Hasdrubal arranged his center in three divisions: Spanish troops as the middle one and an African contingent to their left and right. His elephants were most likely in front. The idea must have been to repeat Cannae: lure the Roman infantry center into pushing the well-drilled Spaniards backward and then strike it in either flank with the Africans while the cavalry and elephants disposed of their own opponents and fell on the Roman center from behind. Neither Hasdrubal's talents, however, nor his soldiery were equal to his elder brother's. The Roman infantry did push the Spaniards back—then swung left and right to knock out the Africans while Hasdrubal's cavalry and elephants unhelpfully fled. Hasdrubal escaped the wreckage; but there would be no march to Italy.

SCIPIOS IN THE SOUTH

What followed is complicated by the sole detailed source, Livy's at times nebulous though narrative, stuffed with miscalculated chronology and puzzling place names. He offers smashing Roman victories after Hibera in 215 and 214, then a two-year standstill in 213–212, and lastly a disaster-strewn final campaign in 211. The account is so unsatisfactory that most reconstructions ditch much or all of it as fanciful Roman fiction. Yet some of his throng of names and datings suggest not shameless invention but fogged misunderstanding. Roman victories in 215, though exaggerated, can be believed. Despite Hasdrubal's heavy defeat, the Carthaginians tried again, moving against a city Livy calls "Iliturgi"— probably confusion for Hibera Ilercavonia (the real Iliturgi stood beside the river Baetis down south). Hibera, guarding the main coastal crossing of the Ebro, had previously resisted the Scipios but may have capitulated after their victory. Driven from there, the Punic army assailed Intibili twenty-seven Roman miles (forty kilometers) south of Hibera, apparently another place that had changed sides. It suffered another defeat, although excited claims that 60,000 Punic troops were involved, led by both Barcid brothers and an otherwise unknown colleague, need scaling down. The colleague, Hannibal son of a Bomilcar, more likely was the only general and in command of much smaller forces, for the defeat had no bad consequences for Carthaginian Spain.

For Livy the next year was adorned with victories in southern Spain, yet was followed by a two-year standstill. In reality his own evidence shows the standstill occurring in 214–213; then in 212 the Scipios invaded the south, to winter there and be obliterated in 211. One clue is that when the brothers (supposedly in 214) took Saguntum and brought its surviving citizens home, our historian himself dates this "in the eighth year" after Hannibal had captured the city. Another is that, despite having the brothers perish in 212, Livy afterward reports Gnaeus Scipio meeting his end "in the eighth year" after coming to Spain; Gnaeus had come in 218. The brothers had reason to halt war-making in 214–213. Already in 215 they had written dolefully to the Senate that they were short of supplies and funds for their troops; this dispatch had prompted Roman suppliers to offer to provide munitions on trust—and the fraudsters among them, led by Pomponius and Postumius, to cheat on these for several years. As mentioned earlier too, Rome suffered even worse financial trouble in 214. As a result the Scipios had to find their own funding and husband their forces. Harder to divine is why Hasdrubal left them alone in the northeast. Renewed rebellion by Tartessii or others may be one reason, though a more mettlesome general might have delegated such annoyances to a subordinate and gone after the Romans himself. Maybe too Hasdrubal was not so eager about marching to join Hannibal even if he could crush the Scipios. In Italy he would be a subordinate once more, after years of independent command. Even after the road was cleared he would show an odd disinclination to go.[2]

The reinvigorated though not reinforced Scipios launched their new offensive in 212. Hasdrubal now had not only Mago with him but a new colleague, Hasdrubal son of Gisco, and the rebels were finally being tamed. Publius and Gnaeus could worry that the Carthaginians would strike at them unless they acted first. Livy narrates that they penetrated deep into the southeast, to the area where Hamilcar Barca had met his end, before being strongly opposed. Then they won over Castulo, the important mining city near the upper Baetis and the home city of Hannibal's wife, along with other places nearby such as the real Iliturgi and Ilugia, a town of the Orissi or Oretani—the people responsible for Hamilcar's death. Three victories followed, one at "Munda" and then two at "Auringis." These look like mistaken versions of two known cities, Unda and Aurgi, again in that region. At some stage in 212, too, came the restoration of the Saguntines to their homes. The brothers then chose to winter at Castulo, we read in Appian, and at "Orson," which plausibly is Orissian Ilugia again (certainly not Urso more than 200 kilometers southeast).

This was a bold challenge to Hasdrubal. It impressed the Celtiberians enough for 20,000 fighters to accept mercenary service with the brothers, allegedly the first mercenary contract in Rome's history. The aim was plainly to push farther down the Baetis valley, harry the enemy from the field, and raise fresh rebellions all the way to the Atlantic. The Scipios had broader ideas too. In 213 or 212 they made contact with Syphax, the enterprising king of the west Numidian Masaesyli whose efforts at making the whole of Numidia his own were at odds with the powerful Massyli in the east. The Massyli's king was Gaia, father of Hamilcar Barca's ally Naravas and also of an equally enterprising younger son named Masinissa. If Naravas did marry Hamilcar's daughter, Masinissa was thus brother-in-law to Hannibal, Hasdrubal, and Mago. Just as it was natural for the Massyli to look to Carthage for backing against Syphax, so too Syphax inevitably would welcome overtures from the invaders of Spain. They sent an experienced centurion, Statorius, to train his soldiers, and over the next few years he would wage inconclusive war against the Massyli and Carthage. A more decisive, and disastrous, impact of the Scipios' link with him was to bring young Masinissa and a body of Numidian cavalry over to Spain to support Hasdrubal.

The Roman generals at Castulo and Ilugia can have had only some 20,000 troops apart from their new Celtiberian auxiliaries, for doubtless they had sustained losses over the last seven years, and they could not have left Tarraco and the northeast ungarrisoned. Undeterred, they split what they had: Gnaeus to confront Hasdrubal at a town Livy calls Amtorgis, Publius to march against Mago and Hasdrubal son of Gisco five days' march away. "Amtorgis" looks like a later copying error either for Iliturgi on the Baetis or for a town rather farther south called Iliturgicola. Gnaeus's already small army became emaciated when the Celtiberians accepted a hefty bribe from Hasdrubal to go home, leaving the Romans no choice but to start a doomed retreat. Publius meanwhile was marching across open country to find Mago and the son of Gisco, under constant harassment from Masinissa's newly arrived Numidians. When word came that Indibilis the Ilergetan, once more in action for Carthage, was approaching with soldiers from northern Spain, Publius led most of his troops in a futile effort to intercept them. Trapped between the newcomers and the rest of the enemy forces, he was killed, and his force was cut to pieces. The victors, Masinissa included, then marched to join Hasdrubal and hunt down Gnaeus. It took four weeks and a day, but in the end the Romans were encircled on a bare hilltop somewhere near Ilugia, with nothing but their saddle packs for a rampart. They were overwhelmed; Gnaeus died fighting like his brother. Some survivors reached Ilugia, only to be murdered by the townsfolk, hastily trying to atone for their defection.[3]

The brothers' whole campaign had been marked by overconfidence. The poor enemy performance the year before encouraged them to take risks that backfired one after the other. Of course they could not foresee the arrival or the relentless energy of Masinissa, but dividing their forces and being outbid for their mercenaries by Hasdrubal would fairly certainly have brought them low anyway. News of their elimination must have been all the more cheering to Hannibal because around the same time he lost Capua. Now he might look forward to Hasdrubal marching to Italy with his victorious veterans. It was surely disappointing to learn instead of his brother's uninspired follow-up to the victory. Roman survivors, collected by an officer named Lucius Marcius Septimus, gamely struck out for the Ebro 500 kilometers away—and got there. They could not have achieved this had the Carthaginians stayed anywhere near. Even Masinissa must have been leashed. By gathering in troops from unnamed strongholds on the way (Saguntum would be one) and those holding the northeast, Marcius put together an army of barely 8,000–9,000 men to hold the Ebro line. Livy then bestows on him a string of sweeping—and fantastic—countervictories against first Hasdrubal son of Gisco and then Mago. At best Marcius may have beaten off a Punic probe or two, for instance at Hibera; perhaps, as the (allegedly conscientious) historian Lucius Piso claimed just seventy years later, he ambushed an incautious Mago and inflicted enough losses to make him retire.

The Romans thus held the northeast—another of Carthage's egregious errors in the war. Hasdrubal nonetheless had a fine opportunity to skirt the skimpy enemy defenses by an easy inland march, for instance through the territory of his Ilergetan allies the brothers Indibilis and Mandonius; then cross the western Pyrenees (as he would finally do in 208) and march for Italy. He did not take it. Hannibal's feelings can only be guessed.

When a dispatch from Marcius reporting the catastrophe reached Rome, the Senate—while taking silly umbrage at him assuming the title "propraetor"—acted decisively, a great contrast to Carthaginian insouciance. The propraetor Gaius Claudius Nero, recently helping to besiege Capua, sailed in the new year with 12,000 foot and 1,100 horse to Tarraco. Supposedly these were the troops who marched out of Rome in 211 by one gate even as Hannibal prowled about outside another—but in fact they left early in 210. Livy recounts that Nero soon managed to entrap Hasdrubal in a mountain pass called Black Stones but was fooled by pretended peace talks into letting the Carthaginians abscond: a tale with the renewed scent of later fiction, decorated with a piece of supposedly typical Punic cunning. Nevertheless the unique place name—and the fooling of a Roman general—may yet hint at a nugget of fact, perhaps a cautious standoff in the stony Maestrazgo ranges south of the Ebro. Nero wisely stayed on the defensive otherwise.

Less excusably, so did Hasdrubal and his colleagues. What their plan may have been for the next year's campaign, in 209, can only be guessed. Maybe they hoped to give Nero enough space to entice him into another march southward, where they could converge on him. Instead they would find themselves facing yet another Scipio and a revolution.

10

CARTHAGE IN RETREAT: 210–206

NEW CARTHAGE, 209

Claudius Nero was a stopgap, even if an effective one. He was probably astonished nonetheless to learn, late in 210, who would be his long-term replacement. With an imposing range of possibilities to choose from— that year's consul Marcellus, his colleague Valerius Laevinus, Fulvius Flaccus the surviving conqueror of Capua, not to mention Nero himself (*in situ* at that)—the citizens in the Comitia Centuriata voted for a young man who put himself forward even though he had held no magistracy higher than aedile. He was Publius Cornelius Scipio, aged twenty-five, the elder son of the dead proconsul, his namesake. He had served with his father and Sempronius Longus in 218, was at Cannae two years after, had been aedile in 213, and no doubt had seen much military service overall. Even so, appointing him to take charge of the precarious Roman position in northern Spain—and removing a steady though unspectacular older commander—was the Romans' biggest gamble of the entire war.

All that young Publius had to recommend him was his kinship with the slain Scipios, which would lend him some influence with northern Spaniards (though it proved useless with the Ilergetes and their tirelessly pro-Punic lords Indibilis and Mandonius). Maybe some voters felt too that his father and uncle had turned Spain into a kind of Scipionic preserve— scarcely a typical Roman attitude to military appointments, all the same, nor a strong argument in logic. For the gamblers to be not the Senate but the citizens in the Comitia was as novel as to choose a twenty-five-year-old, whether or not they were swayed by a knot (not easily identifiable) of leading men. Certainly a couple of precedents from the past could be had: the fourth-century heroes Manlius Torquatus and Valerius Corvus had served in high office illustriously at similar ages (Valerius was first consul reportedly at twenty-three, in 348). But Scipio was unique: currently a private citizen and mere ex-aedile, he received *imperium* as a proconsul. As colleague he was given an ex-praetor, the hardly more eminent Marcus Junius Silanus, who the year before had commanded forces policing Etruria. Silanus's formal *imperium* may have been equal to Scipio's—the evidence is not clear—but in practice he was the younger man's subordinate. Silanus proved a reliable journeyman, but Scipio's most trusted officer was his close friend Gaius Laelius.

No doubt Scipio had strong and influential senior supporters, but it is easier to surmise whom his election annoyed—Nero for a start and probably too Fabius Maximus (who viewed Scipio as a dangerous hot-head even five years later). The able consul Laevinus is not likely to have been delighted either. In a puzzling tussle with the Senate earlier in 210 he had refused to summon the Comitia to choose a dictator for supervising the coming elections, perhaps disgruntled that the choice was being left to voters instead of to the consul (an innovation dating to 217 for Fabius). When the task was transferred to his colleague Marcellus, the voters elected Fulvius Flaccus dictator, and as his master of horse Fulvius chose Scipio's great friend P. Licinius Crassus. Crassus, young as he was, had influence. He had become Pontifex Maximus in 212—beating two more eminent rivals, one of them Fulvius—and then in 210 itself he became censor, though his colleague's death made it impossible to complete all censorial tasks. Crassus no doubt supported Scipio and quite possibly his superior Fulvius did too; whereas Laevinus, already cross with the voters, would likely take a sourer view about electing an untried youngster for a major theater. Marcellus, hounding Hannibal in southern Italy, by contrast made no objection (even if he thought the choice surprising). If the elderly Junius Pera, who had been dictator after Cannae, was still influential and if he liked Junius Silanus, he may have lent his backing too, but this is another surmise. Of the many and varied Cornelii active at the time—a couple of Lentulus brothers, a Sulla, and a Cethegus were recent ex-praetors and another Lentulus was an ex-quaestor—none as yet was very high in rank or military achievement. Nor need all have been friendly to Scipio; some years later one of them as consul would try to take over his role in Africa.

Scipio sailed with 10,000 infantry, 1,000 cavalry, and an ample 400 talents. At Tarraco he started planning his moves. Rome's forces in Spain now numbered about 31,000—four legions with their Latin and Italian allies—a growth that surely could not escape Hasdrubal's notice. Scipio himself built up accurate intelligence about the Carthaginian positions scattered across southern Spain; so he explained in a letter twenty years afterward to Philip V, read later by Polybius. He realized that Hasdrubal and his colleagues were handing him an extraordinary opportunity. Apparently assuming that a youth in his first military command signaled nothing more troublesome than ongoing defensiveness in the northeast, they continued with masterly inactivity. Scipio carefully practiced the same for several months. As a result, for the winter of 210–209 the three Punic generals divided their forces widely. Polybius, relying on Scipio's letter, stations Hasdrubal the non-Barcid near the mouth of the river Tagus, Mago somewhere in the southwest, and his brother in central Spain besieging a town of the restive Carpetani. Small garrisons held important strongholds across the Punic province: for instance, 1,000 regular troops at New Carthage under another Mago.[1]

All this may have been partly to ease commissariat problems, but Polybius puts it down to the generals' quarreling. One dispute may have been over how to deal with their Spanish friends and subjects now that the threat from Rome had (supposedly) been neutered. Hasdrubal son of Gisco opted to ill-treat their loyal Ilergetan allies Indibilis and Mandonius—he tried to extort money from them and, when thwarted, took their daughters hostage—but may not have been cheered on by the more experienced Barcid brothers. All three may have disagreed over what to do about the Romans: for instance, whether Hasdrubal the Barcid should bypass them and march for Italy, leaving the others to keep them busy. Hasdrubal, as was already clear, wished no such thing.

Less clear is what he did wish, unless simply a quiet military life holding southern Spain.

All independent decision-taking was soon forfeited. In spring 209 Scipio mustered an expeditionary force at the Ebro: 25,000 infantry, 2,500 cavalry, and the fleet of thirty-five quinqueremes under Laelius. Leaving Silanus with just 3,500 infantry and cavalry to hold the crossing at Hibera, he set out for New Carthage, the city founded by Hannibal's brother-in-law Hasdrubal and effective capital of Punic Spain, 500 kilometers south. None of the enemy armies lay within ten days' march of that city or knew of his movements. A phenomenally swift advance brought the Romans to the gates of the Barcid capital of Spain. One day later it was in their hands.

Scipio took the city commandant, Mago, totally unawares. Even if Polybius and Livy overdo the speed of the advance—500 kilometers in ten days was impossible, unless in reality Laelius's quinqueremes escorted unmentioned transports bearing the troops—Mago had time only to arm 2,000 able-bodied citizens of New Carthage to help defend it. The city, bounded by its harbor on the south and the saltwater lagoon on the north, was nearly impregnable. Still, coastal fishermen interviewed at Tarraco had told Scipio of a weakness: late every day the lagoon's waters would flow out into the harbor through a canal at the western edge of the city, lowering the depth greatly. The likeliest reason was a strong northerly wind that blew up toward evening (unless improbably Polybius, or Scipio himself, invented this tale, as some suspect). On the day of the assault Scipio improved his charismatic hold on his men by forecasting it as a vision he had had from the sea god Neptune. After preoccupying the enemy in the morning with furious attacks on the east walls and the harbor's, once the lagoon's water sank he sent 500 picked legionaries and *extraordinarii* with scaling ladders through it. They seized the nearly deserted north wall; then the troops on the eastern side broke in too. A spate of indiscriminate killing ensued through the streets until Mago, holed up in the citadel, offered surrender.

Scipio promptly replaced ruthlessness with leniency, and he had his men well enough in hand to enforce it. The 10,000 surviving townsmen and 2,000 noncitizen and slave artisans were perhaps surprised not to be slaughtered or sold off. He left the townsmen and their families in their (admittedly ransacked) homes, while informing the artisans that they were now slaves of Rome but would be freed at war's end if they worked loyally. Massive quantities of plunder were seized—gold and silver goods, coined money, huge stores of wheat, barley, military supplies, armor, artillery, and warships in the harbor—and shared out, though Scipio sequestered the city treasury's 600 talents for military needs along with the ships. With Mago the Romans captured seventeen Carthaginian *adirim*, two of them members of the inner council, and 300 Spanish hostages whom the astute proconsul at once released to their homes. They included the womenfolk of several Spanish lords, including the Ilergetan Mandonius's wife and his brother Indibilis's daughters. Their release had the eminently satisfactory effect of inducing the brothers, early next winter, to switch their allegiance.

New Carthage fell in spring 209. Its capture was one of the most brilliant actions of the whole war, not to mention one of the most decisive. What happened next was anticlimax. Military operations stalled yet again. Scipio remained at his new conquest, putting his troops through a cycle of drill and exercises (day one required a thirty-stadia run—nearly six kilometers—in full armor), while the fleet, enlarged with eighteen captured warships, trained offshore and the city's workshops got busy manufacturing armaments. Meantime Scipio added to his reputation by restoring to her Spanish fiancé a beautiful girl captive whom his men had thoughtfully reserved for him. Laelius was then dispatched to Rome to announce the news and deliver the aristocratic Carthaginian prisoners. Not only did Scipio avoid moving out to challenge the Carthaginian generals, but they too avoided challenging him: no attempt to retake their capital or blockade it to cut him off or to attack him when he left to spend the winter at Tarraco. New Carthage with its Roman garrison remained inviolate too. Not surprisingly, many Spanish peoples besides the Ilergetes started to review their loyalties.

The shoddy performance of these experienced Carthaginian generals, each leading an army at least equal in size to Scipio's, would in older times have led to a crucifixion or three. But they remained in command, merely awaiting his next move. They were temporarily without Masinissa, for during 210 that prince was at Carthage. Even had he stayed in Spain he could have made little difference to the generals' lethargic indecision. The way was open for Scipio to return to the south in 208, this time looking for battle.

BAECULA AND ILIPA

Now faced with mass defections, Hasdrubal finally wanted to fight—not, however, outside the old Punic province, for not only had all of northeastern Spain declared for Rome but so had the powerful Edetani on the coast below the Ebro. Still, operations were slow to start. Scipio took his time about readying his new campaign. He beefed up numbers by transferring suitable men from his warship crews to the army, departed Tarraco sometime in spring, and on the march was joined by Indibilis with his Ilergetans. He seems not to have been in any hurry; in any case his 700-kilometer advance to Castulo's region would have taken time—down the coast past Saguntum and then inland to skirt the wild Alcaraz, Cazorla, and Segura mountains rimming the Baetis valley on the east. More remarkable is how the Carthaginian generals showed no interest in uniting to meet him, even though he cannot have kept his approach secret throughout. Maybe their continued disagreements were allowing their hearts to rule over their heads, or maybe—less stupidly, but more hypothetically—they again had problems with rebellious Spaniards and optimistically trusted Hasdrubal to deal with an upstart who had taken New Carthage only thanks to luck.

Hasdrubal awaited attack with about 30,000 troops near Baecula, a town in the Castulo region. With him too was Masinissa, back from North Africa at the head of a cavalry force—though Masinissa was to play no useful role in what followed. After some skirmishing Hasdrubal positioned his forces on a flat hilltop with steep slopes on either side and a lower flat area in front again edged by steep slopes. A river flowed behind the hill. His camp was on the upper level, while a body of troops held the lower one. The Roman army was perhaps 40,000 strong including the new Spanish allies, but these played little or no recorded part in the battle; Scipio was wary of Spanish auxiliaries after what had befallen his elders in 211. His Roman and Italian troops, naval recruits included, were probably about equal in number to Hasdrubal's.

Hasdrubal's strong position was not a sign that he now wanted to avoid fighting. Rather, he meant the fight to be as hard on the Romans as possible. In the frontal attack that he expected, they would have to climb first one slope and then the next under fire, while his infantry and cavalry could charge downhill against them. He was perhaps expecting too—or at least hoping—that one or both of his fractious colleagues would finally appear (both did catch up with him later). If he could defeat or at any rate weaken Scipio now, then with Mago and the other Hasdrubal he could annihilate the new invader as totally as the old.[2]

Scipio, after two days of reconnoitering, launched his light-armed *velites* and some of his best infantry against the enemy on the lower level. Even though pushing uphill, the disciplined Romans gave their adversaries so much trouble that Hasdrubal started to deploy his main army on the upper hilltop, expecting the rest of Scipio's to join in the frontal attack. Instead, and in defiance of every Roman battle norm, the proconsul had deployed the other legionary and allied infantry in two divisions as his wings. He now led the right wing around to the slope below Hasdrubal's left as Laelius moved up likewise under Hasdrubal's right. With the enemy from Hasdrubal down intent on what was happening in front, these movements were practically invisible—until too late. They struck the stunned Carthaginians in both flanks while these were still deploying to face their foes in front. Hasdrubal's ranks disintegrated. He himself made off with his elephants and whatever troops he could rally; so did Masinissa and most of the Numidians. The river in their rear was plainly no barrier. Some thousands more lost their lives, while 10,000 foot soldiers and 2,000 cavalry—these perhaps hampered by the steep slopes and corralled by Scipio's own, unmentioned cavalry—became prisoners.

Scipio's follow-up was unusually cautious. Pursuing Hasdrubal risked running into the other two generals, who before long joined the beaten Barcid somewhere near the upper Tagus. Scipio did order a force to advance toward the Pyrenees to monitor Hasdrubal but not to try stopping him. Evidently he reckoned that, if Hannibal's brother did make it to Italy, the fifteen or so legions there could cope. He himself remained in the upper Baetis region, welcoming Spanish leaders anxious to emphasize how much they hated their old rulers and how keen they were for Rome. At the same time he refused their cheerful salutation of him as "king"—whatever that might mean to Spanish lords, each a king among his own people—which was not only meaningless to a Roman leader with no plans to settle in Spain but could be political death for him at Rome: for 300 years the concept of kingship had been anathema to Romans, as it would still be in Julius Caesar's day. More agreeable was a unique acclamation from his own men, *imperator*, meaning "commander," but with the extra sense of "battle-winning" commander. He was not to know that it would set a style and, ironically, end as the title of a new series of kings, the Caesars. Another noteworthy gesture was to free a teenaged Numidian prisoner, Masinissa's nephew Massiva, and send him back to his uncle laden with gifts of honor. This created an early link between the Numidian prince and Scipio, one with momentous consequences. Meanwhile, fearful of taking on the victor of Baecula directly, Mago and the other Hasdrubal agreed with the defeated Hasdrubal that it was high time he set out for Italy, while they themselves retreated into the southwest to regroup and revitalize.

The peculiar stop-go character of this Peninsular war continued. Like his elders in 214–213 and the Punic generals in 211 and 210, and his own withdrawal to Tarraco after taking New Carthage, Scipio did not follow up Baecula with any great urgency. Having flattered, and been flattered by, the grandees of eastern Spain and frightened the enemy southwestward, he marched back through the mountains, across the plains, and over the Ebro for his third Tarraco winter. Just as restrained, his opponents made no effort eastward militarily or diplomatically over the rest of 208, even though then or early in 207 another commander from Carthage, named Hanno, joined them with some fresh troops.

This newcomer did not last long. When he and Mago in 207 marched into Celtiberia to raise more soldiers, they and their recruits were caught by Silanus leading a task force. He routed them and bagged Hanno among the many prisoners. Scipio meantime marched south again, now with his younger brother Lucius as his *legatus* (Laelius was absent, perhaps guarding Tarraco and its surrounds). The Romans were sedulously avoided by Hasdrubal the non-Barcid, even when they assaulted a wealthy city that Livy calls Orongis—probably Aurgi southeast of Castulo—and even though this cost them plenty of trouble to capture. The son of Gisco had distributed his forces over various cities in the south (unnamed by Livy as usual) and sat tight. In attacking Orongis Scipio may have aimed at provoking a battle (no success there), as well as at garnering useful booty for the troops and showing the south that strong fortifications were no barrier against Romans. It did not serve as a springboard for a continued offensive through the Baetis valley. To be sure, Hasdrubal's troop dispersals were a potential weakness, for the Romans might have picked off one strongpoint after another, gambling that he would stay passive. Yet Scipio might reckon that that would risk jolting him instead into dangerous activity, should the Roman army get itself into another Orongis-style entanglement—especially if Silanus's large task force was absent. As a result, campaigning stopped once again even though the year cannot have been far advanced. Scipio marched his army all the way back to Tarraco, there to receive the welcome news that Hasdrubal the Barcid had been annihilated in northern Italy. At Gades the same news must have had a depressing impact. Hasdrubal son of Gisco and Mago decided on a make-or-break confrontation—next year.

Early in 206 Scipio came south once again, arriving at Castulo untroubled by the enemy. A Spanish lord in the area, Culchas, banked on a Roman victory and brought in a small but useful reinforcement of 3,000 foot and 500 horse. Together with Spanish contingents that had come in on the march, this gave Scipio 45,000 infantry and 3,000 cavalry (so Polybius reports). He was still wary of Spanish troops, but his Roman and Italian soldiers must have numbered only 35,000 at best: this contributed to the unique tactics that he devised. Hasdrubal, with Mago as his deputy and Masinissa leading the Numidian cavalry, had a formidable force. Livy gives him 50,000 infantry and 4,500 cavalry; Polybius less plausibly gives 70,000 and 4,000 plus thirty-two elephants, figures probably magnified in his source to burnish Scipio's victory.[3]

Just where the battle was fought is debated. Not only do Polybius and Livy give different names, but the names seem corrupt. Polybius calls the nearest town "Elinga" or "Ilinga," and Livy, "Silpia"—none of them known otherwise, and Livy's version could be a misreading of Polybius's Greek text. That the real name was Ilipa is widely accepted. Southern Spain abounded in places called Ilipa and Ilipula—not to mention a Iulipa and a quite separate Iluipa. "Elinga" and the other spellings could conceal an Ilipa or the like nearer Castulo, rather than the much more distant one near Seville.[4]

Reaching his chosen campsite, Scipio easily beat off an attempted cavalry ambush by Mago and Masinissa with a counterambush. Over the following days he left the (seeming) initiative to Hasdrubal, whose unimaginative technique was to lead his forces down to level ground after midday to deploy them in standard style—heavy Libyan infantry in the center, Spaniards and cavalry on the wings, elephants ahead of the wings. Each afternoon Scipio matched him precisely, legions and Italian allies forming his center and Spanish allies (foot and horse) forming the wings. Yet neither general attacked; at nightfall both sides retired to their camps.

Once he had the Carthaginians fixated on this sequence, Scipio acted. Soon after dawn one morning he deployed the army—this time with the infantry forming the wings, the right under his own command and the left under Silanus and the veteran Lucius Marcius, placing the Spanish allies now in the center. His cavalry and *velites* crossed the plain to assail Hasdrubal's camp and jolt him into coming out. With no time even for his men to breakfast, Hasdrubal reacted as desired: he brought them down in their usual formation—and then was made to wait for hours while the armies' light-armed and cavalry skirmished. Even if he could see that the Roman deployment had changed, he could not risk changing his formations to match, for as they moved about they would be open to attack. Nor did he choose to launch his own attack, even though that would have given his troops the initiative and might even have stymied Scipio's plan. Instead the proconsul had time to recall his *velites* and cavalry, place them behind his infantry wings, and order a general advance early in the afternoon.

For the first recorded time, the infantry moved in cohorts: a unit formed of one maniple each of *hastati*, *principes*, and *triarii*, a flexible arrangement (it would become standard later). When his army was four *stadia*, less than a kilometer, from the Carthaginians Scipio had the infantry execute an extraordinary sequence of maneuvers: first wheeling from line formation into marching columns, then—just before reaching the foe—back into lines. This final redeployment, Polybius says, brought the rear ranks up alongside the others. In other words each wing now formed a single long line of cohorts, probably too at an oblique angle to the enemy wings. Meantime the cavalry and *velites* wheeled again into line too and charged straight at the Spanish wings' flanks. All this happened while Scipio's own Spanish allies were marching forward much more slowly toward Hasdrubal's center, which held position as though paralyzed—or hypnotized.

These shifting alignments were Scipio's calculated risk for keeping the enemy nonplussed about what would come next and equally—as Polybius stresses—for enabling the Romans to strike the Spaniards' flanks with infantry as well as cavalry and *velites*. That he simply wanted to close faster with Hasdrubal's less experienced Spaniards, while delaying his own center's advance, is less plausible. Certainly columns could move faster than lines—yet the advantage would have faded once they came to wheeling back into line, within fighting distance of their foes at that. Scipio could not have decided on columns to intimidate Hasdrubal's Libyans from charging out against his Spanish center, for had his columns tried to swing round against the Punic center instead of Hasdrubal's wings, they themselves could be struck in flank and rear by these, not to mention by Hasdrubal's cavalry and elephants (Scipio did not know how initiative-deprived his adversary was).

The maneuvers were hugely risky. Wheeling into columns had caused his cohorts to jut out farther to left and right than the enemy's did, but at the same time it opened a gap between each wing and his center—a gap widening as the cohorts pressed forward. Had Hasdrubal loosed his cavalry and elephants into the gaps, the Carthaginian might have destroyed the Romans. But Hasdrubal was (it seems) as paralyzed as his men. He did not detach troops from his static center (some rear ranks, for instance) to aid his Spaniards or order the Libyan veterans to charge Scipio's slowly pacing Spanish center—which they might have routed, trapping the legions between them and Hasdrubal's wings. A vigorous countermove had at least the chance of making Ilipa a Carthaginian victory—or else a draw: an outcome much worse for Scipio than for Hasdrubal. Instead the

Punic cavalry made no impact anywhere, and Hasdrubal let his Spaniards fight without support against the legionary assaults by Scipio, Silanus, and Marcius. His elephants proved useless too. The Roman cavalry's and light troops' cutting and thrusting attacks so harassed them that they ran wild, damaging their own side as much as the enemy's.

The battle was lost once Hasdrubal's stubbornly resisting, famished wings gave way late in the afternoon. The Libyans had to join in what began as an orderly retreat toward their hilltop camp but ended in a desperate scramble with the Romans wreaking havoc on the collapsing army. It was saved from total disaster only by a colossal rainstorm that put an end to all fighting. But next day, with his remaining Spaniards starting to desert, Hasdrubal abandoned camp to retreat westward under relentless harrying—a contrast to Baecula's aftermath, when Scipio allowed the enemy to march away with his surviving forces. After another clash shattered what forces he still had, he left his last 6,000 men on a steep hilltop near the Baetis and made off by water to Gades, followed not long after by Mago. Masinissa and his Numidians also escaped the debacle.

Ilipa was the most complex clash of the Punic Wars; Cannae's maneuvers were simple by comparison. Scipio's divisions revealed skills in coordination and movement on a level rare in ancient armies and by 206 impossible even for Hannibal's. Their general in turn showed himself a masterful blend of planning, cool judgment, and boldness. Although piecemeal Punic opposition lasted a few months more, Punic Spain was now virtually in Rome's power. It was plain now whom the republic must choose to confront Hannibal.

THE END OF PUNIC SPAIN

Over the spring and summer of 206 Scipio and his lieutenants put paid to what resistance remained. Hasdrubal son of Gisco soon preferred flight to fight: he shipped himself off to Africa. Masinissa, beginning to have second thoughts about his allies, also hastened home to lay claim to his late father's kingdom, taken over by kinsmen abetted by Syphax. Mago did stay on for a time at Gades rallying some troops, while Scipio marched either back to Tarraco (so Livy) or maybe to New Carthage, which better fits his following actions. He distributed some troops into garrisons at key centers: we know of 8,000 Latin and Italian allies at Sucro on the coast eighty kilometers south of Saguntum. Another garrison was probably placed at or near the notable city of Hispalis, for before year's end Scipio settled a body of discharged veterans on a ridge overlooking the Baetis, evocatively naming the new town Italica. Italica would be the hometown of two Roman emperors, Trajan and Hadrian.

The proconsul also sounded out the ambitious Syphax over in Numidia. Although much occupied at home since 211, including war against Masinissa's Massyli, Syphax was now close to taking over all Numidia. This would make him a useful ally against Carthage, if he so chose—but Syphax was being courted by Carthage too. Probably in early summer Scipio himself sailed south from New Carthage across to Syphax's little capital, Siga, on the Numidian coast, hoping to cajole him. There he found another royal guest: none other than Hasdrubal son of Gisco. It must have made for interesting banquet conversation. Supposedly Scipio did persuade the king into allying with Rome, but it would prove not worth any papyrus it was written on.

The rest of 206 was busy. Scipio took the field again, to wreak first-degree vengeance on Ilugia north of Castulo because it had murdered survivors of his uncle Gnaeus's disaster. Ruthless when it suited him just as much as seductive at other times, he slaughtered Ilugia's entire population in a holocaust to Gnaeus Scipio's memory. Bizarrely Castulo, which had done the same to other survivors, was spared. He then returned to New Carthage, leaving the competent Lucius Marcius to demonstrate the power of Rome to the lands of the lower Baetis region. Most centers there surrendered hurriedly, but the rich stronghold of Astapa, in the uplands 150 kilometers northeast of Gades, could not be prized from its Punic loyalty and was taken amid further horrific scenes. After most townsmen made a suicidal sortie, their women and children were slain by a trusted band of warriors, and the dead along with all of Astapa's treasures were set on fire in a vast hecatomb in the central square. So at least the story went (based no doubt on Marcius's own reports). Believable at any rate is the detail that his troops were so eager to lay hands on the gold and silver melting in the pyre that they delved into the flames themselves, some suffering horrible burns.

Scipio meanwhile was taken out of action by falling seriously ill at New Carthage—so seriously that he was expected to die. This encouraged various discontented parties to assert themselves. At Sucro the garrison, restive over their long service and lack of pay—and over missing out on the plunder that others had won—started a mutiny that was in practice very respectful. Led by two ordinary soldiers, Atrius, a Latin, and Albius, an Umbrian, the troops maintained discipline and eventually agreed to come to New Carthage to put their case. By then Scipio had recovered his health, and he acted firmly. The leaders were arrested and executed, but the men received both their back pay and his forgiveness. The episode if anything heightened his hold on his army and on Spaniards, since he did not face any such insubordination again either in Spain or later in much more parlous situations in Africa.

More challenging defiance came from the irrepressible Mandonius and Indibilis in the northeast, angry at not being rewarded more handsomely for their support (for instance, with lordship over all peoples beyond the Ebro). Scipio had to march from New Carthage, cross the Ebro, and bring their forces to battle in hill country. By concentrating the bulk of the Spaniards' attention on his advancing light-armed troops and infantry, he used the hilly terrain to send Laelius with the cavalry behind them unseen to strike Mandonius's and Indibilis's own cavalry, kept on a hilltop above their infantry. Their army smashed, the brothers soon surrendered, accepted by a no doubt skeptical but time-pressed proconsul.

Seemingly tireless despite his recent near-death, Scipio next hastened back south, where Mago with Masinissa was holed up on Gades's offshore island. With Carthage's fortunes evaporating, Masinissa once more hinted at switching sides in a secret interview on the mainland with the Roman general, while Mago received instructions from home to sail with his remaining fleet for north Italy. First he tried capturing New Carthage by sea, which failed, and then found himself and his ships shut out of Gades too by its disenchanted residents (though he lured the city's magistrates out and crucified them). Only now did he sail, just as

Masinissa and his horsemen also left Spain, and Gades opened its gates to Scipio. Ten years of peninsular warfare thus ended, and with them ended the Barcid province founded only thirty-one years before.

It must have been fairly late in the year by now, but Scipio in turn departed, leaving Silanus and Marcius to take over command in Spain. He had his eyes already fixed on still greater prospects: the consulship and with it the long-shelved expedition to Libya.

HANNIBAL AGAINST MARCELLUS

In Italy the fall of Capua in 211 was a body blow to Hannibal's fortunes. Not just Campania was lost. Some Samnite communities had already fallen or capitulated too, and in Apulia in 213 the enemy had won back Arpi. The Roman war effort hardly slackened. In 210 with the operations in Sicily and against Macedon, and Sardinia garrisoned, ten legions were serving outside Italy, while in Italy armies were spread out from Cisalpina to Apulia and Lucania. Of the sixteen legions in the field in 211, there were still eleven at the start of 210—five of them in the south watching Hannibal and the allies that remained.

Tarentum and the other Greek cities of the south were no counter-weight to losing Capua. As noted already, they supplied Hannibal with few if any recruits or naval resources or (it seems) funds. Neither he nor his home authorities made much effort about exploiting Carthage's access to their coasts—to Locri's harbor, for instance. The Romans holding Tarentum's citadel were a continuing frustration, which Bomilcar failed to break: his expedition to Tarentum in 212–211 ended with the Tarentines begging him to leave. The Romans in the citadel, the armies patrolling Apulia and Lucania, and the fleets operating in south Italian waters did not make the Greeks' commerce by land or sea prosperous or even safe. Harassed, increasingly distressed, they like Carthage's other Italian allies needed protecting to maintain Hannibal's strategic position, not to mention his dented prestige. Protecting them had never been an easy task, as the fate of Capua showed above all. Now it would worsen.

Hannibal must have seen that prospects for ultimate victory had dropped nearly to zero. Even during Capua's siege he had essentially been on the strategic defensive. Now he had to look to Rome to help him out by agreeing, at last, to fight some more major battles that he could win. If so, he might still—somehow—switch off their will to resist. The sole alternative was to hang on in the south and urge his brother Hasdrubal to make the long-awaited march to Italy—although that would bring problems of its own, since Hasdrubal would arrive in Cisalpina while Hannibal stood in Apulia or Lucania. By 210 he faced the real possibility that the war would end in a compromise peace, far from the decisive victory and hegemony over the western Mediterranean that he and his countrymen had envisaged when he marched from Spain in 218.

Of the new consuls for 210, Marcellus took command in the south, while his predecessor Gnaeus Fulvius Centumalus continued nearby as a proconsul, each commanding two legions. The year began with another

Claudius Marcellus. (Rom, Capitolinisches Museum.)

FIGURE 10.1
Statue of Marcellus, Hannibal's dogged adversary (done in Roman imperial times).

Punic setback. Salapia in Apulia, which had stayed loyal after its neighbor Arpi returned to Rome, now fell into Marcellus's hands thanks to its two leading citizens. Its 500-strong Numidian garrison did fight, only to be all but wiped out. Marcellus's success, however, was followed in turn by one for Hannibal when he found Centumalus aiming to win over Herdonea nearby. In one of his trademark swift advances he came upon the proconsul's army outside the town and occupied its attention with his infantry, while his cavalry rode right around them unseen to fall on them from behind. The disaster cost Fulvius 7,000 or more killed and at least as many captured. Only some 4,300 men, mostly Latins and allies, got away; their nonreward was to be relegated in 209 to Sicily to join the Cannae legions serving there. Herdonea was emptied of its residents by the resentful victor and then burned; Hannibal made them all transfer south to Metapontum and Thurii, whose citizens he could still rely on.

Losing a two-legion army was a blow as sizable as losing Flaminius's at Trasimene. Yet the impact, seven years on, was minimal. Marcellus, who had been making life miserable for the Hirpini in Samnium, moved into Lucania. At Numistro in the mountains inland from the gulf of Salerno, he gave Hannibal a two-day battle that neither won. Roman losses may in fact have been heavier than Carthaginian, but Hannibal found no reason to stay around and retired across the hills to approach Venusia, one of Rome's Latin colonies. Marcellus did not let him depart in peace, partly perhaps concerned for Venusia but partly too to inflict as much harassment as he could. Taking precautions against possible ambushes— no repeat of Flaminius's and Minucius's errors—he daily encamped close enough to the enemy to carry on a string of skirmishes between cavalry and infantry patrols. Again Hannibal did not stay long. For the rest of the year, the two armies moved around Apulia in the same style, without battles but in skirmishing contact. The only other Roman setback was in the waters off Tarentum, when a small squadron trying to shepherd a supply convoy to the citadel was routed by the Tarentines' minnow navy of twenty-two ships. Hungry as the garrison in the citadel was, all the same, it could not be forced out.

Marcellus turned Fabian tactics on their head. Instead of avoiding contact with Hannibal's army and hounding his allies, he kept in steady contact to probe his outposts, skirmish with his patrols, and at times even meet him in battle. He had small hope of defeating the Carthaginian genius (despite Livy's and other sources' enthusiastic fancies), but, at the head of long-serving and disciplined legions and allies, he in turn could not be defeated. Even if his troops came off worse in clashes, they regrouped. Meantime other forces could take over hounding places that flew Carthage's colors. This approach to war-making was unwelcome to Hannibal. Not only was it becoming still harder to guard his remaining allies, but his own forces suffered continual attrition—a serious matter when refilling the ranks required local recruits who could see that he was going nowhere. Marcellus was not done with Hannibal even when his consulship ended, because next year Rome continued him as proconsul.

Both consuls for 209, Fulvius Flaccus (who as dictator the year before had presided over the elections) and Fabius the Delayer—Fulvius's fourth consulship, Fabius's fifth—and Marcellus all operated in the south. Despite the Herdonea disaster, Hannibal again faced six legions across his reduced territorial base: a base that was about to shrink further. Marcellus with his two legions kept him occupied in Apulia, bringing on near Canusium another two-day battle that cost the Romans heavily (5,700 killed and thousands more wounded) but again failed to put them out of business. Fulvius meanwhile was free to receive capitulations by the Samnite Hirpini and Lucanian communities nearby. Then Hannibal was called to Bruttium to save Caulonia from the Sicilian irregulars whom Valerius Laevinus had brought over and who had been joined by deserters from Hannibal's forces—but while he did so, Fabius began besieging Tarentum. Before the harassed Carthaginians could cover the 250 kilometers from Caulonia, the commander of Bruttian troops in the garrison had allowed the Romans to scale the eastern wall by night, and by noon the next day all resistance was over in Tarentum. In the fighting and after, thousands were cut down (even some of the Bruttians) by the Romans. The garrison commander himself, Carthalo, a family friend of Fabius's, was slain as he tried to reach the consul for safety. Thirty thousand people were collected for slavery. Nothing was going right for Hannibal; when he tried to entice Fabius over to Metapontum with a trick report that it too was ready to submit, the gods intervened with unfavorable omens. Cautious and pious, the Delayer stayed put, returning to Rome only once the campaigning season ended.

The year 209 had not simply been a bad one for Hannibal. It made clear that, without some sharp and spectacular shift of events, he and Carthage were on the way to losing the war. By the time Tarentum fell, he had probably learned that New Carthage had gone too. What Scipio's coup at New Carthage portended for the future surely alarmed him (unless he was determinedly blind to the blatant mediocrity of Spain's Punic generals). He himself now controlled—flimsily in places—just sectors of Apulia, Lucania, and Bruttium and the coastal Greek cities from Metapontum to Locri. Roman armies could thrust into any of these regions at will, whereas he no longer had the strength or security to carry the war into Rome's territories. Even Latin strongholds in the south, such as Luceria and Venusia in Apulia and Brundisium on the Adriatic, continued unbothered because he could not afford to shackle his army to assailing one—if he did, he would have the legions from all over the south converging on him. In practice Hannibal was under strategic siege, a siege he could not break without fresh help. His brother Hasdrubal was supposed to bring it, but he was taking his time.

Rome had her own problems. Punishing the survivors of the battle at Herdonea did not go down well with her allies. It pushed twelve Latin colonies into declaring themselves too exhausted to supply their annual quota of recruits or funds. The Romans were furious—none of the dozen was in a current war zone; most in fact were historic colonies in Latium, southern Etruria, and the Sabine land north of Rome. The Senate nonetheless chose tactful silence over recriminations (penalties would come later, in 204). Strikingly, the eighteen noncomplainers included Brundisium, Venusia, Luceria, and Beneventum, all of them in or near the seat of war. The Senate was less tolerant of restive rumblings among the Etruscans, especially at Arretium; in 208, hostages were taken from there, and two propraetors, one of them the ex-consul Varro, were assigned three legions to watch the region. Finances meanwhile were still so hard-pressed that Rome's final and sacred reserve was brought out: 4,000 pounds of gold, accumulated over a century and a half through a 5 percent tax on slave manumissions. This was worth at least four million *denarii* or forty million *asses*.

Marcellus returned to the consulship in 208 for his fifth time, together with Titus Quinctius Crispinus, one of the previous year's praetors. This was scarcely a hit at Fabius, who must have been nearing his eighties and could rest on his laurels while continuing to offer cautious counsels in the Senate (not with invariable success). Marcellus meant to continue the aggressive strategy in the south, although religious tasks kept him from leaving Rome with his colleague. Hannibal avoided any opportunity to hit at Crispinus while he was on his own. Crispinus advanced into the toe of Italy to besiege Locri but broke off his attempt when he heard that the Carthaginian had moved down to Cape Lacinium near Croton, 150 kilometers northeast. He then marched more than 400 kilometers north, through the largely mountainous lands of Bruttium and Lucania, to join Marcellus, now commanding the legions at Venusia. Had Hannibal corralled Crispinus outside Locri or intercepted him on his long march to Venusia, Marcellus's strategy would have been crippled. Hannibal's one initiative instead was to ambush and smash a large Roman detachment near Petelia as it marched from Tarentum to help a second move against Locri, by the praetor (and future historian) Cincius Alimentus.

Near Venusia the consuls were ready to fight the battle that Hannibal, too, had long awaited. Instead he trapped both men in a small hilltop ambush, when with supreme insouciance they rode out from their camp with a few hundred escorting troops to reconnoiter. Marcellus was killed, and Crispinus so badly wounded that (like Appius Claudius Pulcher three years before) he died before year's end. Hannibal treated his tenacious foe's remains with honor, but he had won a self-defeating success. There would now be no great battle, no chance to recover the initiative with a smashing victory. Hannibal tried to exploit his coup by using Marcellus's signet ring to trick Salapia's magistrates, sixty kilometers away, with a message to expect him, Marcellus, shortly. Crispinus, however, had already alerted surrounding cities against such notices. The Salapians let in 600 of Hannibal's Roman deserters, slammed the gate shut, and made short and unpleasant work of them. The best that the frustrated general could do was to march south again and save Locri a second time.

THE BATTLE OF THE METAURUS

For the first time in Rome's history both consuls had lost their lives in war, leaving it to a dictator, the elderly Manlius Torquatus, who had crushed the Sardinian revolt in 215, to hold the elections for 207. Crispinus had taken his legions north to Capua before he died, leaving his colleague's army at Venusia under Marcellus's wounded son and namesake, a military tribune, whom the younger Fabius Maximus afterwards replaced. All this should have been a prize opportunity for Hannibal to capitalize on the dismay and separation of Rome's forces. As before, he did nothing at all; the year petered out inconclusively. At least he did finally have the cheering news that Hasdrubal was on the march from Spain, though his brother would not arrive in northern Italy until next spring. Meanwhile the Romans, who two years earlier had made an extraordinary choice of general for Spain, now came close to matching this with a strange pair of consuls for 207.

One was no great surprise—Gaius Claudius Nero, young Scipio's immediate predecessor in Spain—even though arguably he was a good deal less proven than, for example, Valerius Laevinus (still proconsul in Sicily) or Fulvius Flaccus, who instead was sent as proconsul to Bruttium and Lucania. His colleague, by contrast, was a phenomenon. Marcus Livius Salinator, the consul of 219 who had been fined for misappropriating Illyrian booty, had lived in embitterment and squalor for years outside Rome. The censors of 210 had made him shave, wash, and attend the Senate again, but even then he spoke once only, to defend his kinsman Livius Macatus, who had lost Tarentum to Hannibal—but so vigorously (Livy avers) that everyone suddenly realized his potential. This tale, whether true or too good to be true, does not explain why everyone thought him the best choice to pair with the man whose testimony had brought him down twelve years before. This was the year when a looming new invasion under a second Barcid general posed the gravest danger to the republic since Cannae. The voters did choose him and again made history.

Hasdrubal crossed the Pyrenees in the second half of 208, with a small army and ten elephants. The Gauls allowed him secure transit through their lands; he was able to recruit soldiers and, clearly feeling no great urgency, wintered comfortably there before crossing the Alps in spring. Again by contrast with Hannibal's much-harassed march, he met no opposition. In Cisalpine Gaul his numbers grew as 8,000 Ligurians came in and probably some local Gauls, but even so, his troops at best totaled 30,000 horse and foot. The Romans were keeping track of him through reports from Massilia and then from the new commander in Cisalpina, the praetor Porcius Licinus. Word of his arrival still caused some rather unseemly panic in the City—no one there knew how mediocre a general Hasdrubal was—but as soon as the consular odd couple entered office on March 15, 207, brisk steps were taken to cope. Claudius Nero received Bruttium and Lucania for his operations, and Livius Salinator, Cisalpine Gaul, each with a consular army fully strengthened. Porcius Licinus, Livius's subordinate, had two (understrength) legions; nearby in Etruria the solid workhorse Varro had two more. Nero's subordinates were the tough Fulvius Flaccus as proconsul in Bruttium, again with two legions, and a propraetor, Claudius Flamen (Tarentum, with two). As in previous years a reserve legion stood at Capua, and two newly levied ones stayed at Rome. The Romans thus had fifteen legions arrayed across the north and south—more than 100,000 citizens and allies.

Hasdrubal's sole hope of joining up with his brother was to evade the northern legions and move fast. His idea was to meet Hannibal in Umbria north of Rome. Yet, instead of advancing fast, he decided to stop to besiege to the Latin colony Placentia on the middle Po. He may have wanted to impress the local Gauls and win some more recruits, but it lost him the strategic initiative. And he was not yet in touch with Hannibal, so now he sent off six horsemen—four Gauls and two Numidians—with a sealed dispatch spelling out his plan. It looks as though he had no Roman or Italian deserters available, but the riders did make their way unnoticed all the way south to Metapontum, seeking his brother.

Hannibal was not having an easy springtime. His prime need was to push northward to link up with Hasdrubal, and he began by gathering in troops from his Bruttian strongholds. Livy's fuzzily unsatisfactory account of what followed makes him zigzag around the south: first and improbably into the Sallentine heel of Italy, then over to Bruttium, and from there northward to Lucania. There he was intercepted by the consul hurrying down from Venusia and made to fight a hard but inconclusive battle at Grumentum. Next, shifting toward Venusia, he was dragged again by Nero into another hectic clash. After this, he swung south—still dogged by his foe—all the way to Metapontum, meantime sending his lieutenant Hanno for fresh recruits from the Bruttians: a sign of the losses inflicted by his untiring foes. With Fulvius Flaccus now patrolling Lucania, his options were narrowing. Nero, determined to hobble him, was using the same tactics as Marcellus in earlier years, again with an army that Hannibal could neither defeat nor distract. The Carthaginian pushed north again (just before his brother's couriers reached Metapontum), Nero cautiously shadowing, past Venusia and up to Canusium. There—undecided, exhausted, or simply pinned down—Hannibal stayed.

Things were already going wrong. Now they went very badly wrong. Hasdrubal had given up besieging Placentia to march 300 kilometers southeast to the Adriatic, coming down toward Livius Salinator and Porcius Licinus not far from Sena Gallica. By now it was June. He did not know that his couriers had finally been captured and Nero had read his dispatch. The consul sent orders to Rome for the urban legions to move out to Narnia on the middle Tiber and the Capua legion to transfer to Rome.

He then took a further, completely unorthodox decision that changed history. Selecting 6,000 infantry, Romans and allies, and a thousand cavalry, and leaving his *legatus* Quintus Catius in command facing the blissfully unaware Hannibal, Nero marched northward with all speed, picking up recruits en route, to join Livius and Porcius 450 kilometers away. If it took six days, as Livy suggests, the infantry must have hitched rides on the wagons bearing their equipment—a not improbable scenario given the emergency. His arrival increased Roman numbers to around 37,000.[5]

Livius hid the reinforcements by cramming them into his existing camp, but Hasdrubal soon caught on—especially when unimaginative Roman protocol required that in the consular camp, unlike in Porcius's, trumpets should now sound twice instead of once. Yet this insight was self-defeating. He assumed that disaster had befallen his brother and decided to pull out. In any case, his realistic options were few and fearful: stand and fight superior numbers, somehow snake around them and then around the Roman forces farther south (a purposeless effort if he had no Hannibal with whom to rendezvous), or retreat to Cisalpina under heavy pursuit—where, even if he made it, he would need to fight off converging Roman armies till the generals in Spain could crush Scipio and march over Pyrenees and Alps to his rescue.

In deciding to move away from the Adriatic coast Hasdrubal was perhaps keeping the second and third options open, but he merely deferred disaster. The army made off at night but, deserted by its local guides and failing to find a usable ford over the nearby river Metaurus, was caught the next morning by the Romans. As the consuls and praetor deployed their troops, Hasdrubal positioned his tired and dispirited Gauls—those who had not deserted during the night—on a steep hilltop opposite the enemy right wing under Nero and massed the Spaniards and Ligurians in closely packed ranks facing Livius and Porcius, with his ten elephants in front. It was June 22, 207, ten years and one day since Trasimene.

His hope was surely to overwhelm the Roman left (neither side deployed a center) while Nero was busy trying to assail the torpid but nearly inaccessible Gauls, and then strike the Roman right. If so, this was his most sophisticated battle plan ever. It had no better success than his past ones. Rather than continue trying to get at the immobile Gauls, Nero took the second most momentous decision of his career. Detaching several cohorts, he led them behind and around the Roman left as it clashed fiercely with Hasdrubal's fighters. The elephants, panicked by the uproar, had already started to run wild and wreak havoc on friends as well as foes (as those at Ilipa would the year after). Now Nero struck the Spaniards and Ligurians in flank and rear, and they collapsed. The Gauls were next to be cut down. Six elephants were killed by their drivers to prevent capture, but the others became Roman prisoners of war. Hasdrubal gave up being a general and charged into enemy ranks to die.

What was left of Carthage's second army to invade Italy scattered. Ten thousand men had been killed, and, Livy reports, 5,400 were captured—a 50 percent loss in all. Many of Hasdrubal's Carthaginian officers were slain, and the others were taken. Livy adds that 4,000 Roman captives were liberated from the enemy camp. If this is accurate, Hasdrubal had shackled his movements to no purpose by dragging them around with him, but where he can have captured so many is so opaque (he had taken no towns and fought no earlier battles) that it may be just a propaganda claim.[6]

Forgivably frenzied exhilaration and religious thanksgiving followed when the news reached Rome. Less civilized was Nero's way of passing it on to Hannibal. The Carthaginian leader had noticed nothing odd, or shrunken, about the army facing him at Canusium. He still waited to hear from his brother. Instead, hurrying back to Apulia from the scene of victory, Nero delivered a grim trophy: Hasdrubal's head, flung by a Roman patrol to one of Hannibal's outposts. Two prisoners were then freed to tell him all that had happened. Hannibal had treated like this none of the Roman generals or other ranks killed in his battles. Supposedly, he said that he now saw the destiny of Carthage; certainly he saw that the invasion was effectively finished, however long he might hold on in the far south. Emptying Metapontum of its people, and the few Lucanian centers still in his power, he moved with them into Bruttium to await events.

Hasdrubal's incursion had been poorly run from start to finish—even, in fact, before it had begun. Had he marched from Spain after annihilating the elder Scipios in 211, he might indeed have propelled his brother to final victory, but by 207 their combined armies would have had trouble coping with opponents no longer afraid of Hannibal (and not needing to fear Hasdrubal) and superior in numbers. Strategically the expedition was foredoomed. Hasdrubal's only route to Italy, by land, put him on arrival more than 800 kilometers from Hannibal. The faster his movements, then, the better—but even by June and without opposition he had got only as far as Sena Gallica. His proposal for uniting their armies came at the eleventh hour instead of much earlier, for instance, via Carthage in 208; Hasdrubal surely did not need to be actually in Italy to know where Umbria, Apulia, and Rome were. Hannibal in turn was strangely passive over his brother's movements. Though in touch with Carthage down to 203, he made no recorded effort to contact him by sea, nor did he try by land even though his own Numidians, after ten years in Italy, should have known its geography well—not to mention his Bruttian veterans and at least a few Roman and Italian deserters. The strategic maneuver that decided the campaign—detaching an elite body of troops from one theater to reinforce another—was Nero's; it could have been Hannibal's. The otherwise uncelebrated Quintus Catius had no trouble hiding his reduced numbers from the Carthaginian. Ten years earlier it would have been a different story.

The consuls for 206, Lucius Veturius Philo and a friend of Scipio's, Quintus Caecilius Metellus, were more cautious souls than Nero and Livius. Assigned to Bruttium, they preferred plundering rebel territory to seeking out Hannibal—until he sprang an ambush on them in a defile around Consentia and frightened them away to Lucania. It was a slight affair (none of their plunder was lost) and, paradoxically, showed that he now posed little threat if left to himself. Veturius and Caecilius made up for it by taming Lucania's remaining rebel districts. The Romans were already looking to the postwar future: before leaving the City the consuls had initiated measures to revive ravaged Italian lands by encouraging absent farmers to go home and get back to work. As fear eased and optimism revived, the news from Spain of Scipio's overthrow of Carthage's power there made it clearer still how—barring some pro-Punic miracle—the war would end.

11

SCIPIO AND ROMAN VICTORY

SCIPIO INVADES AFRICA

Publius Scipio (figure 11.1) returned home late in 206 or early in 205, delivered another huge quantity of Spanish booty to Rome's treasury (14,342 pounds of silver bullion, not to mention coined money), and offered himself for election as consul for 205. He was of course chosen, as was his friend Publius Licinius Crassus, the Pontifex Maximus, and he openly pushed for invading Africa at long last. The idea ran into outraged hostility from the aged, ever-cautious Fabius Maximus senior, who could not imagine taking on such a gamble (as many quite rightly judged it) before Hannibal had been completely erased in Italy. Other veterans, such as Fulvius Flaccus, sympathized with these misgivings; quite likely too some thought Scipio—still only thirty-one—a dangerously overconfident egoist whose luck could run out anytime. Scipio made it clear, however, that he was ready to bypass the Senate and put his plan directly to the Comitia Centuriata: this tamed the recalcitrants. He was assigned Sicily, the necessary jumping-off point for Libya, as his military province—even if the critics did manage to inflict one irritant on him. Instead of levying citizen recruits in normal fashion to supplement Sicily's existing forces, he had to call for volunteers. This was no problem; he left Rome with 7,000 of them.

The legions in Sicily largely consisted of the long-serving and long-suffering survivors of Cannae, whose pleas back in 212 to be demobilized had been brushed away by an unmoved Senate, and those from the

second battle of Herdonea in 210. In spite of some supplements, by now
the army would at best total 15,000–16,000. Scipio's Roman volunteers
were almost certainly augmented, now or in 204, by Latin and Italian
allied troops—volunteers again or conscripts—but invading Carthage's
home territories with scarcely 30,000 soldiers can only have worsened the
forebodings of Fabius and his friends, all the more when Scipio took his
time about doing it. He passed his consulship in Sicily, training the men,
sending Laelius to raid the Libyan coast (the last raid of the war), explor-
ing Sicily's Greek culture, and even intervening across the straits of
Messina in Bruttium to retake Locri as his colleague Crassus's army was
immobilized by an epidemic. Locri wanted to change sides, but its Punic
garrison under Hannibal's friend Mago held out in its fortress while
Hannibal marched up in support. Scipio himself had already arrived in
the city; now he led a surprise sortie against the attackers—and Hannibal
withdrew, taking his garrison along. His army was full of sick men too,
and he chose caution. Still, the Hannibal of old would not have been taken

FIGURE 11.1
Scipio Africanus: probable portrait (gold signet ring of the late third/early second century BC, with
the name of its artist, Heracleides).

aback by a sortie or missed the extraordinary opportunity that was offered of capturing or killing the only Roman general who could match him.

Scipio left Locri under a *praefectus* named Quintus Pleminius, who turned out to be a ruthless thug, pillaging even the sacred shrine of Persephone (Proserpine) and—after Scipio indulgently ignored complaints from not just the Locrians but even two Roman military tribunes there—murdering the tribunes. The scandal, now extending into 204, gave Fabius Maximus a fresh and more justified opportunity for criticism, though to demand Scipio's recall from Sicily, where he was now proconsul, was going rather far. Specially appointed senatorial envoys headed by the praetor Pomponius Matho—a cousin of Scipio's—and including three lesser magistrates and Scipio's friend Caecilius Metellus, consul two years before, had to sort things out, restoring Persephone's sacred treasures and dispatching Pleminius and his many cronies in chains to Rome. They then visited Sicily to investigate complaints about the proconsul's slack handling of his army and excessive fondness for Greek ways but (to the surprise of few) found nothing to criticize and everything to praise. Greek ways, it turned out, meant wearing a Greek cloak and sandals when visiting the gymnasium, going to plays (all this probably at Syracuse), and reading too many, no doubt Greek, books.

One of the complainants, incidentally, was Scipio's own quaestor Marcus Porcius Cato (figure 11.2), a kinsman of Porcius Licinus of Metaurus note, whose attitude both to Romans behaving like Greeks and to Scipio personally was uncompromisingly censorious and would remain so all his life. Rather as the influx of American ways, from chewing gum to informality of manners, into Britain in and after World War II irked many natives, many Romans of Scipio's day—not only elderly ones (Cato was thirty)—resented how attractive Greek culture was to other citizens.

Influences from Greece had in fact started centuries before, but their pace was quickening alarmingly by the end of the third century. The poets Livius Andronicus, Naevius, and Ennius were already exercising their creative skills under Greek literary influences, and the cult of the Great Goddess (or Cybele, non-Greek but venerated by Greeks) had just been imported from Asia Minor through the good offices of the Hellenistic king of Pergamum. Probably in this period too, the comic poet Plautus staged his satiric sendup of braggart general versus resourceful civilians, *Miles Gloriosus*, based in the usual way on Greek models but with plenty of sharp Roman touches. For Roman conservatives, Greek ways meant loose clothing, loose entertainments, and loose morals. Evidently, for Scipio's enemies, bringing him down would have been worth jeopardizing the expedition to Africa. As the choice of investigators shows, a more level-headed viewpoint in the Senate prevailed.

Scipio's leisurely preparations in Sicily are not easy to explain. After all, they offered the Carthaginians (and Hannibal) plenty of time to counter-prepare. The simplest explanation may be that in 205 he chose to train his men as thoroughly as possible and so left too little time for crossing to Africa before winter set in. He was also in touch with Masinissa, the Massylian prince, whom he wanted as an ally (Scipio was prepared to overlook the Numidian's large role in his father's and uncle's deaths). Masinissa, though, could offer little at this time. After his own father Gaia's recent death, family infighting over who should rule had given the western Numidian king Syphax his chance. Encouraged by Hasdrubal son of Gisco, now the senior Carthaginian general in Africa, he repeatedly defeated Masinissa in battle and made himself master of the Massyli. Hasdrubal was happy to have the king marry his own daughter, Sophoniba,

FIGURE 11.2
Cato the Censor in old age.

to confirm Syphax's alliance. She was the third Carthaginian girl in as many decades to become a Numidian royal. Not only had Naravas probably become Hamilcar Barca's son-in-law, but one of Masinissa's uncles had taken a niece of Hannibal himself to wife; when widowed, she was wed to Masinissa's rival for power before disappearing from history.

Sophoniba (her name, properly Safonbaal, means "Baal Safon has judged") was beautiful, highly educated, musically gifted, and—as Diodorus and Appian gushingly insist—irresistibly seductive. Appian adds extra romantic color by claiming that she had first been betrothed to Masinissa but was wedded to Syphax by the Carthaginian authorities while her father and fiancé were in Spain (thus in 206 or earlier). Diodorus, going improbably further, asserts that she was married first to Masinissa. Appian may be right about the betrothal but not about the sleight-of-hand marriage. Polybius implies that in late 203 it was still recent; Livy confirms this by reporting Hasdrubal himself arranging the marriage during 204. For Sophoniba, her accession to royalty was to start down a road to tragedy, if also to romantic fame in modern times.[1]

Masinissa meanwhile, reduced to living as a wounded fugitive near the coast of the Lesser Syrtis gulf, got in touch with Laelius during the latter's raid but could only promise goodwill and the help of his small band of loyalists.

It was fortune's gift to Rome that Scipio's slowness did Carthage little good. When his armada finally sailed in June or July 204 to land near Utica—400 transport ships escorted by just forty quinqueremes—there was no enemy navy on station to block it or attack it at its moorings. The only land force anywhere near was a body of 500 horse sent out from Carthage under an officer named Hanno. Scipio had been joined by Masinissa with 2,000 horsemen—or according to another of Livy's sources, with 200. Like most officers of his name in the war, this Hanno did not shine. His riders were quickly routed and he himself was slain. A second Hanno, sent out with 4,000 cavalry, was ambushed and suffered the same fate. While all this was happening Hasdrubal son of Gisco was far inland organizing an army—something he should have done at least twelve months earlier—and linking up with Syphax, now firmly and fatally on Carthage's side.

Scipio therefore had time to range through the countryside inland from Utica, capturing a place called Salaeca and amassing piles of plunder to send off to Sicily on the transport ships. Only as winter was approaching did Hasdrubal, Syphax, and their armies make an appearance. Scipio broke off besieging Utica to establish himself just three kilometers east of the city, on a small high promontory later known as Castra Cornelia (today an inland hill), with his forty warships on the beach alongside. Rather than assail him, the new arrivals settled down comfortably for the winter in two camps not far to the south. Winter was no doubt mild, for both camps were lightly constructed with wood and branches and (in Syphax's) partly with just reeds from nearby swamplands. Scipio, with about 30,000 men, and Masinissa, even if he led 2,000, were facing 33,000 under Hasdrubal son of Gisco and (says Polybius, followed by Livy) 60,000 under Syphax. These figures are probably exaggerated, like some others offered by Polybius (his Roman ones at Cannae, for example). Still, the Carthaginians and Numidians plainly outnumbered their foes: Livy's casualty figures from their ensuing catastrophe suggest something like 47,500.

Winter now cut the invaders off from fresh supplies, not to mention any reinforcements. At Carthage, the authorities—again long after they should have—were finally putting a reasonably sized fleet into readiness. This was exactly the nightmarish predicament that Fabius had envisaged. All that Carthage needed was energy and planning: a vigorous land and sea assault (which Polybius claims they did plan for the winter) on the Romans and their handful of Numidian allies would demolish the invasion and revive Hannibal's prospects in Italy. Yet nothing happened. The weather may have turned against any naval move, but Hasdrubal's and Syphax's supineness is hard to understand—and from the Punic point of view even harder to justify. Rather than bother the Romans, they began to think favorably of negotiating peace when Scipio artlessly offered to talk. Syphax believed that he could act as honest broker, and Hasdrubal perhaps did want peace, although Syphax's proposed terms—Rome and Carthage to withdraw from each other's territories but to keep what they currently held elsewhere—would confirm Carthage's loss of her Spanish province and effectively leave Rome the dominant power in the west.

Neither Hasdrubal nor Scipio was in a hurry. Recruiting agents from Carthage had sailed to Celtiberia in Spain to hire more mercenaries, but these could not arrive until after winter. Scipio happily spun things out, ensuring that when his spokesmen visited the opposing camps their attendants included some shabbily dressed and sharp-eyed centurions. Once spring began, he broke the talks off with the message that he favored the terms but his war council did not. That night he attacked both camps simultaneously, setting the flimsy structures ablaze as their occupants slept and slaughtering those who got out of the inferno. As Livy tells it, 40,000 men were killed by fire or the sword, and only some 5,000 were taken, including Carthaginian aristocrats (eleven of them members of the *adirim*).[2]

The Romans, who down the ages would characterize Hannibal as the soul of treachery, had no such hard words for Scipio. He himself insisted that his final message freed him from the existing truce, though Roman writers afterward decided to help him along by claiming—quite unconvincingly— that at the last minute Hasdrubal had added some new and impossible demands. Polybius describes Syphax and Hasdrubal as inferring from his message that they would have to fight it out after all, which, if true, is something of an absolution for Scipio. Nonetheless, resorting to an unheralded night ambush was definitely more in the style of the Hannibal depicted by Rome than of a scrupulous old-style Roman hero. What the censorious quaestor Cato thought of it is, sadly, not known.

PEACE ABORTED, 203

Scipio's coup freed him from immediate peril. It left Carthage without a field army: Hasdrubal and Syphax escaped with a mere 2,500 men, many badly burned. At Carthage, all the same, Hasdrubal and the Barcid faction moved the republic to fight on. Because Scipio preferred not to close on the city but to continue besieging Utica—Polybius claims that he reckoned Hasdrubal and Syphax to be spent forces, a strangely obtuse notion if true—the two were able to put together new forces in the interior. Thirty days after linking up, they positioned themselves on the

Great Plains, a wide region edged by uplands along the middle Bagradas river. The best part of their 30,000 men, paradoxically, were not their African levies but the 4,000 Celtiberian mercenaries who had finally found their way over. Why they took their stand on these inland plains, rather than hasten to the coast against Scipio, is not obvious. After all, for all they knew, reinforcements might be on their way to him. No more obvious is why he decided to march 120 kilometers inland to confront them, necessarily leaving part of his army outside Utica, when defeat so far from his base would mean a fate like his father's. He may have reckoned that Hannibal, now holed up in Bruttium, might return at any moment and it was vital to strike down Hasdrubal and Syphax first—so if they would not come to him, he would go to them.

After some days' skirmishing, the armies clashed in what proved a lopsided fight. Neither Polybius nor Livy makes it clear what happened, but it seems that on the cavalry wings Laelius and Masinissa quickly got rid of their opponents (no elephants are mentioned), and in the center Scipio used part of his infantry to demolish Hasdrubal's Libyan and Syphax's Numidian soldiery. In the very center of their line stood the Celtiberians, refusing to retreat, whom Scipio chose to engage with only the first line of one legion, the *hastati*, while its *principes* and *triarii* moved out to left and right behind this and then swung in against the Celtiberians' flanks to destroy them. The maneuver put the gritty discipline and matchless expertise of the men of Cannae and Herdonea on a par with Scipio's army at Ilipa. Hasdrubal got away to Carthage—to be stripped of command and banished—while Syphax was pursued to Cirta by Masinissa and Laelius, defeated again, and captured. Scipio himself accepted the capitulation of one Libyan town after another on his march back to the coast (though not sparing them from looting).

Next he moved down with most of the army to Tunes, close by Carthage. But he had to backtrack hurriedly when the Punic fleet of sixty quinqueremes sailed out to attack his own, moored outside Utica and outnumbered. The Carthaginians had been fitting out these warships since the winter, and it was now late spring if not early summer, but— having sportingly forgone the opportunity to make a raid during Scipio's absence inland—their ships now dawdled long enough over the twenty-five or so nautical miles (in fact overshooting their target and overnighting at Cape Farina to its north) to let the proconsul put both his warships and his transports into a strong defensive array. The attackers were beaten off, though they dragged away sixty of the 400 Roman transports: the Punic navy's last spasm. When Scipio once more encamped at Tunes, the sufetes and *adirim* sent envoys asking for talks. At the same time, they had sent Hannibal a recall notice—a conundrum with dangerous potential.

Syphax and his wife had already been brought to Tunes by the triumphant Laelius and Masinissa. Masinissa, now in control of his ancestral realm and looking to take over western Numidia from his rival's son Vermina, had also taken over Sophoniba—to Laelius's great annoyance and Scipio's concern. The antiromantic story of the marriage interested only ancient historians, but Livy's emotive retelling captivated imaginations in the Renaissance and later: how Masinissa, improbably portrayed as a hot-blooded youth (he was thirty-seven), fell in love at first sight and married his beautiful captive on the spot but, after being avuncularly admonished by Scipio (pointing out that as a Carthaginian and Hasdrubal's daughter she was actually a Roman prisoner), salved her and his honor by sending her poison.

The outline of events may well be true, but the reality was more ruthless. Sophoniba's father might have been currently on the run, but he still had political allies and the chance of a comeback. For Masinissa, who already had Punic links of his own, to marry into a leading family at Carthage was a risk that Scipio would not run with the war far from finished and Masinissa's kinsman-by-marriage Hannibal on the horizon. At the same time it would have been a grave humiliation to Rome's new and needed ally if his wife were taken off to captivity in Italy, as Syphax soon was. It suited both Masinissa and Scipio that she should die. In return, Scipio in front of the entire army proclaimed him king of all Numidia, and then let him leave to impose his rule there with the help of a Roman cavalry force. To Masinissa this was well worth Sophoniba's loss.

Carthage was offered terms that (from a Roman point of view) were reasonable. She must evacuate her forces from Italy, Cisalpine Gaul, and the islands; renounce Spain; hand over all Roman prisoners and deserters and all but twenty warships; and pay a war indemnity of 5,000 talents (thirty million *denarii*). Like Syphax's proposals the previous winter, these terms in effect swept away Carthage's overseas power. The ban on a sizable navy would prevent future ventures outside Africa, and Masinissa, whose kingship depended on Rome's backing, would keep her under watch at home. On the other hand, the city of Carthage and her own territory were left alone; so was her rule over Libya.

The Carthaginians accepted the terms, agreed on an armistice with Scipio, and sent envoys off to Rome to ratify the peace. Laelius too set off to deliver the captive Syphax there. A series of peculiar and poorly recorded events ensued.

Livy is chiefly responsible for the muddle (Polybius's narrative does not survive here). As he tells it, the Carthaginian envoys assured the Senate that the war had been wholly Hannibal's doing and asked for the peace treaty of 241 to be renewed—in other words, they ignored the terms just accepted from Scipio. Laelius and others bitterly attacked them, accusing them of being spies, asserting that Scipio had given terms on the premise that Hannibal and Mago would not be recalled— both brothers, supposedly, had now sailed for Africa—and urging that the envoys be sent packing. This mishmash of misstatements and allegations must come from some source that Livy preferred to use rather than Polybius: a source unhappy with telling a straight story. For in this version not only do the envoys forget what they came to ratify, but nobody in the Senate seems interested in learning Scipio's terms either. Laelius blithely ignores that those terms did require Italy and Cisalpina to be evacuated. Finally, Polybius in a surviving excerpt states—in so many words—that Scipio's peace was ratified. So does a report in a surviving fragment of papyrus from Egypt, dating to Polybius's own time but by an unknown Greek author, reporting the envoys' return to Carthage to announce the ratification.

The true sequence of events at Rome may be that after the Senate and People ratified Scipio's terms, word came that Hannibal and Mago had finally sailed for Africa. A revulsion of Roman feelings may have followed—even among some senators—prompting loud accusations against the envoys (these may not yet have left Rome) as deceivers merely playing for time. Livy's chosen source could reshape this into a scenario of sharp-witted senators seeing through the enemy's supposed deceit from the very start and therefore refusing to accept a false peace. To Livy, unenthusiastic at times over Polybius's dry accounts of treaties (we recall Hannibal's with Philip V), this scenario might appeal for exactly the same reason.

Whatever the facts, a genuine issue existed that neither state addressed. Neither the peace talks nor the peace treaty specified when Hannibal should leave Italy and Scipio Africa. The treaty merely implied that both would do it around the same time. Hannibal had been sent his recall after—if not before—the Great Plains, and he sailed once the Carthaginians had accepted Scipio's terms but before word reached them of Rome ratifying them. Scipio meanwhile was making no matching preparations to vacate Africa. All he did was to withdraw to Castra Cornelia, his camp outside Utica.

Maybe partly for this reason, by the time the ratification news did arrive his relations with the Carthaginians were worsening. Just when all the events happened is magisterially vague in the sources, but the news from Rome must have come in late 203. It was just ahead of a supply convoy for Scipio, which contrary winds forced to beach at Aegimurus island off Cape Bon and along the Cape Bon peninsula's western shores. Putting the news and convoy into spring 202 would have left him unsupplied at Utica throughout the winter and kept both him and the Carthaginians in diplomatic limbo for up to six months. Besides, when the news and the convoy arrived Hannibal was already in Libya: and this certainly happened before winter 203. When the laden transports were abandoned by their crews, warships from Carthage seized the ships and brought them to the city. Scipio promptly sent over spokesmen from Utica by ship to remonstrate and to inform the authorities of the ratification; but the spokesmen were met with popular abuse and dismissed without any official reply. Then off Utica their returning quinquereme was almost sunk by Punic triremes—a deliberate act, Polybius insists, by the war party. He can mean only the Barcid faction. Even if the act was committed just by some aggressive hotheads, the outcome was what pro-war Carthaginians wanted. Scipio resumed hostilities.[3]

HANNIBAL'S RETURN

After failing at Locri in 205, Hannibal had retreated into Bruttian gloom. His limited operations had become an irrelevance to the war overall. As though sensing this, he chose to inscribe an account of his campaigns in the temple of Hera at Cape Lacinium, in both Punic and Greek; it survived long enough for Polybius to study it half a century later. It is a puzzle why he did not abandon his Italian enterprise at once and return to Carthage with his remaining forces. Scipio in 205 was plainly preparing to invade Libya, and (Hannibal surely knew) the generals there such as Hasdrubal son of Gisco and the various Hannos would be outclassed. Neither had he any way of helping his brother Mago, now essentially marooned—by the brothers' own choice—in Liguria and Cisalpine Gaul: in other words even farther from Hannibal than Hasdrubal had been in 207 and with absolutely no chance of reaching him (or vice versa). Yet that had supposedly been the whole point of Mago's operation. In the face of strong Roman forces it stalled. After lengthy inaction, in summer 203 he finally confronted a praetor's and proconsul's armies near Mediolanum to suffer utter defeat, sustain a severe thigh wound, and retreat to the Ligurian coast for a desperate embarkation for home with his surviving troops. On that journey he died.

In 204 and 203 Hannibal kept his army in being—what was left of it—and could still inflict pain. In 204 when one of the consuls, Sempronius Tuditanus, stalked him Marcellus-style in a running fight near Croton, Hannibal killed 1,200 of Tuditanus's men and forced him back to his camp. It was another small, sterile victory. The consul summoned Licinius Crassus, now proconsul commanding in Bruttium, to join him and then stalked again. Livy's cheerful claim that they now badly defeated Hannibal can be scaled down to another drawn clash at best, or fiction at worst, but Hannibal was in no position to do more. For the rest of 204 Tuditanus turned to harassing Carthage's few remaining allies in Bruttium, a pressure continued in 203 by his successor Servilius Caepio. Caepio suffered so little interference that one of Livy's immediate predecessors, Valerius Antias, would concoct one last victory over the Carthaginian to liven up events. In reality Hannibal was preparing to evacuate Italy at last, spending the first part of 203 readying a transport fleet.

If Hannibal could have seen his way to leaving in 205 or even 204, Scipio's invasion might have met a different fate. He stayed on in Italy perhaps hoping that Rome's need to keep armies watching him would lessen the forces assigned to Africa and deter reinforcements later. Scipio certainly received no reinforcements, but by mid-203 it was plain that he did not need them to wreak havoc. Hannibal had, perhaps, hoped too that staying in Italy would counterbalance Scipio's presence in Africa in any peace talks. If so, that hope also was dead after the Great Plains. In paradoxical contrast, the Romans could see that it was now in their interest to keep him. The consuls of 203, maybe those of the previous year too, were ordered by the Senate not to let either brother leave Italy, and it excited much annoyance when both did.[4]

Hannibal's army cannot have consisted only—or even mainly—of veterans of the long march to Italy, now fifteen war years past. Campaign losses and wounds, desertions, and diseases such as the epidemic in 205 will have cut down their numbers. Over the years Italian recruits had joined up in sizable numbers, as his Samnite allies' complaints had shown as early as 215, and so too the many Bruttians in his garrisons. Livy actually calls Hannibal's returned troops Bruttians when he narrates the final battle (Polybius does not say who they were). By 203 most of them must have been as seasoned as his surviving Africans and Spaniards. In all he seems to have carried over 10,000–12,000 men. Stories about him massacring thousands of troops who did not want to go and who had sought sanctuary in his favorite temple, Hera's at Cape Lacinium, look compellingly like Roman fiction (Hannibal the murderous miscreant again) based on the slaughter, recorded by Diodorus, of some thousands of pack animals that could not be taken aboard ship.

Sometime late in 203 Hannibal returned to his homeland after thirty-four years away. He and the army landed at Leptis Minor in Byzacium. Remarkably his crossing was not pursued or intercepted by any Roman fleet, despite the Senate's order. He was still chief general of Carthage. Barcid generalissimos were appointed for indefinite terms, and in any case Carthaginian generals could hold peacetime commands, like Hanno the Great in the 240s after his Libyan campaigns ended. Not long after he disembarked, word came that Rome had ratified the peace treaty. This meant that he was now a general commanding a superfluous army. Carthage and Rome were at peace.

Anomalously, Hannibal acted as though there was no peace—or at least not one that applied to him. He did not communicate with the sufetes and *adirim*. Nor did he disband his army; in fact, bringing over the Bruttians showed that he planned to keep it. Moreover he began acquiring fresh horses and supplies. It might be that he simply meant to protect Carthage from any mistreatment or chicanery of Scipio's; but staying aloof, with a veteran army at his back, hardly conformed to the spirit of renewed peace. Tellingly, the people of Carthage and their leaders were—Polybius states—already regretting that they had made peace. Certainly they could see that Scipio was in no hurry to return Hannibal's favor and go home, while with Hannibal returned they themselves felt renewed hope for victory. Realistically, they could hope only for victory over Scipio and a compromise peace on terms like Syphax's; but even if they were hoping so far ahead, that would be bliss compared with the terms dictated by Scipio.

All ancient accounts take it for granted that Hannibal returned to make war on Scipio. At the same time they are all vague on how this squared diplomatically with the ratified peace. They do not claim that the Carthaginians repudiated the treaty, still less that they declared war anew. Supposedly it was their shameless transgressions in the waters outside Carthage that caused the proconsul to decide that the truce was over and react by taking fire and sword again into the countryside of Libya. In short, it is Scipio, not Hannibal, who restarts hostilities. This scenario scarcely looks like one that pro-Roman or pro-Scipio sources would want to invent: they could have blamed the breakdown of the peace much more blatantly on Carthage by inventing (for example) a war declaration from the *adirim* or a message from Hannibal to Scipio that the war was not over after all. The hostile behavior toward Scipio's spokesmen, orchestrated by the Barcid faction or not, can be believed.

Scipio may not, in fact, have been averse to the peace breaking down. Since the Romans blamed the war on Hannibal—as many fearful Carthaginians were also beginning to do—a peace that left that general controlling Carthage and keeping a devoted veteran army might not look like a peace likely to last. By contrast, Scipio was confident of his own ability to defeat Hannibal. Paradoxically, then, the restart of hostilities was probably welcome to both sides. The peace recently negotiated turned out to be a waste of effort, but the blame was not solely Carthage's or Hannibal's.

Odd as the events leading up to the new hostilities were, what followed was just as strange. Scipio stood at Utica with his veteran army, and Hannibal stood at Hadrumetum with his. They were within fifteen days' march of each other, and neither viewed the recent peace as valid. The date can only be guessed, but, like Hannibal's return, the collapse of the peace must have come before winter shut down overseas communication. The two generals must, therefore, have waited inactive until winter ended—Hannibal more comfortably than Scipio, who had lost his supply convoy. In the spring, however, rather than confront Hannibal, Scipio marched off into the Libyan countryside to loot, burn, enslave, and generally spread terror. Naturally, the farther west the Romans advanced, the more distance they opened up from their coastal bridgehead. If Hannibal were to imitate his father's tactics against Spendius and Autaritus that culminated at the Saw—or those of Marcellus and Nero against himself—he might well reduce the invaders to ruinous straits even without pushing them to battle. Or he could have put paid to the Roman forces remaining outside Utica (they cannot have been very large) and cut Scipio off even from the Mediterranean. Instead he stayed in his east-coast camp levying forces that included mercenaries, adding Mago's survivors to his army, acquiring elephants, and drilling his recruits.

Scipio had another reason for moving toward Numidia. He needed auxiliary troops promised by Masinissa, who was busy taking over western Numidia from Syphax's son Vermina—and taking his time about heeding his Roman patron's repeated summons. Hannibal had Numidian allies too. A kinsman of Syphax, Tychaeus, had already brought him 2,000 excellent cavalry, and Vermina was rallying an army in western Numidia—another reason for Hannibal to move. Nevertheless he dismissed the increasingly agitated appeals from Carthage for action until the year was quite advanced. Then at last—after what must have been one of ancient history's lengthiest military training programs—early in October 202 he decided that his army was ready. From Hadrumetum he marched cross-country to Zama, a stronghold about fifty kilometers southeast of Sicca. Thanks to his clumsy biographer Nepos, this temporary stopover has given the decisive battle of the Second Punic War the wrong name, imperishably.

Scipio had 23,000 foot and 1,500 horse in western Libya. Even after Masinissa came in, almost too late, with another 6,000 infantry and 4,000 cavalry, the invaders were outnumbered by Hannibal's 40,000 men, about 4,000 of them cavalry. Hannibal also had eighty elephants, his largest elephant corps ever. Scipio was undeterred, or put on an undeterred face. Three detected spies were shown all round his camp and then sent back to Zama. As Masinissa was yet to arrive (he came in the next day), they took back an underestimate of the Roman forces. Next the proconsul occupied a hilltop near a town Livy calls Naraggara—Polybius calls it Margaron—and Hannibal in turn encamped not long after on another hill barely six kilometers away. As the only known Naraggara, today Sakiet Sidi Youssef, lies in hilly country at Tunisia's border with Algeria, their clash is commonly located well to the east, near Sicca. All the same, around Sakiet Sidi Youssef much of the country seems undulating and open enough to accommodate a major ancient battle, so the only topographical certainty about the battle of Zama is that it should not really be named Zama.[5]

The day before the battle, Hannibal and Scipio had a personal meeting, suggested by Hannibal, on neutral ground. Both could speak Greek, but protocol required interpreters for Punic and Latin. As an event the meeting stands unique, for no other opposing commanders in history—certainly no first-class ones—did the same. This is hardly a reason to judge it a Polybian fiction: if anything, it makes the parley more believable. Of course Polybius, Livy, and all other sources dramatize it shamelessly, yet its essence is credible. Hannibal proposed that bloodshed could be avoided through a peace that gave Rome Spain and recognized her rule over Sicily, Sardinia, and the other Mediterranean islands (a meaningless gesture, for Carthage had yielded all these in 241 and 237). This was in practice Syphax's old peace proposal again, with Hannibal carefully ignoring the recent treaty's indemnity and other penalties. Implicitly too it left Carthage a free hand in Africa, which would be bad news for Masinissa. What Hannibal offered thus contained nothing to attract the Romans into peace. Had he been serious in seeking this, he would have offered more.

Had Scipio feared defeat in the coming battle, he might have accepted nevertheless. Instead he made no counteroffer, nor mentioned the new and broken treaty, but said that battle would decide. This very probably was what Hannibal wanted too. If he could decisively defeat the enemy, then a peace such as he proposed could be won—and that was realistically the best that Carthage could achieve. For Scipio the stakes were plainly much higher, but plainly too he was absolutely confident of a victory. The essential reason for their meeting was probably curiosity. Hannibal surely knew that Scipio had once met and conversed (at Syphax's dinner table) with Hasdrubal son of Gisco. It was an opportunity—Scipio obviously thought the same—to form an impression of the other general, maybe also to gain an idea of how he might react in battle.

ZAMA AND PEACE

Next day came the battle. If the solar eclipse in Zonaras can be trusted, the date was October 19. Carthage's army included the dead Mago's Ligurians and Gauls as well as some Mauretanians and Balearic slingers—12,000 mercenaries in all—forming the first line of three, with the eighty elephants in front. The second line consisted of Libyan recruits and Carthaginians, one of the rare occasions that citizen soldiers formed a contingent. Livy unblushingly adds 4,000 Macedonians to this line, complete with a kinsman of Philip V as commander, but these are fanciful Roman inventions; no one else mentions them, and even Livy forgets them until they suddenly reappear as alleged captives. Forming the rearmost line were Hannibal's veterans from Italy: the Libyan and Spanish survivors of Hannibal's fifteen-year epic and their Bruttian comrades.

Scipio faced them with the standard three-line array of *hastati, principes*, and *triarii*, comprising the survivors of Herdonea, his volunteers, and—outnumbering both—the men from Cannae. Polybius states that these three lines together were about equal in strength to Hannibal's veterans: probably then some 12,000–15,000 men. Unusually, the maniples of all three stood in file, each behind the one in front, instead of their regular checkerboard formation, with the *velites* in the spaces between the *hastati*. The indispensable Laelius led the Roman and Italian cavalry on the left wing, opposite Hannibal's Carthaginians, and Masinissa with the Numidian cavalry stood on the right opposite their countrymen and Tychaeus.

Hannibal's tactical plan can only be guessed. The aim was, perhaps, to disarray the legionaries with his elephants and his first two lines, neutralize or rout Scipio's cavalry with his own, and then deliver the finishing blow with his veterans. A suggestion that he really wanted Laelius and Masinissa to chase his own riders off the field, leaving his infantry free to take on Scipio's—in other words, to turn the Roman's superiority in cavalry against him—is less plausible. After all he could not be sure that Laelius's and Masinissa's riders would disappear indefinitely. Scipio's own battle plan was not much subtler. He would batter the opposing lines until they gave way; then, if fortune favored, his cavalry would crush Hannibal's and then join in against the enemy infantry.

So it turned out. For a start, Hannibal's elephants proved useless. The Roman and allied light troops goaded and terrified them into running amok, as at Ilipa. Some crashed into Hannibal's left wing just as Masinissa launched his charge, others fled down the lanes that Scipio had thoughtfully laid out between his maniples, and still others went straight into Hannibal's right wing, which Laelius promptly attacked. Both Punic wings were swept away. Meanwhile the Roman front line furiously engaged Hannibal's mercenaries until these were forced back into the ranks of the Carthaginians and Libyans behind. The second line had stayed in place rather than advance to reinforce the first—maybe part of Hannibal's plan, but if so, it backfired. Some enraged mercenaries turned round to fight their supposed comrades, and as the two Punic lines squashed together Scipio's hard-pressed *hastati* were reinforced by the *principes* to continue their attack. The Carthaginians and Libyans now managed to resist as vigorously as the aggrieved mercenaries, yet did no better. After heavy fighting, those in both lines not slaughtered by the Romans hurried backward toward where Hannibal himself stood with his veterans.

As the carnage, graphically described by Polybius, progressed in front of him, Hannibal waited. All the cavalry and elephants were off the field, and both armies' first two lines were in close combat. Only Scipio's *triarii* and their matching allied units, 3,000 or 4,000 men in all, remained disengaged—and the perhaps 15,000 veterans with Hannibal. Almost certainly he had time to swing these out—in one division or even in two like Scipio at Baecula—bypass the flanks of the combatants, and strike hard. As so often in this last campaign, Hannibal did not act. When the shattered mercenaries, Libyans, and even his fellow Carthaginians streamed toward his veterans, these leveled their spears to force them off to the sides and (it seems) into flight. This left Hannibal's army of Italy alone face to face with the legions.

Again his veterans did not move. Hannibal stood completely passive, allowing Scipio plenty of time to halt his own troops, remove the wounded, and reorganize his formations by ordering the *principes* and *triarii* to move out to left and right—much as at the Great Plains—and position themselves on either side of the *hastati*. With their front now more than doubled in extent, and with no reserves left, the men of Cannae and Herdonea and their comrades closed with Hannibal's veterans.

In a face-to-face slogging match against troops as seasoned as his own, without cavalry support or a waiting ambush, Hannibal doubtless knew that prospects for victory were thinning out. His elephants had disappeared like the men from his first and second lines (unless some of these had regrouped and been allowed to join the veterans). He had little hope of his cavalry being able to shake off their pursuers and come back to help. When cavalry did reappear behind him—under Laelius and Masinissa— he could not have been wholly surprised. Equally he was helpless to prevent their assaults on the veterans' rear breaking up his array as the battlefield became Cannae in reverse. Disdaining to throw his life away like his brother Hasdrubal, once the battle was clearly lost he rode away at full speed with a couple dozen companions. Behind him on the battlefield he left 20,000 of his men dead and nearly as many taken prisoner. Within forty-eight hours Hannibal was at Hadrumetum 200 kilometers away.

Carthage's last army was effectively annihilated. By contrast Scipio incurred 1,500 Romans and Italians killed and perhaps a thousand of Masinissa's men. Hannibal over the next several days gathered in what survivors he could, yet he knew that it was the end. He soon set off for Carthage, returning there after thirty-five years away, to urge negotiations.

In this closing campaign Hannibal's generalship was much inferior to his prime. Throughout he left initiative and maneuverability to Scipio, whose mastery of tactics and battlefield discipline he could not equal. Polybius, dutifully imitated by Livy, showers enthusiastic praise on his actions before and during the battle—offering peace to Scipio, placing the elephants in his front, holding back his third line to tire out the enemy—to conclude that the Carthaginian showed matchless skill in taking every available step for victory. In reality, none of the praised measures worked. The peace offer was foreseeably pointless. The elephants not only were as ineffective as their kin had regularly been against Romans but materially contributed to defeat by disrupting his cavalry. Worst of all, the Hannibal of Zama showed himself painfully static in tactics and bereft of the resourcefulness that had won him Trebia, Trasimene, and Cannae, when the war and he were young.

At Castra Cornelia a Roman fleet and a new supply convoy awaited Scipio. Better still, peace envoys came from Carthage once more. By then Syphax's tardy son Vermina had appeared somewhere in the hinterland with an army supposedly of some 16,000 horse and foot, but when Scipio sent off troops against him those forces were almost entirely annihilated. According to Livy this happened on December 17, the first day of the Saturnalia festival (he does not say where), but if the Roman calendar was somewhat out of kilter by 202, as is often surmised, the true date may have been during November. The main Roman army moved down at Tunes, from where Scipio dispatched his demands to Carthage.

His new terms were more punitive than those of 203, yet still did not touch on Carthage's self-government or even her possession of Libya. Nor did Scipio—or anyone at Rome afterward—call for Hannibal or his leading supporters to be handed over or even exiled. Along with restoring captives and delivering up deserters, Carthage had to become Rome's friend and ally, surrender her right to wage war outside Africa, seek Roman permission for any war within Africa, and pay an indemnity of 10,000 talents (sixty million *denarii*) over fifty years. The navy was to shrink to ten triremes—no quinqueremes—and war elephants were banned. Another clause, seemingly modest, would come to be explosive: the Carthaginians must restore to Masinissa all the territory and property once owned by him or his ancestors, "within the boundaries to be assigned." Scipio afterward demarcated the boundaries between Punic Africa and Masinissa's now united kingdom, but the wily king would find ways to extend them. Meanwhile there was to be a three-month armistice. During it the Carthaginians had to pay reparation for their plunder of the Roman transports—plainly a sore point with Scipio—to the fairly sizable sum of 25,000 pounds of silver. They must also provide grain and pay for his forces and yield as hostages a hundred young Carthaginians, no doubt from aristocratic families (we may wonder whether any were Barcids).

Even at this desperate stage and even with her general arguing for peace, not everyone at Carthage wanted to give in. In the senate Hannibal personally forced one Gisco (father or brother of the late Hasdrubal, maybe) off the dais to silence his opposition to the terms and then had to mollify the astounded and angry *adirim*—clearly many shared Gisco's continuing fever for war—by explaining that as a returned old soldier he was unversed in protocol and needed to ram home the absolute need for peace. Envoys were duly sent off to Rome, led not by a Barcid supporter but by one of Hanno the Great's younger associates, a Hasdrubal nicknamed obscurely "the Kid." After braving the winter sailing conditions, the Kid and his colleagues were nonetheless made to wait at Rome until late March or early April 201. Clearly the Romans were in no hurry to conclude matters. Indeed one of the new consuls, Gnaeus Cornelius Lentulus, brashly sought to take over the African command and with it the glory of terminating the war, until public common sense stopped him.

Finally given a Senate hearing, the Kid played the losers' usual card of deflecting blame. The war was all the fault of Hannibal and his faction; the right people (meaning his and Hanno's faction) had never been listened to; and Carthage ought not to be punished for the wrongdoing of a few. This disingenuous ploy led to no easing of the peace terms. Yet it would have an impact. One of the likely listeners was the senator Fabius

Pictor, probably already at work on his history of Rome and having his own family contacts at Carthage. Fabius would insist that not only Hanno's group but all her leading men had opposed Hannibal's war. However implausible, that claim is still often put.

When news that Rome had ratified the peace reached Africa, Scipio took his final measures. The Carthaginian navy, reportedly 500 ships large and small, was burnt to ashes in the gulf of Tunis within sight of the grieving city. He received Carthage's Roman war prisoners, as well as all deserters and runaway slaves (these for execution); the first installment of the war indemnity; and a prescribed number of hostages, who under the treaty terms would be replaced later by others and these in turn by still others, until the indemnity was paid off. He also delimited her borders with Numidia—by now he must have known Libya well, after all his ravages—before at last sailing laden with booty and glory to celebrate a grand triumph at Rome and take on the congratulatory added name of Africanus. The African booty on display in the procession included no less than 123,000 pounds of silver, while each legionary soldier received 400 *asses* as a bonus. The captive Syphax, according to Polybius, walked among the prisoners—a humiliation that Sophoniba had escaped by taking Masinissa's poison—and, Livy mentions, behind Scipio marched an ex-prisoner of war, a senator named Quintus Terentius Culleo. He ostentatiously wore the symbolic freedom cap of a manumitted slave, to mark his gratitude to the victorious general. Hannibal in his turn eventually gave up the generalship that he had held for twenty years, to retire (for the time being) into private life and watch his political foes regain their long-lost control of affairs.[6]

HANNIBAL'S WAR: ASSESSMENT

Appian makes the Romans claim that Hannibal had killed 300,000 people and destroyed 400 cities in Italy. Like a great deal else in Appian, the figures must be taken as exaggerated if not imagined, but undeniably the war had cost the Romans, their allies, and also the defectors dear. Whereas in 225 the register of Roman citizens was 273,000, the census of 204—carried out with exceptional thoroughness, covering even troops abroad—listed just 214,000, and even ten years later it had risen to only 243,000, although in both cases rebel Campanians still surviving were of course not counted. As mentioned earlier, in 209 twelve Latin colonies had said that they were too worn out to supply their troop and supply quotas. Great cities such as Capua and Tarentum and smaller ones too many to count were captured, looted, and punished with large-scale enslavements. The southern countryside suffered plunder and ravaging by both sides, which meant that rural populations were impoverished and often uprooted (if not put to the sword). Much the same misery befell Sicily, where not only did Agrigentum suffer its usual fate of being sacked but so did once-impregnable Syracuse. The freebooting desperadoes removed from Sicily to Bruttium in 210 were no doubt only the biggest and best-organized body of such persons produced by four years of Sicilian war. Spain, too, did not miss out on towns sacked, from Saguntum to Astapa; lands looted; and people made slaves.[7]

In Italy and Sicily at least, various recovery measures did start early, for instance, the push in 206 to encourage Italian farmers back to their land (Livy records the push but, unhelpfully, not whether it worked) and Valerius Laevinus's similar steps in Sicily four years earlier. By 204 the Latin recalcitrants had recovered enough to provide—with much complaining—doubled recruitment quotas, and in the same year the treasury started to repay, in installments, the money contributions made in 210. The *res publica populi Romani* could enjoy faster recovery, not only because its own territories (rebel Capua apart) were rarely invaded or ravaged after 217 but also thanks to the riches garnered from booty, prisoner sales, confiscated rebel property and territories—much of Capuan territory and of Bruttium became Roman state land, for example—and of course the Punic indemnity. But in a sign of improving Sicilian cultivation, so much Sicilian as well as Sardinian grain was imported to Rome in 202 that it left importing merchants frustratingly out of pocket.

Carthage and her African lands suffered much less until the last two years of the war. The eight Roman naval raids from 217 to 205 had done damage to several coastal areas but did not penetrate far beyond. Only Scipio's expeditions into Libya in 203 and 202—their details studiously vague in the sources—spread pain and fear more widely, yet they were short-lived by comparison with the relentless warfare in Italy from 217 to 203. The Romans sensibly avoided attacking Carthage directly, a city even stronger in its defenses than Syracuse. Certainly the war put Carthaginian finances under heavy strain: she poured money into fighting Rome on many fronts, as late as 205 lavishing funds as well as troops uselessly on Mago in his Ligurian enclave. Moreover her foreign trade must have been harmed by the raids and by Roman naval forces prowling out of Lilybaeum. All the same, Hannibal was probably right to laugh bitterly at his fellow aristocrats' groans and grumbles when they were called on to contribute to the first indemnity installment.

The war decided that Rome would be the mistress of the western Mediterranean and Carthage at best her compliant satellite. If there were discussions among Romans or Greeks on whether the result could have gone the other way, they have not survived. Polybius's only extant comment is that Hannibal foredoomed his enterprise by taking on Rome before he had properly subdued other regions—perhaps meaning the rest of Spain plus Gaul, maybe Numidia and Mauretania too. This notion is facile. Taking the time to conquer all of Spain and even the southern half of Gaul (not to mention the rest of North Africa) would have brought the general to old age, besides putting Rome very much on the alert, and all for limited or minimal benefit. Livy does judge Hannibal's decision not to march on Rome after Cannae as "the salvation of the City and the empire" and later depicts him lamenting that he had not; but he goes no deeper into the matter.[8]

In terms of resources Carthage could have defeated Rome. While Rome could draw on more than three-quarters of a million male citizens and allies for her armies and fleets, so could Carthage, with her Libyphoenician, Libyan, and Spanish allies and subjects. At the outset in 218, and at least down to the defeat of Hasdrubal in 207, she was able to field armies—and fleets—of similar strength. Punic finances were at least as well grounded as Roman, since they could fund forces and expeditions at least down to Mago in Liguria, and of course in Hannibal the state had a military genius with no Roman equal before Scipio Africanus. At one stage Carthage was allied with the premier military power of the Aegean world and had reduced the reach of Rome to peninsular Italy's center and north, some of Sicily, and the northeast coast of Spain—redoubts of resistance threatened at every point by Carthage or her allies. Failure and defeat were not preordained. They happened from miscalculations and wrong decisions, exploited by better Roman choices.

The worst miscalculation of all was to reckon that a sequence of heavy defeats would be enough to overturn Italians' support for their hegemon and compel the Romans to peace on Punic terms. Where Hannibal got this belief from is not obvious. Not against Pyrrhus, nor in the previous war with Carthage, nor during the Gallic invasion of 225 had Roman allies defected. He seems not to have made any advance soundings of Italian attitudes, even though he did sound out the Cisalpine Gauls. Perhaps he was told what he wanted to hear from Italian merchant sailors. Another serious flaw was the absence of a proper navy in 218, compounded by Carthage's constantly fumbled use of the naval resources she then created. True, even with a navy in being Hannibal would still have had to invade Italy overland—or run the unpleasing risk of the Romans intercepting his invasion fleet—but after that, properly handled fleets could have reinforced him as needed and could have countered Rome's more tellingly than actually happened. Even when grown to fighting size, Punic fleets performed hopelessly, above all if led by Bomilcar—although other commanders came close to his standard, for instance at the battle of the Ebro in 217 and in the clumsy attack in 203 on Scipio's fleet outside Utica.

On land, most though not all of the major mistakes were Hannibal's: in prime place, first his heavy losses of men between the Pyrenees and Cisalpine Gaul and then his refusals to march on Rome after Trasimene (even with a supporting fleet on its way) and again after Cannae. The strategies of sending Hasdrubal from Spain to Cisalpine Gaul and later Mago to Liguria were disasters preordained, no matter whether their purpose was to reinforce their brother a thousand kilometers to the south and separated from them by half a dozen Roman armies or just to draw away some of his tormentors (Hasdrubal certainly did so and suffered for it). These were Hannibal's decisions as chief general; Polybius rightly stresses that he was in charge of military policy in all theaters. In his later campaigns Hannibal's own once-sharp military skills seemingly lost their edge. He could not find a way to defeat Marcellus and Nero, did not discover and therefore did not exploit Nero's audacious absence in 207, took a year in Libya to collect and train an army that—his veterans apart—still proved substandard at Zama, and in that battle practiced the most uninspired tactics of his career against his younger and nimbler antagonist.

On the other hand, Hasdrubal's seven-year delay in obeying his marching orders was not Hannibal's doing, nor was the joint failure by the three generals in Spain to exploit to the maximum their shattering double victory over the elder Scipios in 211; nor again was Himilco's alienating treatment of Mottones in Sicily, which materially contributed to disaster there. Overall, Carthage's conduct of the war was dragged down by the second-rate (when not third-rate) abilities of virtually all of her other army commanders. Energetic and devoted to their cause though they were, the two Hasdrubals (the Barcid and the son of Gisco) proved quite unequal to their tasks. Mago the Barcid was both more energetic and still less capable—and Bomilcar with the navy and Himilco in Sicily made Mago look good by comparison. Even Hannibal's lieutenant and nephew Hanno, a vigorously effective subordinate at the crossing of the Rhône in 218 and on later errands, fell easy prey to the Romans when given his own army. Other capable lieutenants—Maharbal, Carthalo, the quartermaster Hasdrubal who helped to win Cannae—all vanished from the record by 209. One other, Mottones the non-Carthaginian, changed sides. And Hannibal was not well served at Zama by whoever were his subordinates.

According to Livy, he transferred the blame for his failure in Italy onto the authorities at home plus Hanno the Great's machinations, a defense still accepted by many well-wishers. Allegedly, he would have won the war if only the sufetes and *adirim* had supported him with proper reinforcements—not just the miserable few thousand in 215—instead of regularly dispatching forces to Spain, Sardinia, Sicily, and Liguria and leaving their premier general in their premier war theater to scrabble for local conscripts and unreliable allies. If true, it follows that Hannibal and his supporters were not in control at Carthage but were outdone, and repeatedly wrong-footed, by a more powerful faction—an assessment harking back in essence to Fabius Pictor. Thus it would be this supposed anti-Barcid faction that made Mago the Barcid commander of two of these other expeditions (to Spain in 215 and Liguria ten years later); appointed a Barcid kinsman, another Mago, as one of the Sardinia expedition's leaders in 215; all the while kept Hasdrubal the Barcid in overall command in Spain even though he kept disobeying its order to leave for Italy; and found no reason to replace their likely kinsman Bomilcar as admiral: in short, an anti-Barcid faction that paradoxically relied heavily on the Barcids.

It is equally flawed to see Hasdrubal son of Gisco as hostile to the brothers. If in 210–209 he had disagreements with Hasdrubal and Mago, so had they with each other; and after the catastrophe of the camps outside Utica early in 203, he and the Barcid faction at home were united in rallying their fellow citizens for a fresh effort. Hannibal's supposedly masterful opponents could not make their opposition heard even when all was lost. If anything, the mood at Carthage after Zama remained defiant, as Hannibal found when he shut Gisco up. In the speech Livy composed for Hasdrubal the Kid at Rome, the self-pitying claim that the Barcids' opponents had never been listened to is a sounder insight.[9]

Rome began the war overconfidently and badly, taking for granted that she would do the invading and then, when invaded, that Hannibal would fight with standard battle tactics and be beaten by the same. The resulting disasters forced on her the thoroughly untraditional strategy devised instead by Fabius Maximus, varied from 210 on by Marcellus's and Claudius Nero's aggressive harassment of Hannibal himself. At very great cost, it worked. Even before the southern Greeks began defecting in 212, the Romans had begun to claw back lost strongholds and territories. Then the fall of Capua confined Hannibal strategically under siege in southern Italy, an unstable bailiwick that from 207 shrank into southern Bruttium and made him irrelevant to the wider war. Yet, if bolder Roman decisions had been made in 218, they could have saved Italy from fifteen years on the rack. Had the Senate not aborted the planned expedition to Africa and instead recalled the one to Spain, even though the defeats at the Trebia and Trasimene might still have occurred, at the same time Carthage's own heartland would have been under invasion. Of course Sempronius Longus was very far from being a Hannibal, but (as just noted) all other Carthaginian generals were just as far, even his brothers.

A moderately competent invader could have put Carthage under enough threat to force Hannibal's early recall—and even had he then put paid to the invaders, he would have had to re-create the Punic navy and learn naval tactics before making any renewed venture against Italy.

Instead, Rome persisted with the Spanish expedition, which before 209 was essentially a sideshow. The usual defense for it is that for ten years it kept the Carthaginians in Spain from sending reinforcements to Italy; but Hasdrubal, year after year, showed marked unenthusiasm anyway for leaving Spain or even sending someone else, such as Mago. In any case, had he set out while Rome was invading Africa, his arrival in Cisalpine Gaul would have been counterbalanced—or checkmated—by a Carthage under Roman sea and land siege. Speculative as this is, it suggests that while Rome's persistence with Spain was certainly bold, replacing it with Africa would have been bolder and could have been decisive.

Two exceptional initiatives did mark Rome's conduct of the war: the republic appointing a twenty-five-year-old in 210 to take over the distant and by then disastrous Spanish theater, and then three years later Claudius Nero deciding to take a task force from his own army facing Hannibal to join Livius Salinator against Hasdrubal. Neither act on its own decided the war, but both tilted it further in Rome's favor: the first as the debut of Scipio Africanus, the second effectively reducing Hannibal from a menace to a nuisance. It was Rome's good fortune too that in commanders she did better overall than Carthage. Only Scipio was a military genius, but many others—Fabius, Marcellus, Gnaeus Scipio, Gracchus, Fulvius Flaccus, Laevinus, and Nero—were distinctly abler, despite lapses, than their Carthaginian opposites. Another advantage was the strength of Rome's bonds with her Italian allies. It took three shattering defeats for Hannibal to snap even some of the links, and even that did not prove enough. The Latins and other allies who stayed loyal bore the grinding load of war service to the end (save for the twelve recalcitrants in 209–204). Carthage could not match this doggedness. Three defeats in two years, even without any allied defections, drove her to seek terms.

Scipio's appointment in 210 had extra historical moment. For the first time in history a senior military command was entrusted to someone not an ex-consul or even ex-praetor (he was merely a former aedile). This was an advance on the practice of extending some consuls' and praetors' *imperium*—like that of the elder Scipios in Spain and Marcellus in Italy— beyond their year of office. Scipio's was one of many occasions where the Romans showed how flexible they could be with their revered institutions. The first, in 217, was to have Fabius Maximus elected dictator, not nominated by a consul, which was soon to be followed by the still more unprecedented elevation, through popular election again, of his master of horse to the same level. This nearly caused a catastrophe, but it did not deter the Romans from again having two simultaneous dictators, Junius Pera and Fabius Buteo after Cannae (one for the war, the other for replenishing the ravaged Senate: so no clash).

In 217 too, when the shock of Trasimene drove home the unprecedented gravity of Hannibal's invasion, a law was enacted that so long as there was war in Italy, any ex-consul could be elected as often as the People wished—a suspension of normal bans and conventions, clearing the way for the multiple consulships of Fabius, Marcellus, Fulvius, and Gracchus between then and 208. It also made possible what would normally have been odd and questionable: Fabius being chosen consul two years running (215–214) and Fulvius as dictator in 210 presiding over consular elections that returned him for 209 along with Fabius. This and the repeated extensions of *imperium* meant that trusted (if not always inspired) generals operated more or less continuously over several years: Scipio, the prime example again, held *imperium* as proconsul, consul, and once more proconsul from 210 until 201. It was a sharp contrast to the regular changes of consuls during the First Punic War and constituted a Roman way of matching the lengthy tenures of Carthaginian generals—although in this at least, Hannibal, with over twenty years of supreme command, outdid his Roman rival and conqueror.

PART FOUR

THE LAST CONFLICT

12

ROME, MASINISSA, AND CARTHAGE

ROME AND ITALY AFTER 201

The ravages of Hannibal's war were repaired for Rome during the first quarter of the new century. Romans and to a smaller (and decreasing) extent their Italian allies benefited from the steady flow of plunder, war indemnities, and provincial revenues after 200. Even though the state was at war in one land or another, and often in several at once, virtually without cease, none of the glorious and profitable eastern wars from 200 to 167 lasted more than four years, nor were occasional defeats in them catastrophes. In newly annexed Spain wars did grind on for years, often with setbacks and casualties—conscription for Spain became highly unpopular—but the scale was nothing like Hannibal's war. Citizen numbers began to rise again: 243,000 by 194, twenty years later 269,000, and by 164 a sharp rise to 337,000. In other words, by 174, a quarter-century after the peace with Carthage, the Roman citizenry—in raw figures anyway—was as numerous as in 225. These factors enabled the republic to maintain astonishing numbers of citizens serving in armies and fleets across much of the Mediterranean: between 200 and 168 never fewer than 33,000 even in a peacetime year, sometimes over twice as many during major wars.

The City's growth was marked by large-scale public works launched by various censors. Cato and his colleague Valerius Flaccus in 184 spent six million welcome *denarii* renovating its sewers; then an aqueduct in 179 and a much grander one in 143 multiplied the water supply. Meanwhile from the 190s to 170s colonies, Latin and Roman, were placed in Cisalpine

Gaul at new sites or added to old ones, as well as others elsewhere—
Saturnia in northern Etruria, for instance; Pisaurum on the Adriatic
south of Ariminum; Puteoli near Naples; and Paestum, Copia, and Vibo
Valentia in the south. These meant new opportunities for Roman and
Italian grantees, as did individual land grants in annexed Cisalpine territory in 173 and land in Samnium and Apulia (and maybe elsewhere)
allocated to army veterans soon after 201.

What benefited Romans and some Italians came at a cost to others,
especially ex-defectors. Capua, Tarentum, and the Bruttians lost much of
their lands to confiscations. The Samnites, Pentri excepted, had to accept
settler-veterans and then, after 180, nearly 50,000 deportees from the
Ligurian Apennines. Many Samnites migrated; Fregellae, a Latin colony
in southern Latium, complained to Rome in 177 about being swamped by
4,000 of them. Much earlier (in 199) another Latin city, Narnia in the
upper Tiber valley—one of the twelve defaulters from 209 to 204—
already found itself an equally unwilling host to arrivals from elsewhere,
and at Fregellae in 177 other unwanted newcomers were Paelignians,
neighbors of Samnium, whose homeland had been lastingly loyal to
Rome but who obviously saw opportunity beckoning in Latium. Rome
attracted thousands of migrants from nearby regions, affecting her Latin
kinfolk so painfully that these persuaded the Senate to order their missing residents home—12,000 in 187 and an unstated number ten years
later. But nothing could halt the growth of the City.

ROME THE MEDITERRANEAN SUPERPOWER

Victory over Carthage did not leave Rome with a longing for peaceful times.
The very next year, in 200, she was at war all over again: now with Macedon,
on the ground that Philip V (figure 12.1) was molesting her friends Athens,
Rhodes, and Pergamum. Philip's historic mistake in 215—allying with
Hannibal against Rome—now rebounded on him. Even after he was totally
defeated at Cynoscephalae in 197 and forced to give up his hegemonial
ambitions over Greece and the Aegean, he failed to shake off Roman suspicions; and when he died in 179 they were transferred to his son Perseus.

FIGURE 12.1
Philip V of Macedon, Carthage's ally.

The Second Macedonian War opened an extraordinary twelve-year period that transformed Rome from one of the Mediterranean's many leading states into its paramount power. The Seleucid Great King of the East, Antiochus III (figure 12.2), was crushed in 189 because his territorial ambitions clashed with the settlement of affairs that Rome had set up for the states of Greece and the Aegean. Her one-time allies the Aetolians, shortsightedly chafing at their meager returns from that settlement, had incited Antiochus and likewise paid a humbling price. For in 196 at a packed Isthmian Games in Corinth, the young and personable proconsul Titus Quinctius Flamininus, victor of Cynoscephalae, had staggered the Greeks by proclaiming Rome's bestowal of universal freedom on them: that is, freedom from any hegemony. Reality was of course different, whether or not the Romans wanted it. While Egypt remained a carefully loyal friend, the swarm of lesser Greek and barbarian states from the Adriatic to the shrunken Seleucid realm promptly transferred their hopes, fears, and endless squabbles to the new hegemon from the west.

With wars and other concerns to keep them busy in Cisalpine Gaul and Spain, the Romans avoided annexations east of the Adriatic, but could neither ignore the appeals and demands of their trans-Adriatic clients nor cure themselves of rancor toward Macedon. In the 180s and 170s the situation gradually soured. When Perseus continued his father's measures to restore the kingdom as a major eastern power, it ended with a Third Macedonian War from 171 to 167. His catastrophic defeat at Pydna in 168 by Lucius Aemilius Paullus, son of the consul slain at Cannae, in turn ended the ancient monarchy. Rome replaced it with a Macedon parceled out into four unhappy republics (which paid her a yearly tax).

This war and its aftermath brought the grimmer side of Rome's hegemony to the wider Greek world too. Cities, including some allies, were sacked by loot-hungry Roman armies or fleets. Rhodes and Pergamum, which had misguidedly tried to mediate peace, now paid for it with loss of territories and revenues—and threats of war. Because the Achaean League in southern Greece had shown less than impressive enthusiasm for Rome against Macedon, 1,000 leading Achaeans whom the Senate judged too unenthusiastic were shipped to Italy in 167 for indefinite detention. One of the victims—a neat irony of fate—was the future historian and admirer of Rome, Polybius. Fate dealt Epirus, Pyrrhus's homeland, a much more savage blow in return for some Epirotes' pro-Macedon sympathies: by order of the Senate, Aemilius Paullus's troops sacked seventy towns on a given day and took away 150,000 people to sell as slaves.

A no less dramatic portent of changing times had been given a year earlier, to the Seleucid Antiochus IV (notorious as the foe of the Maccabees of Judaea) when he was on the verge of making himself master of Egypt. Roman ambassadors met him on the shore of Eleusis, a seaside suburb of Alexandria, to deliver the Senate's decree that he should withdraw. He was granted no time for discussion—the chief envoy, Popillius Laenas, used a staff to draw a circle in the sand around him and told him to reply before moving from it. Both the Great King and the envoys knew of Pydna, fought a few weeks before. Antiochus obeyed. The Greek world was stunned.

Luckily for the Hellenistic states, Rome's high-handed petulance cooled. She paid the Seleucid realm only sporadic, if unhelpful, notice once it began to fall apart through internal strife and outside attacks (the Maccabees secured a token Roman alliance). Similarly intermittent attention was paid to Greece and Asia Minor. Still, most Greek leaders remained acutely aware of the danger of crossing Rome. The long-lasting Achaean leader Callicrates warned his countrymen in the 150s not to think of undertaking war, anywhere, without seeking Rome's advice. The unspoken addendum was that war was best avoided entirely. In Pergamum around 155 King Attalus II and his council—so he wrote in a surviving letter—decided against an attractive war against neighboring Galatia after a saner adviser noted that not consulting the Romans about it would give them a pretext for unfriendly intervention.[1]

After 150 some people flung aside this restrictive wisdom. The Macedonian republics in 149 welcomed a fake, or possibly bastard, son of Perseus as their ruler and reuniter, defeating and killing the praetor who intervened. The revived Macedon was short-lived: a year later "Philip VI" was overwhelmed, appropriately enough near Pydna, by Quintus Caecilius Metellus, son of Scipio Africanus's friend. Rome then took a momentous step. Now ruling many subject territories north and west of Italy, she imposed the same condition on Alexander the Great's ancient kingdom. It became her first annexation east of the Adriatic.

FIGURE 12.2
Antiochus III, the Seleucid Great King.

To Macedonia's south, the Achaean League took on more assertive leaders after the 300 surviving exiles came home in 151 and Callicrates died. Rome was distracted by wars in Spain and North Africa; the league chose to imagine itself once more a great power in Greece—to no benefit. Its war in 147 on a seceding Sparta, against Rome's wishes, ended the illusion. Metellus marching from Macedonia overwhelmed resistance; then in the fateful year 146 Metellus's successor, the consul Lucius Mummius, sacked and razed Corinth (where Roman envoys had been attacked) and abolished the league. He left its cities independent, partly thanks to the saving influence of Polybius, but—with the rest of Greece—under the supervision of the praetor governing Macedonia. In 133, when the last king of Pergamum bequeathed his wealthy realm to the Roman People, Rome's mastery of the Greek and Aegean world was confirmed for all to see.

ROME'S WESTERN PROVINCES AFTER 201

The end of Hannibal's war left unfinished business north and west of Italy. Cisalpine Gaul had to be subdued all over again; the new Spanish territories had to be organized. Subduing Cisalpina was complicated at first by the diehard skills of a Carthaginian officer, Hamilcar, who had stayed on as a freelance and helped the Insubres in 200 to capture Placentia (something that had eluded Hasdrubal). He even created a diplomatic incident when the Romans complained to a powerless Carthage. They did capture him three years later, completed the reconquest by 191, and then made it permanent by refounding Placentia and Cremona on the river Po and planting other Latin and Roman colonies over the Boian plains south of these, colonies such as Parma, Mutina, and Bononia. At the head of the Adriatic, among the friendly Veneti, was founded a large Latin colony, Aquileia, to guard the eastern approaches to Cisalpina. Land grants to individual Romans and Italians were made later, in 173, once again south of the Po. In the end the unfortunate Boii, like the Insubres in the northeast, were largely thrust out to live in the Alpine foothills.

The Ligurian communities of the northern Apennines suffered likewise, but it took much longer to break them. Roman commanders sometimes treated them savagely, as in 173 when the consul Popillius Laenas (the arrogant envoy's brother) let 10,000 believe that they would be leniently treated if they capitulated and then sold them all as slaves. Earlier, in 181–179, 50,000 were forced to migrate from their homes, most to Samnium in central Italy. Close to the Etruscan coast the Latin colony of Luca and the Roman Luna, both sizable, were founded to help control Liguria's decreasingly lawless highlands.

Having ended Carthage's rule over southern and eastern Spain, the Romans chose not to leave. The territories were populous, well developed, and (in the south) rich in silver and other ores. From 197 on two new praetors were elected every year to govern the provinces of Nearer and Further Spain, as they were termed, though at critical times a consul could come out as their superior, as Cato did in 195. Warfare was a regular event, for the Spaniards, unimpressed at receiving Roman overlords in place of Carthaginians, put up a great deal of resistance over several decades. The irrepressible Ilergetan lords Mandonius and Indibilis fought the generals who replaced Scipio until Indibilis was killed and his brother executed in 203. Resistance elsewhere climaxed in a total revolt of the new territories in 197, and this went on for years, despite Cato's victories in 195 (which he loudly publicized). When the provincials were finally subdued around 191, governors looked outside for fresh opportunities to win military glory and booty.

Beyond the Tagus and Ebro lived unconquered peoples, broadly termed Celtiberians (in the center and northeast) and Lusitanians (in the west), with still others beyond these, such as Hannibal's one-time foes the Vaccaei. The Celtiberians and Lusitanians, warlike and far from primitive, were nearly as prone to raid the Roman Spains for loot and renown as governors were to raid them. This set the scene for two decades of intermittent hostilities, until the praetors Quintus Fulvius Flaccus and Tiberius Sempronius Gracchus (sons of the generals who fought Hannibal) brought about peace with mutually respectful treaties. A quarter-century of fairly steady quiet ensued, although later ambitious and scruples-free consuls and praetors would provoke even worse wars. Even then Rome's influence over central Spain, Lusitania, and the north-west was never powerful or permanent until the early years of the emperor Augustus. Taxes, courts, and Italian immigrants stayed closer to the Mediterranean, where the border between the two provinces began just west of New Carthage to run northwest.

In the decades following 201 the Romans, by fair means and foul, took a great deal of wealth out of Spain. Livy's text, if trustworthy, supplies startling figures: down to 168, consuls and praetors carried home 5,900 pounds of gold (equating to 3.8 million or so *denarii*) and more than 333,000 pounds of silver (around twenty-eight million), plus Spanish coined money worth at least another million and a half. Some of the precious metals may have been from the provinces' mines, but all were presented to Senate and People as war booty. By Polybius's time the rich silver mines around New Carthage alone yielded 25,000 *denarii* a day to Rome, roughly nine million a year. Roman and Italian entrepreneurs flocked in to run the provinces' mining leases, digging deeper and farther than their Spanish and Punic predecessors and, as Diodorus records, showing profit-minded insouciance to the desperate suffering of their imported slave workers.[2]

From 205 governors levied what funds they wanted, including some mining output. Cato in 195 set up a more regulated extraction of mining revenues in the Ebro region; in 180–179 Gracchus and Fulvius reportedly institutionalized a range of taxes everywhere. Yet, with governors and soldiers effectively free to do as they liked, the provincials felt burdened enough by a 5 percent tax on their grain harvests to protest to the Senate in 171, and they protested too about continuing arbitrary exactions in both money and kind by military prefects. The Spaniards were given a sobering lesson in how Rome responded to inconvenient truths. The arbitrary practices were banned for the future (whether the ban worked is unknown), but the governors they accused of maladministration were only rapped on the knuckles. Meantime another phenomenon, rather predictable, presented itself in 171 too. Delegates from 4,000 sons of Spanish mothers and Roman soldier fathers—plainly Scipio's troops had not spent all their time warring—went to Rome seeking recognition. The Senate authorized them to settle at Carteia (near Gibraltar), a town thenceforth classified, mystifyingly, as a Latin colony "of freedmen." They, with Carteia's existing residents, became the first colony of Latins not born in Italy; many more would follow, not only in Spain, and with notable impact on Roman history.

New towns as well as new taxes marked Rome's rule, much as they had marked Barcid rule. Tarraco, the elder Scipios' work, developed into the Nearer province's capital, while the younger Scipio in creating Italica in 205 gave Roman and Italian settlers their first dedicated Spanish foundation. Other towns too were founded on governors' initiative: Gracchurris established by Tiberius Gracchus on the middle Ebro for loyal Spaniards—he also refounded Iliturgi in the south, or so that center later claimed—and Corduba on the middle Baetis by Marcus Claudius Marcellus, grandson of Hannibal's tormentor and twice governor of Further Spain, with both Roman and Spanish settlers. Corduba became Further Spain's capital. Then in 138 the consul Decimus Junius Brutus, closing off another round of Lusitanian wars, founded a city on the Mediterranean coast near restored Saguntum, probably again with Romans and Spaniards and with an auspicious name: Valentia, meaning "Strongpoint." Fifteen years later another consul, Quintus Caecilius Metellus (son of Macedonia's annexer), finally subdued the Balearic islands and planted Roman citizen colonies in Majorca with names once again auspicious and enduring, Palma and Pollentia ("Palm" of victory and "Fruitfulness").

Other Roman influences took hold during the second century. From very early on Roman governors applied Roman legal usages where they felt it suited. In January 189, a small bronze tablet records, Aemilius Paullus, the future victor of Pydna, then praetor in Further Spain, decreed freedom for the inhabitants of Turris Lascutana, north of Gades, from neighboring Hasta, which had counted them as slaves even though they possessed (and now kept) their own town and land. A century later, Contrebia Belaisca, a country town near the middle Ebro, recorded on another bronze Latin inscription how its senate, praetor, and magistrates arbitrated a dispute about water rights between nearby villages, a verdict confirmed by the provincial governor. Contrebia's officials all bore proper Celtiberian names, but the appeal that Roman forms of law and local government had, even for provincials a long way from Tarraco, is plainly shown.

Sicily was also open to Roman influences without forfeiting its old cultures. With the fallen kingdom of Syracuse part of the province, Valerius Laevinus (it seems) applied island-wide Hiero's efficient system for taxing agriculture—his famous "one-tenth" levy in kind—and the Sicilian grain tithe became crucial for supplying Rome's constantly active armies. A pasturage tax was levied, as well as customs dues (5 percent in Cicero's day) at Syracuse and other ports. Even with all these exactions, the island prospered. During the second century rich Romans and Sicilians were able to build up large estates to meet the demand for foodstuffs, using ever-larger numbers of slaves. Imported mainly from the east, though other Roman wars must have contributed (including the Third Punic War), these were as usual harshly exploited—so harshly that Sicily suffered massive slave rebellions twice in the last decades of the century, also crushed harshly. Nonetheless the island's productivity was maintained, while its Roman population grew and Latin or Roman status was granted widely.

Sardinia and Corsica were not so amenable. Repeated risings punctuated the second century on both islands; the Romans countered with repeated harshness. Tiberius Gracchus, who had settled the Celtiberian war on intelligently mild terms, handled rebel Sardinians differently two years later—he killed or captured 80,000 of them, by his own boast anyway. The captives sold as slaves were plentiful enough to produce a proverb, "Sardinians going cheap, each worse than the next." Gracchus's younger son was fighting Sardinian rebels half a century later still. Yet the island became another important granary for Rome, and its towns prospered. Corsica interested Romans less; they occupied the coastal towns and passed most of the last two centuries BC in intermittent fights with the defiant peoples of the interior.[3]

CARTHAGE AFTER THE WAR

Zama and the peace discredited the Barcid faction, not surprisingly, even if Hannibal may have continued as general for a year or two more. A late Roman report casually mentions him occupying his unemployed troops— maybe Zama's survivors—in planting olive trees. By 196, however, a group that Livy calls "the class [ordo] of judges" was in full and unethical control of the state. He can hardly mean anything but the Court of 104, once the terror of failed generals but after 237 Barcid-tamed. Most of its members, like most other officials and magistrates, must have owed their judgeships to Barcid backing, some probably through political bargains to keep potential critics quiet. Now even once-friendly fellow aristocrats could feel free from Barcid pressure and aim to feather their own familial nests. Nonetheless Hannibal and supporters still loyal to him were too strongly based to be attacked. Instead of finishing up on a cross or banished, he retired into private life to watch the judges make up for lost time.[4]

Their dominance lasted half a decade, marked by a rising tally of greed and incompetence. State finances went into a nosedive. As early as 199, when that year's indemnity installment was sent to Rome, fifty of the 200 talents' worth of silver were found to be adulterated with base metal; the embarrassed envoys had to borrow from Roman moneylenders to make up the amount (no doubt at high interest). By 196 so much was being raked off Carthage's revenues that a special tax was mooted to fund the coming year's installment. Attempts to prosecute delinquent officials— many or most of them probably judges, since citizens could hold several positions simultaneously—foundered for obvious reasons. Then a quarrel

FIGURE 12.3
The "Hannibal quarter" on Byrsa hill, Carthage: twentieth-century excavations.

broke out with the Numidian king Masinissa, most likely over disputed boundaries.

With popular feeling running high, Hannibal sought and won election as sufete for 196–195 (the Punic year, like the Phoenician and Egyptian, began in late spring or in summer). Unresisted by whoever was his colleague, he trumped the judges by using the *ham* to legislate abolishing their lifetime tenure. Henceforth a judge would be elected for one year at a time and could not be reelected for the next, a reform that most probably took effect at the elections for 195–194. This opened the way for an entirely new roster of judges, many no doubt on his side. He then carried out a full review of Carthage's much-abused finances to claw back all the thieved funds he could and set revenues on a secure footing. Just four years later, the republic could offer to pay off the entire remaining indemnity—forty years' worth, equivalent to forty-eight million *denarii*—in one lump sum.

This Barcid resurgence was brief. Hannibal's furious enemies colluded with their Roman senatorial friends to force him into exile after his sufeteship ended. He never saw Carthage again. For seven years he served Antiochus III, first as a (largely disregarded) military adviser against Rome and then, bizarrely, as a naval commodore in the eastern Mediterranean in 190 against a Rhodian fleet—which crushed his; then from 188 to 183 he moved from one lesser eastern kingdom to another, until driven to suicide in Bithynia to avoid being seized by the still vengeful Romans. At Carthage the Barcid faction disappeared after 193, though some members perhaps took on a different guise. Some form of competitive politics did last till the 150s, suggesting again that the judges' old domination had gone. In this and in his financial reforms Hannibal served Carthage well—much better in fact than in his twenty-two years as generalissimo.

Suicide in 183 delivered Hannibal to history and legend. The legend soon overshadowed the history: it focused on a boyhood oath of hatred; epic elemental struggles against Alpine snow, ice, and savages; amazing victories against superior numbers; the one-eyed general on his one surviving elephant; the frenetic but foiled March on Rome in 211; and the poison ring that ended it all in a Bithynian villa. Having finally removed him, the Romans with their Greek admirers began to respect him (of course some, notably Scipio Africanus and Polybius, always had). Roman schoolboys for centuries would apply their rhetorical lessons to showpieces urging him to march, and not to march, on the City after Cannae. Juvenal satirized him as an exemplar of the folly of grand ambitions. Roman and Greek historians in turn were ready to accord him a tempered greatness—cruel, full of faithlessness, yet charismatic and almost awe-inspiring. It made him, too, a worthy enemy for Scipio to crush. Modern times often view him in a different but still almost legendary guise: as one of history's greatest commanders; the exemplar of surprise tactics, unpredictable maneuver, and annihilating envelopment; and a continuing inspiration to military academies—sometimes even the champion of Hellenistic cultural values against Roman crudities. As we have seen, none of these views, ancient or modern, offers a complete—still less an accurate—verdict.

Hannibal was also an exemplar of history's might-have-beens. Had he taken Carthage to victory over Rome, his leadership skills marshaling the potential of Africa, Spain, and Italy could have achieved for his city the rocketlike rise to eastern Mediterranean hegemony that Rome, instead, achieved by 188. Not only the Romans' grit and resilience but her and Carthage's mistakes and limitations too prevented it—above all their failure with the navy, their lack of other properly talented generals, and more than one of his own strategic decisions.

With no fleet or large army to maintain, with Rome's favor constantly if sometimes painfully cultivated, and with her advantages of position and enterprise, Carthage made a steady return to prosperity. In refusing her full-repayment offer in 191 for political reasons—the yearly indemnity and the hostages associated with it usefully emphasized who had won the Hannibalic War—Rome may have done her a favor, for paying 8,000 talents in one go would surely have strained her reviving resources. Her offer in the same year of a million bushels of wheat and half a million of barley was declined as a gift; instead the Romans insisted on paying the going price, a tidy amount.

Scattered archaeological finds suggest a vigorous commercial life—second-century Punic coins found in Illyria, a merchant making his mark at Istrus (sometimes called Histros) on the Danube beside the Black Sea, another at a coastal station in the Red Sea, and Punic black-figured pottery postdating the year 200 found in Spain, Sicily, and Italy. On the southeastern slope of Byrsa hill, a new residential and business quarter was created early in the century, perhaps thanks to Hannibal's reforms (hence its nickname today, the "Hannibal quarter"; figure 12.3). Comfortable stone buildings housed ground-floor shops, upper-level apartments, and underground cisterns for rainwater, along a grid of rammed-earth streets. The site, destroyed in 146 and covered by rubble from later Roman building on Byrsa, thus survived for recent rediscovery. Then, probably in the 150s, came the ambitious refurbishment (or possibly creation) of the famous artificial ports below Byrsa.

Around 190 the Roman playwright Plautus not only made a small-scale Carthaginian merchant the title character of his comedy *Poenulus* (naming him Hanno, predictably) but gave him some lines actually in Punic. Hanno's fairly sympathetic role, searching for and finally finding his kidnapped daughters, suggests that Roman audiences within a generation after Hannibal's invasion could follow a bit of Punic and see ordinary Carthaginians as open to cheerful teasing rather than lasting hate. The links between Punic and Roman aristocrats, and Carthage's carefully continued services to her ex-enemy, are other signs that relations could thaw somewhat as Hannibal's war receded in time.[5]

MASINISSA AND CARTHAGE AFTER 201

This was not to the liking of the ambitious king of Numidia. The wiliest ruler of his age, Masinissa first unified Numidia and then spent fifty-three years developing and extending it (figure 12.4). Although Syphax's son Vermina was for a time ensconced in an enclave (maybe Syphax's old capital, Siga, in the far west) and even made his peace with Rome, his lordship too was eventually absorbed into a Numidia that stretched from the borders of Libya 1,000 kilometers west to the Mauretanian border at the river Mulucha and from the Mediterranean down to the beginnings of the Sahara. Masinissa lived to be ninety, vigorous and calculating to the end, consolidating Numidia from a mosaic of widely spread and often fractious peoples into a single enduring monarchy.

Massinissa.
(Rom, Capitolinisches Museum.)

FIGURE 12.4
Masinissa, Musei Capitolini, Rome.

The peoples and minor kings in Numidia were not equally keen on being unified. Syphax's family remained powerful and (predictably) aggrieved; around 152 a grandson, with the unexpected Persian name Arcobarzanes, went over to the Carthaginians with a sizable body of armed followers. Earlier, around 165, Masinissa obtained Carthage's leave to pursue a rebel lord named Aphther and his followers through the Emporia region, though whether he caught them is not recorded. In 150 again, two of his own vassals would defect to Carthage with their horsemen. To reinforce his and his dynasty's position, Masinissa had to develop prosperity at home and his prestige abroad. For prestige nothing matched Greek culture and connections: so he fostered friendly relations with Egypt, Rhodes, and the sacred island of Delos (which honored him with statues as a reward for gifts). His sons Micipsa and Mastanabal became noted for their knowledge of Greek literature, Mastanabal also for his legal learning—and, as an inscription list records, for his chariot team's victory at Athens's Panathenaic festival in 166. Micipsa's forte was philosophy; possibly he was acquainted with a young Punic thinker,

Hasdrubal, before the latter left home around 162 for Athens, a name change to Cleitomachus, and greater prospects.

Masinissa had no animus against Carthaginians. He had been educated there in his youth, probably his brother Naravas had taken a sister of Hannibal's as his bride, and more recently an uncle had married a niece of Hannibal's. One of his own grandsons would be a general at Carthage in her final war with Rome. Punic was the language of second-century Numidian official inscriptions and coins, and Carthaginian names were given to members of his family, like his son Mastanabal. But to increase Numidia's wealth he also needed to aggrandize his territories. The only ones worth taking were Carthage's.[6]

The peace of 201 had entitled Masinissa to all lands once possessed by his forebears. Very usefully, neither the lands nor the forebears were specified. He could argue that originally the Carthaginians had held none of Libya outside their walls (the Massyli had not either, but that was not a detail to worry him). He began prodding her in 196 as mentioned, and by 193 the dispute was bad enough to bring over a Roman embassy led by the king's friend and benefactor Scipio Africanus. Livy unconvincingly dates the Aphther episode now and has the king harrying the Emporia region soon afterward, but Polybius's date of thirty years later is much likelier. The earlier dispute more likely concerned some of western Libya—for instance, the Theveste region, conquered only half a century before. Scipio's embassy avoided giving a verdict, thus (it seems) maintaining the status quo, no doubt to Masinissa's frustration. Scipio had determined what the Punic–Numidian borders were in 201 and would scarcely be minded to see them changed only eight years later.

In 183 or close to that year Scipio died, in voluntary exile away from Rome under pressure from his rancorous political foes—Cato among them. Thus, by a historical irony, he suffered a similar though gentler humiliation to the one that had befallen Hannibal twelve years before (as we have seen); by another irony, both men died around the same time. Scipio was Rome's greatest general before Julius Caesar and Caesar's rival Pompey. Like Caesar, and unlike Hannibal and Pompey, he never lost a battle. His armies reached a level of precision and maneuverable skill beyond even Hannibal's and not reached again for more than a century. The golden glow that enfolds him in the ancient sources—Polybius admired him, Livy makes him a showpiece of Roman virtue much like the fourth-century paradigm Camillus, and for the epic writer Silius he is a chivalric nonpareil—does not completely overpaint his capacity for ruthlessness: the Astapa holocaust and the night attack on the enemy camps at Utica could not be hidden. Nevertheless his contribution to winning the Second Punic War and to mastering the west for Rome outdid every other Roman's.

In 181, with Scipio dead, Masinissa seized another tract of Punic territory (perhaps the same one), but another embassy from Rome in effect made him give it up: Livy writes merely that the envoys secured peace for Carthage with both Rome (this must mean by confirming their peace treaty) and Masinissa, but nine years later the Carthaginians complained to Rome that he had again occupied the same area plus others—more than seventy towns and strongholds in all. The Senate instructed the king's envoy, his son Gulussa, that Rome would not tolerate such seizures or any changes to the existing boundaries. The snub plainly forced Masinissa to curb his predatory instincts afresh. Rome was equally disappointingly skeptical of his diplomatic machinations. When in 174 he wrote that Carthage was dealing secretly with Perseus of Macedon, and again when, via Gulussa two years later, he direly denounced her as building a war fleet, the tepid Roman reaction warned him that he was pushing his special relationship rather too far.

Livy describes the king's calculations at the outbreak of the Third Macedonian War in notably cold terms. If Rome won, he would be secure but with no prospect of expansion, because Rome would shield Carthage; contrastingly, if Rome lost, all of Africa would be his. This description is not a later concoction, for Rome won and yet Numidia did soon expand, at Carthage's expense. Instead Livy, using Polybius or some other informed source, is plausibly reproducing the Senate's assessment in 172 of their unsentimental ally. An episode four years later confirms it. Masinissa, via yet another son, pushily reminded the Senate how much support he had given Rome in the war just ended (soldiers, grain, elephants), averred that his kingdom was really Rome's possession, and asked to be allowed to come to pay his respects. He also wanted the Senate to make the Carthaginians send to Rome one Hanno son of Hamilcar (probably a personal enemy), to replace an existing hostage. He was put firmly in his place: denied permission to visit and told that the Senate did not select hostages at someone else's behest.[7]

MASINISSA VERSUS CARTHAGE, 162–152

For thirty-three years after 201, therefore, Rome treated her ex-enemy Carthage with rather surprising considerateness. Masinissa, her official ally, was repeatedly stopped from aggrandizing at Punic expense. Yet within a few years this balanced attitude tilted, and not in Carthage's favor.

The flimsy surviving accounts—scattered Polybian excerpts, Livy's epitome, Plutarch, and the sometimes suspect summary by Appian—do not make clear why. Carthage had been no less zealous than Numidia in lavishing wheat and grain on Rome and her armies down the decades, and the Senate had not taken Masinissa's allegations seriously. Yet around 162 he got away with seizing the Emporia region, occupying its countryside first and then calling on Rome to adjudicate ownership, as did the Carthaginians too. Even though he had previously recognized Punic possession by asking leave to pursue Aphther—not to mention that Emporia, far to the east of Libya, lay farther still from Numidia—nevertheless the Senate declared him the owner. It then piled insult on injury by instructing Carthage to pay Masinissa 500 talents, the income that he supposedly had foregone over the year or more of the dispute. Theveste's region, which lay between Numidia and the new acquisition, either was included tacitly (if so, the Senate was defining Emporia very elastically) or more probably was afterward handed over to him in 157 when—says a one-sentence report in Livy's epitome—Roman envoys settled yet another land dispute. Theveste pretty certainly was in the king's hands by 152, when he grabbed the Great Plains and the Thusca district still nearer to Carthage. All this reduced Scipio's original boundary-settings to nonsense.[8]

Impatience with Numidia, therefore, had faded as irritation with Carthage grew. It was partly at least due to her reviving prosperity, particularly visible in the work on the artificial ports but also in her wide-ranging trade. Letting Masinissa wrench territories away was a neat way of impairing her at no cost to Rome, an exercise in tune with Rome's hardened mid-century international attitudes. Even a decade after Pydna the Romans could still act harshly to suit what they considered their interests: thus in 157 senators judged that Roman character was suffering badly from too much peace, so a war in Dalmatia, north of the now obedient Illyrians, would be a good thing. In mid-century Spain, Roman praetors and consuls thought little of breaking sworn agreements with the free Spaniards or attacking them without provocation for booty and slaves and massacring many who had surrendered. Most of the perpetrators avoided punishment. Favoring Masinissa against Carthage fit the same pragmatic pattern. Later writers then found it easy to generalize, wrongly, that Rome had taken this line from 201 on.

Appian has a story of Masinissa in Spain with a son in 153, helping the Romans in their new Celtiberian war and by his absence tempting Carthalo, a Carthaginian territorial general or "boetharch," into raiding Numidian-occupied Libya. Envoys from Rome turn up to adjudicate, with secret orders to favor the king, but they merely arrange a ceasefire and then vanish. None of this is believable. No earlier source corroborates Appian, whose own fuller narrative elsewhere on these Spanish wars makes no mention of Masinissa. Even less believably, the story shows Carthage breaking the treaty of 201 twice over—she wages war without consulting Rome and against Rome's ally—yet drawing no fire. The item is either another of Appian's many confused fancies or a Roman invention. The aggressive initiative was firmly Masinissa's.

When he next moved, probably in 152, it was to seize areas of Carthage's Libyan heartland: the Great Plains along the middle Bagradas river, site of Scipio's victory in 203, and the Thusca region with fifty towns centered on the city of Mactar. These may well have been the same lands that he had been balked of in 172. In practice they comprised virtually all of western Libya including Sicca and Zama—leaving to Carthage, at best, only the intervening region of Gunzuzi around the major city of Thugga. This was barely a hundred kilometers from Carthage. With a new Roman arbitration embassy on the way, including Cato and probably another eminent ex-consul, Publius Scipio Nasica (descendant of Africanus's uncle Gnaeus), the wily monarch showily retired from the disputed area. He had no need to worry: Cato and company pronounced in his favor. The Carthaginians' bitter complaint that they were the wronged party was carefully ignored. In later times stories were made up to sugarcoat the business—at Carthage the envoys supposedly were threatened by a furious mob stirred up by the sufete Gisgo (a tale blatantly modeled on the attacks on Scipio's spokesmen in 203); the Carthaginians were already warring against Masinissa (with not only an army but a fleet too); and they refused to stop. Not a word of this is credible, save maybe that one sufete in 152 was named Gisgo.

Forced to acquiesce, the Carthaginians knew that this grab would not be the king's last grasp. If still theirs, Gunzuzi now formed a tempting salient between the Great Plains and Thusca. If not, there were other parts of Libya still under their rule. They resolved to react differently next time.[9]

13

THE TRIUMPH OF ROME

CARTHAGE'S NUMIDIAN WAR

Political life at Carthage had become more open and more flexible by the 150s than ever before, even if it can be viewed only through Appian's erratic historical lenses. Cramming the politics of four decades into ten lines, he offers three factions: one pro-Rome, with Hanno the Great at its head; another, pro-Masinissa, under a Hannibal nicknamed "the Starling"; and a "democratic" third group led by Hamilcar, nicknamed "the Samnite"—conceivably his father had been one of Hannibal's Italian officers—along with the Carthalo from the tale of the Punic raid into Numidian Libya. Appian (as usual) must be read with caution. For one thing, Hanno the Great must have gone to his grave long before. Not that Appian mentioned him when writing about the Second Punic War—instead he lowers Hanno and his feeble faction down to these decades, mentions it and him once, and then forgets about both. Even minus Hanno, a supposed pro-Roman group existing simultaneously with a pro-Numidian one is suspect: it would have had practically the same policies. Perhaps a group championing good postwar relations with Rome had existed for some decades earlier, as the aristocrats who got rid of Hannibal with Rome's help would have formed its core. Close, indeed subservient, relations with Rome paid off after 195, as shown above: down to 168 she kept Masinissa on a leash. Once her attitude changed, however, a pro-Roman policy would be virtually identical to a pro-Masinissa policy.

Appian's remaining factions raise questions too (assuming he has not simply made them up). If one supported Masinissa in foreign relations and the other supported "democracy" at home, that need not logically pit them against each other. Likely enough one group did advocate good relations with the king through thick and thin—an appeasement policy, giving him what he wanted each time and hoping he would not come back for more. Inexorably, its standing must have waned when losing Emporia was followed by losing Theveste and after that the Great Plains and Thusca—even if constantly turning the other cheek to the king continued to appeal to some who feared what could happen if it were not turned.

The "democrats" by contrast enjoyed greater popularity if their epithet means anything. Yet such a term covers internal politics, not foreign policies. In any case, before 153 there was no call by anyone to resist the city's relentless neighbor with force. Every Carthaginian, democrat or otherwise, knew that that would range the Romans wrathfully on Masinissa's side. The "democratic" hue of Hamilcar's and Carthalo's faction should imply that they backed fuller participation in state affairs by ordinary citizens in the *ham*, against opponents insisting on the old supremacy of the *adirim* or, as in Aristotle's time, the *adirim* and sufetes in collaboration. That recalls Hannibal's challenge to the judges' oligarchy forty years before and would make the "democrats" the heirs of the old Barcid faction, even if no Barcids themselves survived. For dealing with Masinissa, however, they like any opponents must have looked to Rome, at any rate down to 168. After that, maybe they did talk of resisting him—but if they did, nothing came of it for seventeen years.[1]

Masinissa's successful land-grab in 152 envenomed Carthage's political life. Hamilcar's and Carthalo's opponents were cornered. Any renewed call to humor him looked not only farcical but treacherous. The democratic faction—now more like a strident nationalist movement—was soon able to have forty of them exiled, among them no doubt the Starling himself (who is never heard of again). Citizens were made to swear an oath never to recall them and never to raise even the question of recall. Appian implies that all this was done through the *ham*. No doubt the democrats' grip on the *adirim* was less firm, though getting rid of opponents must have helped. Their action, all the same, was a spectacular own goal.

Quite predictably the banished men fled to Numidia, giving the king just the wedge he wanted. Not only were his sons Gulussa and Micipsa refused entry to Carthage when they came to demand the exiles' restoration, but—icing on the cake—Hamilcar the Samnite took it into his head to ambush Gulussa's party on the journey home. He killed some, but not the prince, and Masinissa had his pretext. Eighty-eight years old, vigorous (one of his wives had just borne him another son) even if toothless, he arrived with 52,000 men to besiege a Carthaginian town that Appian calls "Horoscopa," probably in spring 151. Horoscopa is unknown otherwise but could be a distortion of Thubursicu Bure (modern Teboursouk), in fertile country near Thugga, if the Gunzuzi region was still Carthage's. A strategic gain in itself, it was a pawn in a bigger game too. The Carthaginians had readied an army, as the king no doubt knew—it could scarcely be hidden while being recruited, trained, and equipped. If they now sent it out to fight, the treaty of 201 would be broken.

Masinissa, and surely the Carthaginians too, knew that the Romans were on alert. The eighty-two-year-old Cato had returned from Africa infuriated at the prosperity he found at Carthage and in the Libyan countryside. He made up his mind that Hannibal's city, the enemy of his youth, was a menace once more and had to be dealt with. Famously, he showed three-day-old African figs to an astonished Senate to dramatize how fast a Punic fleet could strike at Rome; even more famously, he closed every speech, whatever the topic, by opining that "Carthage ought not to exist" (later generations rephrased it into *Carthago delenda est*—Carthage must be destroyed). That he lyingly used locally grown figs (a revisionist modern view) assumes that his fellow senators were easily fooled—or wanted to be. Yet at first Cato made little headway, partly because his fellow envoy Publius Scipio Nasica opposed his demands (even after Cato brandished figs) and probably too because the Carthaginians did seem resigned to being Masinissa's permanent prey. But in 151 war in Libya galvanized the debate and turned it round. Polybius indicates that the Senate decided that fighting Carthage was inevitable: all that Rome needed was a plausible pretext.[2]

The Carthaginian army against Masinissa was led by another boeth-arch named Hasdrubal. He and his "democrat" allies must have reck-oned that if Masinissa could be defeated quickly—better still, captured or killed—an accommodation could be reached with Rome despite the treaty breach and that would free Carthage from further harassment. The risk was great. Plainly they believed that passiveness was worse. The core of the army, 25,400 citizen horse and foot, was joined on the march by about the same number of Libyan recruits; many Libyans were not happy about exchanging Carthage's rule for Numidia's. It was also about now that two of the king's cavalry leaders, Hagasis and Suba, decamped with 6,000 men to Hasdrubal. Arcobarzanes and his fighters perhaps came in too. The boetharch's confidence climbed when his opponent stopped besieging Horoscopa to retreat into nearby hill country.

There Masinissa received an honored visitor, a Roman military tribune seeking elephants for warfare in Spain: Scipio Nasica's cousin Publius Cornelius Scipio Aemilianus, the adoptive grandson of Africanus and therefore the king's hereditary friend and patron. With him came his friend, the Achaean ex-hostage Polybius (figure 13.1), who had the good fortune to enjoy a lengthy conversation (or more than one) with the ancient king. That probably occurred in the aftermath of the battle in which Masinissa decisively shattered the Punic army.

Hasdrubal's beaten troops fled to their camp on nearby heights, from where their commander appealed to Scipio to broker terms. The tribune was not minded to upset the victor. In effect, Carthage through her boetharch agreed to be punished for being victimized. She promised fur-ther territorial cessions and a 1,000-talent indemnity (but taking back Hannibal the Starling and his fellow exiles, the nominal origin of the quarrel, was not mentioned). Yet, because the boetharch, honorably enough, refused to hand over the Numidian deserters, the parleys collapsed. Trapped on the heights with summer wearing on, his army underwent torments of starvation, sickness, and mounting deaths—a nightmare recalling that of Spendius's rebels at the Saw ninety years before. In the end Hasdrubal capitulated. He now had to hand over the deserters and promise that Carthage would take back the exiles and pay a far bigger indemnity. The agreement was promptly broken once his surviving troops, unarmed, started out for Carthage. The vengefully treacherous Gulussa fell on them; only a few made it to safety. One who did (unfortunately for his city) was Hasdrubal.

ROME REACTS

Throughout this disastrous campaign Rome had not intervened. No new embassy put in an appearance. There were plenty of regular sources to keep her informed—merchants plying the African trade, Carthaginian aristocrats with Roman friends, members of Masinissa's court, traveling Greeks. In similar ways word reached Carthage about Rome's hardening attitude, and then came news of the disaster inland. Both the *ham* and the *adirim* revolted against the discredited "democrats," condemning all to death. That was the end of Carthalo, Hamilcar the Samnite, and (if he ever existed) Gisgo. The only leader to escape, the incompetent but agile boetharch, established himself somewhere in the hinterland with what forces he could pull together. Masinissa chose not to assail him or his city, nor even to send to the Carthaginians to demand surrender. He knew how strong their city's defenses were, hoped perhaps that a Punic push for peace would follow the overthrow of the "democrats," and—above all—wanted to see what the Romans would do. What they did was more, and worse, than he expected.[3]

Carthage's new authorities sent an abject embassy to Rome, probably early in 150 as soon as sailing became feasible, to offer explanations, announce the punishments, and—in effect—promise not to reoffend. The envoys found the Senate's mind made up and hostile. Polybius stresses that the Romans had been waiting only for a plausible pretext to appease foreign opinion. Now they had one: the treaty of 201, shattered. Who supported Cato's famous demand that "Carthage ought not to exist" and who joined Scipio Nasica against it is unknown, except that another Cornelius, Lucius Lentulus, who had been consul in 156, likewise opposed the bellicose octogenarian while other, unnamed leading men backed Cato. Among these must have been one or both of the new consuls (consuls now entered office on January 1), Titus Quinctius Flamininus, son of the liberator of Greece, and Manius Acilius Balbus, for there was no strong opposition to the truculent line that the Senate now took. Scipio Aemilianus, now returned from Spain, though a junior senator was no doubt another hard-liner.

First the envoys were told that they had not explained matters satisfactorily. When they asked what penalties they would incur if judged to have acted wrongly—of course they knew that the Romans did so judge, and they expected penalties like those in 152—the answer instead was curtly delphic: "The Carthaginians must give satisfaction to the Romans." This pronouncement, taken home by the frustrated envoys, perplexed and frightened the sufetes and *adirim*. They sent a second embassy, surely selecting for it the most manifestly pro-Roman aristocrats possible, to ask what that satisfaction should be. These envoys received a flat statement even more opaquely terrifying, "The Carthaginians know perfectly well," and were sent home. It may have been now, not in 152 as Livy's epitome has it, that the Senate went on to resolve that unless Carthage did give satisfaction, the coming consuls should put forward a proposal for war.[4]

The envoys could not have missed the heightened and hostile atmosphere in Rome or have been left totally in the dark by their guest-friends about what could follow. Any prospect of a new clash with Carthage excited ordinary Romans, mainly because such a war (unlike the hugely unpopular ones dragging on in Spain) raised expectations of lavish booty. When the call went out for troops early the following year, the new consuls had no trouble recruiting men. If Carthaginians felt still unclear after their second embassy about what satisfying the Romans meant, they were given a demonstration early in the new year 149. From their sister city Utica, staunchly loyal throughout Hannibal's war, an embassy sailed to Italy to offer what Romans called *deditio*: unconditional surrender to the will of Rome. A *deditio* did not have to occur after a defeat—Saguntum before 218 and probably Messana in 264 had, in practice, offered it to win Rome's support. Whatever role Utica had played (or shirked) in the recent war, it recognized an oncoming clash with Rome when it saw one—and one that its sister and hegemon was guaranteed to lose. The formal terminology was "to give oneself over to the good faith [the *fides*] of the Roman People"; and if it was done at a moment pleasing to the Roman People, the yielders could hope for a mild reception. Utica certainly received one. Without doubt the same absolute submission was the "satisfaction" that the Senate called for from Carthage.

The Carthaginians could have offered it after their second embassy, yet they hesitated. No doubt they feared that a *deditio* would be harshly used. There would be nothing, for example, to stop Rome from installing a garrison—or letting Masinissa install one, even though he and his army had by now gone back to Cirta. Their fears were correct, even though the full extent of what the Romans did want was still hidden. At Rome as soon as the new consuls, Lucius Marcius Censorinus and Manius Manilius, entered office in January, the Senate resolved that war be declared and Africa be their military theater.

LIBYA INVADED

Once war was decided on, preparations went smoothly. Cato, soon to die, could rest satisfied that his wish would be fulfilled. In Sicily a massive armament came into being—two consular armies at full strength under Manilius, and Censorinus commanded fifty quinqueremes and a hundred smaller warships plus transports. Among their twenty-four military tribunes were Scipio Aemilianus and two of his kinsmen, Nasica's son Publius Scipio Serapio and nephew Gnaeus Cornelius Hispanus. Now at last Carthage submitted. As soon as news of the war declaration reached the thunderstruck city, a third embassy sailed for Rome. Its members' names are recorded: Gisco, Hamilcar, Mago, and two others with (it seems) Libyan names, Gilimas and Misdes. The Senate graciously accepted their city's *deditio*—and promptly laid down terms: 300 sons of senators to be taken within thirty days to Manilius and Censorinus at Lilybaeum, then the consuls' further orders to be carried out. On those terms Carthage would keep her freedom, laws, territory, and all other possessions. Largely reassured—though not entirely—the city complied. The young hostages were delivered (they were sent off to Rome). Then the news came that the Roman fleet had anchored at Utica and the army was ashore.[5]

The Carthaginians discovered that they were in a Roman game of cat and mouse. Their fourth set of envoys, this time to Utica, was received by Censorinus and Manilius amid the legions deployed in battle array. The consuls stated a new order: that the city hand over all its military stockpile. When the envoys pointed out the threat from the outlawed Hasdrubal's army, they were simply told that the Romans would handle him. Supervised by the military tribunes Scipio Serapio and Cornelius Hispanus, the Carthaginians then surrendered an imposing arsenal—200,000 sets of armor, great quantities of javelins and arrows, and 2,000 catapults. With these safely in hand, Censorinus delivered Rome's final order: the Carthaginians must abandon their homes to settle at least ten Roman miles (fifteen kilometers) inland, for the Romans intended to raze the city save for its temples and tombs. He rejected a plea to let Carthage send one last mission to Rome. If Appian is right, Censorinus with disingenuous cheek added that ten miles would still leave the Carthaginians nearer the sea than Rome's twelve. In reality—as he and his entourage knew—it would have to be more. Tunes, still beside the sea, lay that distance away amid hills and salt marshes stretching north to south from behind Utica to the Catadas river, today's Miliane, south of Tunes.

This step-by-step rigmarole of exactions must have aimed at sapping Carthaginian morale as well as military resources. It caused the opposite. Desperation and defiance seized the disarmed city. Murderous mobs fell on the envoys after they reported to the *adirim*, on senators who had urged submission, and on any Italians met on the streets. On the same day what was left of the *adirim* declared war, freed the slaves in the city, and mobilized all residents, women as well as men. Masinissa's grandson Hasdrubal was chosen general to defend the city—he was no doubt a leading opponent of submission—and messages were sent to his exiled namesake, now at the head of 30,000 men south of the Gulf of Tunis, annulling his outlawry and imploring him to forgive and forget.

Manufacturing armor, weapons, and artillery started up at once in temples and public spaces. The city had always been full of craftsmen and artisans, and by now refugees were probably streaming in from the country-side, in fear first of the Numidians, next of the Romans. Many of these arrivals would be able-bodied farmers and workers. Appian gives a detailed—maybe overschematic—set of statistics: every day saw a hundred shields, 300 swords, 500 javelins, 1,000 catapult missiles, and plentiful catapults produced. Likely enough, merchant ships trapped in the enclosed ports were broken up for timber and rope, while Appian famously tells how women cut off their long hair to be twisted into catapults' cords.

The consuls took their time about reacting—from compunction at their distasteful task, later propaganda suggested, but more likely because they now had to work out military tactics instead of comfortably receiving a capitulation. They also (it seems) performed the solemn ceremony of *evocatio*, calling on the gods of Carthage to abandon her and travel to Rome for new honors. Baal, Tanit, Eshmun, and their fellow gods were not listening. To the consuls' chagrin, when they then moved on to the attack, their troops were driven back. It happened both at the isthmus fortifications where Manilius stationed his army and at the sea wall—the weakest part of Carthage's defenses—south of the hidden ports. There Censorinus had occupied the Taenia, a narrow tapering peninsula extending from outside Carthage's southeastern wall into the lake of Tunis (today, in enlarged form, the districts of Le Kram and La Goulette). He left alone the quadrilateral-shaped quay outside the walls just below the artificial harbors. Even though his next assault broke through the wall using huge battering rams, it was then repulsed. The rams were burnt, and his overbold troops were saved only by the wary Scipio Aemilianus, who brought up a reserve force just in time.[6]

There was more chagrin to come. Masinissa was unwilling to help. Rome had not consulted him about the invasion, and that he resented being effectively elbowed aside (as Appian claims) is believable. Besides, he saw that Carthage was not to be punished by being forced—for example—to cede him still more ground, but then left intact to pursue economic and cultural dealings with Numidia. Instead she was to cease existing, and hundreds of thousands of Carthaginians would be displaced inland: a potential problem not for the Romans but for him.

To add to consular frustration, Hasdrubal moved up to the southern shore of the lake of Tunis, at or near the seaside town of Maxula. He did not challenge the Romans in battle, but his young cavalry general Himilco (or Hamilcar) Phameas repeatedly harassed soldiers sent out on foraging expeditions. Phameas's troopers, on horses small, swift, and hardy, were probably Numidians from Hagasis's and Saba's contingents. Nor was Hasdrubal's field army operating on its own. Apart from some cities that had declared for Rome—notably Utica, Leptis Minor, Hadrumetum, and Acholla—Libyans continued loyal to their embattled hegemon.

Meanwhile, summer heat and the packed quarters of Censorinus's sailors and soldiers on the Taenia were ideal for bringing on sickness. Then the besieged Carthaginians set ablaze and launched a flotilla of skiffs, all but incinerating his fleet. He was probably relieved to sail home in September or October 149 to hold the elections for 148, leaving Manilius in sole command. This did not help the invasion: Manilius, eminent in legal studies, deployed modest military talent. Operations, all the same, would probably have gone no better had Manilius sailed and Censorinus stayed.[7]

STALEMATE

If Appian's unashamedly partisan reportage can be believed, the only Roman officer with serious leadership skills was the military tribune Scipio Aemilianus, who, over and over, had to save situations created by the incompetence of others. He scared off a daring night sortie from Carthage against Manilius's poorly fortified camp—after which the consul thought it a good idea to put a wall around it instead of a palisade. Scipio then figured scintillatingly during a large-scale expedition that the consul led into the countryside, probably along the lower Bagradas valley since Hasdrubal lay over to the east. Phameas's cavalry once again harassed foragers—except those carefully guarded by Scipio. The tribune also protected local communities that had submitted and yet were being attacked by other Roman forces, earning Libyan gratitude; and on the return to camp he chased off another nighttime raid from Carthage's defenders.

Manilius next launched a botched expedition against Hasdrubal, now at Nepheris, a hill town thirty kilometers southeast of Tunes and standing probably on the slopes of the high mountain Jebel Ressas. Crossing a steep-banked river, Manilius fought a drawn battle, lost heart, and had his troops retreat across the river under Hasdrubal's counterattack. Scipio rallied cavalry to harass and distract the enemy—barely getting his horsemen to safety afterward—and the next day capped this by rescuing four cohorts that had gotten themselves trapped on a hilltop. Fortunately for him Phameas seems to have been elsewhere, but even Scipio could not prevent Phameas's cavalry from then assailing the dispirited Romans as they trudged back to the isthmus. Operations ran down after this fiasco—it must now have been late 149—but they had gone so badly that a commission of senators came over from Rome to see what was going on. Manilius was lucky. His embarrassed officers and troops deflected the envoys' attention to the glorious deeds of Scipio. The commissioners' report inspired Cato, just before he died, to overpower his long-standing dislike of all Scipios and praise the young hero in a verse from the *Odyssey*: "Only he has wits; the rest flutter as shadows."[8]

Scipio himself was now given a unique nonmilitary mission: to visit Cirta, at Masinissa's dying request, to arbitrate on who was to succeed him as king. It was not an easy task because there were three surviving legitimate sons, Micipsa, Gulussa, and Mastanabal (a plethora of bastards could be ignored). Scipio compromised, opting for all three: the eldest, Micipsa, to administer Cirta and the kingdom; Gulussa to head military affairs; and the learned youngest, Mastanabal, to be Numidia's supreme judge. This tripartition could have been a recipe for fission, but it turned out well, Micipsa surviving the others to die in 118 (more than a decade after Scipio himself). Along with finding roles to keep all three brothers busy, Scipio may have particularly wanted Gulussa to have the military one. His brothers, "friends and allies" of Rome though they were too, were as minimally keen on helping the Romans as their father had been.

Gulussa by contrast was happy to bring a cavalry contingent to aid operations. His men soon proved a match for Phameas's; before winter was over, the Carthaginian's harassments had ended. Even more important, so had Phameas's loyalty to his city, which he saw as doomed. His decision to defect was helped by a long friendship between his family and Scipio's, going back to the time of Africanus. A winter's day parley with Africanus's grandson, person to person, led at the start of spring 148 to the Carthaginian chevalier and some 2,200 of his men deserting to the Romans. This happened during a second, equally unsuccessful effort by Manilius against Nepheris. The pro-consul (as he now was) at least avoided losses this time, but his troops were starving on the retreat—provisions had run out—until the ener-getic Scipio, Gulussa, and their new friend Phameas rode out to scour the countryside for food (and of course loot).

The war had reached a virtual stalemate. The besiegers could make no impression on Carthage's fortifications or on Libyan support for her. Hippou Acra to the north, despite its nearness to the Roman bridgehead at Utica, handily harassed Roman supply ships to add to the expedition's troubles. Even though the army was encamped outside Carthage, people were still able to come and go between city and mainland. More impor-tant, provisions could still get in (so Appian stresses), just as venture-some traders could do despite the Roman fleet on watch. Yet the Carthaginians in their turn were stymied. Hasdrubal's strength at Nepheris is not known, but he did nothing with whatever forces he had. It was a missed opportunity, for Manilius was more or less the ideal opponent—especially after Scipio left for Rome to seek election as aedile, the next stage in a political career. Almost as unhelpful to the invasion and a good deal harder to justify, the tribune took Phameas with him to receive handsome rewards from the Senate. Phameas did promise to come back but is never heard of again.

The stalemate hardly shifted after Manilius in spring 148 gave place to Lucius Calpurnius Piso, one of the new consuls. Failed assaults on Clupea on the Cape Bon peninsula and then Hippou Acra used up the campaign season while showing the world that Piso's talent in war was fully at Manilian levels. His one success was to sack a town near Clupea, perhaps Neapolis—and that by treachery, for its people had surrendered when promised good treatment. The Romans' setbacks were bad enough to prompt one of Gulussa's lieutenants, Bithya, to desert to Hasdrubal with 800 of his riders, a modest compensation for Phameas.

SCIPIO AEMILIANUS IN COMMAND

The Romans' total failure to accomplish a brief and booty-filled war encouraged the Carthaginians to hope again. Their commander in the city, Gulussa's nephew Hasdrubal, sent out envoys to keep up the spirits of Libya's loyal communities and others to urge his uncles in Cirta, and even the ruler of Mauretania, to join Carthage in resisting Roman imperialist designs on Africa. The Numidian kings had no mind to help, but something came of the Mauretanian mission: a force (it seems) set out from there to join the field army, although it was intercepted and destroyed. The Carthaginians even managed to send off an embassy by sea to promise funds and a fleet to the temporarily successful Macedonian claimant "Philip VI," not that this was more than a gesture of defiance.

At the same time Carthage's successful stand offered a damaging opportunity to her field general Hasdrubal. He matched mediocrity with lack of scruples, and for both reasons he may have feared being sacked. He abruptly accused his namesake, the city general, of scheming to betray Carthage to his uncle. Supporters among the *adirim* flared into murderous—no doubt prearranged—frenzy to bash the man to death with their benches. The slaughtered Hasdrubal, if he had sinned at all, had perhaps offered peace feelers via Gulussa; certainly his people's sole (though slim) hope of avoiding annihilation was to negotiate while the Romans were stalemated. Instead, the brutal killing left the city under the other Hasdrubal's unchallenged sway, and he was in no mind for talks.

Carthage's reprieve was almost over anyway. When Scipio Aemilianus in Rome stood for the aedileship for the coming year, popular enthusiasm insisted on electing him consul—the modern rule that only ex-praetors were eligible was waived—and entrusting him with the African command (the normal casting of lots with his colleague was waived too). On taking office at the start of 147, the new consul levied fresh troops to bring the damaged army up to strength, gathered auxiliary forces from Sicilian cities and foreign states—even as far away as Side in Pamphylia and the Black Sea kingdom of Pontus—and sailed via Sicily to Utica. With him came his close friends Gaius Laelius (son and namesake of Scipio Africanus's confidant), Polybius, and his cousin Tiberius Sempronius Gracchus, grandson of the Hannibalic War hero.

Piso was off ravaging the countryside. The fleet commander, Hostilius Mancinus, was in trouble. It was yet another case of a good opportunity misused—he had scaled cliffs by night at a weak section of Carthage's sea wall, probably the cliffs just above today's Sidi Bou Said, but then was trapped just inside the wall with a poorly armed force. Very luckily for them Scipio arrived that same evening at Utica. He sailed down with troops as dawn broke, frightened off the defenders, and saved Mancinus and his men.

All the same, boundless as the new consul's energy was, it made little difference at first. Far from being paralyzed with fear of Piso's ominously named successor, the besieged Carthaginians chose to plant a camp on the isthmus, outside their walls and not far from his. Hasdrubal and Bithya then came in with 6,000 foot and 1,000 horse. How this substantial force got there without falling foul of the besieging Romans Appian fails to say. It was a notable feat by Hasdrubal, but he did nothing to exploit it. He had left the rest of his army at Nepheris under an officer named or nicknamed Diogenes, but the two generals made no effort to concert any operations; they might well have done damage to the invaders had they tried. Scipio could perhaps argue that he failed to prevent Hasdrubal's feat because he was hampered by indiscipline and defeatism plaguing Piso's and Mancinus's men. Some had even defected to the Carthaginians. The consul had to spend time rebuilding morale with drilling and exhortations, not to mention ejecting the motley horde of traders and hangers-on who had battened on the expedition. At least he could count on his opposite number staying firmly inactive amid all this.

Scipio's next offensive borrowed Mancinus's idea of breaking in at a weak point—this time on the landward side of the garden district Megara, protected by only a single wall. Like Mancinus's, his attack made headway at first, helped by a feint assault farther along the same wall. Roman troops crossed into Megara to open a nearby gate, causing alarm that Appian and Zonaras exaggerate into a universal Punic panic. Prudent to a fault, Scipio then decided that semirural Megara was not a good area to fight in after all and called off the operation. Its one positive result was that it spooked Hasdrubal into abandoning the short-lived camp outside the walls and retiring into the city. He vented his discomfited rage by parading Roman prisoners on the walls and dismembering them alive for the besiegers to see—an atrocity calculated too to emphasize to his own citizens that any hope for mildness from Scipio was dead. He underlined the lesson by arresting and executing leading critics among the *adirim*. In effect he made himself dictator of Carthage.

Her situation worsened steadily. Despite defenders' sorties, Scipio over three weeks built up an elaborate double-walled fortification across the entire isthmus to cut her completely off from the mainland. People began to run low on food. Bithya had made it into the countryside to collect supplies but could send them in only on ships that ran the Roman blockade, as did some risk-taking foreign traders. Naturally Hasdrubal channeled most of what supplies did come in to his 30,000 soldiers, not to mention himself. To block access to the enclosed ports, Roman soldiers and seamen built up a mole of rocks and boulders from the Taenia out into the sea toward their entrance. The besieged responded with notable resourcefulness, for which some credit has to be given to their general. In total secrecy, using timbers and other materials left in the ports, they constructed fifty triremes, even perhaps a few quinqueremes, and some smaller craft. At the same time other Carthaginians, women and children as well as men, worked to pierce a new opening in the naval port's sea wall. When the improvised armada sailed out one morning at dawn, it took Scipio completely off guard.

His fleet was badly undermanned because crews had been largely diverted to building the mole. The attackers could have made short work of it—not that that could have decided the war, but it might have bought breathing space to reprovision the city, perhaps even to renew their overtures to outside powers. Instead, having revealed themselves to their dumbfounded enemies, the ships turned back into their refuge. Why this was done is hard to fathom. Shabby leadership, the curse of Carthage in this war, is the obvious suspect. Who commanded the last war fleet in Carthage's long history is not known—probably not Hasdrubal himself but a subordinate of the same clumsy mold. When the fleet rowed out again three days later, of course it found the Romans ready for it.

Yet the Carthaginians fought a stubborn battle all day until sunset, inflicting losses as well as suffering them. Sunset brought disaster. The surviving ships, ordered to retire into port for the night, created a bottleneck at the makeshift entrance and had to anchor instead alongside the fortified quadrilateral quay nearby. There too they put up fierce resistance. Scipio's legate Serranus finally overcame them only thanks to the five warships from Pamphylian Side. What was then left of Carthage's improvised fleet limped back into port, never to leave. Scipio over the next two days assaulted the quadrilateral against bitter resistance. Commando teams swam up to set his catapults and rams on fire as the troops operating them broke and ran. The consul himself had to face and kill some of the runners to restore order. But once the quay was taken, his artillery could rain missiles into the area behind it. Carthage was at last completely cut off. With winter approaching, Scipio turned to another target: Nepheris.

Diogenes's army was strongly encamped near the town, which had a separate garrison. Nothing is known of Diogenes; the name might suggest a Greek mercenary, but Greeks had not been in Carthage's military service for a hundred years. He was maybe a Carthaginian of part-Greek descent, like Hannibal's half-Syracusan officers Hippocrates and Epicydes. His army was large, apparently too large to fit into Nepheris, although Appian's numbers must be doubted—they add up to 84,000 soldiers and camp followers. If at all believable, this total perhaps covered Diogenes's army including Nepheris's garrison, along with camp followers and townspeople. The troops in the camp put up feeble opposition to Scipio's and Laelius's well-planned assault from two sides. Diogenes's men ran, to be cut down by Gulussa's waiting cavalry, now complemented by elephants. Nepheris by contrast sustained a siege of twenty-two days. It was clearly well fortified, bravely defended, and helped by atrocious winter weather. On its fall, however, the rest of Libya swiftly capitulated to forces sent out by Scipio. So it seems did Bithya, and it was perhaps now, somewhere inland, that the contingent sent from Mauretania met its fate. By spring 146, with his troops rested and his command extended as proconsul, Scipio could concentrate on Carthage.

THE DEATH OF CARTHAGE

The city under Hasdrubal's rule was suffering torments. He and his confidants lived the high life, and he made sure that his soldiers, including 900 Roman deserters, were fed. Amid arrests and executions, ordinary Carthaginians starved. The numbers perishing from hunger grew, and so did desertions—plainly not just by disillusioned, even if pampered, troops but also by any citizens who could find ways to get out. Hasdrubal himself could see what was looming. Before the disaster at Nepheris he took the same step that his murdered namesake had been virtually accused of: to sound out the Romans for peace terms. Ironically, given his earlier accusation against his rival, he did so through Gulussa.

Hasdrubal was counting on Scipio being eager to wrap up the war before the next consuls entered office, lest one or both try to supersede

FIGURE 13.1
Relief portrait of Polybius, in the Peloponnese, Greece (set up by a second-century AD descendant[?], T. Flavius Polybius).

him. Yet he then rejected the offer of safe departure for himself, his family, and ten of his friends with their families—together with their slaves and funds—as the consul refused to ease the ultimatum of 149. Polybius (perhaps an eyewitness) in sourly memorable style describes Hasdrubal, red-faced, potbellied, his armor swathed in a purple cloak, slapping his thigh to insist with appeals to the gods that he would rather perish with his city. Polybius may overdraw the scene to underline its irony (Hasdrubal notoriously failed to perish as promised), but the Carthaginian did not renew peace feelers even after Diogenes's disaster. Instead he and his fellow citizens simply waited for the end.

In early spring Scipio launched the final assault. Hasdrubal tried to block off the city's southern sector by setting the commercial port on fire one night—another miscalculation, for it took defenders' attention away from the whole area. The abandoned circular port fell to a picked force under Scipio's *legatus* Laelius. Two military tribunes, the proconsul's young cousin Tiberius Gracchus and Gracchus's friend Gaius Fannius, were the first to scale the wall. Scipio himself followed with more troops; then the Romans seized the nearby main square as night was falling. Although Hasdrubal's soldiers virtually encircled the square, they were too famished and dispirited to try counterattacking. The next morning the proconsul brought in 4,000 fresh legionaries to secure the area—and promptly lost control when they realized that in the square's temple of Reshef (Apollo to Greeks and Romans) a shrine of beaten gold held Reshef's statue, itself of solid gold. Appian records the gold as worth 1,000 talents: six million *denarii* in Roman money. Shrine and statue were hacked and smashed to pieces with swords—in the unstoppable frenzy, some men's hands were even sliced off—before centurions and tribunes could restore discipline.

Once more the defenders took no advantage. Hasdrubal had already moved into the citadel on Byrsa hill with the diehard Roman deserters. His citizen soldiers were now retreating into the citadel and the streets and buildings below it, along with tens of thousands of civilians. The streets from the square up to Byrsa, one passing through the new "Hannibal quarter," were lined by closely set buildings up to six stories high. Here at last the Carthaginians stood and fought for the last time, in the streets and inside the buildings, each turned into a minifortress and each crowded with trapped civilians. Scipio worked his troops in relays to stave off exhaustion, for each street and every building had to be fought through. When one house was taken, soldiers laid planks from its upper stories across to the next one against bitter resistance, while more fighting raged in the streets below. It took three or four days to reach the walls of Byrsa, leaving behind Carthaginians dead and injured, civilians as well as soldiers. Then Scipio had the buildings along all the streets set on fire.

Why he did this is not obvious. With the entire sector of Carthage between the main square and Byrsa aflame, he and his troops were effectively cut off, facing thousands of the enemy in the citadel still armed and desperate. The arson could have waited as Carthage was to be razed anyway. Its only purpose now can have been to intimidate the soldiers and refugees packed into Byrsa. Appian paints a vivid picture of confused mayhem—the houses burning, Roman troops hurrying on the destruction by making them crash down (maybe using the battering rams), those people still in them being crushed or burned. Then clean-up squads went in with axes, mattocks, and forks to drag bodies, rubble, and wreckage from the streets. Carthaginians lying dead—or injured—in the open were shoveled into holes and trenches (many of the makeshift tombs were no doubt the underground cisterns); some of their bones have been found in modern diggings. It would all be visible from Byrsa.

The operation, from the Romans' advance from the main square to these Dantesque scenes, lasted six days and nights. On the seventh morning, men bearing olive branches came down from the citadel to offer surrender in exchange for its occupants' lives. The exhausted but exultant proconsul agreed, save for the Roman deserters; desertion was an inflexibly unforgivable military offense.

From a narrow gate in the walls no fewer than 50,000 men, women, and children filed out, to spend the rest of their lives as slaves. Not so their beaten leader, who emerged with his own olive branch, knelt at Scipio's feet, and begged for mercy. Hasdrubal had stolen away without telling even his wife. It was too much for the deserters in the great temple of Eshmun whom he in turn had now deserted. As Scipio launched a new attack they set the temple afire, while some of them on its roof jeered and cursed Hasdrubal for cowardice, depravity, and treachery (they could have added incompetence). Then they made room for his wife: dressed in her finest robes and leading her and his two small boys by the hand, she vilified him in the same words before stabbing each boy to death in front of her appalled audience. She cast their bodies into the blazing building and leapt after them. With her perished the 900 deserters.

The fallen city was thoroughly plundered in systematic Roman style to yield masses of treasure. Collected too were the spoils that Carthaginians of earlier times had taken in their Sicilian wars: artworks, sacred objects, even Phalaris of Agrigentum's four-century-old bronze bull, which he had used to roast opponents alive. What still remained standing was then set on fire. So were remaining military stocks and the last ships of Carthage's last fleet, as dedications to the gods Mars and Minerva, Rome's gods of war and wisdom.

As Scipio and Polybius stood watching Rome's rival burn, Scipio wept. Polybius asked why, when it was so splendid a sight. The conqueror quoted Agamemnon's forecast and Hector's foreboding of the coming fate of Troy in the *Iliad*—"The day will surely come when mighty Ilion shall be destroyed with Priam and Priam's people"—and explained that he feared the same for Rome. He was not completely wrong. In one of history's most pungent ironies, six centuries later a Vandal armada sailing from refounded Carthage would sack his own city.[9]

THE TRIUMPH OF ROME

Amid almost hysterical rejoicings at Rome, the Senate authorized making Carthage's territory into a new province. Ten senatorial commissioners were sent to join Scipio in settling Libyan affairs. Carthage was not literally flattened—its burned and shattered structures remained for the Roman exile Marius to sit in sixty years later—but Scipio pronounced a solemn curse on the site, imposing the wrath of heaven on anyone trying to settle there. The same would be done a few months later over the wreckage of Corinth in Greece. Unaware that a modern myth would also force him to sprinkle biblical salt on the ruins, he and the commissioners then turned to the congenial job of punishing pro-Punic Libyan loyalists such as stubborn Hippou Acra, rewarding the timely turncoats including Utica and Phameas, and organizing *provincia Africa*.[10]

This extended from fifty to at most 100 kilometers inland to cover perhaps 25,000 square kilometers, about as much as Sicily. Though smaller than old Punic Libya, the province still enjoyed most of Libya's fertile and populous regions. The taxes levied, one on the land and one on persons, were most likely the old Punic ones, though the practical sums they brought in were limited by plentiful exemptions. Seven cities received autonomy and tribute-free status, as a surviving Roman law from the year 111 attests: Utica, Hadrumetum, Leptis Minor, Leptis's neighbor Acholla, and a trio—Thapsus on the east coast, Uzalis and Theudalis close to Hippou Acra—that must likewise have submitted to Rome early. Utica became owner of most of Carthage's territory from near Hippou over to parts of Cape Bon and would serve as provincial capital for the next century. Scipio's supple friend Phameas and his 2,200 men received land too.

Masinissa's latest seizures were ratified, Scipio and the commissioners marking out the new boundary with a ditch—still traceable—that wound across the countryside southeastward from Thabraca, on the north coast, to Thaenae eighty kilometers below Acholla. Within *provincia Africa* Gulussa and his brothers were granted estates as personal possessions. Clearly Scipio preferred to reward Gulussa's sterling service in the war and overlook his brothers' lukewarm attitude. In fact the Numidian kings received an extra and portable gift: all of Carthage's libraries (which Scipio had taken care to salvage), save a twenty-three-book encyclopedia of agriculture by one Mago, judged useful enough to be kept for translation into Latin. The contrite Hasdrubal and his friend Bithya benefited too. After being shown off in Scipio's triumph, they with other important captives were allowed to live out their lives under passably comfortable supervision in Italy.[11]

Scipio Aemilianus celebrated a magnificent triumph at Rome, though thanks to his generosity to his troops and allies he brought only 4,370 pounds of silver to the treasury (about a quarter of what Africanus had delivered without the benefit of a sack). He too was accorded the honorific extra name Africanus. From now on he was Rome's foremost citizen and a wielder of influence across the Mediterranean world unparalleled even by his great ancestor. He remained the man to turn to when more ordinary generals failed. After the small but indomitable town of Numantia in Celtiberian Spain embarrassingly forced a consular army to surrender (and then equally embarrassingly freed it), Aemilianus, once more consul and then proconsul in 134–133, besieged it into capitulation, enslaved the survivors, and so once again added destroying an enemy state to his record of feats.

Carthage's site, cursed yet geographically alluring, was not reoccupied for a hundred years, although Tiberius Gracchus's brother Gaius as tribune in 123–122 set up a project—thwarted in the end—to refound it with Roman colonists. The province all the same continued to draw settlers, traders, and investors from Italy; then in 44 BC the iconoclastic dictator Caesar arranged for a proper Roman colony to be established at Carthage, and the new city swiftly rose to be again the dominant center of North Africa—indeed one of the greatest cities of the empire, alongside Alexandria, Antioch, and Rome herself. The new Carthage lived long after the collapse of Rome's western empire: first as the capital of a Vandal kingdom (it was that kingdom's founder, Geiseric, who in AD 455 sailed to seize and sack a nearly defenseless Rome) and then under Byzantine rule, until it was permanently annihilated by North Africa's new Arab rulers in 698. The one-time fishing town of Tunis took, and still holds, its primacy.

OVERVIEW OF THE WAR

Carthage's annihilation did not, then or later, arouse wide or lasting condemnation. To Scipio and his admirer Polybius it was a splendid sight; the Romans at home celebrated. Only an occasional descendant, such as the historian Sallust a hundred years on, saw it as a moral error. As Polybius shows, some contemporary Greeks considered it justified, and others judged it an arrogant hegemon's act; but to all Greeks, sacking and even razing cities were recognized if deplorable war events, practiced by the most respectable states. Athens had destroyed Melos; Alexander the Great sacked Thebes, Tyre, and Persepolis; Philip V's uncle Antigonus Doson obliterated Mantineia in the Peloponnese. To Polybius's Greek contemporaries and Polybius himself, the catastrophe of Corinth was a great deal sadder than that of Carthage.[12]

Cato had insisted that the Carthaginians were once more a threat, that they were already Rome's enemies because they were readying war—an argument based on a lie, for the most that he and his fellow envoys can have seen would have been the artificial harbors and (maybe) the armament being readied against Masinissa. Nasica's counterarguments were that nothing had been proven, Rome should not leap to conclusions, and morally moreover she needed to have a counterweight to her burgeoning hegemony. Without it, hegemony could lead to injustice and corruption. In the end Nasica was overborne. His strictures, though, were remembered.

Polybius, who was to watch Carthage burn three years later, enigmatically proffers a range of (he says) contemporary Greek verdicts on Rome's decision that Carthage must be destroyed, without attaching himself to any. He lists four. It was rational for Rome to destroy a long-standing enemy; it was a ruthless use of her supremacy; it was totally deceitful and out of keeping with the Romans' normal virtuousness; it was entirely lawful, because Carthage did make a *deditio* and this meant that the Romans could legally do what they liked with her. In reality, not only do the four boil down to two pairs—the first compatible with the fourth, the second with the third—but none of them logically invalidates any of the other three, even if Polybius presents each as separate and distinct.

Modern explanations entwine other factors with one or other of these Greek verdicts: Rome's fear of a Punic resurgence, for example, plus modern awareness of Romans' greed for plunder (Polybius's Greeks failed—apparently—to notice this permanent appetite); resentment still rankling against the invaders of Italy, coupled with fear that it could happen again as Cato claimed; or mere greed for Carthage's wealth as it was nearly twenty years since the last major plunder-orgy in the Third

Macedonian War. Or did Rome act not from fear of Carthage but to fore-stall Masinissa from taking over the city, because this would have given him the supremacy over North Africa that Livy claims he wanted as far back as 172?[13]

Even Romans who felt as Cato did could not realistically view Carthage as an urgent threat, whatever the old man's fervid rhetoric or the stocks of arms stored in the city. These, if not stuff left over from the last years of Hannibal's war, had much more likely been gathered for fighting Numidia. Sources of professional mercenaries for a war, meanwhile, were now nearly all closed off thanks to Rome's Mediterranean domi-nance. Above all there was no fleet (essential to Cato's alarmism), despite Gulussa's and later Roman propaganda. On land, the Carthaginian army's and its leadership's performance against Masinissa was reassur-ingly mediocre. Again, the idea that the Romans nursed an unsated hatred of Carthage for half a century and it erupted at long last in 150–149 does not easily fit their cool but consistent support for her against Masinissa for more than thirty years or fit the king's belief in 172, if Livy is right, that they would go on supporting her.

As for the view that Rome launched war on Carthage out of fear of Masinissa, it posits bizarrely convoluted policymaking and does not accord with Rome repeatedly acquiescing in his recent land-grabs. Deterring him, moreover, would have been simple: to declare Carthage a friend and ally of the Roman People. That would make her untouchable and—a bonus—would virtually guarantee permanent political supremacy to her pro-Roman leaders. It is true that Masinissa was furious when Rome's decision turned out to be that Carthage must be emptied, her citizens relocated inland, and the city razed. Feeling that he should have been consulted, he balked at sending military help when the consuls requested it. All this, nonetheless, is a long way from showing that Rome feared his ambitions. If she was anxious about a danger arising in North Africa, it might have been about the reverse—not Masinissa taking Carthage but Carthage taking advantage of his inevitable death to exploit, or foment, strife among his mature sons so as to push Numidia into disunity and Punic hegemony. But this was not a motive suggested at the time, nor did it occur even to later Roman propaganda.

Greed as a motive is more inviting. The eager response to the consuls' call for volunteers shows that the lure of Punic plunder struck a Roman chord—and members of the elite were no purer about plunder than the man in the Roman street. Carthage's prosperity itself seems to have rankled. Rome demanded that her citizens desert their ancient home to dwell inland. Even though Appian's voluble version of the ultimatum is his invention—eulogizing the simple and secure pleasures of living off agriculture, as against the troublesome uncertainties of commerce—the demand in effect was that Carthage forego the topographical and mercantile advantages that made her rich. Not that Rome would expect Carthage's Mediterranean trade to switch itself 600 kilometers north to Ostia (nor did she take steps afterward to encourage this). The greed operated in a narrow time range. After 146 Carthage's site was left derelict, in defiance of its economic potential; Gaius Gracchus's sensible move to resettle it, two decades later, was bitterly opposed and annulled. Cities loyal to her were (so Appian says) thoroughly razed too, a decision again defiantly uneconomic but typical of Roman vengefulness. As for what remained of Punic Libya, it was parceled out. Most of the land became the tribute-paying province called Africa, but, as noted earlier, seven cities that had taken Rome's side were left independent and tax-free; Utica was granted much of her annihilated neighbor's territory; while some western districts of Libya were gifted to Numidia. All in all, it was a notably low-key settlement after three years of effort and expense devoted to destroying Carthage. Serious economic lust for the produce and wealth of North Africa could have exploited the victory much more—heavier tribute, many fewer exemptions and grants—and Rome could even have clawed back Masinissa's most lucrative seizures to give greater body to the new province.

The resentment simmering since the 160s against her old enemy's recovery had become more acerbic amid stress from the grindingly unpopular and costly wars against the free Spaniards and from the renewed Greek and Macedonian defiance of Roman hegemony. Lessons had to be taught. As a result the 140s would recall, and outdo, the 160s in ruthless treatment of irritants all around the Mediterranean. What the Senate, the consuls, and their enthusiastic recruits did not expect was how long and how frustrating it would be to teach the lesson to the Carthaginians.

The Third Punic War was unnecessary and unwanted. It was unnecessary because Carthage was not a threat to Rome, as the Romans knew (even if alarmists chose not to know), and without war would have continued as a satellite forced to go along with whatever her hegemon required. The Carthaginians showed that they accepted this reality with their *deditio* and obedience to Censorinus's and Manilius's demands, save the last. Their future obedience would have been ensured by the unspoken threat of otherwise being left to the ongoing tender mercies of the Numidian kings. Like the Macedonian republics after 167, Carthage too could have been obliged to pay Rome regular tribute or been subordinated to her economic interests by restrictive trade treaties (reverse versions of their earliest treaties with her). A neutered but rich Carthage would have added to Rome's burgeoning Mediterranean-wide wealth from trade.

The war was not wanted by the Carthaginians (obviously)—or paradoxically the Romans. These expected their powerful invasion armament and step-by-step erosion of Carthage's armed resources to bring about her bloodless capitulation. Polybius himself had expected it. Originally Censorinus and Manilius when in Sicily had summoned him from Greece, but, en route, news of the *deditio* convinced him that there would be no war, so he returned home. When Carthage refused to capitulate, the consuls had to devise a military response instead. Plainly they did not have one ready—for instance, isolating the city by land and sea from the start and collaborating with Masinissa, who had a battle-tried army but whom instead they chose to estrange (only to realize too late that he would have been an asset).

Roman military strategy, in turn, in both 149 and 148 proved so inept that the Carthaginians resisted it successfully with continuing support and therefore supplies from many or most of the Libyans. Scipio Aemilianus himself had as little success at first as the previous commanders. Plainly it was not so much their strategic choices that were wanting—Carthage's field forces had to be crushed, her city walls had to be pierced—as properly thought-out tactics for them. As a result, for a time the besieged had the confidence even to reach out to the pretender "Philip VI" in distant Macedonia. Noteworthy, too, is how so many Libyphoenicians, such as those in Hippou Acra, and even Libyans preferred to back their hegemon *in extremis*, rather than yield to either Numidia or Rome.

The Carthaginians—even before being disarmed—had no hope of winning this war. They had no allies, their manpower and money were no match for Rome's, and their city was at Rome's strategic mercy. Deciding to fight stemmed from shock and rage at the demand that they abandon their ancestral homes and sacred places (even though the consuls, maybe disingenuously, had promised that they could continue to visit these). The Roman setbacks that followed only slowed the inevitable outcome, something that rational Carthaginians no doubt always realized.

Even so, the city could hardly have made a more misguided choice of military leader than the one whom Masinissa outgeneraled and who could not make use of his unexpected success over Manilius outside Nepheris, or interfere with Piso's attempt against Hippou Acra, or hold himself back from treachery, butchery, and terrorism at home. A more skillful commander, helped by the resourceful Phameas and Bithya in the countryside and the competent Hasdrubal in the city, might have inflicted enough hurt to make the Senate rethink what it wanted from Carthage, especially with the troubles brewing in Macedonia, Greece, and both provinces in Spain. At the very least, some strong Punic victories might have won back for Carthage in 148 the terms that the consuls had offered in spring 149: the city's destruction but the people's survival. Instead, her continued resistance under Hasdrubal—who as late as 147 still hankered after the impossible, Carthage's continued existence—guaranteed the destruction of both.

Sacking and depopulating Carthage and Corinth did not create Rome's dominance over the Mediterranean world; that already existed. But the gutted corpses of two of the ancient world's greatest cities somberly climaxed her ever more high-handed attitude to states and peoples who irritated her. Most ancient combats did not end with the utter liquidation of one combatant—not even those between Athens and Sparta or, later on, Rome and Parthia. The demolition of Carthage and the Carthaginian state put paid, in glaring paradox, to a relationship that had begun long before with two and a half centuries of peaceful association. Sallust, at least, judged it to be the starting point for the self-destruction of the Roman Republic.[14] For him it marked the start of a perverted era of ruthless greed and aggrandizement that would finally turn Roman against Roman until the state itself was subverted. The Third Punic War, in a real sense, opened the road to the Caesars and despotic monarchy: a bleak vengeance for the fate of Carthage.

CONCLUSIONS

I N 146 BC CARTHAGE was destroyed, the Carthaginian state was nullified, and scores of thousands of captured Carthaginians were turned into slaves (many of them at Rome). Yet the victors inflicted no ethnic cleansing. Other Carthaginians survived besides those enslaved: dwellers in the countryside and small towns who had not fled from their homes, residents of Carthage who had managed to get out before the end, and Carthaginians living in aggrandized Numidia and abroad. All were consoled (perhaps) by a tract from the Carthaginian-born Hasdrubal Cleitomachus in Athens, who one day would head Plato's Academy, on easing their sorrows through philosophy. Impartially, Cleitomachus dedicated a work on aspects of epistemology to none other than Lucius Marcius Censorinus, consul in 149.

The Punic language and religion survived the cataclysm too. Many if not most Libyan communities used Punic for official purposes, as did the Numidian kingdom. Places once under Carthage's hegemony, such as Thugga and Mactar in North Africa and Carales in Sardinia, had their own sufetes well into Roman times—and magistrates could still bear Punic names. Across Roman North Africa even the well-to-do went on speaking Carthage's language. The sophisticated second-century AD author Apuleius, from Madauros in Numidia, claimed that his wayward stepson spoke Punic alone; not many decades later, the emperor Septimius Severus from Lepcis Magna was too embarrassed at his Punic-speaking sister's poor Latin to let her live at Rome. Two hundred years later, ordinary people spoke Punic in and around Hippo Regius 300 kilometers west of Carthage, as the local bishop Saint Augustine (another Numidian sophisticate) could hear; and a century later still the historian Procopius would attest it in what had been Libya and Numidia. Religion was not proscribed either and flourished as Phoenician/Punic deities were identified with Roman ones: Baal and Tanit with Saturn and Juno, for example; Reshef with Apollo; Eshmun as Aesculapius, Rome's name for Asclepius.[1]

Over the 120 years of the Punic Wars Rome moved through widening stages of hegemony, first over Italy and then beyond. By 146 she dominated, one way or another, virtually the entire Mediterranean world. Regions directly ruled or occupied—Cisalpine Gaul, the major Mediterranean islands, eastern and southern Spain, Macedonia—were now joined by the small but rich possession of *provincia Africa*. In the next twenty years she would link Cisalpina and Spain by the new province of Transalpine Gaul. Even sooner, in 133, a territory richer even than *provincia Africa*, the kingdom of Pergamum, would find itself bequeathed to her by its childless king. Old Polybius, still hale, could see the Mediterranean world's unprecedented unification under Rome—the theme of his analytical history—growing ever firmer. He need not have judged it with full favor. Romans, he found, were now more ruthless and less selflessly patriotic than in the great days of the wars against Carthage. Worse still, the inevitable destiny of even a reasonably balanced constitution like theirs was to evolve into imbalance: civil strife, mob rule, even dictatorship. For a Greek who died in 118 this was not a bad, even if unhappy, forecast.[2]

The Punic Wars began almost out of the blue. Rather like the war of 1914, when a quarrel between two old antagonists in southern Europe inflated into a global great-power collision, the enmity festering between two Sicilian city-states evolved—over just a few months—into a clash between two Mediterranean powers that both backed the same city-state. After their first, surprised clash in 264, Rome and Carthage did not get around to serious hostilities until 262 (this very much in contrast to AD 1914) and then chose to fight a geographically circumscribed war, mostly in and around Sicily, for two decades. The second war was different: it engulfed eventually all western Mediterranean lands and even the nearer Greek world. Yet it too started—it can be argued—in a misunderstanding, if one more deep-rooted and malign than in 264. In contrast to both was the third, the product of a Roman rancor that revived after a long remission and took to a new level Rome's brutalist second-century approach to peoples weaker but irritating.

None of the wars was a clash over cultures, ideologies, or race. The commercial and social links that predated 264 were promptly reforged after 241 (even supposing they had been completely snapped) and again after 201. Carthaginians and Romans always had ties of friendship and hospitality at the highest social levels. We know of the luckless Carthalo's family ties with Fabius Maximus (though these did not save him from a common soldier's sword at Tarentum); in 195 it was when Hannibal's enemies at home and their equally embittered friends at Rome put their heads together that the reforming ex-general found himself exiled; and the friendship that Scipio Africanus had formed with the forebears of Himilco Phameas helped that young cavalryman decide that he could do better as a collaborator with Scipio Aemilianus. Plautus's comedy about Hanno the "little Carthaginian," about a dozen years after the greatest war yet in Rome's history, offers Carthaginian characters—not just old Hanno the merchant—whom his audiences could find sympathetic as well as funny.

The Punic Wars were never a struggle between west and east (the popular portrayal) but, rather, between two western powers each under the powerful, and constantly growing, influence of the Hellenistic east. Both Rome and Carthage found Greek cultural forms appealing, Carthage earlier than Rome. Guest-friends in the two cities most likely communicated in Greek. Before Fabius Pictor and Cincius Alimentus began composing their national histories in Greek, Hannibal was writing up his campaigns bilingually in southern Italy, and Silenus and Sosylus were taking notes for their eventual histories of his wars. Twenty years later Hannibal dedicated to the Rhodians an account (probably not glowing) of a Roman proconsul's recent booty-hunting expedition into Galatia. It was not his only work in Greek, says his biographer Nepos.

Aristotle in the 330s had treated Carthage as almost a Greek political entity; Polybius in the 160s judged Rome in effect as a polity that Greeks could learn much from. Rome's conquest of the Mediterranean world fixed history in a mold whose shaping power endures to the present. We can wonder whether conquest by Carthage would have shaped history all that differently.[3]

APPENDIX: THE SOURCES

NEARLY ALL OUR INFORMATION on the wars comes from Greek and Roman writers. Polybius, the earliest, watched the catastrophe of Carthage in person. Most surviving authors by contrast lived generations or centuries later and necessarily relied on preceding accounts—as Polybius himself did for the First and Second wars. They did have plentiful narratives, memoirs, and other materials from those times and on both sides; without these their job would of course have been impossible.

Of the sources used by our sources, Carthage in the First Punic War was favored by the Sicilian Philinus of Acragas/Agrigentum, and in the Second, by Hannibal's literary friends Silenus, another Sicilian, and Sosylus of Sparta. The Roman senators Quintus Fabius Pictor, kinsman of the Delayer, and Lucius Cincius Alimentus, Hannibal's one-time prisoner, included the Second war in their histories of Rome—which they wrote in Greek. When recording the war Livy cites Fabius and Cincius only once each, as he does Polybius. Yet we can tell, from his copious borrowings, that Polybius was one of his principal sources; he quite likely used Fabius and Cincius more extensively too. Cato the Censor in old age wrote *The Origins*, the first history in Latin, starting with the beginnings of Rome and other Italian states and coming down to his own day—inserting his own speeches as a bonus and minimizing the naming of individuals.

After Cato, Roman historians wrote in Latin: broad histories dealing with events annalistically (year by year) or monographs treating specific, and normally military, topics. The first Latin monograph, by Lucius Coelius Antipater between 120 and 100 BC, was a seven-book study of Hannibal's war, which Livy cites often. Coelius took pains—sometimes, anyway—to evaluate sources both Roman and Punic and form his own verdict on disputed points. He could also give fancy free rein, for instance embroidering Scipio's crossing to Africa in 204 with a huge storm and almost drowning Scipio in it. The poets Naevius and Ennius, earlier in the century, had already written verse accounts of the First Punic War (thus Naevius) and a general history of Rome down to 187 (Ennius's). Ennius was the first Latin poet to bring in Greek-style hexameters for his epic, an example every successor followed.[1]

Large-scale prose histories of Rome were regularly produced during the century after Cato, but nothing survives apart from some citations in later writers: notably Piso, a kinsman of the consul besieging Carthage in 148, and sometime after 100 Claudius Quadrigarius and Valerius Antias. These two put together very lengthy histories from earlier sources including supposedly official documents. Livy cites them more often than any other of his predecessors—often in frustration (for example, over Valerius's grossly exaggerated battle losses and booty quantities). Neither can have been Livy's main source anyway: Quadrigarius began at 390 BC and was at Cannae by book 5, Valerius probably started with 753 (Rome's foundation) and was in the year 137 by book 23 (Livy arrived there only in his book 56).

POLYBIUS

Polybius, of Megalopolis in the Achaean League, was one of the 1,000 political detainees shipped to Rome in 167. He made friends among the consular aristocracy—particularly Scipio Aemilianus and his circle—and developed a powerful admiration for the Romans' way of life, military methods, and political system. Originally in forty sizable books, the *Histories* survive now only in disjointed blocks: books 1 to 5 in full, then plentiful extracts, short or lengthy, preserved by medieval Byzantines (though none from books 17, 19, or 37). Books 1 and 2 give a fairly compressed narrative of the period from 264 to 219, as Polybius viewed it as a preliminary to his real purpose of covering the half-century that followed.

His work is unusual for its constant authorial comments and digressions—from lengthily discussing earlier Hellenistic historians and their many failings (in Polybius's eyes) to his famous analysis of the Roman Republic as a political system balanced almost ideally among Senate, consuls, and People; and to expounding why the Roman military system was superior to Greek and Macedonian ones. Originally he aimed to explain, not just narrate, how and why the Romans became masters of the Mediterranean world in the fifty-three years from 219 to 167. Then he expanded the scope from 167 to 146 to tell how they used their mastery. He drew on a wide range of sources (though all in Greek), not only documents, books, and letters but sometimes participants themselves, such as Masinissa, who reminisced about Hannibal, and eyewitnesses to the Alpine crossing. When his narrative diverges from those in Livy, Plutarch, Appian, or other writers, as it often does, his version generally proves the most plausible and consistent.

As his history ranges across the Mediterranean world, the Punic Wars form only part of its content; but Polybius was fully aware of their importance. The war of 264, he noted, was Rome's first venture overseas; her victory in the Second war emboldened her, he insists, to aim at world dominance; and the Third, paralleled by the crushing of Greece, marked the latest and most emphatic stage of that dominance. Strikingly, while at first almost wholly favorable to the Romans and their virtues civic and military, later on he grew rather less enchanted. He saw flaws appearing both in their treatment of foreign states, especially Greek ones, and at home, where (he avers) not every Roman leader in his own day was immune to bribes and too many young men were besotted with improper pleasures taught to them by Greeks—including costly banquets and sex with boys or prostitutes; quite unlike his virtuous friend Aemilianus. Polybius did not hide, either, how deviously calculated Rome's dealings with Carthage were in the 150s, if—as is likely—Appian's narrative draws basically on his.[2]

The work has limitations: very little on Roman or Carthaginian internal politics and social structures, for example. Personal partialities often color his treatments, such as his admiration for Hamilcar Barca, disdain for the populist tribune and consul Flaminius, and the pained, not to mention inaccurate, comment that by 218 Carthage had become overdemocratic. His account of why and how the First Punic War broke out is both brief and logically unsatisfactory. The war of 218 he blames simply on Hannibal's and his father's supposed anger against Rome, plus a hint that Rome in turn feared the Barcid empire. He demands, rightly, that historians must supply accurate geographical data yet goes almost out of his way to leave in darkness Hannibal's route through the Alps.[3]

LIVY

The other chief informant, Livy (Titus Livius, a contemporary of the emperor Augustus), survives only in part too. Of *From the Foundation of the City's* 142 books, which took him most of a long life to write, only thirty-five remain: the first ten on early Rome and books 21 to 45 on the period 219 to 167 BC—by coincidence Polybius's own original choice. A set of later epitomes (*Periochae*) of nearly all 142 books does convey— sometimes erratically—what the lost ones covered.

For Hannibal's war his ten-book account (21 to 30) is the fullest extant, drawing as mentioned above on Polybius and a range of other predecessors. Though he was not given to in-depth analysis any more than to regular admonitions to his readers, Livy's genius lies in vivid narrative, imaginative character-drawing, emotive rhetoric, and patriotic moralizing, with famous episodes such as Hannibal's boyhood oath, his crossing of the Alps, Cannae, the later March on Rome, Scipio's chaste treatment of the women hostages at New Carthage, Sophoniba's story, and the meeting between Scipio and Hannibal. At the same time, he regularly has trouble combining literary brilliance and often contradictory sources, not to mention handling military details. His mishmash telling of Hannibal's Alpine crossing, discussed earlier, is a vivid paradigm. Later, to help the Carthaginian attack on Nola in 215 a corps of elephants materializes, only to disappear again. Carthage's treaty with Philip V in 215 comes in a boldly pro-Roman version—and rather than acknowledge the verbatim and very different version in Polybius, he ignores that. At Zama he equips Hannibal's array with a powerful Macedonian division allegedly sent by Philip; it then disappears until it reappears captured. On the Roman side, he is unclear much too often and can make obvious errors: at the Metaurus he donates to each army a supposed center division that—being imaginary—does nothing and then vanishes. Quite often (though not with Philip V's treaty) he stops, baffled, to complain how difficult his task is when sources offer him contradictory versions of the same item: the year that Hannibal sacked Saguntum, whether Fabius in 217 was dictator or "pro-dictator," how Gracchus met his end in 212 and Marcellus in 208, what quantities of equipment and booty Scipio garnered from New Carthage in 209 (a feat he misdates to 210).

Drawbacks and all, however, Livy's year-by-year narration paints the Second Punic War on a canvas broad, vivid, and detailed. We meet each year's senior magistrates with their fields of duty, the legions and fleets in their war theaters, laws, Senate debates and decrees, controversies and scandals, occasional economic data (such as the munitions that Etruscan cities contributed to Scipio's expedition to Africa), and a wealth of religious information— priestly appointments, omens and portents, and the arrival in 205 of the Phrygian goddess the Great Mother represented by a sacred meteor stone, enabling Rome to win the war at last. Livy's information is even preferable to Polybius's on occasion, as with his numbers for Roman casualties at Cannae—just under 50,000 to Polybius's 75,000—and for both armies at Ilipa. Where Polybius's work does not survive, he is essential.

OTHER WRITERS

Most of the other noteworthy extant sources for all three wars wrote in Greek. Diodorus, a Sicilian contemporary of Julius Caesar, wrote a forty-book *Historical Library*, which for events after 301 survives only in disjointed excerpts. Yet some can be important, such as the diplomatic foreplay at the straits of Messina in 264, the sieges of Lilybaeum and Drepana in the 240s, and Hamilcar's and Hasdrubal's Spanish empire-building. Diodorus's Roman contemporary Cornelius Nepos offers very short biographies of famous foreign generals, Hamilcar Barca and his son among them. Historically wayward—Nepos puts Fabius Maximus's 217 dictatorship after Cannae and has enduringly misnamed Hannibal's last battle Zama—still he alone mentions Silenus and Sosylus as Hannibal's historian friends.

Plutarch, about a century after Livy, included Fabius Maximus and Marcellus among his short biographies of famous Greeks and Romans, in which moralizing character-depiction was his prime interest. He must have read not just sources with a mainly Roman viewpoint but at least one friendly to the Carthaginians, since he includes a few unique anecdotes about Hannibal: a cheering comment to Gisco, for instance, an officer friend anxiously surveying the huge Roman army at Cannae: "You haven't noticed—not one man in all that crowd is named Gisco." He is not an independent or very sophisticated historian, but the biographies add welcome extra personal detail to their main figures and their great adversary.

Appian, a retired imperial official from Alexandria in the late second century AD, wrote a series of military histories of Rome's wars down to Augustus's time, arranged by region or theme. There is one book on Hannibal in Italy, one on all of Rome's wars in Spain, another on those in North Africa down to 146, and so on. Overall Appian on the Punic Wars follows the general record of events as in Polybius and Livy, but discrepant details large and small crowd in, most garishly of all a dramatic battlefield duel between Hannibal and Scipio at Zama. For the first two wars his narratives vary sharply from good to deplorable. He has strange ideas, apart from mythical duels: Saguntum sited north of the Ebro and, once sacked, refounded by Hannibal as New Carthage; a Hannibalic bridge made of slaughtered prisoners; Cannae adorned with the ambush from the Trebia. With the Third Punic War, abruptly he improves. A few surviving Polybian extracts show that Appian used him as his main source, even if this was accompanied by lengthy invented speeches and a few other distractions. The result is largely coherent and credible—particularly welcome as it is the sole substantial narrative that survives of the death throes of Carthage.[4]

Of the early third-century AD ex-consul Lucius Cassius Dio's Greek history of Rome in eighty books, only Byzantine-era extracts survive before book 36, but they include a Thucydidean-style discussion on why Rome and Carthage went to war in 264—with all other ancient historians, Dio assumed that they intended to—and his famous, if conventional, character sketch of Hannibal. Around AD 1130 John Zonaras compiled a world history that on Rome is largely a précis of Dio and can be useful: only they name Rome's war envoy to Carthage in 218 as Marcus Fabius (everyone else impossibly says Quintus), for instance. To the fourth-century AD résumé of Roman history by Eutropius, another retired official, we owe the date for the battle of the Aegates, March 10, 241, and useful census figures. Meanwhile, in a class of its own is Latin's vastest epic poem: Silius Italicus's first-century AD *Punica* in seventeen books. Yet another retiree (an ex-consul), Silius was inspired to turn Hannibal's war into hexameter verse, modeled on Vergil, with everything told in approved epic manner—deities intervening (pro-Carthage Juno saves Hannibal from Scipio's sword at Zama, for example) and language of sonorous elevation. Silius's historical contribution boils down to only a few items, notably Hannibal's supposed descent from Dido's family, his Spanish wife's name Imilce, and the point that in 264 Rome's aid to the Mamertines was aimed against Syracuse.

COINS AND INSCRIPTIONS

Carthage's coinage, from its start in the late fifth century, was influenced by Greek styles and featured standard motifs on varied shekel denominations of silver, bronze, electrum, and (less often) gold: a goddess's (probably Tanit's) profile, a lion, a horse or horse's head, or a palm tree. In times of stress like the Punic Wars, silver and electrum issues suffered debasement with copper to allow a greater output. As mentioned earlier, the Truceless War rebels overstruck Punic coins with similar images (figure A.1), issued much-debased coins of their own as well, and often incised the Greek word for "Of the Libyans."

(a)   (b)

FIGURE A.1
Truceless War rebel coin, overstruck on Carthaginian coin.

Barcid Spain's silver and bronze coinage over the three decades from 237 was a different phenomenon (figure A.2). Along with excellently crafted traditional motifs or sometimes a carefully pictured African elephant, some silver issues display handsome profiles, again in Greek style, of older and younger men, sometimes complemented by a club or a lion skin—the standard emblems of Hercules, who in turn was seen as equivalent to Melqart. Whether the profiles were meant to be seen too as portraying Hamilcar (a bearded older face), Hasdrubal, and Hannibal (younger and differing faces) remains a popular and regularly disputed theory. During Hannibal's stay in southern Italy, coins were struck by or for him, including some electrum and silver ones of fine artistic quality (figure A.3). All bear the usual Punic images and especially Tanit—but not Melqart. His Italian allies, all the same, such as the Bruttii, Tarentum, and Metapontum, continued striking their own coinage on the model of Rome's.

Carthage's final half-century saw mostly bronze issues of varied weights, with a small quantity of gold and silver shekels (whether to pay for public works such as refurbishing the artificial ports or for the wars of 150 and 149). The conflagration of 146 left behind melted or half-melted coins to be found in the debris, including a little group of three perhaps from a lost purse, again with the head of Tanit—the last survivors of Carthaginian money.

At Rome, coining money began relatively late, not long before 300, with some Greek-influenced silver coins conventionally called didrachms (double drachmas), their subordinate issues, and bronze pieces for which

FIGURE A.2
Barcid silver shekel, Spain, later third century BC.

the standard unit of value was the *as*. These all become more frequent from Pyrrhus's time (along with solid bars of cast and stamped bronze— these clearly not for small transactions). Then around 211 the needs of war led to a new silver system, with the standard unit being the "ten-*as* piece"—the *denarius*—together with subordinate values such as a quarter-*denarius* called the *sestertius*. This much improved the quality and stability of Roman finances at a crucial stage in the war; the influx of booty and confiscations from Syracuse and then Capua and other places no doubt helped the reform to be launched. At some stage in turn the *denarius* was reset to sixteen *asses* (without changing its name), making the *sesertius* worth four. After Hannibal's war Roman silver money virtually replaced the issues of her Italian allies and of course began to circulate, or be imitated, in the new provinces alongside their own local output.

The images on coins were limited. Usually Jupiter in a four-horse chariot figured on silver didrachms; the personified goddess Roma appeared in profile on *denarii* and *sestertii*, and on their reverses, types such as the divine brothers Castor and Pollux, a ship's prow, or the goddess Victory (figure A.4). Only after 150 BC or so did more varied reverse types start appearing, such as a famous *denarius* depicting the she-wolf of Rome, the infants Romulus and Remus, and the shepherd Faustulus, who rescued them. Even so this stood in contrast with the constant announcements of accessions, victories, largesses, and other activities that typified emperors' coinage in later eras.[5]

FIGURE A.3
Tarentum: silver coin from Hannibal's occupation period.

FIGURE A.4
Early silver *denarius*: goddess Roma (obverse), Dioscuri twins Castor and Pollux (reverse).

Not many inscriptions survive from the third century, and fewer re-
flect the wars with Carthage. Had it survived, the most notable inscription of all would have been Hannibal's memoir in bronze of his campaigns
down to 206, which he placed in Hera's temple at Cape Lacinium (today
Capo Colonna) near Croton. All we have from it is the information that
Polybius cites about the Punic military arrangements in 219–218. Earlier
Gaius Duilius, consul in 260 and Rome's first naval conqueror, narrated
his victories in an inscription originally set up in the Forum; the damaged surviving version was made perhaps three centuries later. Duilius
states his successes on land before his naval victory at Mylae, reserving
his greatest achievement for the climax, a common Roman habit in such
documents; this has caused unnecessary criticism of Polybius's reverse
order of events. The tomb epitaph of Lucius Scipio, consul the following
year, records his magistracies, his (no doubt impressive) virtue, and his
capture of "Corsica and the city of Aleria." Then probably in 217 or early
216 Fabius Maximus's unruly colleague Minucius made a dedication to
Hercules, the base of which survives with its inscription styling him
"dictator." In turn, the lists of Republican consuls and triumphs set up by
Augustus in his temple of Mars Ultor, though damaged, illustrate the
pride and propaganda of Rome's historical traditions.[6]

TIMELINE

814/813 BC	Traditional date of Carthage's foundation.
753	Traditional date of Rome's foundation.
509	First Roman–Carthaginian treaty (Polybius's date).
348	Second Roman–Carthaginian treaty (probable date).
279	Third treaty, officially an addendum to the second.
278–276	Pyrrhus of Epirus leads the Greek Sicilians against Carthage but quarrels with them and leaves.
275–264	Rise to power of Hiero of Syracuse, finally becoming king there.
272–270	Rome completes dominance of peninsular Italy with surrender of Tarentum and Rhegium.
265(?)	Birth of Rome's earliest poet, Gnaeus Naevius, author of a verse history of the First Punic War.

THE FIRST PUNIC WAR

264	The Messana crisis and outbreak of war among Rome, Carthage, and Syracuse. Consul Appius Claudius Caudex unsuccessfully attacks Syracuse.
263	Hiero accepts peace terms with Rome. Consul Valerius Messala raids Punic western Sicily, prompting Carthaginian military buildup at Agrigentum.
262	New consuls besiege Agrigentum, harassed by Carthaginians.
261	Agrigentum sacked, and Romans decide to expel Carthaginians from Sicily. Carthaginian naval raids on Italian coasts impel Romans to create a war fleet.

260	Naval victory of consul Duilius off Mylae.
259	Carthaginian general Hamilcar (not Barca) defeats Roman allies at Thermae Himeraeae. Consul Lucius Cornelius Scipio raids Corsica.
258	Romans take Camarina and Enna in Sicily and defeat Carthaginian fleet off Sulcis (Sardinia).
257	Roman naval victory off Tyndaris and raid on Malta.
256	Invasion of Libya under consuls Manlius and Regulus, defeating Carthaginian fleet off Mt. Ecnomus (southern Sicily). Manlius is recalled home, but Regulus defeats Carthaginians near Adyn, seizes Tunes, and blockades Carthage.
255	Peace talks fail. Regulus's army destroyed by Carthaginians under Xanthippus of Sparta, and Regulus captured. Roman rescue fleet defeats Carthaginians off Cape Bon but on return voyage is largely sunk in sea storm near Camarina (July).
254	Romans capture Panormus, and Carthaginians destroy Agrigentum.
253	Roman fleet raids Libyan coast but loses half its ships in storm north of Sicily.
252	Carthaginians lose Lipara island and Thermae Himeraeae; Romans reduce their forces in Sicily.
251	Generally quiet war year.
250	(June) Hasdrubal defeated by proconsul Caecilius Metellus at Panormus. Consuls Atilius and Manlius lay siege to Lilybaeum and Drepana, Carthage's last strongholds in Sicily.
249	Adherbal crushes consul Publius Claudius Pulcher's fleet outside Drepana. Carthalo shepherds the other consul Junius Pullus's fleet to destruction on the shore near Camarina, later capturing Junius at Mt. Eryx outside Drepana. Rome abandons naval operations.

248	Sieges of Lilybaeum and Drepana continue deadlocked. Hiero becomes "friend and ally" of the Roman People.
247	Hamilcar Barca takes command in Sicily, seizes height of Heircte near Panormus, and harasses Romans without succeeding in freeing Lilybaeum and Drepana from siege. In Libya, Hanno "the Great" expands Carthaginian rule west and southwest, taking Theveste. Heavy oppression of Libyans to pay for the war.
246–244	Continuing fruitless siege of Lilybaeum and Drepana.
244	Hamilcar Barca moves to Mt. Eryx, wedged between Drepana's besiegers and Roman force on Eryx's summit.
243	Sieges drag on, amid skirmishes between Hamilcar and Romans. Rome decides to build a new war fleet by raising a public loan.
242	Consul Gaius Lutatius Catulus and praetor Publius Valerius Falto blockade Lilybaeum and Drepana by sea and land.
241	(March 10) Hanno (not Hanno the Great) defeated with heavy loss off the Aegates Islands near Drepana. Hamilcar Barca has to negotiate peace terms, which require Carthage to give up western Sicily and pay a war indemnity. Rome crushes rebel ally Falerii. (Autumn) Truceless War breaks out in Libya.

THE INTERWAR YEARS

241–237	Truceless War threatens Carthage with ruin, but Hamilcar Barca, reappointed general, finally shatters the rebellion.
240	(approximately) Livius Andronicus from Tarentum begins to offer Latin adaptations of Greek poetic works.
239	Quintus Ennius, author of the epic poem *Annals* on Rome's history, born at Rudiae in Apulia.

237	Rome declares war on Carthage to force her to cede Sardinia and pay another heavy indemnity. Hamilcar Barca, with his son Hannibal and son-in-law Hasdrubal, leads expedition to southern Spain after causing Hannibal to swear "never to be friendly to the Romans."
237–229/228	Hamilcar extends Carthaginian dominance over southern Spain and founds new city, Acra Leuce, at or near Alicante(?).
235	Rome opens efforts to subdue Sardinia and Corsica, with varying success.
232	Plebeian tribune Flaminius carries hotly disputed proposal to distribute annexed Gallic land in northeastern Italy.
231	Alleged, but unlikely, Roman embassy to Spain supposedly to ascertain Hamilcar Barca's activities.
230–229	Dispute with Illyrian kingdom across the Adriatic and First Illyrian War.
229/228	(Winter) Hamilcar, killed in ambush, is replaced by son-in-law Hasdrubal as general in command over Libya and Spain.
227/226	Hasdrubal founds New Carthage in southeastern Spain while steadily expanding Carthaginian rule, ultimately to the river Tagus.
225	(less probably 226) Roman envoys make the "Ebro agreement" with Hasdrubal. Possible date of Saguntum's unofficial friendship with Rome. Invading Gauls from the north reach Etruria but are wiped out at Cape Telamon by the consuls.
224–222	Romans invade Cisalpine Gaul to conquer Boii and then Insubres.
221	Rome intervenes in Istria at the head of the Adriatic. (Autumn) Hasdrubal assassinated; Hannibal elected general in his place and subdues Olcades in eastern-central Spain.

220	Hannibal's first major campaign, defeating the Vaccaei and Carpetani in central and northwest Spain. (Autumn) Roman envoys at New Carthage demand that he respect Saguntum and the Ebro agreement.
219	Rome launches new expedition under both consuls against Illyria. Hannibal opens siege of Saguntum but takes nearly eight months to capture it, untroubled by Rome.

THE SECOND PUNIC WAR

218	(March?) Roman embassy to Carthage pronounces war. (May/June) Hannibal marches north from New Carthage to invade Italy via Pyrenees and Alps. (Late October or early November) Hannibal arrives in Cisalpine Gaul, to be joined by Gauls in revolt against Rome. (November–December) Consul Publius Scipio with cavalry is defeated at river Ticinus, and then colleague Sempronius Longus with both consular armies defeated at the river Trebia.
217	Hannibal invades Etruria. (June 21) Flaminius defeated and killed at Lake Trasimene, but Hannibal does not march on Rome. Fabius Maximus elected dictator, with Minucius Rufus as master of horse. Fabius fails to entrap Hannibal in Campania; Hannibal, to destroy Minucius in Apulia. Gnaeus Scipio wins first successes in northeast Spain, and Publius Scipio arrives as his colleague.
216	(August 2) Battle of Cannae. Hannibal again does not march on Rome. Most of the Samnites join his side.
215	Capua defects; so do Arpi, Salapia, Locri, and other cities in the south. Hannibal makes alliance with Philip V of Macedon and receives small reinforcements and funds from Carthage. Larger Punic forces sent to Spain and Sardinia. Marcellus at Nola resists Hannibal's attacks. In Cisalpina, consul-elect Postumius and his army are slaughtered by the Boii.

Carthaginian-sponsored revolt in Sardinia is quashed. (Early 215) Scipios in Spain badly defeat Hannibal's brother Hasdrubal on land and sea at mouth of Ebro. Hiero, king of Syracuse, dies, succeeded by grandson Hieronymus, aged fifteen.

214   Hannibal in Campania fails to take Puteoli or Nola, but Fabius Maximus retakes Casilinum near Capua. Secondary Punic army under Hannibal's kinsman Hanno routed by Tiberius Gracchus in Samnium. Revolutionary turmoil at Syracuse with assassination of Hieronymus, enabling Hannibal's Syracusan friends Hippocrates and Epicydes to bring the city over to Carthage. Marcellus takes command in Roman Sicily. Valerius Laevinus discomfits Philip V in Illyria. In Spain, two-year pause in Roman operations while Carthaginians stand on the defensive.

213   Fabius Maximus retakes Arpi; Hannibal fails at Tarentum. Marcellus and praetor Appius Claudius besiege Syracuse.

212   New successes of Hannibal: Tarentum (without its Roman-held citadel), Metapontum, and other Italian Greek cities defect from Rome; praetor Gnaeus Fulvius defeated at Herdonea. Hanno is defeated by consul Quintus Fulvius Flaccus near Beneventum in Samnium, but Gracchus is ambushed and killed. Consuls Flaccus and Appius Claudius open siege of Capua, beating back Hannibal's efforts to relieve it. After an arduous siege Marcellus captures and loots Syracuse; Archimedes is slain; Syracusan independence ends. In Spain, the Scipio brothers resume offensive and spend winter in the south.

211   Hannibal's failed March on Rome does not save Capua from capitulation; he retreats into the south. The Aetolian League allies with Rome. Marcellus campaigns against hostile or suspect communities in Sicily and

condones preventative massacre at Enna. Gnaeus and Publius Scipio are separately defeated and killed in southern Spain, but some Roman forces escape to the Ebro. Gaius Claudius Nero arrives to hold the northeast for Rome.

210   Marcellus retakes Salapia, but Hannibal destroys the proconsul Centumalus and his army in second battle of Herdonea. He and Marcellus fight furiously but indecisively at Numistro in Lucania. In Sicily Valerius Laevinus captures Agrigentum thanks to turncoat Punic commander Mottones; Carthaginian forces evacuate Sicily. Laevinus takes steps to restore the island's wrecked economy. Roman expeditionary forces active in central Greece and in the Aegean sea. Young Publius Scipio, aged twenty-five, is appointed to take command in Spain as proconsul.

209   Scipio seizes New Carthage. Fabius Maximus captures Tarentum despite Hannibal's efforts. Marcellus continues harassing Hannibal's army in the south; pro-Roman irregular forces from Sicily harass his Bruttian allies. Many Samnites and Lucanians surrender to Fulvius Flaccus. Twelve of the thirty Latin colonies refuse further support to Rome, pleading exhaustion.

208   Ambush and death of consul Marcellus in Apulia, and colleague Quinctius Crispinus mortally wounded. Hannibal remains unable to exploit the success. Scipio again invades southern Spain and defeats Hasdrubal at Baecula but does not pursue him. Hasdrubal winters in southern Gaul en route to Cisalpine Gaul.

207   Hasdrubal enters Cisalpine Gaul and marches south; Hannibal, harassed by consul Claudius Nero, is not able to leave Apulia. (June 22) Consuls Livius Salinator and Nero, arriving from Apulia, destroy Hasdrubal and his army at the river Metaurus. Hannibal retreats into the far south of Italy. Inaction in Spain.

206   Small-scale fighting around southern Italy; Lucanians and some Bruttians capitulate to Rome. In Spain Scipio ends serious Carthaginian resistance with victory at Ilipa over Hasdrubal son of Gisco and Hannibal's brother Mago; pro-Carthaginian cities are captured or surrender. Scipio suffers severe illness but then puts down a resulting mutiny by restive troops and founds Italica (near Seville). Hasdrubal returns to Africa to compete, successfully, with Scipio for alliance with Syphax, the western Numidian king; Syphax marries Hasdrubal's daughter Sophoniba. Aetolians make peace with Philip V.

205   Scipio as consul prepares expedition in Sicily to invade Libya. Scipio recovers Locri, in southern Italy, against Hannibal's efforts and then tolerates his subordinate Pleminius's vicious acts there. Mago lands with troops and elephants in Liguria but makes little progress. In Spain, revolt of Ilergetes under Mandonius and Indibilis is crushed; Rome controls eastern and southern Spain. Peace of Phoenice with Philip V.

204   Scipio as proconsul invades Africa and besieges Utica near Carthage. Masinissa, Syphax's enemy, joins him; Hasdrubal son of Gisco and Carthage's ally Syphax, both encamped nearby, open peace discussions with him.

203   (Spring) Scipio's night attack massacres the Carthaginians and Numidians in their camps. He then defeats new enemy armies at the Great Plains inland. Masinissa and Laelius pursue Syphax to capture him and his capital Cirta; Masinissa marries Sophoniba but forces her to suicide to avoid Scipio's wrath. Scipio then declares him king of all Numidia. Carthaginians conclude peace on Scipio's terms but also recall Hannibal. Rome ratifies the peace, but the Carthaginians overconfidently reject it on Hannibal's return.

202	After long delay Hannibal marches from Leptis to the Sicca region and confers fruitlessly with Scipio the day before the battle. (October 19?) Hannibal defeated and his army destroyed at "Zama" (in fact near Naraggara). Carthaginians, pressed by Hannibal himself, accept harsher peace terms.
201	Peace ratified at Rome. Return and triumph of Scipio, now additionally named Africanus.

THE FIFTY-YEAR PEACE

200	(probable year) Polybius, historian of the rise of Rome to world power, born at Megalopolis, a city of the Achaean League in the Peloponnese.
200–196	Second Macedonian War costs Philip V his dominance in Greece and the Aegean. (July 196) Proconsul Titus Quinctius Flamininus proclaims freedom of all Greeks.
200–191	Rome recovers Cisalpine Gaul and begins to found several Latin and Roman colonies across the region, including Bononia, Mutina, and Parma.
197	Roman Spain is put under two regular praetors, leading to formation of provinces of Nearer and Farther Spain. Extensive but eventually unsuccessful revolt by Spaniards. Masinissa of Numidia opens first of many territorial disputes with Carthage.
196–195	Hannibal sufete at Carthage; reform of state finances and weakening of the corrupt "order of judges" (probably the Court of 104). His enemies collude with Rome to force him into exile despite the protests of Scipio Africanus.
191–188	War with Antiochus III, Seleucid Great King; Rome drives him out of Asia Minor. Hannibal forced to flee Antiochus's court to wander through eastern lands. Carthage's offer to pay off her war indemnity rejected by Rome.

181, 172–170, 168	Repeated efforts by Masinissa to take over Carthaginian territories in Libya, each disallowed by Rome.
171–168	Third Macedonian War, against King Perseus; Aemilius Paullus's decisive victory at Pydna (June 22, 168) leads to breakup of the kingdom into four separate republics. Harsh Roman treatment of lukewarm allies such as Achaea, Pergamum, and Rhodes; attitude toward Carthage also gradually hardens.
167	One thousand suspect Achaeans are deported to Italy, remaining there until 151; Polybius is one.
162(?)	Masinissa's seizure of Emporia from Carthage is approved by Rome, and Carthage is also required to pay him an indemnity. Increasing dissatisfaction at Carthage over relations with Numidia and Rome.
152	Masinissa (now eighty-seven) takes over some of Carthage's Libyan heartland, the Great Plains and Thusca district; Roman envoys, including Cato (now eighty-two), approve. Factional struggles at Carthage lead to flight of pro-Numidian group to Masinissa.
151	Masinissa's attack on further territory draws a military response from Carthage, but under his leadership the Numidians annihilate the Punic army. Romans debate how to punish Carthage for violating the peace of 201.
150	Repeated embassies from Carthage to Rome plead her case but are rebuffed. Utica declares submission to Rome.

THE THIRD PUNIC WAR

149	Consuls Manius Manilius and Lucius Marcius Censorinus land at Utica with troops and warships. Carthaginians surrender all their stockpiled armaments and supplies and then are bidden to vacate the city and move ten Roman miles inland. They declare war and improvise weapons, aided by many Libyan communities and by surviving Carthaginian forces inland.

149–148	Fruitless Roman siege of Carthage, marked by incompetence and growing malaise; but outstanding leadership qualities are shown by Scipio Aemilianus, grandson of Africanus, as a military tribune.
148	Death of Masinissa, aged at least ninety; succeeded by sons Micipsa, Gulussa, and Mastanabal.
147	Scipio Aemilianus, now consul, restores discipline and reinvigorates both siege and field operations.
146	Fall of Carthage; Polybius present as friend and mentor of Aemilianus. Much of remaining Punic territory is annexed as *provincia Africa*; some is granted to Masinissa's successors, and privileges go to Utica and other defector cities. In Greece, Corinth is sacked in hard-line treatment of Greek efforts against Roman hegemony.

AFTER THE WARS

122	Reformer Gaius Gracchus's foiled scheme to settle Roman colonists on site of Carthage.
59(?)	Birth of the historian Livy at Patavium, Cisalpine Gaul.
46	Julius Caesar decides on founding a Roman colony at Carthage; developing swiftly, it again becomes the premier city of North Africa.
AD 455	Vandal rulers of North Africa sail to Rome and sack the city.
535	North Africa reconquered by eastern Roman emperor Justinian's general Belisarius.
693	Carthage captured by the Arabs; five years later, it is dismantled and abandoned.

GLOSSARY OF SPECIAL TERMS

---

adirim "The Mighty Ones," the Punic name for the senate of Carthage; see also "Sufete" below.

as, plural *asses* Roman bronze coin and money value (the original *as* weighed one Roman pound); the top level of the Comitia Centuriata required a property minimum of 100,000 *asses*. When the *denarius* (see below) was issued from about 211 BC on, it was set as worth ten of the much-lightened bronze *asses*; later the equivalence was increased to sixteen.

boetharch Greek term (the Punic one is unknown) for the military administrator of a Carthaginian-ruled territory. The Greek means "bringer of help," which must be a euphemism; the Punic probably did so too.

Comitia The two most regularly active of Rome's many assemblies for all citizens were the Comitia Centuriata and Comitia Tributa (see also "Concilium Plebis").

The Centuriata, evolving out of the citizen army in array, met on the Campus Martius outside the city walls, elected senior magistrates like the consuls and praetors, and voted on laws proposed to it by the senior magistrate who convened it; it could also judge serious criminal cases. In it, citizens were allocated among 193 "centuries," each originally comprising a notional 100 voters. The centuries themselves were organized in five groups ("classes") plus some extras; membership depended on how much a citizen was worth in property, and the Centuriata was structured to give better-off and wealthy Romans a dominant role. The classes' centuries were very unequal in numbers: the first class, for citizens worth at least 100,000 *asses*, had nearly as many as the other four. Each century had one vote, decided by its members. All Romans owning no property at all were assigned to a single century outside the classes. Apparently after 241, it was slightly reorganized to align itself with the Tributa; details are debated.

In the Comitia Tributa Romans were assigned to districts (*tribus*, "tribes") according to where they lived. Four tribes covered the City itself, and a growing number, the rest of Roman territory until there were thirty-one of these plus the City's four. Each tribe had one vote, decided by its members. The Tributa was convened by a senior magistrate, elected quaestors and aediles, and could also legislate. It may have come into existence once the Concilium Plebis was recognized as another legal body; unlike the Concilium, the Tributa included patrician Romans. Attending it was of course hard for members of more distant tribes.

Concilium Plebis This was limited to plebeian Romans (a massive numerical majority in the state) and organized by *tribus* (see on "Comitia Tributa" above). It elected the plebeian tribunes and plebeian aediles (see "Magistrates, Roman" below). Early in the third century it gained the right to legislate for all citizens.

Court of 104 The most powerful institution at Carthage, according to Aristotle; it judged accusations against defeated generals and, over time, probably others. Hannibal as sufete in 196 broke its political dominance.

denarius The silver coin, originally worth ten *asses* (*deni asses*, "ten *asses* each"), first issued by Rome during the Second Punic War. Its main fraction was the *sestertius*, a quarter of its value and so originally equal to 2.5 *asses*. Later the *denarius* was retariffed at sixteen *asses*, making the "sesterce" worth four.

eques, plural *equites* Roman cavalrymen; they were subsidized for the horse but had to meet the costs of armor, forage, etc. themselves. Obviously only affluent men could be *equites*. Later on *eques Romanus* became a courtesy designation for such men, whether they actually served in war or not.

flamen The special priest of particular gods at Rome: Mars, Quirinus, and above all Jupiter, with one *flamen* apiece. A very ancient priesthood hedged about with taboos, including a ban on leaving Rome, the flaminate was nonetheless held by men in public life.

gens, plural *gentes* Patrician families claiming the same distant, usually legendary ancestor belonged to family groups called *gentes*: the Cornelii, Postumii, and Valerii are examples. A patrician *gens* shared specific religious rites that were carefully guarded. In time, as plebeian families also became politically powerful, the *gens* concept was taken up by them too (to patrician annoyance). See also "Names, Roman" below.

ham "The people" in Punic and the name given to the citizen assembly at Carthage, which passed laws when consulted by a sufete and (in later Carthaginian times at any rate) elected sufetes and generals.

imperium The "power to command" held by consuls, praetors, and the dictator (see "Magistrates, Roman"). Consular *imperium* outranked a praetor's; the dictator's outranked everyone's. If a consul's or praetor's year of office expired while he was still on military service, the Senate could extend his *imperium* for another year, sometimes more, making him a proconsul or propraetor.

interrex A patrician senator appointed by the Senate to arrange consular elections if the consuls had died. As elections could be held only once the correct omens (the auspices) were seen, the first *interrex* after five days had to appoint another, and so on until the auspices for elections were obtained.

magistrates, Roman Forming several colleges, from consuls down to quaestors, all except censors held a single year of office. The consuls' year in the third century BC seems to have run from May 1 to April 30; by 217, from March 15 to the next March 14. In 153 this was changed to January 1. In practice a magistrate had to be of well-known family and good personal reputation, especially through military service. It became customary to hold one or more junior offices first (quaestor, tribune, aedile) before trying for the senior ones; this was made a formal requirement during the second century. See also "Tribunes."

names, Carthaginian Even though Punic inscriptions show hundreds of male names, high-ranking Carthaginians confined themselves to a small number. The commonest were Adherbal, Bostar, Carthalo, Gisco, Hamilcar, Hasdrubal, Hannibal, Mago, and Maharbal. All names, like Phoenician ones, honored one or other deity: for example, Carthalo = "(Mel)qart has saved (me)," Hamilcar = "Servant of Melqart," Hannibal = "Baal's favor," Mago = "Gift (of heaven)," Sophoniba (Punic *Safonbaal*) = "(Baal) Safon has judged." Some Carthaginians in later centuries bore nicknames, most famously Hamilcar Barca (apparently "Thunderbolt"); Hannibal the Gladiator, a close friend of Hannibal the general; and Himilco Phameas in the 140s.

names, Roman Unlike most ancient peoples, Romans evolved a complex naming system that could perplex even their Greek friends. Its basis was the personal first name (*praenomen*), such as Gaius and Marcus, followed by the family or *gens* name, such as Cornelius or Sempronius. As only a small number of first names was used, the *praenomen* was almost always abbreviated in writing to a single initial or two (L. = Lucius, M. = Marcus, T. = Titus, Ti. = Tiberius, etc.; Gaius and Gnaeus were abbreviated C. and Cn.). A third name, or *cognomen*, was increasingly often taken on too, to mark out a particular family within a *gens* or sometimes just an individual person.

In rare cases a further *cognomen* might arise as a joke (as with Scipio Asina) or to distinguish between aristocrats with the same three names— thus Publius Cornelius Scipio Nasica ("Big Nose") in the second century, whose cousin was Scipio Aemilianus—or to recall an adopted son's birth *nomen*. For instance, Scipio Aemilianus, the son of Aemilius Paullus, conqueror of Macedon, was adopted in boyhood by the childless son and namesake of Hannibal's foe. Another extra *cognomen* was triumphal, as with Scipio Africanus (see "Triumph"). After 146 Scipio Aemilianus too gained this triumphal *cognomen* to add to his many existing names. By contrast, daughters had only the feminine form of their family name (such as Claudia) and did not change it when married.

patricians The oldest Roman aristocracy, with special religious cults and public privileges (see "Gens" and "Interrex" above). The patrician *gentes* were few by the third century BC, but many were immensely influential and prestigious. One consul each year was a patrician, sometimes both.

plebeians All Roman citizens not patricians were plebeians; there were wide social and wealth differences among them, and it was wealthier plebeians who tended to attain consulships. Some established their families lastingly in the consular elite, for instance, the Atilii, Caecilii, and Sempronii, and in the second century Cato the Censor's Porcii. Other plebeian leaders, such as Gaius Duilius, were the only consuls in their families but played major roles all the same.

rab mahanet Punic for "head of the army," meaning a general. There were often several generals, but how the chief *rab mahanet* was termed is unknown.

res publica Latin for "state" or "country," above all used of Rome, whose proper epithet was *res publica populi Romani*, "the *res publica* of the Roman People."

senatus consultum, plural *s. consulta* A resolution voted by the Roman Senate on the motion of the convening magistrate. Technically it was advisory only, but the Senate's political authority made disregarding a *senatus consultum* unwise for the magistrate.

sufete The Roman form of *shophet*, "judge," the title of the two chief magistrates of Carthage. By the third century, and probably from much earlier, they were elected by the *ham* for one year at a time. Originally the sufete may also have held command in war, but once the generalship was brought in the sufeteship became civilian only. According to Aristotle, if the sufetes and the *adirim* agreed on a question, the decision could be enforced without consulting the *ham*.

tribunes, military The senior officers of a legion, normally young men of well-to-do families. Each legion had six; those for the first four legions levied by the consuls were elected by the Comitia Centuriata, while for any further legions the magistrate in command chose them. Not to be confused with the civilian plebeian tribunes.

tribunes, plebeian Ten in all, elected annually by the Concilium Plebis; naturally only a plebeian could be elected. They entered office on December 10. Evolving from their fifth-century origins as spokesmen for the plebeians, they became active watchdogs over affairs, and many were innovative and sometimes controversial reformers, such as Gaius Flaminius.

tributum The direct tax on property levied on citizens. The Senate each year decided whether it should be levied (occasionally it was not) and if so, what the year's rate should be. It was abolished in 167 because Rome was acquiring so much loot from abroad.

triumph The march of a victorious consul or proconsul with his army from outside Rome into the City to display their captives and booty and offer the required share of booty to Jupiter in his temple on the Capitoline Hill. A very ancient ritual, it saw the commander clothed in special garb, with red-painted face, in a splendid chariot followed by his troops, who sang coarse and satirical songs at his expense (to ward off divine jealousy). It could be granted only by the Senate and was the high point of a Roman leader's military career. From Scipio Africanus on, a victorious commander occasionally won an extra, "triumphal" name commemorating the land or people he had defeated (see "Names, Roman").

NOTES

Abbreviations in the Notes are listed at the head of the Bibliography

INTRODUCTION

1. Pol. 1.13.10–14 and 63.4–9, 5.33.1–8.

2. Ennius, *Annals* 363 (O. Skutsch edition). Unforgiving Aemilianus: in 133 BC, learning in Spain that his cousin, the supposedly radical tribune Tiberius Gracchus, had been murdered on the Capitoline Hill, he reportedly quoted Homer: "So perish too whoever else does the like" (Diod. 34/35.7.3; *Odyssey* 1, l. 47).

3. Population of Italy around 224 BC: Pol. 2.24; Walbank, *Comm.* 1.96–203; Brunt 1971, 44–66; Scheidel 2004, especially 1–4, 11–12.

1. TWO REPUBLICS

1. Third-century Rome and Carthage: (e.g.) Sznycer 1978; Starr 1980; *CAH²* 7.2,.486–537, 573–624; Staveley 1989; Ameling 1993; Cornell 1995; Lancel 1995a; Palmer 1997; Peters 2004; Hoyos 2010; Miles 2010; Hoyos 2011, 1–57.

2. Patrician *gentes* fifth to second centuries: Scullard 1973, 9 nn. 3–6. *Equites* in 224 BC: Pol. 2.24.14.

3. Intricacies of Rome's political system: Lintott 1999. *Asses*: a bronze currency; in Polybius's time a legionary soldier was paid 1,200 a year (6.39.12) and probably the same a century earlier (Daly 2002, 51, 214). Before 211 the highest-class qualification was 10,000 "heavy *asses*," an old value that after 211 translated into 100,000 *asses*, which were linked to the new ten-*asses* silver coin, the *denarius*. On early Roman coinage: Cornell 1995, 394–97.

4. Italian population: Brunt 1971, 44–60; Erdkamp 2011; Hin 2013. Vigorous third-century Rome: Cornell 1995, 369–98; Palmer 1997.

5. Roman–Punic treaties and dealings before 264: Walbank, *Comm.* 1.336–56; Scullard 1989, 517–37; Scardigli 1991; 2011, 28–38; Hoyos 1998, 5–16; Bringmann 2001b; Serrati 2006; Steinby 2007, 78–84.

2. FIGHTING THE ENEMY

1. Carthaginian warfare: Connolly 1978, 34–67; Wise and Hook 1982; Goldsworthy 2000, 25–36; Daly 2002; Koon in Hoyos 2011.

2. Quinqueremes and other warships: Murray 2012, especially 13–30, 143–70. Limitations of sea warfare: Rankov 1996.

3. On mid-republican Roman warfare, notable are Kromayer and Veith 1928, 288–376; Connolly 1981, 86–207; Sabin 1996; Daly 2002; Dobson 2008, 47–121; Koon 2011; Sage 2013.

4. Food supply and its problems: Erdkamp 1998, especially ch. 1; 2011, 58–76.

3. SICILY AND ITS SEAS: 264–257

1. Why war broke out: (e.g.) Molthagen 1975, 1979; Harris 1979, 111–14, 182–90; Huss 1985, 216–22; Hoyos 1998, 17–66; 2011, 131–48; Bleckmann 2002, 57–63, 110–17; Gehrke 2002, 153–62; Loreto 2007, 9–43.

2. Hiero's treaty with Rome: Walbank, *Comm.* 1.68–69; Lazenby 1996a, 52–53; Hoyos 1998, 104–8.

3. Valerius's foray: Diod. 23.4–5.1; Zon. 8.9.12 (erratic); Molthagen 1979; Hoyos 1998, 108–12.

4. Rome's new fleet and the "raven" (Greek *korax*, Latin *corvus*): Pol. 1.20.9–22.11; Wallinga 1956; Walbank, *Comm.* 1.72–79; Lazenby 1996a, 61–70; Steinby 2007, 87–104; Rankov 2011, 152–55; Vacanti 2012, 64–74 (desiring Archimedes as inventor).

4. AFRICA AND AFTER: 256–249

1. On D-Day reportedly 351,000 personnel went over: thus http://en.wikipedia.org/wiki/Normandy_landings#Allied_order_of_battle (accessed October 26, 2013).

2. Regulus's terms: Dio, frg. 43.22–23; Hoyos 1998, 116–18.

3. Xanthippus's later career: Walbank, *Comm.* 1.94.

4. "Between the risings": Pol. 1.37.4; Walbank, *Comm.* 1.96–97; Lazenby 1996a, 111–12.

5. Diod. 23.18.5.

6. Regulus's widow: Sempronius Tuditanus (second century BC) in Gellius, *Noctes Atticae* 7.4.5; Diod. 24.12.

7. Hannibal the Rhodian: Pol. 1.47.3; Murray 2012, 258. Not a Rhodian captain—many Carthaginians eked out their narrow use of names with sobriquets. Vacanti 2012, 82–86, unpersuasively speculates that he sailed a quadrireme of (completely unattested) Rhodian revolutionary design.

8. "Let them drink": Cicero, *de Natura Deorum* 2.7; Livy, *Per.* 19; *MRR* 1.214. His colleague, who also lost a fleet, incidentally was named Pullus, "Chicken" (Polybius carelessly calls him one of the next year's consuls: 1.52.5).

5. STALEMATE AND CHECKMATE: 249—241

1. Census figures: Livy, *Per.* 18 and 19. Hanno "the Great": only Appian (*Iber.* 4.16; *Lib.* 49.123) and Zonaras (8.22) so name him (*megas*).

2. Privateers attack Hippou Acra: Zon. 8.16 (imagining "Hippo" as Hippo Regius, 300 kilometers west of Carthage). Bleckmann (2002, 209–14) stresses the privateers' importance but, less persuasively, sees their ships forming most of the new fleet in 242.

3. Pol. 2.7.6–11 (Gallic deserters). Hamilcar's chivalry: Diod. 24.9.

4. The battle site lay between Marettimo (Hiera) and Levanzo islands. Recent underwater finds off Levanzo include three bronze ships' rams, one with Punic lettering and one bearing the names of the two Roman commissioners (*sexviri*), Gaius Sestius and Quintus Salonius, who certified its fitness for use (Vacanti 2012, 87–88 n. 205).

5. Peace of 241: Schmitt 1969, 175–81; Scardigli 1991, 205–43; Hoyos 1998, 118–23; Bleckmann 2002, 218–24.

6. Polybius on Hamilcar: 1.64.6 (tr. Waterfield).

6. BETWEEN THE WARS: 241—218

1. Camarina's and Phintias's interstate pacts with Cos: *Supplementum Epigraphicum Graecum* 12.370; Hoyos 1998, 114, 122. Hiero's and Rome's postwar aid to Carthage: Pol. 1.83.2–10; Hoyos 2007, 126–29, 192–93.

2. See now Waterfield 2014, chs. 1–4.

3. Cato's esteem: Plutarch, *Cato the Elder* 8.14. Barcids and Carthage after 237: Hoyos 1994 (with detailed earlier bibliography, 247 n. 2), 2003, and Hoyos 2011, 211–14; Günther 1999; Barceló 2004, 66–68, 96–99; 2011, 357–62.

4. Melqart as the Barcids' preeminent god and his supposed role in Hannibal's anti-Roman propaganda: Huss 1986; Barceló 2004, ch. 1, and likewise in Barceló 2011, 360–61, 363; Miles 2010, especially 103–6, 246–55, also Miles 2011, 260–79; Brizzi 2011, 483–98. Barcid silver shekels: e.g., figure 6.1; Lancel 1995b, plates 2, 9; Peters 2004, 307 no. 46, 311 no. 74. Melqart at Gades: Livy 21.21.9 (Hannibal's vows); Strabo 3.5.7; Pliny, *NH* 2.242, 19.63; Silius Italicus, *Punica* 3.1–44. Hannibal's treaty with Macedon: Pol. 7.9 (actual text).

5. Hasdrubal's accord: (e.g.) *StR²* 3.1.400–404, 416–20; Walbank, *Comm.* 1.168–72; Scardigli 1991, 245–96; Rich 1996, 20–23; Hoyos 1998, 150–73; Bringmann 2001a; Barceló 2004, 87–92; Serrati 2006; Erdkamp 2009; Beck in Hoyos 2011, 230–32; Hoyos in Hoyos 2011, 216–21; Loreto in Hoyos (ed.) 2011, 193–96. On Saguntum and Rome: (e.g.) Harris 1979, 201–5; Schwarte 1983; Huss 1985, 281–93; Rich 1996, 24–34; Hoyos 1998, 174–95, and 2003, 84, 92–100; Burton 2011, 238–41; Zimmermann in Hoyos 2011, 281–83.

6. M. Fabius: Dio, frg. 55.10; Zon. 8.22; *MRR* 1.241. Not "Q. Fabius" (Livy 21.18.1), i.e., the Delayer; for the embassy, complete with M. Fabius's hugely famous toga gesture, is never given to the Delayer by any source, even Plutarch.

7. HANNIBAL'S INVASION

1. "Honor and power": Livy 22.58.2 (Hannibal), 28.19.6–7 (Scipio). Carthaginian resentment over Sardinia (and the extra indemnity): Pol. 3.10.3–5, 13.1, 15.10, 28.1–3.

2. Livy 21.1.2 (tr. Yardley). Initial force strengths: Pol. 3.33, 35 (Hannibal's, most or all from the general's own record); Livy 21.17 (Rome's). For Roman legions enrolled during the war the standard catalog remains de Sanctis, *StR²* 3.2.613–19; see also Brunt 1971, 416–22, 645–57; also 666–69 (fleets), 677–81 (Italian allies).

3. Orpheus's magical singing persuaded the gods of the Underworld to let him lead his untimely dead wife, Eurydice, back to the land of the living; but when he disobeyed their warning not to look back at her until they both returned to the world, she was obliged to go back forever to the land of the dead (e.g., Vergil, *Georgics* 4.453–506).

4. Scipio's speech in 218: Livy 21.41.7. For claims of Hannibal's supposed Heracles-based propaganda, see chapter 6 note 4.

5. Hannibal's march: Pol. 3.50–56; Livy 21.30–38; Appian, *Hann.* 4.13–17; Zon. 8.23; Silius 3.464–645 (with various divine orations). Date: Hannibal was at the final pass in early November (the rising of the Pleiades: Pol. 3.54.1; Livy 21.35.6). On modern efforts to get him to it in September: Hoyos 2003, 259 n. 23. Notable modern discussions: (e.g.) Walbank, *Comm.* 1.361–95; Proctor 1971; Lazenby 1978, 32–48; Connolly 1981, 153–66; Seibert 1993a, 191–213; Lancel 1995b, 99–133; Hoyos 2006; Mahaney 2010.

6. Hannibal's possible plan: so too Seibert 1993b, 67 n. 29, 156.

7. As the oldest living augur (since 265), Fabius may also have been judged the best choice for appeasing the gods irritated by Flaminius's alleged disregard of ill omens (a point gratefully owed to the anonymous assessor of this work).

8. Callicula: maybe at Pietravairano north of ancient Capua (Walbank, *Comm.* 1.427–30; Lazenby 1978, 70; Connolly 1981, 178–79; Frederiksen 1984, 238) or else the broader but still block-able pass at Marzanello just to the west; this too leads into Samnium, with a narrow saddle under Mt. Caievola on its east side (*StR*² 3.2.122–23; Seibert 1993a, 224, dismissing unpersuasively the cattle ruse as fiction).

9. Fabius "pro-dictator": Livy 22.31.8–11; refuted by Walbank, *Comm.* 1.434; Beck 2005, 284–86.

10. Gisco: Plutarch, *Fabius* 15.2.

11. On the Cannae campaign: (e.g.) *StR*² 3.2.126–59; Walbank, *Comm.* 1.435–49; Lazenby 1978, 73–86; Seibert 1993a, 227–32; Goldsworthy 2001; Daly 2002. Maharbal's advice: J. Lazenby 1996b, 39–48; Hoyos 2000 (dating it after Trasimene, repeated after Cannae). Livy's and Polybius's admiring comments: Livy 22.54.10–11; Pol. 3.118.8–9.

8. HANNIBAL'S ZENITH

1. "Because he had not despaired of the state" (*quod de re publica non desperasset*): Livy 22.61.14. Italian commoners' alleged pro-Punic sympathy: 23.14.7, 24.2.8 (gloomily terming it a sort of disease).

2. Capua's expectations: Livy 23.6.1–3, 10.2; accepted by (e.g.) Frederiksen 1984, 240; cf. Fronda 2010, 119–25. Feuds—the Bruttians versus Croton: Livy 24.2–3; on Petelia versus its Bruttian neighbors, cf. Fronda 2010, 153–58.

3. Guarded Greek fascination: Pol. 5.102–5. Hannibal's treaty with Philip V: Pol. 7.9; Livy 23.33.10–12; Schmitt 1969, 245–50. God list: Walbank, *Comm.* 2.46–52; Barré 1983.

4. Hannibal "the Gladiator": Pol. 9.24.5–8. Livy's "a young nobleman" (24.6.2) hardly rules him out despite Geus 1994, 95. Even Hannibal the general was only thirty-two in 215.

5. The contracts saga: Livy 23.48.10–49.4, 25.3.8–4.11 (doubted by Erdkamp 1998, 114; Ñaco del Hoyo 2011, 388–89). *Mensarii*: Livy 23.21.6, 24.18.12, 26.36.8. Sailors privately supplied: 24.11.7–9.

6. Carthage's enclosed ports: though commonly dated after 200 (Hurst in Ennabli [ed.] 1992, 83–85; Lancel 1995a, 172–82, 189–90; Le Bohec 2011, 433), this is not certain (Hurst and Stager 1977, 341–44; Hurst 1979, 27; Picard and Picard 1983, 34–37). Falbe's Quadrilateral: Lancel 1995a, 179–80, 189.

7. Felsnas Larth: Bonfante (ed.) 1986, 83–84, 204.

8. Bomilcar: Livy 25.27.10–12 (avoids battle); Pol. 9.9.11, Livy 26.20.7–11 (fleet at Tarentum); Lazenby 1978, 117.

9. Centenius's and Gnaeus Fulvius's much-debated defeats: (e.g.) *StR*² 3.2.282–83, 445 n. 28; *MRR* 2.268, 271 n. 2; Lazenby 1978, 114; Kukofka 1990, 87–91; Fronda 2011, 253; Rawlings 2011, 300, 302.

10. *Legiones Cannenses* supplemented: Livy 23.25.8, 24.18.8–9, 27.7.12–14, 29.24.13. Shortage of available recruits: 22.57.11, 25.5.5, 26.25.2 (naval crews).

11. Treatment of Capua: Livy 26.16.5–11; better version, 26.34.1–12; Frederiksen 1984, 244–50.

9. THE WAR BEYOND ITALY

1. Archimedes's flammables: Lucian, *Hippias* 2 (ca. AD 160); Galen, *De Temperantia* 3 (ca. AD 200). Shields or mirrors burning ships from afar are Byzantine fancy: Simms 1991, 91–96; Kayser 2002, 183–96.

2. "In the eighth year": Livy 24.42.9–11 (Saguntum), 25.36.14 (Gnaeus Scipio).

3. "Amtorgis" perhaps Iliturgi or Iliturgicola: Hoyos 2001, 83–84. Gnaeus perished twenty-nine days after Publius: Livy 25.36.14. Ilugia: Pol. 11.24.10–11 ("Ilourgeia"); Appian, *Iber.* 32.128 ("Ilurgia"); Livy's "Iliturgi" (28.19.1–4) is another mistake.

10. CARTHAGE IN RETREAT: 210—206

1. So Pol. 10.7.3–5. Yet Livy's locations (26.20.6) look more strategically plausible: Mago near Castulo, the other Hasdrubal near Gades, and Hasdrubal the Barcid seemingly at Saguntum, which could be a copyist's mistake for Segontia in Celtiberia.

2. Baecula's battle site is traditionally placed outside Bailén, but a corrugated hilltop near Santo Tomé, seventy kilometers farther east, has late third-century Roman military items (Bellón Ruiz et al. 2009).

3. Scipio's forces: Pol. 11.20.8; Livy has 45,000 (28.13.5). Carthaginian: Pol. 11.20.1, echoed erratically by Appian, *Iber*. 25.100.

4. "Elinga" etc.: Pol. 11.20.1; Livy 28.12.15; Hoyos 2002. The best-known Ilipa, later called Ilipa Ilia, is the favorite candidate: Alcalá del Río, sixteen kilometers north of Seville and 250 kilometers west of Castulo. But it is hard to believe that Scipio could have advanced so far into Punic Spain without any interference at all. Another Ilipa seems to have stood about thirty-five kilometers west of Castulo; and Iluipa—known from its later coins—was in the same region. All these sites have suitable hills and level plains. For Alcalá: *StR²* 3.2.483 n. 86; Scullard 1970, 262–63; Seibert 1993a, 266–67. Near Castulo: Hoyos 2002. The battle: Walbank, *Comm*. 2.17–18, 296–304; Scullard 1970, 86–95; Lazenby 1978, 145–50; Connolly 1981, 199–201; Millán León 1986, 283–303; Goldsworthy 2000, 279–85.

5. To Livius's two strong legions and Porcius's two weak ones, Nero brought in maybe 9,000 after recruiting extra volunteers on his march (Livy 27.46.3).

6. Date of the Metaurus: Ovid, *Fasti* 6.770. Livy kills an impossible 57,000 invaders (27.46.6), but 5,400 prisoners is believable (Walbank, *Comm*. 2.273–74, and Lazenby 1978, 190, want 10,000). Their sale realized 300 talents (Pol. 11.3.2)—1.8 million *denarii*, averaging a plausible 333 *denarii* per head (on prices: Frank 1933, 100–102).

11. SCIPIO AND ROMAN VICTORY

1. Sophoniba: Pol. 14.1.4, 14.7.4–7; Diod. 27.7; Livy 29.23.1, 4 (date and marriage), 30.7.8–9, 30.12.11–15.8; Appian, *Iber*. 37.150; Appian, *Lib*. 10.37, 27.111–28.119; Zon. 9.11, 13; Geus 1994, 200–201. "Sophonisba" is a later misspelling of the Latinized form.

2. Livy's figures for Punic and Numidian losses (30.6.8) are bigger than Appian's more economical 30,000 killed and 2,400 taken (*Lib*. 23.94). Carthaginian plan for a land and sea offensive: Pol. 14.5.6–7.

3. Hannibal already in Africa when supply convoy seized and Scipio's envoys mistreated: Pol. 15.1.10–12. That a panicky Rome first heard of the restarted hostilities at the time of the Ludi Apollinares, i.e., in July 202 (so Livy 30.38.6–7), does not look very plausible.

4. Consuls ordered not to let Hannibal or Mago depart: Livy 30.21.1.

5. Battle of Zama: *StR²* 2.336–39, 3.572–82; Walbank, *Comm*. 2.446–50; Scullard 1970, 271–74; Lazenby 1978, 218–21; Seibert 1993a, 309–16; Fields 2010, 61–62. "Zama": Nepos, *Hannibal*. 6.3.

6. Vermina defeated: Livy 30.36.8. Peace terms: Pol. 15.18; Livy 30.37.1–6; Appian, *Lib*. 54.234–38; Walbank, *Comm*. 2.465–71; Schmitt 1969, 291–308; Scardigli 1991, 297–326. Scipio's triumph: Livy 30.45; he cites Polybius ("an author not at all to be disregarded") on Syphax—but only after reporting that the fallen king had already died at Tibur. Polybius's account does not survive.

7. Appian's claim about Hannibal wrecking Italy: *Lib*. 134.635.

8. Hannibal foredoomed his enterprise: Pol. 11.19.6–7. Livy on Hannibal's decision (or indecision) after Cannae: 22.51.4, 30.20.7–9.

9. Hannibal blamed home authorities: Livy 30.20.1–4. Hasdrubal the Kid: Livy 30.42.12–19; Geus 1994, 150.

12. ROME, MASINISSA, AND CARTHAGE

1. Attalus II's letter: Austin 2006, no. 244.

2. Rome's Spanish silver mines: Diod. 5.36.3–38.1.

3. Sicilian grain tithe fed Rome's armies: Erdkamp 2011, 288–89. "Sardinians cheap": Cic., *ad Familiares* 7.24.2.

4. Hannibal's olive trees: Victor, *de Caesaribus* 37.3 (original source unknown).

5. The Punic in *Poenulus*: Adams 2003, 204–5. Sympathetic features in *Poenulus*: Franko 1996; Syed 2005, 366–70; Le Bohec 2011, 432–33.

6. Micipsa and Mastanabal: Diod. 34/35.35; Livy, *Per.* 50; *Inscriptiones Graecae* 2².2316, ll. 41–44 (Panathenaic victory). Hasdrubal Cleitomachus: Diogenes Laertius, *Lives of the Philosophers* 4.67; G. Schmidt in *Kleine Pauly* 1975, 3.235–36. Masinissa's Carthaginian grandson Hasdrubal: Livy, *Per.* 50; Appian, *Lib.* 93.439.

7. Masinissa, Carthage, and Rome: Livy 34.61.16–62.18 (in 193, with Aphther episode); 40.17.1–6, 34.14 (181); 42.23–24 (172); 42.29.8–10 (171); 43.3.5–7 (170); 45.13.12–14.9 (168); Harris 1989, 145–47; Desanges 1995; Burton 2011, 112–14; Kunze 2011, 396–411.

8. Emporia dispute: Pol. 31.21; Walbank, *Comm.* 3.489–90. Roman embassy ca. 157: Livy, *Per.* 47; probably too Appian, *Lib.* 67.302–3 (impossibly dating it ca. 200).

9. Carthalo's alleged raid: Appian, *Lib.* 68.306–8; Walbank, *Comm.* 3.653–54; Harris 1989, 149; Storm 2001, 72–73. Great Plains and Thusca: Appian, *Lib.* 68.309. Cato's and Nasica's embassy in 152: Livy, *Per.* 48; Plutarch, *Cato Maior* 26; Appian, *Lib.* 69.310–14; Zon. 9.26.

13. THE TRIUMPH OF ROME

1. Punic politics in 150s: Appian, *Lib.* 68.304–5. Picard and Picard 1968, 281, see the Starling's group aiming to unify Carthage and Numidia.

2. Cato's African figs: Pliny, *Natural History* 15.74; Plutarch, *Cato Maior* 27.1; Günther 2008. For Meier 1984, senators knew that Cato had grown the figs himself, but they played along. "Horoscopa": Appian, *Lib.* 70.319. "Carthage ought not to exist": Plutarch, *Cato Maior* 27.2; Diod. 34/35.33.3; Dubuisson 1989. Senate had decided on war "long before" 149: Pol. 36.2.1.

3. Zonaras brings over a Roman embassy before the battle (9.26; trusted by Harris 1989, 151)—but makes Nasica its leader, ignores Aemilianus, and seemingly squeezes it and everything else into 149; he should not be believed.

4. L. Lentulus: Cic., *Tusculan Disputations* 3.51. Carthage's embassies to Rome: Appian, *Lib.* 74.344–46; cf. Pol. 36.3.1 (Carthaginians' perplexity).

5. For the Third Punic War the prime source is Appian, *Lib.* 74.336–136.648, extensively but not solely drawn from Polybius. Important others: Pol. 36.1–11, 16; 38.7–8, 19–22; Diod. 32.1, 3, 6–14, 16–18, 22–25; Livy, *Per.* 49–52; Dio, frg. 70; Zon. 9.26–27, 29–30.

6. *Evocatio*: Macrobius, *Saturnalia* 3.9.7–8; Servius, *Commentary on Aeneid* 12.841; Fraenkel 1963, 237–38. Huss 1985, 455 n. 128, doubts it.

7. Phameas: perhaps a sobriquet derived from the name of the Phoenician god Pumay (Huss 1985, 445 n. 64). Pumay: *DCPP* 364.

8. *Odyssey* 10.495.

9. Scipio's emotion: Pol. 38.21–22 (surviving partly in Appian, *Lib.* 132.629–30); *Iliad* 4.164–65 (= 6.448–49).

10. The salt story was invented, by biblical inspiration, by B. L. Hallward in his narrative of the Third Punic War in vol. 7 of the *Cambridge Ancient History*'s first edition (1928). See Ridley 1986, 140–46; Baldwin 2003, 289–94.

11. Size of *provincia Africa*: Harris 1989, 160 n. 288; Mattingly 2011, 147–49 with map. Taxes: Appian, *Lib.* 135.640–41. Hasdrubal and Bithya postwar: Eutropius 4.14.3; Zon. 9.30.

12. Polybius laments fall of Greece: 38.1.1–2; Baronowski 2011, 117; McGing 2010, 149–57.

13. Cato versus Nasica: Astin 1967, 272–81, and 1978, 127–30, 283–86; Harris 1989, 152–55. Greek views: Pol. 36.9; Walbank, *Comm.* 3.663–70; Harris 1979, 271–72; Baronowski 1995, and 2011, 101–4; Champion 2004, 163–65, 195–96; Burton 2011, 305–23. Preliminaries to the war: Huss 1985, 433–39; Harris 1989, 151–57; Kunze 2011, 407–9; Le Bohec 2011, 430–35.

14. Sallust, *Catiline* 10; *Jugurtha* 41; *Histories* 1.10, 12 (McGushin).

CONCLUSIONS

1. Carthaginian slaves at Rome, Cleitomachus's consolation: Cic., *Tusculan Disputations* 3.53–54; Diogenes Laertius 4.67. Cleitomachus and Censorinus: Cic., *Academica* 2.32.102–4. Survival of Punic language: Apuleius, *Apology* 98.6–8; *Historia Augusta, Severus* 15.7. Saint Augustine and others: Millar 1968. Punic culture after 146: Bénabou 1976; Lancel 1995a, 428–46; Fantar 2011. Magistrates' Punic names: *ILS* 6095 (near Hadrumetum); Miles 2010, 370 (Hannibal Tapapius Rufus of Lepcis Magna, 8 BC). Baal as Saturn differed from the older, Greek identification with Zeus/Jupiter. Tanit became "Juno Caelestis," Juno being queen of heaven as wife of Jupiter; Apollo was the multitalented god of music, poetry, and prophecy and was identified too as Phoebus the sun god; Asclepius/Aesculapius was god of healing.

2. Polybius on Rome's decline: 6.9.12–14; Champion 2004, especially 144–88; McGing 2010, 157–67; Baronowski 2011, 153–59; cf. Erskine 2012, 17–32.

3. Hannibal's writings: Pol. 3.33.18, 56.4; Livy 28.46.16; Nepos, *Hannibal* 13.2. Polybius on Roman political excellences: 6.43–56; Walbank 1972, 144–56; Baronowski 2011, 159–63; McGing 2010, 169–89.

APPENDIX

1. Early sources: Champion 2011, 98–102; Mineo 2011, 111–17. Early Roman historians: Badian 1966; Goldberg 2005, 21–22; Kraus 2005, 241–42. Naevius: Goldberg 1995, 58–82. Ennius's *Annals*: Elliott 2013.

2. Pol. 2.56–63, 12.3–28 (criticizing Hellenistic predecessors); 18.28–32 (phalanx versus legion); 10.43–47 (fire signals); 18.35.1–2 (bribing modern Romans); 31.25.2–8 (follies of young Romans); 38.1.5 (Carthaginians not wholly in the wrong in 149). Roman army: 6.19–42; see Kromayer and Veith 1928; Walbank, *Comm.* 1.697–723; Connolly 1981; Goldsworthy 2000; Daly 2002; Dobson 2008.

3. Carthage too democratic in 218: Pol. 6.51.5–6. Sufferings of Greece in 146: 38.1.4–8. Vagueness on Alpine route: 3.36.1–4; Hoyos 2006.

4. Bridge of corpses: *Hann.* 28.121; contrast Livy 23.5.12 (Varro states as rumor).

5. Carthaginian coinage: Visonà in Krings 1995, 166–81; Baldus in Peters 2004, 294–313. For excellent reproductions online, see Markowitz [2012]. Roman coinage: Crawford 1974; Kent 1978; Marchetti 1978.

6. Duilius's inscription: *ILS* 65. For the naval victory as narrative climax, not chronological, compare Lucius Scipio's epitaph (*ILS* 2–3) and a still more august match, the emperor's climax in *Res Gestae Divi Augusti* 34–35, recording what happened in 28–27 BC. Minucius: *ILS* 11 = *ILLRP* 118.

BIBLIOGRAPHY

ABBREVIATIONS

Appian, *Hann.*	Appian, *Hannibalica*
Appian, *Iber.*	Appian, *Iberica*
Appian, *Lib.*	Appian, *Libyca*
ca.	circa
CAH²	*Cambridge Ancient History*, 2nd edn., vol. 7, part 2: *The Rise of Rome to 220 BC*, ed. F. W. Walbank, A. E. Astin, M. W. Frederiksen, and R. M. Ogilvie; and vol. 8: *Rome and the Mediterranean, 220–133 BC*, ed. A. E. Astin, F. W. Walbank, M. W. Frederiksen, and R. M. Ogilvie (Cambridge, CUP: 1989)
cf.	compare
ch., chs.	chapter, chapters
Cic.	Cicero
CUP	Cambridge University Press
DCPP	*Dictionnaire de la Civilisation phénicienne et punique*, ed. E. Lipiński (Tournai, Brepols: 1992)
Diod.	Diodorus
ed.	editor, edited by
edn.	edition
eds.	editors
frg.	fragment
ILLRP	*Inscriptiones Latinae Liberae Rei Publicae*, 2 vols., ed. A. Degrassi (Florence, La Nuova Italia: 1963, 1965; 2nd edn., 1972)
ILS	*Inscriptiones Latinae Selectae*, 3 vols. in 5, ed. H. Dessau (Berlin, Weidmann: 1892–1916)
Livy, *Per.*	Livy, *Periocha* (book epitome)
MRR	*Magistrates of the Roman Republic*, 3 vols., ed. T. R. S. Broughton (Atlanta, American Philological Association and Chico, Scholars Press: 1951, 1952, 1986)
OUP	Oxford University Press

Pliny, *NH*   Pliny, *Natural History*

Pol.   Polybius

*StR*²   G. de Sanctis, *Storia dei Romani*, 2nd edn., vol. 3, parts 1–2 (Florence, La Nuova Italia: 1967–68) [1st edn., Torino: 1916]

tr.   translated by, translation, translator

UP   University Press

vol., vols.   volume, volumes

Walbank, *Comm.*   F. W. Walbank, *A Historical Commentary on Polybius*, 3 vols. (Oxford, Clarendon Press: 1957–79)

Zon.   Zonaras

MODERN WORKS CITED

Adams, J. N. 2003. *Bilingualism and the Latin Language* (Cambridge, CUP).

Ameling, W. 1993. *Karthago. Studien zu Militär, Staat und Gesellschaft* (Munich, Beck).

Astin, A. 1967. *Scipio Aemilianus* (Oxford, OUP).

Astin, A. 1978. *Cato the Censor* (Oxford, OUP).

Austin, M. M. 2006. *The Hellenistic World from Alexander to the Roman Conquest: A Selection of Ancient Sources in Translation*, 2nd edn. (Cambridge, CUP).

Badian, E. 1966. "The early historians," in T. A. Dorey, ed., *Latin Historians* (London, Routledge and Kegan Paul), 1–38.

Baldwin, B. 2003. "Keep the kings, shake the salt, coals to Scipio: a methodological auto-da-fé," in A. F. Basson and W. J. Dominik., eds., *Literature, Art, History: Studies on Classical Antiquity and Tradition in Honour of W. J. Henderson* (Bern and Frankfurt-am-Main, Peter Lang), 289–94.

Barceló, P. 2004. *Hannibal: Stratege und Staatsmann* (Stuttgart: Klett-Cotta).

Barceló, P. 2011. "Punic politics, economy, and alliances, 218–201," in Hoyos 2011, 357–75.

Baronowski, D. W. 1995. "Polybius on the causes of the Third Punic War," *Classical Philology 90*, 16–31.

Baronowski, D. W. 2011. *Polybius and Roman Imperialism* (London, Bristol Classical Press).

Barré, M. L. 1983. *The God-List in the Treaty between Hannibal and Philip V of Macedon: A Study in Light of the Ancient Near Eastern Treaty Tradition* (Baltimore, Johns Hopkins UP).

Beck, H. 2005. *Karriere und Hierarchie. Die römische Aristokratie und die Anfänge des cursus honorum in der mittleren Republik* (klio Beiträge zur Alten Geschichte, N. F. Band 10: Berlin, Akademie Verlag).

Beck, H. 2011. "The reasons for the war", in Hoyos 2011, 225–41.

Bellón Ruiz, J. P., Gómez Cabeza, F., Ruiz, A., Molinos, M., Sánchez, A., Gutiérrez, L., Rueda, C., Wiña, L., García, M. A., Martínez, A. L., Ortega, C., Lozano, G., Fernández, R. 2009. "Baecula. An archaeological analysis of the location of a battle of the Second Punic War," in N. Hanel, A. Morillo Cerdán, and E. Martín Hernández, eds., *Limes XX. Estudios sobre la frontera romana* (Madrid, Consejo Superior de Investigaciones Científicas y Ediciones Polifemo), 239–52.

Bénabou, M. 1976. *La Résistance africaine à la romanisation* (Paris, Maspero).

Bleckmann, B. 2002. *Die Römische Nobilität im Ersten Punischen Krieg: Untersuchungen zur aristokratischen Konkurrenz in der Republik* (Klio Beiträge zur Alten Geschichte, N. F. Band 5: Berlin, Akademie Verlag).

Bonfante L., ed. 1986. *Etruscan Life and Afterlife: A Handbook of Etruscan Studies* (Detroit, Wayne State UP).

Bringmann, K. 2001a. "Der Ebrovertrag, Sagunt und der Weg in den zweiten punischen Krieg," *Klio* 83, 369–76.

Bringmann, K. 2001b. "Überlegungen zur Datierung und zum historischen Hintergrund der beiden ersten römisch-karthagischen Verträge," in Geus and Zimmermann 2011, 111–20.

Brizzi, G. 2011. "Carthage and Hannibal in Roman and Greek memory," in Hoyos 2011, 483–98.

Brunt, P. A. 1971. *Italian Manpower, 225 BC–AD 14* (Oxford, OUP).

Burton, P. J. 2011. *Friendship and Empire: Roman Diplomacy and Imperialism in the Middle Republic (353–146 BC)* (Cambridge, CUP).

Campbell, B., and Tritle, L. A., eds. 2013. *The Oxford Handbook of Warfare in the Classical World* (Oxford, OUP).

Champion, C. B. 2004. *Cultural Politics in Polybius' "Histories"* (Berkeley, University of California Press).

Champion, C. B. 2011. "Polybius and the Punic Wars," in Hoyos 2011, 95–110.

Connolly, P. 1978. *Hannibal and the Enemies of Rome* (London, Macdonald).

Connolly, P. 1981. *Greece and Rome at War* (London, Macdonald).

Cornell, T. J. 1989. "The recovery of Rome" and "The conquest of Italy": chs. 7–8 *in CAH*² 7.2. 309–419.

Cornell, T. J. 1995. *The Beginnings of Rome: Italy and Rome from the Bronze Age to the Punic Wars (c. 1000–264 B.C.)* (London, Routledge).

Crawford, M. H. 1974. *Roman Republican Coinage*, 2 vols. (Cambridge, CUP; repr. 2001).

Daly, G. 2002. *Cannae: The Experience of Battle in the Second Punic War* (London, Routledge).

Desanges, J. 1995. "Masinissa et Carthage entre la deuxième et la troisième guerre punique: un problème de chronologie," in *Actes du IIIe Congrès international des Études phéniciennes et puniques, Tunis, 11–16 novembre 1991* (Tunis, Institut National du Patrimoine), *1*.352–58.

Dobson, M. 2008. *The Army of the Roman Republic: The Second century BC, Polybius and the Camps at Numantia, Spain* (Oxford, Oxbow).

Dubuisson, M. 1989. "*Delenda est Carthago*: remise en question d'un stéréotype," in *Studia Phoenicia 10: The Punic Wars*, ed. H. Devijver and E. Lipiński (Leuven, Peeters), 279–87.

Elliott, J. 2013. *Ennius and the Architecture of the "Annales"* (Cambridge, CUP).

Ennabli, A., ed. 1992. *Pour Sauver Carthage: exploration et conservation de la cité punique, romaine et byzantine* (Paris, UNESCO/Tunis, Institut National d'Archéologie et d'Art).

Erdkamp, P. 1998. *Hunger and the Sword: Warfare and Food Supply in Roman Republican Wars (264–30 B.C.)* (Dutch Monographs on Ancient History and Archaeology, 20: Amsterdam, J. C. Gieben).

Erdkamp, P. 2007. *A Companion to the Roman Army* (Oxford, Wiley-Blackwell).

Erdkamp, P. 2009. "Polybius, the Ebro treaty, and the Gallic invasion of 225 BCE," *Classical Philology* 104, 495–510.

Erdkamp, P. 2011. "Manpower and food supply in the First and Second Punic Wars," in Hoyos 2011, 58–77.

Erskine, A. 2012. "Polybius among the Romans: life in the Cyclops' cave," in Smith and Yarrow 2012, 17–32.

Fantar, M. H. 2011. "Death and transfiguration: Punic culture after 146 BC," in Hoyos 2011, 449–66.

Fields, N. 2010. *Roman Conquests: North Africa* (London, Pen and Sword).

Fraenkel, E. 1963. *Horace* (Oxford, OUP).

Frank, T. 1933. *An Economic Survey of Ancient Rome*, vol. 1: *Rome and Italy of the Republic* (Baltimore, Johns Hopkins UP).

Franko, G. F. 1996. "The characterization of Hanno in Plautus' *Poenulus*," *American Journal of Philology* 117, 425–52.

Frederiksen, M. W. 1984. *Campania*, ed. N. Purcell (London, British School at Rome).

Fronda, Michael P. 2010. *Between Rome and Carthage: Southern Italy during the Second Punic War* (Cambridge, CUP).

Fronda, M. 2011. "Hannibal: tactics, strategy, and geostrategy," in Hoyos 2011, 242–59.

Gehrke, H.-J. 2002. "Die Römer im ersten punischen Krieg," in J. Spielvogel, ed., *Res Publica Reperta: Zur Verfassung und Gesellschaft der römischen Republik und des frühen Prinzipats. Festschrift für Jochen Bleicken zum 75. Geburtstag* (Stuttgart, Franz Steiner), 153–71.

Geus, K. 1994. *Prosopographie der Literarisch Bezeugten Karthager (Orientalia Lovaniensia Analecta, 59*: Leuven, Peeters en Departement Orientalistiek Leuven).

Geus, K., and Zimmermann, K., eds. 2001. *Punica—Libyca—Ptolemaica. Festschrift für Werner Huß, zum 65. Geburtstag dargebracht von Schülern, Freunden und Kollegen* (Leuven, Peeters).

Goldberg, S. M. 1995. *Epic in Republican Rome* (New York, OUP).

Goldsworthy, A. 2000. *The Punic Wars* (London, Cassell).

Goldsworthy, A. 2001. *Cannae* (London, Cassell).

Günther, L.-M. 1999. "Carthaginian parties during the Punic Wars," *Mediterranean Historical Review* 14, 18–30.

Günther, L.-M. 2008. "Catos Feigen aus Karthago: Zur Interpretation einer Anekdote (Plutarch, *Cato maior*, 27, 1)," in J. González, P. Ruggeri, C. Vismara, and R. Zucca, eds., *L'Africa Romana: Le Ricchezze dell'Africa* (Sassari, Carocci), *1.*151–56.

Harris, W. V. 1979. *War and Imperialism in the Roman Republic, 327–70 B.C.* (Oxford, OUP; repr. 1985).

Harris, W. V. 1989. "Roman expansion in the West," *in CAH² 8.*107–62.

Harrison, S., ed. 2005. *A Companion to Latin Literature* (Malden, Blackwell).

Hin, S. 2013. *The Demography of Roman Italy. Population Dynamics in an Ancient Conquest Society 201 BCE–14 CE* (Cambridge, CUP).

Hoyos, D. 1994. "Barcid 'proconsuls' and Punic politics, 237–218 BC," *Rheinisches Museum* 137, 246–72.

Hoyos, D. 1998. *Unplanned Wars: The Origins of the First and Second Punic Wars* (Berlin, W. de Gruyter).

Hoyos, D. 2000. "Maharbal's *bon mot*: authenticity and survival," *Classical Quarterly* new series 50, 610–14.

Hoyos, D. 2001. "Generals and annalists: geographic and chronological obscurities in the Scipios' campaigns in Spain, 218–211 BC," *Klio* 83, 68–92.

Hoyos, D. 2002. "The battle-site of Ilipa," *Klio* 84, 101–13.

Hoyos, D. 2003. *Hannibal's Dynasty: Power and Politics in the Western Mediterranean, 247–183 BC* (London, Routledge).

Hoyos, D. 2006. "Crossing the Durance with Hannibal and Livy: the route to the pass," *Klio 88*, 408–65.

Hoyos, D. 2007. *Truceless War: Carthage's Fight for Survival, 241 to 237 BC* (History of Warfare, 45: Leiden, Brill).

Hoyos, D. 2010. *The Carthaginians* (London, Routledge).

Hoyos, D., ed. 2011. *A Companion to the Punic Wars* (Oxford, Wiley-Blackwell).

Hoyos, D. 2013. "The Second Punic War," in Campbell and Tritle, 688–707.

Hurst, H. 1979. "Excavations at Carthage 1977–9: fourth interim report," *Antiquaries' Journal* 59, 18–49.

Hurst, H. 1992. "L'îlot de l'Amirauté, le port circulaire et l'avenue Bourguiba," in Ennabli 1992, 79–94.

Hurst, H., and Stager, L. E. 1977. "A metropolitan landscape: the Late Punic port of Carthage," *World Archaeology* 9, 332–46.

Huss, W. 1985. *Geschichte der Karthager* (Munich, C. H. Beck).

Huss, W. 1986. "Hannibal und die Religion," in *Studia Phoenicia 4: Religio Phoenicia. Acta Collo-quii Namurcensis Dec. 1984*, ed. C. Bonnet, E. Lipiński, and P. Marchetti (Namur, Société des Études Classiques), 223–38.

Kayser, R. 2002. "Archimède, défenseur de Syracuse contre les Romains," in J. Althoff, B. Herzhoff, and G. Wörle, eds., *Antike Naturwissenschaft und ihre Rezeption 12* (Trier, Wissenschaftlicher Verlag Trier), 183–96.

Kent, J. P. C. 1978. *Roman Coins* (London, Thames and Hudson).

Kleine Pauly, Der: *Lexicon der Antike in fünf Bände*. 1975. 5 vols., ed. K. Ziegler and W. Sontheimer (Munich, A. Druckenmüller; repr. 1979, Deutscher Taschenbusch Verlag).

Koon, S. 2011. "Phalanx and legion: the 'face' of Punic War battle," in Hoyos 2011, 77–94.

Krahmalkov, C. R. 2000. *Phoenician–Punic Dictionary* (Leuven, Peeters).

Kraus, C. S. 2005. "History and biography," in Harrison 2005, 241–56.

Krings, V., ed. 1995. *La Civilisation phénicienne et punique: Manuel de recherche* (Leiden, Brill).

Kromayer, J., and Veith, G. 1928. *Heerwesen und Kriegführung der Griechen und Römer* (Munich, C. H. Beck).

Kukofka, D.-A. 1990. *Sud-Italien im Zweiten Punischen Krieg* (Europäische Hochschulschriften Reihe 3, Nr. 432. Frankfurt-am-Main, Peter Lang).

Kunze, C. 2011. "Carthage and Numidia, 201–149," in Hoyos 2011, 395–411.

Lancel, S. 1995a. *Carthage: A History*, tr. A. Nevill (Oxford, Blackwell) [original French edn., Carthage (Paris, Fayard: 1992)].

Lancel, S. 1995b. *Hannibal* (Paris, Fayard) [English tr. A. Nevill, Oxford, Blackwell, 1998].

Lazenby, J. F. 1978. *Hannibal's War: A Military History of the Second Punic War* (Warminster, England, Aris and Phillips) [2nd edn., Oklahoma UP, 1998].

Lazenby, J. F. 1996a. *The First Punic War: A Military History* (London, Batsford).

Lazenby, J. F. 1996b. "Was Maharbal right?" in T. Cornell, B. Rankov, and P. Sabin, eds. *The Second Punic War: A Reappraisal* (London, Institute of Classical Studies), 39–48.

Le Bohec, Y. 2011. "The 'Third Punic War': the siege of Carthage (149–146 BC)," in Hoyos 2011, 430–45.

Lintott, A. 1999. *The Constitution of the Roman Republic* (Oxford, OUP).

Loreto, L. 2007. *La Grande Strategia di Roma nell'Età della Prima Guerra Punica (ca. 273–ca. 229 a.C.): L'inizio di un paradosso* (Naples, Jovene).

Loreto, L. 2011. "Roman politics and expansion, 241–219," in Hoyos 2011, 184–203.

Mahaney, W. C. 2010. "Hannibal's invasion-route: an age-old question revisited within a geoarchaeological and palaeobotanical context," *Archaeometry* 52, 1096–1109.

Marchetti, P. 1978. *Histoire économique et monétaire de la Deuxième Guerre Punique*. Académie de Belgique, Mémoires de la Classe des Beaux-Arts, 2ᵉ série (Brussels, Palais des Académies).

Markowitz, M. [2012]. "The coinage of Carthage: an introduction," at https://www.academia.edu/3455640/The_Coinage_of_Carthage_An_Introduction (accessed November 20, 2013).

Mattingly, D. J. 2011. *Imperialism, Power, and Identity: Experiencing the Roman Empire* (Princeton, Princeton UP).

McGing, B. 2010. *Polybius' "Histories"* (Oxford Approaches to Classical Literature: Oxford, OUP).

Meier, F. J. 1984. "Cato's African figs," *Mnemosyne* 37, 117–24.

Miles, R. 2010. *Carthage Must Be Destroyed: The Rise and Fall of an Ancient Civilization* (London, Allen Lane; New York, Viking).

Miles, R. 2011. "Hannibal and propaganda," in Hoyos 2011, 260–79.

Millán León, J. 1986. "La batalla de Ilipa," *Habis* 17, 283–303.

Millar, F. 1968. "Local cultures in the Roman Empire: Libyan, Punic and Latin in Roman North Africa," *Journal of Roman Studies* 58, 126–34.

Mineo, B. 2011. "Principal literary sources for the Punic Wars (apart from Polybius)," in Hoyos 2011, 111–27.

Molthagen, J. 1975. "Der Weg in den ersten punischen Krieg," *Chiron* 5, 89–127.

Molthagen, J. 1979. "Der Triumph des M'. Valerius Messalla und die Anfänge des ersten punischen Krieges," *Chiron* 9, 53–72.

Murray, W. M. 2012. *The Age of Titans: The Rise and Fall of the Great Hellenistic Navies* (New York, OUP).

Ñaco del Hoyo, T. 2011. "Roman economy, finance, and politics in the Second Punic War," in Hoyos 2011, 376–92.

Nicolet, C., ed. 1977–78. *Rome et la conquête du monde méditerranéen*, 2 vols. (Paris, Presses Universitaires de France).

Palmer, R. E. A. 1997. *Rome and Carthage at Peace* (*Historia*-Einzelschriften 113: Stuttgart, F. Steiner).

Peters, S., ed. 2004. *Hannibal ad Portas. Macht und Reichtum Karthagos* Sonderausstellung des Landes Baden-Württemberg im Badischen Landesmuseum, Schloss Karlsruhe, 25.9.2004–30.1.2005 (Stuttgart, Theiss).

Picard, G.-C., and Picard, C. 1968. *The Life and Death of Carthage* (London, Sidgwick and Jackson = 1969, New York, Taplinger).

Picard, G.-C., and Picard, C. 1983. *Karthago: Leben und Kultur* (Stuttgart, Reclam) [revised edn. of *La Vie quotidienne à Carthage au temps d'Hannibal*, Paris, Hachette: 1958].

Proctor, D. 1971. *Hannibal's March in History* (Oxford, OUP).

Rankov, B. 1996. "The Second Punic War at sea," in T. Cornell, B. Rankov, and P. Sabin, eds. *The Second Punic War: A Reappraisal* (London, Institute of Classical Studies), 49–57.

Rankov, B. 2011. "A war of phases: strategies and stalemates 264–241," in Hoyos 2011, 149–66.

Rawlings, L. 2011. "The war in Italy, 218–203," in Hoyos 2011, 299–320.

Rich, J. 1996. "The origins of the Second Punic War," in T. Cornell, B. Rankov, and P. Sabin, eds. *The Second Punic War: A Reappraisal* (London, Institute of Classical Studies), 1–37.

Ridley, R. T. 1986. "To be taken with a pinch of salt. The destruction of Carthage," *Classical Philology* 81, 140–46.

Sabin, P. 1996. "The mechanics of battle in the Second Punic War," in T. Cornell, B. Rankov, and P. Sabin, eds. *The Second Punic War: A Reappraisal* (London, Institute of Classical Studies), 59–79.

Sage, M. 2013. "The rise of Rome," in Campbell and Tritle, 216–35.

Scardigli, B. 1991. *I Trattati Romano-Cartaginesi* (Pisa, Scuola Normale Superiore).

Scardigli, B. 2011. "Early relations between Rome and Carthage," in Hoyos 2011, 28–38.

Scheidel, W. 2004. "Human mobility in Roman Italy, I: the free population," *Journal of Roman Studies* 74, 1–26.

Schwarte, K.-H. 1983. *Der Ausbruch des Zweiten Punischen Krieges—Rechtsfrage und Überlieferung* (*Historia*-Einzelschriften 42: Wiesbaden, F. Steiner).

Schmitt, H. H. 1969. *Die Staatsverträge des Altertums*, vol. 3: *Die Verträge der griechisch-römischen Welt von 338 bis 200 v. Chr.* (Munich, C. H. Beck).

Scullard, H. H. 1970. *Scipio Africanus: Soldier and Politician* (London, Thames and Hudson).

Scullard, H. H. 1973. *Roman Politics*, 2nd edn. (Oxford, OUP).

Scullard, H. H. 1989. "Carthage and Rome," ch. 11 in *CAH²* 7.2.486–569.

Seibert, J. 1993a. *Forschungen zu Hannibal* (Darmstadt, Wissenschaftliche Buchgesellschaft).

Seibert, J. 1993b. *Hannibal* (Darmstadt, Wissenschaftliche Buchgesellschaft).

Serrati, J. 2006. "Neptune's altars: the treaties between Rome and Carthage (509–226 BC)," *Classical Quarterly* 56, 113–34.

Simms, D. L. 1991. "Galen on Archimedes: burning mirror or burning pitch?" *Technology and Culture* 32, 91–96.

Smith, C., and Yarrow, L. M., eds. 2012. *Imperialism, Cultural Politics, and Polybius* (Oxford, OUP).

Starr, C. G. 1980. *The Beginnings of Imperial Rome: Rome in the Mid-Republic* (Ann Arbor, University of Michigan Press).

Staveley, E. S. 1989. "Rome and Italy in the early third century": ch. 9 in *CAH*[2] 7.2.420–55.

Steinby, C. 2007. *The Roman Republican Navy: From the Sixth Century to 167 B.C.* (Commentationes Humanarum Litterarum, 123: [Helsinki], Societas Scientiarum Fennica).

Storm, E. 2001. *Masinissa: Numidien im Aufbruch* (Stuttgart, F. Steiner Verlag).

Syed, Y. 2005. "Romans and others," in Harrison 2005, 360–71.

Sznycer, M. 1978. "Carthage et la civilisation punique," in Nicolet 1977–78, vol. 2: *Genèse d'un empire*, 545–93.

Vacanti, C. 2012. *Guerra per la Sicilia e Guerra della Sicilia. Il ruolo delle città siciliane nel primo conflitto romano-punico* (Naples, Jovene).

Walbank, F. W. 1972. *Polybius* (Sather Classical Lectures, 42: Berkeley and Los Angeles, University of California Press; repr. 1990).

Wallinga, H. T. 1956. *The Boarding-Bridge of the Romans* (Groningen, Wolters).

Walsh, P. G. 1965. "Masinissa," *Journal of Roman Studies* 55, 149–60.

Waterfield, R. 2010. *Polybius: The Histories*, with introduction and notes by B. McGing (Oxford, Oxford World's Classics).

Waterfield, R. 2014. *Taken at the Flood: The Roman Conquest of Greece* (Oxford, OUP).

Wise, T., and Hook, R. 1982. *Armies of the Carthaginian Wars, 265–146 BC* (Oxford, Osprey; repr. 1999).

Yardley, J. C., and Hoyos, D. 2006. *Livy: Hannibal's War. Books 21 to 30* (Oxford World's Classics: Oxford, OUP).

Zimmermann, K. 2011. "Roman strategy and aims in the Second Punic War," in Hoyos 2011, 280–99.

INDEX

All dates in parentheses are BC (unless AD shown). Romans are listed by their second (family) names.
Cross-references to 'Hannibal' refer to Hannibal son of Hamilcar Barca

CPSIA information can be obtained
at www.ICGtesting.com
Printed in the USA
BVOW09s0147310717

490592BV00001B/2/P